FAMILY GROWTH IN METROPOLITAN AMERICA

Family Growth
in
Metropolitan
America

BY CHARLES F. WESTOFF

ROBERT G. POTTER, JR., PHILIP C. SAGI

AND ELLIOT G. MISHLER

PRINCETON, NEW JERSEY

PRINCETON UNIVERSITY PRESS

1961

Printed in the United States of America

To 1,165 American couples

Foreword

This book is the product of a research program that began its active life in 1954. The project was conceived at a Round Table that was part of the 1952 Annual Conference of the Milbank Memorial Fund; its gestation was a work-conference sponsored by the Fund in June 1953 at Princeton, and the subsequent deliberations of a steering committee founded there; its birth occurred with the assignment to the staff of the new study in 1954–1955 of Charles F. Westoff (then at the Milbank Fund and currently at New York University) and Elliot G. Mishler (then at the Office of Population Research of Princeton University).

The study has continued under the sponsorship of the Milbank Fund, with grants from the Carnegie Corporation of New York, the Population Council, and the Fund. Since the fall of 1955 the technical work has been centered at the Office of Population Research. In 1955 the staff in Princeton consisted of Elliot G. Mishler, Robert G. Potter, and Charles F. Westoff. In 1957 Mishler left Princeton to accept a position with the Joint Commission on Mental Illness and Health, and Philip C. Sagi was added to the staff. Mishler, Potter, and Westoff, with the advice of the steering committee, formulated the framework of the study and designed the questionnaire for the sample survey conducted in 1957 by National Analysts, Inc. of Philadelphia. Potter, Sagi, and Westoff then designed and carried out most of the analysis of these interviews— the analysis reported in this book. Clyde V. Kiser, of the Milbank Memorial Fund and the Office of Population Research, has participated in every phase of the study, and has analyzed the relation of fertility to residence and migration.

The writing of this book has been a fully collaborative effort, which has included conferences and informal exchanges of ideas at every stage. In a sense, all of the persons named on the title page shared in producing every part of the book. However, each chapter was drafted first by some one person. The three introductory chapters were drafted by Westoff, Potter, and Sagi, in that order. The part on fertility variables (Chapters IV–IX) was drafted by Potter. Chapter VI was based largely on a paper written by Sagi for the 1958 Annual Conference of the Milbank Memorial Fund.

The first five chapters and the last two (X–XIV and XVIII–XIX) of the part on social and psychological determinants were prepared by Westoff, while Kiser did the chapter on residence and migration (XV) and Sagi the chapters (XVI–XVII) on family composition and social relations within the family. The final chapter on the next phase was drafted by Westoff.

This book summarizes the outcome of the first phase of continuing research. Interviews with 1,165 metropolitan couples who had a second child in September 1956 provided the underlying data. In this volume variations in *attitudes toward fertility* and in aspects of *fertility performance* to date are analyzed for couples at a critical milestone in family building—the birth of the second child. The continuing program will record and analyze subsequent fertility behavior and attitudes of these same couples.

The research reported in this volume has been remarkably thorough and careful. Three years of preparatory staff work, expert guidance by a distinguished steering committee, and several pretests underlay the schedule of the first interview. The authors have tried to maintain the same high scientific standard in analyzing the data gathered in the survey. Their colleagues at the Office of Population Research believe that this book shows that they have succeeded.

ANSLEY J. COALE, *Director*
Office of Population Research
Princeton University

Preface

To an unusual extent, this study has depended on the help of others. A steering committee has furnished guidance; a survey research organization of national reputation has done the field work; and even the analysis and writing of results has been fundamentally influenced by the commentary of a small group of experts who have read preliminary drafts of each chapter. Hence, it is a particular pleasure to acknowledge our many debts.

The Family Growth in Metropolitan America Study formally began with the formation of the Steering Committee on Plans for New Studies of Social and Psychological Factors Affecting Fertility. Throughout the six years necessary to bring the study to its present stage, the completion of the first phase, the committee met once or twice a year, usually for two-day sessions. At these meetings, virtually all of the basic decisions about study design were made, including the decision to precede the main field operation with one year of hypothesis formulation and two years of pretesting. Members of this committee have provided valuable ideas on nearly every aspect of the study and, perhaps more importantly, have dissuaded us from some of the worst of our own ideas. The committee has consisted of:

Frank W. Notestein, Chairman	—	Office of Population Research, Princeton University
Ansley J. Coale	—	Office of Population Research
Ronald Freedman	—	University of Michigan
Philip M. Hauser	—	University of Chicago
Dudley Kirk	—	The Population Council, Inc.
Clyde V. Kiser	—	Milbank Memorial Fund
Frank Lorimer	—	American University
Donald G. Marquis	—	Social Science Research Council
Frederick Osborn	—	The Population Council, Inc.
Lowell J. Reed	—	Johns Hopkins University

P. K. Whelpton — Scripps Foundation for
Research in Population
Problems, Miami
University

During long periods of the study, Ansley Coale, Clyde Kiser, and
Frank Notestein have acted as an informal subcommittee, furnishing
advice and supervision between meetings of the Steering Committee.
The connection of Clyde Kiser with the study has been especially
close, as evidence by his authorship of one of the chapters contained
in this volume. Frederick F. Stephan, serving as a consultant to the
Office of Population Research, has advised us on many methodological problems and earlier assisted us on questions of sampling
design.

Actual execution of this study has been a collaborative effort
between the writers and National Analysts, Inc. of Philadelphia.
This collaboration has encompassed such aspects as sample design,
construction of questionnaires and their pretesting, interviewing,
coding, punching, and preliminary tabulation. If high quality has
been attained in these areas, as we believe it has, it is due in large
measure to the experience and high standards of National Analysts.
The collaboration has not included analysis of results and report
writing, so that any deficiencies here are entirely our responsibility.

Many persons at National Analysts deserve acknowledgement. The
task of converting an unwieldy questionnaire into a well-knit field
operation fell intially to Charles F. Sarle as original study director.
Considerable progress had been made when this responsibility was
taken over by Jean K. Szaloczi. Since that time, Jean Szaloczi has
steered the study through successive stages of execution with skill,
ingenuity, and enthusiasm. Undoubtedly our single greatest debt is to
her. We are also indebted to Robert K. MacMillan, who, with the
assistance of Raymond O. Nelson, devised and executed the sampling plan, and to Jane M. O'Donnell, who coordinated operations.
Others who have made important contributions are Frank J. Fulvio
in charge of interviewing, Genevieve Timm in charge of coding, and
Sidney Binder in charge of punching and tabulation. Thanks are
also owed to Franklin P. Kilpatrick, whose many valuable suggestions improved the questionnaires.

Each chapter of this manuscript has been read by several persons, and
as a result of their criticisms most chapters have gone through successive drafts. Among the individuals who have read all, or nearly all,
of the chapters are Ansley Coale, Clyde Kiser, Frank Notestein,
and Frederick Stephan, all persons already acknowledged

in other connections. Another such reader is Professor W. D. Borrie, Visiting Professor at the Office of Population Research. In addition, Christopher Tietze, Research Director of the National Committee of Maternal Health, kindly read Chapters IV and V and their accompanying appendices. Needless to say, the commentary of this group of experts has done much to strengthen the report.

The design of this study, which called for sampling a highly specialized sample of couples, would not have been feasible without the cooperation of several State Commissioners of Public Health and Vital Statistics Registrars. These individuals not merely cooperated with us in securing certain information, but generously gave their time in order to work out the procedural details for obtaining this information in a mutually satisfactory manner. Persons involved in these negotiations and their official positions during the fall of 1956 were: Malcolm H. Merrill, Director of Public Health, Berkeley, California; Paul W. Shipley, Chief, Bureau of Records and Statistics, Department of Public Health, Berkeley, California; Roland R. Cross, Director, Department of Public Health, Springfield, Illinois; O. K. Sagen, Chief, Bureau of Statistics, Department of Public Health, Springfield, Illinois; J. E. Holwager, Director, Division of Vital Records, Indianapolis, Indiana; Albert E. Heustis, Commissioner, Michigan Department of Health, Lansing, Michigan; F. S. Leeder, Director, Division of Disease Control, Records and Statistics, Michigan Department of Health, Lansing, Michigan; Doris L. Duxbury, Chief, Statistical Methods Section, Division of Disease Control, Michigan Department of Health, Lansing, Michigan; Daniel Bergsma, Commissioner, Department of Health, Trenton, N.J.; F. Merton Saybolt, Chief, Bureau of Public Health Statistics, Department of Health, Trenton, N.J.; Marguerite F. Hall, Director, Division of Vital Statistics and Administration, Trenton, N.J.; Anna P. Holkovich, Division of Vital Statistics and Administration, Trenton, N.J.; Carl L. Erhardt, Director, Bureau of Records and Statistics, Department of Health, New York City; Herman E. Hilleboe, Commissioner, Department of Health, Albany, New York; J. V. Deporte, Director, Office of Vital Statistics, Department of Health, Albany, New York; Berwyn S. Mattison, Commissioner, State Department of Health, Harrisburg, Pa.; Albert E. Bailey, Director, Bureau of Statistics and Records, State Department of Health, Harrisburg, Pa. We wish to thank particularly the four persons named from New Jersey. These officials were the first approached and upon them fell the main burden of helping us to devise a plan which could be followed in the other registries.

Other individuals who deserve acknowledgement are Joseph

Bensman, of William Esty and Company, New York, who contributed a number of ideas during the stage of hypothesis formulation, and Ruth Riemer, formerly of the University of California (Los Angeles), who offered valuable suggestions at various times. It has been necessary to make extensive use of electronic data processing. Jonathan Robbins of New York University has done most of this work, with additional assignments performed by Carl Helm of Princeton University and Educational Testing Service. Their competence and versatility have greatly facilitated the analysis.

We also wish to thank David R. Saunders of Educational Testing Service in Princeton for permitting us to use, in abbreviated and modified form, his Personality Research Inventory, then in a stage of development.

Inevitably in a study of this size, a heavy load of clerical detail fell upon the study secretary. For two years Margaret MacDonald filled this trying post. For the past two years, Hazel Chafey has patiently coped with the endless details. We are also indebted to Erna Harm and Wanda Pieslak for their computing.

Finally and certainly not least, a large measure of thanks is owed to the resourceful interviewers and the cooperative interviewees for furnishing the data upon which this report is based.

CHARLES F. WESTOFF
ROBERT G. POTTER, JR.
PHILIP C. SAGI
ELLIOT G. MISHLER

December 1959

Contents

PART IV. RESURVEY

APPENDICES

Tables

xix

APPENDIX TABLES

FAMILY GROWTH IN METROPOLITAN AMERICA

PART I

INTRODUCTION

Chapter I. Background, Objectives, and Approach

This is a study of human fertility. Essentially, it is a study of why American couples differ in the number of children they have. More specifically, this book reports the results of the first stage of research into social and psychological factors which are thought to relate to differences in fertility among American couples living in the largest metropolitan centers of the nation. At the time these couples were initially interviewed, they all just recently had their second child. The second stage of the research, now in process, will provide further results obtained from reinterviews with the same couples three years later.

BACKGROUND

The development of the present research program was based on two primary considerations. The first was the set of questions stimulated by the unprecedented postwar upsurge and sustained high level of the national birth rate following the minimum reached in the 1930's. This apparent radical change in the child-spacing patterns and family-size orientations of American married couples has confounded demographers and has posed a challenge to students of social change. During the late 1930's and even well into the 1940's, the accepted expert view (a position which has only recently become unfashionable) was that a temporary recovery of the birth rate was to be expected as a result of births postponed during the depression, the high marriage rates following the war, and other demographic consequences of the nation's postwar readjustment. The consensus was that the long-term social factors which had produced a steadily downward trend in the national birth rate for several generations could not be reversed easily, particularly in view of the continued increase in the use of methods of family limitation. The popularization of birth control carried the implication that large segments of the population would be able to restrict their fertility even further by reducing the number of unwanted pregnancies.

Available evidence makes it clear that the downward trend of fertility has been genuinely interrupted. In spite of the probable increased availability of techniques of family limitation, the high level of fertility has been maintained to date without any hint of a return to the prewar pattern. Not only are children now being born earlier and more rapidly in marriage, but the long-term decline in completed family size has also been reversed. Evidently this fertility

5

increase has been the result of voluntary decisions by couples who presumably *want* more children than did their parents in the previous generation; at least, it can be plausibly inferred that there has been enough change in the socio-cultural factors relevant to fertility levels to cause a relaxation in the vigilance of contraceptive practices. For example, the economic recovery and prosperity of the past 20 years might be conceived as encouraging an optimistic attitude where couples are more willing to risk a pregnancy.

Thus, the widespread and significant changes in American fertility have provided one of the major inducements to undertake this study. However, even if one accepts the point of view that historical demographic change can be understood in terms of the behavior and motivations of individuals, our study is not designed to permit inferring reasons for the postwar changes in fertility since it does not cover this time span. Surveying these couples again in 1960 will only facilitate analyses of the presumed effects of intervening events on the reproductive behavior of this group over a three-year period of time. The basic sociological and demographic parameters of postwar fertility have been investigated in a representative national survey by Freedman, Whelpton, and Campbell,[1] a survey that is also to be repeated in 1960. Our study concentrates more on assessing the motivational connections between our modern environment and fertility decisions and behavior. This orientation derives from the findings and questions posed by the Indianapolis Study of Social and Psychological Factors Affecting Fertility[2] which constitutes the second consideration prompting our study.

The Indianapolis Study, the first large-scale investigation of the subject, opened the door to knowledge of the cultural and motivational variables underlying contraceptive practice and family size. As is often true, especially with studies in new areas, the research raised many more questions than it answered and has been subjected to a considerable amount of retrospective criticism, most of which has been self-criticism. A number of the original members of the Indianapolis Study group provided the impetus to launch a new investigation which would extend the knowledge accumulated from the early study, benefit from the mistakes it had made, and utilize some of the more recent developments in social science methodology.

Many of the analyses of the Indianapolis data had highlighted the importance of socio-economic status as the dominant factor relevant

---

[1] Ronald Freedman, P. K. Whelpton and Arthur Campbell, *Family Planning, Sterility and Population Growth*, McGraw – Hill, New York, 1959.

[2] P. K. Whelpton and Clyde V. Kiser, eds., *Social and Psychological Factors Affecting Fertility*, 5 Vols., Milbank Memorial Fund, New York, 1946–1958.

to differences both in the use of contraception and the efficacy of its practice. This factor consistently tended to override other relationships discovered between effective fertility planning and such variables as marital adjustment, interest in religion, adherence to traditional values, feelings of personal adequacy, and other characteristics. The persistent influence of socio-economic status stimulated curiosity about the nature of the variable and the kind of social psychological variables that might mediate between having a certain occupation, income, or education and being more prone to use techniques of family limitation more regularly and more effectively. Kiser and Whelpton wrote: "The Indianapolis Study presents a challenge to learn the reasons for the overriding influence of socio-economic status. There is good reason to believe that it is not socio-economic status *per se* but rather the underlying attitudes and psychological characteristics of these classes that account for the fertility behavior."[3] One of the speculations advanced concerned the influence of social mobility aspirations on fertility. Hypotheses on this subject played an important part in the design of the new study.

A number of variables from the Indianapolis investigation have been retained in the present study after methodological refinements. Among these are feelings of economic security, liking for children, patterns of husband–wife dominance, and a number of personality characteristics. Others are described in succeeding chapters. Variables which did not produce significant relationships in the Indianapolis Study and for which no persuasive theoretical rationales remained were, of course, eliminated.

The Indianapolis research experience has exerted other influences besides content on the type of study formulated. These will be noted briefly under the following topics: theory, sample design, study design, and analysis.

THEORY

A criticism directed frequently toward the Indianapolis Study has been that the hypotheses were generated in an unsystematic *ad hoc* fashion and were unintegrated. If one accepts the assumption that a single systematic theory existed whose utilization would have provided more fruitful hypotheses, the criticism would be valid. This alleged shortcoming of the Indianapolis Study formulation was foremost in the minds of the individuals concerned with the development of the new study and much time and energy was consumed during

---

[3] Clyde V. Kiser and P. K. Whelpton, "Resumé of the Indianapolis Study of Social and Psychological Factors Affecting Fertility," *Population Studies*, 7 (1953), pp. 95–110.

the first year of the project in the search for a unified body of thought that could serve as the source of hypotheses. It soon became apparent, however, that there existed no single sociological or psychological theory that would encompass all the factors relevant to fertility. The reasons for this are many. First and perhaps most significant is the fact that research into the social and psychological factors affecting fertility is still at a stage where the primary needs are for gaining more information. When a body of empirically established relationships is secured from research guided by whatever unsystematic hunches and insights occur, then the development of a theory will be much more meaningful and useful.[4]

Secondly, the level of fertility is a complex result of many events. The antecedents to these events can be approached from the perspectives of several sciences and, even excluding the biological sciences, there remains the wide diversity of orientations represented among the behavioral disciplines of sociology, social psychology, and psychology. Moreover, even among the systematic theories extant in the literature relevant to our interest, the perspectives or interpretive models are not reducible one to the other nor are they wholly independent. The only recourse seemed to be to select and combine among them, developing general hypotheses in the process. In effect, this path was followed. The theoretical organization, described in Chapter X, consists of a number of basic themes relating fertility to general sets of propositions represented operationally by specific variables and hypotheses. These independent variables have been further organized by a conceptual classification.

SAMPLE DESIGN

Only a few observations are included here on the subject of the sample design. A more technical account is reported in the next chapter. There are two important differences in the characteristics of the population surveyed in this study compared to that in the Indianapolis Study. The latter was restricted, in its intensive aspects, to native-born, white Protestants with at least eighth grade education, residing in one city. This set of restrictions was by no means arbitrary; it was deemed necessary for several reasons, the dominant one being that an analysis of the social psychological factors affecting fertility

---

[4] For recent statements on the status of theory in fertility research, see: Kingsley Davis, "The Sociology of Demographic Behavior," in Robert K. Merton, Leonard Broom, and Leonard S. Cottrell, eds., *Sociology Today*, Basic Books, New York, 1959, pp. 309–333; Norman B. Ryder, "Fertility," in Philip M. Hauser and Otis Dudley Duncan, eds., *The Study of Population*, University of Chicago Press, Chicago, 1959, pp. 400–436; and Wilbert E. Moore, "Sociology and Demography," *ibid.*, pp. 832–851.

necessitated, with limited resources, eliminating the gross cultural differences involved in nationality and race. This rationale has been retained in the present study.

The exclusion of all religions other than Protestants was based on similar grounds plus the added fear that interviewing Roman Catholics on a subject such as family limitation might involve difficulties. In the current study, this anxiety proved unfounded; although occasional sensitivities were reported, Catholic women proved as cooperative as women of any religious persuasion. This was initially confirmed in a preliminary sample of 100 interviews before the final design was completed. Because of the vital importance of securing information about the patterns of differential fertility among Catholics and the nature of the response of Catholics to the situations in the recent past that have produced such radical changes in the birth rate, it was decided to include religious groups other than Protestants in the present study. Including all religious groups in the sample has complicated the statistical analysis more, but the potential theoretical advantages were conceived to outweigh the analytical inconvenience.

The restriction of the Indianapolis sample to couples with at least elementary school education was prompted by the expectation that the subject of the interview was sufficiently complex that the quality of responses might be impaired by including persons with little education. Our pretest experience did not indicate any such difficulty in 1956 and the final sample design contained no restrictions of any kind on education.

The city of Indianapolis was selected as the site of the first study for various reasons but mainly on the assumption that it was as "typically American" as any city of comparable size. A decision to confine the study to one city, no matter which particular city, would limit the generality of the findings. Although the design of the present study reflected the budgetary necessity of restricting the sample to an urbanized population, it was agreed that a broader base than a single city was highly desirable. The result was to define the base as those eligible couples living in the largest Standard Metropolitan Areas of the country. All cities and their adjacent suburban counties with total populations of at least two million persons were included with one exception:[5] New York–New Jersey, Camden–Philadelphia, Pittsburg, Detroit, Chicago, Los Angeles, and San Francisco–Oakland are the metropolitan areas included. The larger metropolitan area rather than the central city proper was selected deliberately in order

---

[5] Boston was excluded only because birth order was not recorded in their vital statistics, which made the location of eligible couples impractical.

to represent the suburban areas which have mushroomed during the last 15 years.

STUDY DESIGN

The Indianapolis Study was conceived as research into the social psychological factors affecting *completed* family size and the sample was accordingly restricted to couples whose childbearing periods were virtually completed. The focus of the current study and that of Freedman, Whelpton, and Campbell, although ultimately pointed toward completed fertility, is directed more toward current fertility and the intermediate processes of family building. The Freedman, Whelpton, and Campbell investigation has concentrated on the fertility expectations of women at all ages within the childbearing period at all different stages of family formation. The present inquiry has singled out one particular parity and birth interval for study— all the couples have had two children only, the second child being born in September 1956—with differences in fertility beyond the second birth as its primary interest. This particular stage of the fertility process was chosen mainly because of its demographic significance for population replacement and the fact that the recent history of fertility in this country suggests a shift in the modal desired size of family toward more than two children.

The reasons for designing the study to include couples all of a single parity, however, are more complex. In our initial thinking about the ideal design it was felt that the study should sample a single marriage cohort and follow the sample throughout their reproductive span with repeated interviews. Although this plan was very attractive, it was considered impractical at this stage of research. In addition, there was an interest in studying the fertility performance and values of couples who were actively participating in the recent baby boom, which meant fertile marriages contracted since 1946. This consideration, in combination with the demographic interests in the future fertility of couples with two children already born, determined the final decision.

The basic theoretical rationale for limiting the study to women of a particular parity was the evidence indicated by the Indianapolis Study that family size might not be susceptible to investigation as a unidimensional phenomenon. That the Indianapolis analysis was able to account for only 18 per cent of the variance of the size of completed families among couples who planned all pregnancies suggested that some reevaluation of the dependent variable was appropriate. This result should not be construed to mean that

10

focusing on completed size of family is necessarily a mistake nor that eventually it will be impossible to analyze completed fertility as a meaningful social psychological variable. It does suggest, however, that perhaps the Indianapolis Study (as an example of this country's major research effort in this direction) set its sights prematurely high and failed to appreciate effectively that the variable of completed fertility is a deceptively simple net result of an extremely complex series of antecedents—specific birth orders—which may be only loosely connected (in cultural, motivational, and personality terms) in the net result of a given number of children by the end of the reproductive period.

This point of view had led to the current study design, which emphasizes the family-building process *per se* and is based on the assumption that fertility itself has self-generating consequences for family-size preferences and, more specifically, attitudes toward another child. Affective reactions to a given child, the second child in this case, have an influence on whether or not a third child is desired. Such factors as whether or not preferences for children of a given sex have been satisfied, the parents' age, the length of the interval between the first and second child, are some of the considerations involved. In short, attitudes toward family size are a compound function not only of generalized affection for children as such, but also of the discrete family situation created by the addition of the last child. The implication of this thesis is that fertility plans, where they exist in any rational sense, may be subject to periodic or even continuous reevaluation. The compatibility of another child may be defined in relation to the complex of existing family and sibling relationships, to specific circumstances (e.g., financial or housing), and to the extra-familial interests of the parents (e.g., work and leisure interests).

An intriguing aspect of this position is the possibility that the psychological distances between children may be very unequal. The potential consequences for the style of life and the adjustment of the couple are certainly greatest on the arrival of the first child. There may be a decreasing psychological interval with increasing parity, a subject that has never been explored systematically, although it appears frequently in the folklore of fertility. To the extent that this reevaluation is a significant factor in producing differences in ultimate family size, it would seem that a fruitful analysis of fertility requires studying the patterns of reaction to specific birth orders in an attempt to isolate the *general* factors responsible for a positive orientation toward additional children and those conducive to fertility restriction. The assumption postulated here is that the low level of

11

generalization and prediction now available to account for completed fertility differentials has resulted from a failure to recognize the possibility that the same family size can be reached by a number of different paths and that generalizations about particular birth orders may be the most promising avenue to ultimate greater knowledge of completed fertility.

Another often repeated criticism of the Indianapolis Study design is that the interpretation of relationships was frequently obscured by the fact that the social-psychological data were collected after the event (fertility) to be explained. Thus, one could never have any confidence in the sequence of relationships. In order to avoid some of the pitfalls of *post factum* interpretation, this study has incorporated a longitudinal design. The reinterview of the same couples, scheduled for three years after the first interview, will permit the correlation of data collected in the first interview with fertility variation during the interval. However, as amplified below, the analyses of the first interview data still contain some of the problems of *post factum* research.

THE ANALYSIS

The analysis of the data collected in this study has been divided into two main parts as a result of the longitudinal design of the study. Following the second interview, the behavioral criterion of whether or not another pregnancy has occurred will be available. This will be the main test criterion. The situation is quite different, however, with respect to the fertility data available from the first interview. By definition, all of the couples have had the same number of children at this point in time. Which fertility variables at this stage are either significant in their own right or presumably indicative of future fertility performance?

Among the behavioral criteria are the lengths of the intervals between marriage and the first pregnancy and between the first and second pregnancies. The sum of these two, the interval between marriage and the birth of the second child (plus 4 to 6 months between the second birth and the interview) constitutes marriage duration for this sample. The length of these intervals has significant relationships with completed family size and with desired size of amily. The most likely determinants of child spacing, aside from variations in fecundity, are the effectiveness of contraceptive practice and attitudes toward having more children as well as preferences about the spacing of births.

Effectiveness of contraceptive practice can be assessed for every couple in the sample in connection with each of the two conceptions.

The length of exposure to the risk of conception during periods of contraceptive practice can be measured and the comparative effectiveness of use determined. A more general classification of the extent to which fertility has been successfully planned to date, incorporating attitudes toward the circumstances under which each conception occurred, has also been developed. The advantage of using this type of classification in addition to measures of contraceptive effectiveness instead of simply the latter is that it permits categorizing couples who did not use any contraception along with those who did. Thus, a couple who did not use any method prior to the first conception because they desired a baby right away reflects just as successful planning from one point of view as a pregnancy following the deliberate interruption of contraception for that purpose. The fundamental criterion of this classification is the extent to which the conception results from rational and successful planning, regardless of the number of children desired.

All of these criterion variables—the spacing of births, the effectiveness of contraceptive practice, and the extent of fertility planning—are *post factum* in nature; they relate to past events and are measured by responses affected by recall error of both a biased and unbiased nature. By design, this study is directed toward the prediction of fertility, specifically the eventuation of a third pregnancy. What criteria are available from the data collected in the first interview, aside from past performance, which would give some indication of the couple's future fertility orientations? A number of questions were included in the interview schedule expressly for this purpose. These relate to ultimate size of family desired and to preferences and expectations about the spacing of the third child. Two reservations about this type of variable must be noted. First, there is some evidence that family-size preferences are not good predictors of actual fertility over the long term—that is, from engagement to the approximate completion of the family nearly twenty years later.[6] The couples sampled in the present research, however, present a very different situation. These are couples married for an average of over five years, who already have had the experience of two children; thus their future fertility preferences and expectations can be assumed to be much more realistic than those of young couples just engaged who have not yet experienced the realities of marriage and children and whose economic futures are far from clear. In all probability, the majority of couples just entering marriage do not have any meaningfully

---

[6] Charles F. Westoff, Elliot G. Mishler, and E. Lowell Kelly, "Preferences in Size of Family and Eventual Fertility Twenty Years After," *American Journal of Sociology*, Vol. LXII (1957), pp. 491–497.

crystallized idea of how many children they want; no doubt they have only a vague idea of general limits on family size. They want to have a "family"; they have been sensitized to the alleged psychological handicaps of the "only child"; the husband has stereotyped ideals for a son; his spouse has visions of a little girl, although she also wants a boy; and so forth. It may very well be true that explicit questions about ultimate family size are not raised until after the experience of several children. The fact that the proportion of couples who do not practice contraception drops very sharply after each successive pregnancy is at least consistent with this hypothesis. Inevitable biological consequences can be ignored only so long.

There is a point of view that is critical of the family-size attitudinal variable on more serious grounds than its questionable stability. This position maintains that fertility and family size are the consequences of sexual behavior, which is essentially nonrational behavior. Thus, the questions of how many children are desired or when the next child is preferred are irrelevant.

It is undoubtedly correct that many pregnancies result from a casual practice of contraception; rather than being planned in any deliberate manner, conception occurs because another child is not regarded as a disaster. To some unknown extent, such behavior may be motivated by an unconscious desire to have a child, while simultaneously avoiding the psychological responsibility of making the decision explicit. The theory of the unconscious can be pushed to the extreme position of denying the very existence of an accidental pregnancy, though this is an unnecessary exaggeration.

Although these reservations and criticisms are at least partially valid, they are not sufficient to negate the importance of analyzing fertility preference variables and their correlates at this point in the study. The longitudinal design will permit an examination of the reality and stability of these preferences. It should be emphasized that we are not depending upon the validity and reliability of statements about desired family size of couples just married; the main use of such verbal preferences is to index the probable fertility performance of a sample of mature couples in the near future.

ORGANIZATION OF THIS BOOK

The book has been divided into four sections. Part One, the Introduction, is continued in Chapter II which elaborates further the study and sample design. The various decisions about the selection of couples to study, the sampling procedures, the pretests, the interviewing program, the experience with supplementary mail questionnaires, and other facets of the research process are detailed. Chapter III, Methodology, concentrates on the problems of the measurement of attitudes and the decisions about and implications of the extensive correlational analyses undertaken.

Part Two is devoted to a series of intensive analyses of the dependent variables. Variations in the time required for conception is the focus of Chapter IV, Fecundity. In Chapter V, Contraception, details of the use, availability, choice of method, the acceptability and effectiveness of various forms of contraception, and fertility-planning success are presented. A division of birth intervals into voluntary and involuntary components is the theme of Chapter VI, Birth Intervals. In the following chapter, the factors that mothers consider in spacing births are presented. In Chapter VIII, the variable of desired family size is analyzed with particular attention paid to its interrelations with other fertility and contraceptive practice variables. The section is concluded in Chapter IX with a summary of the preceding chapters in Part Two.

The third section of the book is devoted to testing numerous hypotheses about the relations between social and psychological variables and number of children desired, fertility-planning success, and length of birth intervals. The nature of the basic themes and over-all theoretical organization is outlined in Chapter X. Chapters XI through XVIII include the substance of these analyses and are organized around the following topics respectively: religion and class, religiousness, socio-economic status, social mobility, residence and migration, age and sex composition in the family, social relations within the family, and personality characteristics. The outstanding empirical relationships reported in these chapters are brought together in a series of multivariate analyses presented in Chapter XIX.

This report of the first phase of the study ultimately aims toward understanding the social and psychological factors underlying actual fertility. Thus, the book concludes in Chapter XX with a summary of the implications of our analyses for the second phase of the longitudinal study—the phase in which we shall test the validity of our theories against the actual record of fertility performance.

Chapter II. Study and Sample Design

As the introductory chapter has already indicated, the basic design of this study is longitudinal, calling for a probability sample of two-child couples to be interviewed shortly after the birth of their second child and then reinterviewed approximately three years later. This chapter describes the design and field work connected with the first set of interviews.

First of all, the population of interest is defined. Then the listing of the members of the population is discussed and the manner in which names were selected from the list is described. Following the explanation of the sampling, there is an account of the field work as it was carried out by personnel from National Analysts, who completed interviews with 1,165 eligible wives and administered two mail questionnaires to each wife and her husband. Procedures of data processing and analysis are reviewed in the next chapter.

UNIVERSE

The population sampled is a highly specialized one. All couples had their second birth in September 1956, 5 to 7 months before the interview. Both at the time of second birth and at interview, they resided in one of the eight largest Standard Metropolitan Areas of this country, excluding Boston. In addition, both spouses were white, born in the continental United States, once-married, and still living together and with no early expectation of being separated 6 months or longer. Prior to interview, the couples' family building had been uncomplicated by illegitimacy, plural births, adoption, child death, or pregnancy wastage in excess of one miscarriage. Finally, at time of interview, the wife did not believe herself pregnant and she did not report her husband as having a military or farm occupation.

As a result of these many restrictions, the group sampled is only a small fraction of the United States population—at least in a strictly numerical sense. Even in the seven metropolitan areas included in the sampling universe, the ratio of eligible couples to general population is of the order of 1 in 4,000. This low ratio arises chiefly from the requirement that a second child be born in September 1956. In metropolitan America there are about 1,800 persons for every second birth occurring in September.[1] All the other eligibility

[1] In metropolitan United States, approximately 230 live births occur annually per 10,000 population. This amounts to a ratio of 43 persons per one live birth. It requires approximately 150 persons to provide one second birth, and therefore about 1,800 persons to produce one second birth in September.

16

criteria—race, nativity, marital status, pregnancy wastage, etc.—
merely reduce the ratio by a rough factor of 2.

But the group sampled is much less specialized than might first
appear from the very low ratio of eligible couples to general population. For purposes of this monograph, couples recently having a
second birth in September may be taken as representative of couples
recently having a second birth in any calendar month. The present
sample comes close to representing native-born, white couples,
resident in large metropolitan areas, who have recently had a second
birth and whose family growth hitherto has been uncomplicated by
such factors as divorce, separation, death, extensive pregnancy
wastage, plural birth, or adoption. As such, they constitute an
important subgroup among contemporary two-child families in
metropolitan America. Moreover, precisely because their family-
building has been so free of complicating conditions, they make
ideal subjects for a study like the present one, investigating a broad
range of factors in relation to fertility.

Diverse considerations led to these sample restrictions. Early in the
planning stage, for reasons discussed in the previous chapter, it was
decided to focus on a single parity, with preference given to the
period starting shortly after the second birth.

Another decision reached early was to exclude rural communities
in favor of an urban population which included suburbs as well as
central cities. In the interest of economy in sampling, this urban
sector was confined to the eight largest Standard Metropolitan
Areas of 2,000,000 or over, excluding Boston—that is, New York,
Chicago, Los Angeles, Philadelphia, Detroit, San Francisco–Oakland
and Pittsburgh. The census definition of Standard Metropolitan Area
provides a generous periphery of suburbs. Also, restriction to the
largest metropolitan areas increases the ratio of Catholics and Jews to
Protestants, and so makes important interreligious comparison easier.

The lead of the Indianapolis Study was followed in imposing a
number of eligibility criteria aimed at eliminating subgroups that
would have to be handled as special cases in many analyses, thereby
reducing that the effective size of the sample. Despite its disadvantages,
such a course appeared necessary because of the intensive analyses
contemplated in conjunction with a sample of only moderate size.
On these grounds, nonwhites and foreign-borns were excluded, as
well as couples whose family formation had been complicated by
remarriage, prospective separation, child death, plural birth, adoption, or extensive pregnancy wastage. Regarding pregnancy wastage,
the dividing line of eligibility and ineligibility was set between a
single miscarriage and either multiple miscarriages or a stillbirth,

the rationale being that a single miscarriage, while relatively frequent, usually does not greatly alter fertility. On the other hand, more ·extensive pregnancy wastage is both less common and more likely to influence significantly fertility behavior. It also seemed advisable to eliminate the few currently pregnant wives since their attitudes toward future family size would be so much influenced by their present pregnancy.

Sheer expediency dictated the remaining eligibility criteria. The Boston metropolitan area was excluded because it did not offer the same facilities for listing the specialized population of interest as did the other metropolitan areas of 2,000,000 or over. The requirement that both spouses be born in the continental United States was imposed to avoid the language problem associated with Puerto Ricans. Husbands in military occupations were excluded because of the low chance that their wives would be available for reinterview three years later. Finally, to reduce field costs, couples moving out of the seven metropolitan areas between second birth and interview were declared ineligible, though couples moving from one of the 7 metropolitan areas to another during this period retained eligibility.

As noted already, the many sample restrictions result in a low ratio of eligible couples to general population, approximately 1 in 4,000, even in the 7 metropolitan areas. Thus, eligible couples are at once relatively rare and highly scattered. Needless to say, these two properties have greatly influenced both the techniques followed in listing the population and the way this list has been used in the field to generate a probability sample.

Listing the Population

The very low ratio of eligible couples to general population made it impractical to locate respondents by means of house-to-house canvassing. Some special way of listing eligible, or at least partially eligible, couples was essential. With the generous cooperation of several State Vital Statistics Offices such a procedure was developed. This procedure permitted identification of couples having a second live birth during September 1956 and, beyond that, permitted screening these couples on such characteristics as residence, nativity, race, occupation, and the plurality and legitimacy of birth.

A pretest conducted in Camden, New Jersey, demonstrated that this screening was efficient enough so that fewer than 150 partially eligible names were needed to produce 100 completed interviews with fully eligible couples. On the basis of this ratio of 3 partially eligible names to 2 usable interviews, it was estimated that a 20 per cent sample of partially eligible names from the 7 metropolitan areas would be more than enough to produce 1,150 usable interviews. Accordingly, 20 per cent of the partially eligible names in each metropolitan area were selected randomly for inclusion in the final listing.

A final step in the listing process was to type each name and address on a separate index card, successively numbering the N cards belonging to a single metropolitan area from 1 to N. Then, with the aid of a random number table, the N numbered cards were successively sampled (without replacement) and the sample number "s" assigned to the sth card drawn. These sample numbers determined the names to be used in the field. For example, if the sample plan called for n names from metropolitan area X, then the N cards belonging to that area and having sample numbers 1 to n were used.

Sample Plan

In its final form, the sampling plan called for 1,150 interviews with eligible wives, sampled randomly within metropolitan areas in numbers proportional to the eligible couples residing in those areas. Originally a somewhat larger sample had been contemplated but cost considerations forced a reduction of the sample size to 1,150. With eligible couples so dispersed as to make it usually unfeasible for an interviewer to obtain more than one or two interviews per day, the savings in interviewer costs to be had from cluster sampling appeared small. Consequently, it was felt that the luxury of simple random sampling within metropolitan areas could be justified. By representing the 7 metropolitan areas proportionally, it was hoped to increase sample efficiency without materially increasing field costs or forfeiting the self-weighting property of the sample.

Two main problems stood in the way of realizing the objective of a proportionately stratified random sample. First, the number of eligible couples in each metropolitan area was not known precisely. Only an estimate of partially eligible couples based on a one-in-five systematic sample was available. Second, the field staff needed to know in advance the numbers and addresses of names to be used in each metropolitan area so that they could plan interviewer trips to the very scattered respondents, some of whom would demand repeated call-backs.

To solve these problems, the sampling section of National Analysts devised a scheme involving the taking of two successive samples, hereafter termed Sample A and Sample B, which together produced a good approximation to the desired sample. Seventy-five per cent of the names anticipated as needed were used in Sample A, with these names allocated to the metropolitan areas in proportion to the total numbers of partially eligible names received from them. From the results of Sample A, two parameters were estimated for each metropolitan area: the number of eligible couples and the ratio of completed interviews to partially eligible names. In turn, these estimates provided the basis for calculating how many names should be used from each metropolitan area in Sample B in order to achieve as closely as possible a total of 1,150 interviews distributed among the metropolitan areas proportionally to the estimated numbers of eligible couples residing in those areas.

Table 1 reproduces the work table used to derive the number of names needed for Sample A and B as well as their allocation by metropolitan area. The New York area may serve as an example.

TABLE 1

Worktable Determining Allocation of Sample A and B Names to Seven Metropolitan Areas

	New York	Chicago	Los Angeles	Phila-delphia	Detroit	San Francisco	Pitts-burgh	Total
Total names	947	513	458	295	319	149	210	2,891
Sample "A" Total names	423	230	206	132	142	68	94	1,295
Sample "A" Actual interviews	289	152	121	94	96	45	77	874
Sample "A" Per cent completion	68.3%	66.1%	58.7%	71.2%	67.6%	66.2%	81.9%	67.5%
Sample "A" Per cent eligible	82.7%	81.2%	74.8%	81.5%	75.0%	72.6%	84.6%	
Estimated number of eligibles	783	416	342	240	239	108	178	2,306
Per cent allocation	34.0%	18.0%	14.8%	10.4%	10.4%	4.7%	7.7%	100.0%
Interview allocation	391	207	170	120	120	54	88	1,150
Number interviews needed for Sample "B"	102	55	49	26	24	9	11	276
Names needed for Sample "B"	149	83	83	36	36	14	13	414

20

Altogether, 947 partially eligible names were received from the Vital Statistics Offices of the New York area. This 947 was 947/2891 or 32.8 per cent of all partially eligible names received from the seven metropolitan areas. For purposes of determining the number of Sample A names to allocate to New York, the provisional assumption was made that the ratio of completed interviews to partially eligible names would be the same in all 7 metropolitan areas. It was hoped that Sample A might produce .75 (1,150) or 862 completed interviews, of which New York's share was .328 (862) or 282. On the basis of Camden pretest experience, it was estimated that 150 names would be needed to complete 100 interviews. Accordingly 1.5 (282) or 423 names were allocated to New York.

The results of Sample A showed that in the New York area 423 names produced 289 completed interviews, for a completion rate of 289/423 or 68.3 per cent. Among the New York couples interviewed, 82.7 per cent proved eligible, so that the number of eligibles among the total New York names received was estimated as .827 (947) or 783, which represents 34.0 per cent of the estimated eligibles for all seven metropolitan areas. The number of interviews desired for New York, then, was .340 (1,150) or 391 interviews. This was 391−289 or 102 more interviews than obtained in Sample A. These extra interviews had to be obtained from Sample B, and judging from the completion rate observed for New York in Sample A, 102 more interviews would require the use of 102/.683 or 149 names. Therefore, Sample B included 149 names from the New York area.

Theoretically with perfect execution in the field, the sampling plan just described would provide every eligible couple with an equal chance of getting into the sample.[2] In practice, of course, this ideal is

[2] The chance of an eligible couple getting into the sample may be viewed as a product of two probabilities: (a) the probability of being included in the 20 per cent subsample and therefore appearing on the final list; (b) the probability that their name, if listed, will be chosen for use in the field. Having their name chosen assures that they will be included in the sample, since, under the assumption of perfect field execution, there are no refusals or failures of contact. The first probability is fixed at .2 for all couples. Obviously too, the second probability is constant for all eligible couples belonging to the same metropolitan area, by virtue of simple random sampling being used within metropolitan areas. It is less obvious that the second probability is equal for eligible couples belonging to different metropolitan areas. Consider the ith metropolitan stratum with N_i partially eligible names listed. On the basis of Sample A, the eligibility rate in this stratum is estimated as p_i. Hence the number of interviews to be allocated to this stratum is $(N_i p_i / \Sigma N_i p_i) \; 1150$; and the number of names needed to produce this many interviews is estimated at

$$(1/p_i) \; (N_i p_i / \Sigma N_i p_i) \; 1150.$$

Letting $N = \Sigma N_i$ and $p = \Sigma N_i p_i / N$, this number of names may be rewritten as $N_i \; (1150/N_p)$ or more briefly yet, as $N_i C$, since in any single sample p and N are constants. Now the chance of a single name being drawn from a list of N_i names in $N_i C$ random draws without replacement is $N_i C / N_i$ or C, constant for all metropolitan areas.

not reached inasmuch as some couples refuse to be interviewed; others are repeatedly away, ill, or unlocated. Hence, bias is to be expected, its magnitude closely linked with the frequency of refusals and failures to make contact. It is also evident that in the present sampling plan the number of interviews being allocated to each metropolitan area is only approximately proportional to the number of eligible residents. Consequently, the efficiency of the design is not exactly that of a proportionate stratified sample but most likely is intermediate between such an efficiency and that of a simple random sample of the same size.

Because of costs, it was not regarded as feasible to interview husbands or to let the interviews with the wife average much longer than one hour and twenty minutes. Instead it was planned to leave with the wife, at the end of her interview, a personality inventory for her to fill out and mail back and an attitude questionnaire for her husband to complete and mail back. Various follow-up procedures would be employed to increase the rate of returns.

Field Plan

The sampling plan just described necessitated a rather elaborate field plan. All interviewing was done by experienced members of the interviewing staff of National Analysts. In each metropolitan area, a small group of interviewers attended a three day training school and then conducted the interviews of Samples A and B in about two months time. Care was taken to complete all prescribed call-backs on Sample A names before starting with Sample B names so that the completion rates estimated from Sample A would not be biased.

With the names forwarded to the interviewers representing only partially screened couples, a way had to be found of screening these couples on the several remaining eligibility criteria, such as marital status and pregnancy wastage. This problem was solved by a one-page eligibility form stapled on to the front of the questionnaire. If the interviewer ascertained ineligibility, she terminated the interview as soon as she completed the eligibility form. As a precaution against inaccurate information on the birth certificates, the 14 questions of the eligibility form covered the entire list of eligibility criteria. However, the number of birth certificates detected as inaccurate proved negligible.

Special instructions were given about movers. If the interviewer found that the respondent had moved, she made every effort to learn the new address. If the new address belonged to the same Standard Metropolitan Area or one of the other six metropolitan areas, then arrangements were made to contact the household at its new location.

Only if the new address fell outside the universe of seven metropolitan areas was the couple concerned regarded as ineligible.

To reduce losses from such categories as not-at-home, ill, busy, and the like, a maximum of four personal call-backs were employed, when necessary, to complete an interview. To lower the refusal rate, a letter of introduction was sent out to each potential respondent ahead of the interviewer. (See Appendix C.)

A number of precautions were taken to have the interview run smoothly. Good rapport between interviewer and respondent was deemed essential, not only to improve interview content, but to win the respondent's interest in the study and so increase the chances that she would return her mail questionnaire and encourage her husband to do likewise. Toward this end, the questionnaire was pretested in a series of field trials including a pretest of 100 interviews with eligible couples taken in Camden, New Jersey. In addition, every interviewer attended a three-day training session, conducted jointly by a representative from National Analysts and one from the Office of Population Research. Instruction covered the general purposes of the study, objectives and handling of specific questions, as well as field procedures. As aids, an instruction manual was prepared and a study comprehension test administered. Trainers remained in the area long enough to review personally the first two interviews of each interviewer. Following these initial reviews, completed schedules were mailed into National Analysts twice a week for review prior to coding, followed up by direct letters to correct individual errors or omissions.

After each interview was completed, the wife was given two questionnaires, a personality inventory titled "Report of Personal Likes and Interests" to be filled out by herself and a second questionnaire titled "Study of Attitudes Toward Work" to be filled out by her husband. It was hoped that interest generated by the interview would lead most wives to mail back completed questionnaires and to induce their husbands to do the same. The procedure followed to increase the rate of mail returns was to use a reminder letter and a maximum of two personal call-backs, when necessary, to secure completion of the mail questionnaires. However, the interviewers were instructed not to press to the point of jeopardizing future relations with the respondents.

RESULTS

Interview Results

The interview results were highly gratifying. Interviewers reported high levels of cooperation and interest on the part of most respondents, thereby duplicating the experience of Freedman, Whelpton, and Campbell in their national fertility survey and the earlier experience of Whelpton and Kiser with the Indianapolis Study.

A total of 1,165 interviews were completed with eligible respondents, distributed among the seven metropolitan areas as indicated in the first two rows of Table 2. Altogether, 1,709 partially eligible names were used to achieve these interviews, with this ratio of 146 names to 100 interviews coinciding closely with the ratio encountered in the Camden pretest.

Of the total listing of 1,709 names and addresses forwarded to the sample area, 103, or 6 per cent, could not be contacted because they had moved out of the universe of seven metropolitan areas. In Table 2 these moves are distinguished from all other types of ineligibility. The rate of such moves varied significantly from one metropolitan area to another, with a high of 9 per cent for Los Angeles and a low of 2 per cent for San Francisco–Oakland.

There was a total of 1,457 respondents who were asked the questions on the eligibility form. Of this total, 292 respondents, or 20 per cent, were found to be ineligible. Corresponding rates in the sample areas varied from a high of 25 per cent in Detroit to a low of 15 per cent in Pittsburgh. A previous marriage on the part of husband or wife constituted the most important source of ineligibility. Two other consequential sources were pregnancy wastage in excess of one miscarriage and a number of living children other than two.[3]

About 6 per cent of all contacts with potential respondents resulted in a final refusal to be interviewed. In no sample area did the refusal rate reach as high as 10 per cent. Freedman, Whelpton, and Campbell encountered a similar over-all rate of refusals in their survey. The rate reported in the Indianapolis Study was almost twice as high. A break-off almost never occurred after the interview was started. Miscellaneous attrition—chiefly in the form of not-at-home, no-such-address, no-respondent-contact, or illness—led to a loss of 66 cases, fewer than the number of refusals.

These results raise hopes that the sample of wives interviewed is not seriously biased. The ineligibility rates, varying from one metropolitan area to another partly as a result of sampling error, are one reason why the seven metropolitan areas are not represented exactly proportionally. However, these ineligibility rates are not a direct source of bias since they in no way affect the representativeness of eligible couples interviewed in each area. Refusals and miscellaneous

---

[3] Besides these characteristics mentioned in the text as major sources of ineligibility, only three other criteria disqualified as many as 10 couples. They were: expecting a six month separation in the near future, wife currently pregnant, and neonatal mortality, in that order of importance.

TABLE 2

Interview Results, by Metropolitan Area

	Total sample	New York	Chicago	Los Angeles	Phila-delphia	Detroit	Pitts-burgh	San Fran-cisco
Total number of names used	1,709	572	313	289	168	178	107	82
Per cent distribution	100.0%	33.5%	18.3%	16.9%	9.8%	10.4%	6.3%	4.8%
Number completed interviews	1,165	406	207	169	120	118	88	57
Per cent distribution	100.0%	34.8%	17.8%	14.5%	10.3%	10.1%	7.6%	4.9%
Number moved out of area	103	27	26	27	8	10	3	2
Per cent distribution	99.9%	26.2%	25.2%	26.2%	7.8%	9.7%	2.9%	1.9%
Attrition rate (moves)[a]	6.0	4.7	8.3	9.3	4.8	5.6	2.8	2.4
Number of ineligible respondents	292	80	50	57	30	40	15	20
Per cent distribution	100.0%	27.5%	17.2%	19.6%	10.3%	13.7%	5.2%	6.5%
Ineligibility rate[b]	20.0	16.5	19.5	25.2	20.0	25.3	14.6	24.7
Number of refusals[c]	83	35	15	19	7	5	0	2
Per cent distribution	100.0%	42.2%	18.1%	22.9%	8.4%	6.0%	0.0%	2.4%
Refusal rate[d]	5.7	7.2	5.8	8.4	4.7	3.2	0.0	2.6
Miscellaneous attrition[e]	66	24	15	17	3	5	1	1
Per cent distribution	100.0%	36.4%	22.7%	25.8%	4.5%	7.6%	1.5%	1.5%

[a] Number of moves divided by number of names used.

[b] Number of ineligible respondents divided by number of completed interviews plus ineligibles. The ineligible respondents appearing in this table are those found ineligible at the time of interview only. They do not include the cases eliminated at the Vital Statistics Offices.

[c] Includes 3 respondents "too busy" to be interviewed.

[d] Number of refusals divided by number of completed interviews plus number of ineligibles.

[e] The total 66 cases includes 19 where no one was home (despite up to 4 calls); 18 where no such address could be located; 16 where there was no respondent contact; 11 cases of illness; 1 vacant dwelling; and 1 language difficulty.

attrition presumably do contribute bias because it is likely that the eligible couples thereby lost differ systematically from those actually interviewed. But the fact that the refusal and attrition rates are so low greatly reduces the likelihood of serious bias.

For purposes of generalizing to the seven Standard Metropolitan Areas included in this study, the sampling efficiency of the set of 1,165 interviews may be put at roughly that of a simple random sample of the same size. In an auxiliary analysis, not reproduced here, covariance analysis was utilized to investigate the extent to which the seven metropolitan areas differed, within religious groups, with respect to sixteen variables, including most of the principal dependent variables. The contrasts proved consistently small. This outcome means that small gains in sample efficiency were obtained by stratifying the present sample on metropolitan area; and these gains were probably further reduced by the imprecise allocation of interviews to strata. Accordingly, it seems appropriate to base any standard error pertaining to the total sample on the model of a simple random sample of the same size.

Questionnaire Results

The generally favorable response of the respondents is nowhere better shown than in the high rate of returned questionnaires. Most of these returns preceded the reminder letter and, indeed, the two personal call-backs netted relatively few additional questionnaires.

Of the total of 1,165 wives, 961, or 83 per cent, returned completed personality inventories. A total of 941, or 81 per cent, of the husbands returned usable questionnaires. Among the 961 wives and 941 husbands returning questionnaires there were 938 joint returns. Thus, there were only 3 husbands returning questionnaires unaccompanied by the wife's, as compared to 23 wives whose husbands were uncooperative.

Though a nonresponse rate of 20 per cent is low as mail questionnaires go, it is still high enough to allow appreciable bias. An analysis of this bias, summarized in Table 3, is based on a comparison of the 938 couples who did return questionnaires with the 227 couples who did not, including the few cases where only one spouse cooperated. Distributions on 16 variables are compared and the statistical significance of differences evaluated by chi-square. Chi-square values identified by two asterisks indicate probability values below 1 per cent; a single asterisk indicates a probability between 1 and 5 per cent; values with no asterisk mean that the differences were not significant at the 5 per cent level.

TABLE 3

Significance of Differences between Selected Characteristics of Couples Returning and Not Returning Mail Questionnaires

Characteristic	Degrees of Freedom	Chi-Square
Standard Metropolitan Area	6	19.9**
Religion	3	9.2*
Husband's current occupation	7	7.7
Husband's 1956 earnings	9	12.6
Husband's education	9	20.0*
Wife's education	9	13.9
Wife's vocabulary test score	9	13.6
Marriage duration (interval marriage to second child)	8	10.8
Interval marriage to first birth	8	19.1*
Interval first to second birth	8	9.0
Wife's age at marriage	9	7.1
Husband's age at marriage	9	19.2*
Wife's present age	9	8.0
Husband's present age	9	17.0*
Family size desired	8	12.1
Preferred interval to third child	8	22.6**

NOTE: A single asterisk indicates that the probability of no difference is between 1 and 5 per cent; a double asterisk that it is below 1 per cent.

It is clear that couples returning questionnaires are not the same in a number of important characteristics as those not cooperating. One of two highly significant biases relates to Standard Metropolitan Area. The observed significance level is due primarily to the results in Philadelphia which contributed almost twice its share of non-respondents. When the chi-square value is recomputed without this sample area, it fails to attain significance at the .05 level. The only explanation that can be suggested for the deviation of this city is an administrative one—the field work commenced two or three weeks earlier in Philadelphia than in any other city and this caused an extension of the interval between the interview and the follow-up procedures applied to nonrespondents.

Aside from residence, couples not returning questionnaires tend to exhibit the following characteristics, sufficiently intercorrelated to suggest a general factor: Catholic, lower education, lower income, shorter marriage duration and first birth interval, and shorter preferred interval between second and third children. The converse holds for those returning questionnaires, who, for example, show a greater than expected proportion of Jews in the group.[4]

[4] Cooperating and noncooperating husbands also differ significantly with respect to age, both currently and at marriage. However, these contrasts exhibit no simple pattern, such as cooperating husbands tending to be older or younger.

Fairly well defined biases do exist, then, but in subsequent analyses they will be largely ignored on two grounds. First of all, none of the biases are large absolutely and show statistical significance only because of the moderately large samples, 227 and 938 cases, being compared. Secondly, the crucial question for subsequent analyses is not how much distributions differ in the two groups, but how much relationships between variables differ in the two groups; and it is hard to believe that important contrasts of relationship would ordinarily parallel such minor differences of distribution.

Chapter III. Methodology

This chapter on methodology includes the following aspects: preparation and field testing of two mail return questionnaires and an interview schedule; development of measures of variables; quality controls on field work as well as data processing, and descriptions of some procedures and techniques used in analyzing large bodies of data.

Summaries of these four aspects correspond to the four sections of this chapter. The first section, "Questionnaires and Schedule," is limited to general descriptions of pretests in order to maintain a convenient separation from the topic of the second section, the development of measures of variables. Obviously, the development of measures begins with the items to be included in a questionnaire or schedule which is then pretested. However, the manipulation of items and responses to items in the creation of measures, scales, or indices is a distinct and often a technically complicated procedure.

The second section outlines the rationale behind the choice of procedures and then presents the salient details of a factor analytic approach to the construction of measures. The summary supposes a basic acquaintance, on the part of the reader, with both scalogram analysis and factor analysis.

The subsequent sections, on "Quality Control" and "Analysis of Data," deal with solutions to two problems that become accentuated in large-scale research.

The first problem concerns the prevention and detection of errors of various types. Large-scale research requires the assistance of specially trained interviewers and machine processing of data. These are sources of bias and errors found in lesser degrees in more modest studies.

The second problem is created by the absolute amount of data. The task of reducing raw data to manageable and digestable proportions becomes increasingly difficult—especially in an analytic survey—as the size and scope of the survey are enlarged.

QUESTIONNAIRES AND SCHEDULE

In the course of developing questionnaires and the schedule, several pretests were undertaken. Most of these were small-scale tests requiring few interviews. The largest, the "Camden Pretest," involved 100 interviews. The objectives of this series of pretests included the development of appropriately phrased questions and measures; the test of sampling procedures; the test of interviewing

29

procedures; a first validity check of the more important hypotheses; estimates of time-costs per interview; and finally, the evaluation of coding·procedures.

Three methods of collecting data were incorporated into the over-all design. Each of these, a wife's personality inventory, a husband's questionnaire, and an interviewer's schedule, was subjected to pre-testing. Each involved special problems. Husbands are not at home as much as wives and are therefore more difficult to contact. Pre-sumably the wife is more apt than the husband to recall the details of the couple's fertility history. The personality inventory had to be self-administered and yet provide valid measures of rather subtle aspects of the wife's personality.

Personality Inventory

The first two of these pretests were devoted primarily to the development of adequate measures of personality variables. In this area, a preliminary survey of existing and proven personality in-ventories revealed that these either did not claim to measure the variables of interest or were impractical to administer. Cost factors necessitated the restriction of required measures to a few easily coded items that could be administered by regular interviewers or by mail questionnaire. Necessity, therefore, and some optimism regarding success motivated the initial experimentation with semiprojective (sentence-completion) tests administered under field conditions. After two pretests, and discouraging results, this work with sentence-completion tests was abandoned in favor of adopting portions of a personality inventory which is not yet published.[1]

In addition, two measures were adopted from the *Edwards Personal Preference Schedule* developed by Allen Edwards.[2] In all, 15 measures of various personality dimensions were included in a mail-return questionnaire pretested on a sample of 100 wives selected from the area around Camden, New Jersey. The returns encouraged the use of mail return questionnaires and the retention of most measures (based on internal analyses and correlations with fertility measures).[3] However, following this pretest experience, some items were added as well as eliminated in the efforts to improve measurements.

---

[1] A full description of this experimentation is published. See: Elliot G. Mishler, "A Scalogram Analysis of the Sentence Completion Test," *Educational and Psychological Measurement*, 18 (1958), pp. 75–90.

We are indebted to Dr. Saunders for his permission to use portions of the Personality Research Inventory (PRI) prior to its publication. Of the 25 scales of the (PRI), 13 were judged suitable, by virtue of content, for consideration as predictors of fertility variables.

[2] These measures are labeled Succorance and Nurturance.

[3] See Appendix C for the measures retained.

Husbands' Mail Questionnaire

At the time of the Camden test, the interviewers left a questionnaire with the wife and asked her to have her husband complete and return it in an accompanying self-addressed envelope. This procedure resulted ultimately in a return of 81 of the 100 questionnaires distributed. Analyses of these questionnaires, as well as the wife's personality inventory, included examination of interitem associations prior to the formation of measures and the correlation of these summary measures with fertility variables. (In effect, such analyses are also tests of coding procedures.) In addition, comparisons were made on religion, education, and income between the 81 husbands who returned their questionnaires and the 19 more reluctant and forgetful husbands. Such comparisons revealed selection on education— an indication that nonrespondents may tend to be from the lower educational echelons. Lesser differences were found on the income and religion comparisons.

Interviewer's Schedule

The Camden sample of 100 wives served as the respondents in the major pretest of the interview schedule. Again some emphasis in the analysis of responses pertained to the examination of internal consistency in the construction of measures, locating and sharpening poor items, and the like. In these respects, the analyses of pretest results differed little among schedule, questionnaire, and inventory, except that in the case of the schedule tape recordings of interviews and interviewer's opinions proved valuable adjuncts to the statistical analyses. However, in addition to these analyses, the actual process of locating 100 women who were eligible and cooperative wives provided estimates of refusal rates and a partial test of the sampling procedures. Both aspects were of vital concern. Since the interviewer schedule deals with rather intimate details of family life, a high refusal rate was a damaging possibility. Also, if the number of eligible respondents was small relative to the number of initial contacts, the costs per completed interview could well be prohibitive.

The analysis of the Camden pretest data and procedures allayed most fears, although changes in questionnaires, schedule, and procedures did follow. Interviewing time was cut by pruning the schedule of less promising items. Changes were made among the family structure and personality measures. In turn, these changes were further tested on much smaller samples.

Summary of Camden Pretest

The Camden pretest was a test of instruments as well as of procedures planned for the larger study and generally justified the data gathering procedures and the sampling plan. Briefly, out of 143 women whose names were secured from vital statistics records of second births in a given period, 133 names could be contacted.

Of the 133, only 9 refused to grant an interview. Of the remaining 124, 22 were ineligible, 2 broke off the interview and 100 cooperated fully. The completion ratio, conservatively estimated as 100 over 143 less 22 ineligibles, is over 80 per cent—not prohibitively low.

This high degree of respondent cooperation coupled with moderately encouraging results in the development of measures dissuaded further extensive testing.[4]

DEVELOPING MEASURES

The problems and difficulties attending the development of measures vary with the type of measurement attempted and the variable being studied. On the one hand, income, age, residence, religion, sex, job changes, occupation, and the like appear the most accessible to measurement—partly because there is precedent on which to rely. Attitudes and personality traits, on the other hand, appear as less tangible and more elusive when the development of appropriate measures arises. The immediate consequence of this variation in difficulty is a more elaborate, self-conscious, and formal process of developing measures of attitudes and personality variables.

This process is summarized briefly in following paragraphs beginning with the deliberations and decisions that led to the measures reported in Appendix C.

Objectives

The developing of measures for the more vexatious variables was preceded by defining certain goals. First, it was agreed that the most desirable measures were those that satisfied criteria of unidimensionality—that is, items and responses to items should appear to scale, in the Guttman sense of a scale, or "belong together" in the sense of forming a cluster of high intercorrelations that could be explained in terms of an underlying general factor. The persuasive reasons behind this decision were the substantive assumptions that the personality variables and many of the attitudes were indeed unidimensional. Also, the analytic problem of interpreting correlations is simplified if the contents of measures are pure. Secondly, since the

---

[4] In all, the pretesting program involved five distinct tests and over 350 couples.

number of measures to be developed was large, the technique of developing these had to be efficiently routinized. Finally, if a variable was viewed as being continuous, the measure of the variable should be capable of discriminating among a range of values.

Choice of Models

With these agreed upon objectives in mind, Guttman scalogram analysis was the initial choice from among the acceptable scaling models and procedures. One attempt at developing Guttman scales for the personality dimensions is cited elsewhere in this chapter.[5] In addition to Guttman scaling procedures, alternative, more objective, and more routine procedures, based on these and other early experiences were initiated. A factor-analytic approach to scale or test construction was substituted for scalogram analysis of responses to items.

Factor Analysis

The rationale justifying Guttman scaling also justifies the factor-analytic approach. A test designed to measure a single factor, when factor analyzed, should display a general factor. The more this is true, in the parlance of the factorists, the larger the loading of each item on the general factor and the less variance there is to be distributed among common and unique factors.[6]

In general, the conditions for a pure test and a good Guttman scale agree closely. High positive interitem associations assure a more or less pure test and at least a quasi-scale. Fundamental distinctions revolve around whether, for example, responses to items measuring attitudes are viewed as qualitative or quantitative data. This has a bearing on the selection of appropriate statistical procedures. Further distinctions appear in the importance attached to item response distributions (item marginals), ordering of items, and the reproduction of the pattern of item responses from a respondent's ordinal position. The factor analytic approach is largely indifferent to these refinements. However, with deference to the logic and sophistication of scalogram analysis, the emphases on the qualitative nature of attitude-item responses, and the ability to reproduce patterns of responses is of little practical significance. Within limits, quantitative techniques may be forced on qualitative data without distorting conclusions. Almost without exception, there is little to be gained by

[5] Mishler, "A Scalogram Analysis of the Sentence Completion Test."

[6] The factor-analytic approach to test construction is most familiar to psychologists and psychometricians. Factor analysis is employed both as a device for studying the structure of relationship among items composing a multidimensional measure and as means of selecting items that appear to measure some general underlying dimension.

reproducing the pattern of responses. Greater significance can be attached to the emphasis on item response distribution and the ability to order items, but these emphases are related. If the scale is acceptable, the ordering of items by "difficulty" follows the ordering of items by marginals. The greatest value of the emphasis on item marginals is that it assures discrimination—a dispersion of scores or ordinal positions.

Selecting Items

Items judged to have a common content formed the initial pool of candidates for inclusion. A matrix of interitem tetrachoric correlations was computed and the first centroid factor was extracted.[7]

Items were eliminated in accordance with three criteria:[8]

1. items outside the 10–90 per cent range of item marginals to be eliminated regardless of loadings;
2. items with loadings of .4 or less are to be eliminated from inclusion in the measure being developed;
3. items with loadings of less than .5 but greater than .4 are to be considered for exclusion. Such items are retained if the number of items with loadings of .5 or greater is three or less.

These criteria are based on the results of limited experimentation with three pools of items subjected to a complete factorization and orthogonal rotations to simple structure as well as scalogram analyses. Here it was found that: if the items are highly intercorrelated, differences in the items retained are largely a function of the criteria since a particular number of "errors" in scalogram analysis does not unequivocally translate to a particular factor loading; if items are not too highly intercorrelated or form distinct clusters of correlations, the selected items tend to differ and both techniques reject the

---

[7] The assumption here is that the first factor extracted corresponds most closely to the common content of the items as judged by face validity, provided loadings are appreciable and most, if not all, items exhibit large factor loadings. In essence, this assumption is also made in scalogram analysis with respect to the underlying dimension.

[8] The practice of eliminating items if they contribute to low intercorrelations or to large numbers of errors is to be viewed with suspicion unless otherwise justified by statistical tests or replicating studies. Discussion of this and related problems as well as appropriate preliminary statistical tests are found in: A. E. Maxwell, "Statistical Methods in Factor Analysis," *Psychological Bulletin*, 56, 3 (1959), pp. 228–235; L. A. Goodman, "Simple Statistical Methods for Scalogram Analysis," *Psychometrika*, 24 (1959), pp. 29–43; P. C. Sagi, "A Statistical Test for the Significance of a Coefficient of Reproducibility," *ibid.*, 24, (1959), pp. 19–27. In the current study, since all personality measures and most attitudinal measures had undergone a development program even prior to the pretests on the Camden, N. J., sample, there existed ample evidence to make the statistical tests largely superfluous.

hypothesis of unidimensionality; if the first centroid factor loadings are high (say over .5), the correlation matrix is quickly exhausted and no rotation will alter the conclusion that the items belong together.[9]

Clearly the two techniques, scalogram analysis and factor analysis, need not and do not give the same results except in the case where interitem correlations are perfect. However, the more closely the latter is approximated the less concern need be expressed over theoretical and procedural differences. Conversely, where great differences between techniques do obtain, it is quite likely that items and not theories are at fault. Therefore, no great superiority of technique is claimed in employing the factor approach to the development of measures. Quite simply, the factor approach to item selection and the assessment of the internal consistency of a measure are more susceptible to routinized machine procedures. The specific applications of the techniques are found in Appendix C.

Scoring

Much as the technique of item selection was justified in terms of its correspondence to items selected by scalogram analysis, so was the simplified method of scoring justified through comparisons with the ranks assigned to scale types. Experimentation with measures developed by the alternate techniques indicated that where measures were judged acceptable by either technique, the rank ordering of response patterns agreed closely with scores assigned by totaling the number of items endorsed positively. Even under the worst of conditions with the poorest measures, agreement was fairly close.[10]

---

[9] A number of articles pertain to comparisons of scalogram analysis with factor analysis. See: H. J. Eysenck, "Review of Measurement and Prediction, Vol. 4, 'The American Soldier'," *International Journal of Opinion and Attitude Research*, 5 (1951), pp. 95–102; H. J. Eysenck and S. Crown, "An Experimental Study in Opinion-Attitude Methodology," *ibid.*, 3 (1949), pp. 47–86; N. L. Gage, "Scaling and Factorial Design in Opinion Poll Measurements," *Studies in Higher Education*, LXI (1947); L. Guttman, "Scale Analysis, Factor Analysis and Dr. Eysenck," *International Journal of Opinion and Attitude Research*, 5 (1951), pp. 103–120; and P. H. Kriedt and K. E. Clark, " 'Item Analysis' versus 'Scale Analysis,' " *Journal of Applied Psychology*, 33 (1949), pp. 114–121.

[10] To illustrate this latter point, consider four dichotomous items having marginals of .50 and responses that are statistically independent. Sixteen response patterns are formed of which only 5 conform to ideal scale types or patterns. The remaining eleven patterns are assigned to ideal scale patterns they most closely resemble according to the logic of scalogram analysis. (Even so, not all assignments can be made unambiguously.) The correspondence between ranks so assigned and scores computed by merely counting the number of positive endorsements per respondent is great enough to yield a coefficient of correlation of .79, an appreciable value under the adverse conditions of a nonsense measure. (The assignment of non-scale types on one of five ranks is at times arbitrary. The pattern + + − −, for example, was equally split between to the 5th rank [+ + + +] and to the 1st rank [− − − −]). Limited experimentation with actual data, for example, a four item personality scale with a coefficient of reproducibility of .95 shows the expected improvement with the more favorable marginals and a positive manifold to the association matrix. In this case, a coefficient of correlation of .94 instead of .79 results.

Quality Control

The importance of maintaining quality controls on data collection and processing is evident. Field procedures that maintain a high level of interviewer performance, coding procedures that minimize the introduction of errors, and machine procedures that include checks on computations comprise the essential components of an effective control program. No component can be neglected without obvious hazards.

Controls on Field Work

The following goals were established: (a) maintaining field work at a high level of efficiency and accuracy; (b) maintaining consistent treatment of field situations from respondent to respondent and through time; and (c) assuring adequate internal control for proper administration. To achieve these goals required six distinct steps in the preparation and overseeing of the field work:

1. Interviewer training sessions, in which each field worker received individual training.
2. Practice interviews by each field worker for criticism and correction of early misunderstandings.
3. One hundred per cent editing of first returns from each field worker, followed up by direct letters to correct individual errors or omissions.
4. Memoranda prepared for all supervisors where misunderstandings seemed to be general rather than individual.
5. Maintenance of detailed check in sheets, which controlled not only numbers of returns by identification numbers but kept record of such matters as dates received, completions of husband and wife follow-up questionnaires and the like.
6. Maintenance of a standard field editing procedure (over and above "error editing" mentioned above) to remove ineligible, incomplete, or unacceptable interviews at the earliest possible stage followed by submission of all such rejects to the study director for final disposition.

Controls on Coding

Here, the explicit goals were: (a) to maintain a high level of direct accuracy in "factual-type" questions; (b) to insure a uniformity of coding open-ended or "free-answer" questions; and (c) to avoid coding bias. Several operations furthering these ends were devised. These operations, among others, included the use of detailed coding manuals; 100 per cent checking of all coding and punching; and a series of additional checks on coding by trained supervisors of items judged especially important or difficult.

Controls on Machine Data Processing

Two goals in the control of data processing were: (a) the early location of errors and inconsistencies in the data so as to minimize the interruption of machine running; and (b) the checking of machine calculated statistics for errors in programming and effects of rounding errors. The first of these goals was concerned primarily with the recording of data in IBM cards and hence involved controls on the quality of the card punching operation. The second goal was concerned with a check on the programming of electronic data processing machines and dummy data were used as empirical checks on the programming of formulae and the assessment of rounding error.

ANALYSES OF DATA

Analyses of data, in this study, may be simply classified as bearing on assessment of effects of biases due to nonresponse, testing of hypotheses (analyses of interrelationships among dependent variables and analyses of relationships of independent to dependent variables), and, finally, the summarizing of results in a multivariate statement of relationships.

Early in the planning of the study, commitments were made that were decisive in shaping the form that some of these analyses would take. These commitments were to the development of interval type measures, where warranted and possible, and then to the use of coefficients of correlation (where meaningful) as the preferred statistic describing the relationship between two variables. This preference was based on two considerations—the advantages of employing a statistic that succinctly summarized the degree and direction of association and a statistic that was amenable to a variety of analyses, multivariate as well as bivariate.

These decisions facilitated the efficient and rapid processing of data. Correlation coefficients were computed electronically for the entire sample of 1,165 wives and for the subsample of 938 couples returning all questionnaires. In addition, correlations and all intermediate statistics were computed within:

(a) each of eight class-religion subsamples;
(b) each of two class categories;
(c) each of four religion categories.

These fifteen matrices were subsequently utilized for separete and parallel analyses.

Effects of Nonresponse

Differences between correlation matrices for the sample of 1,165 wives interviewed and the 938 wives interviewed who with their husbands returned all questionnaires were used to assess the effects of possible bias if analyses were restricted to the 938 completely co-operative couples. If differences were small, the 938 could be considered as representative of the 1,165. The convenience of possibly restricting the analysis to 938 couples and not being overly concerned with nonresponse as an important source of bias—could not be overlooked.

Differences between matrices were computed as part of the program yielding the correlation matrices. The distribution of differences between corresponding coefficients of correlations yielded only four differences exceeding .05 out of 1,770 comparisons. No differences exceeded .06. Thus, from the point of view of association—the 938 subsample differs little from the total, 1,165. At least, so far as associations between wife's variables are concerned, the effects of bias seem negligible. This may not be true of the husbands who did not return mail questionnaires. Data on this comparison are wanting.[11]

Hypothesis Testing

Many of the hypotheses in the study, when framed in statistical terms, took the form of an assertion of correlation between two variables.

Where this was true, the several correlation matrices conveniently provided the requisite statistics for hypothesis testing. Two types of tests were employed. The first took the form of denying the hypothesis of no association between two variables. The second test, a test of homogeneity of correlation coefficients, was included in the program for computing correlations. The purpose of this test was to ascertain, in some objective manner, whether correlations differed among religions and class categories. If the variations could be attributed to chance, religion-class designations served no purpose in explaining a given correlation.

These statistical tests served another important function besides hypothesis testing. The fact that there were over 100,000 correlations computed required some efficient method of sorting out those that appeared promising as leads for future investigations. Again this

---

[11] A description of couples not returning mail questionnaires is found in the previous chapter.

sorting procedure was facilitated by identification of "significant" differences.[12]

Of course, not all of the statistical analysis by any means was limited to the examination of these correlation matrices. Wherever there was a strong suspicion that correlations were other than linear, the correlational approach was supplemented by a test of linearity. Also, the relationship between religion-class categories and each variable was examined. These analyses took the form of calculating correlation ratios as a further device for ascertaining the importance of maintaining religion and class as controls.[13]

Finally, since certain variables and hypotheses could not be fitted justifiably into the correlational approach just summarized, additional analyses were necessary. The most detailed and extensive of these analyses was concerned with interrelationships among the dependent variables. To facilitate comparisons with other studies, the analysis of contraceptive data, for example, followed accepted conventional techniques. Also, some independent variables—residence, religious affiliation, and sex of children as examples—are clearly qualitative in character and could be most successfully handled through analyses of changes in proportions or frequencies.

Multivariate Summary

Multivariate summaries of relationships are found in Chapter XIX. Those analyses are restricted in scope by the near impossibility of including, in a single analysis, both qualitative and quantitative variables. However, since tests of homogeneity of correlations indicate important differences among religions, separate and parallel treatments are accorded the three major religious groupings.

In this case, the technique of summarizing relationships—factor analysis—appears the most appropriate choice in view of the questions that are put to these data. First, what are the underlying dimensions that account for the intercorrelations among selected dependent and independent variables and how do these dimensions differ among religions? Second, within religions, how much of the variance of these dependent variables is accounted for by selected independent variables taken simultaneously?

The answers to these questions have been deferred to the end of this report.

[12] The significance levels attached to these differences are .05, .01 and .001, presuming, of course, the assumptions have been met. These probabilities are at best only approximate.

[13] Generally, these results were negative. The instances where religion and class exerted a meaningful influence are made clear in later chapters.

PART II

FERTILITY VARIABLES

Introduction to Part II

The six substantive chapters of this section deal entirely with aspects of fertility and their interrelations. More facets of fertility are distinguished than is customary in order to exploit the detailed fertility histories collected in the interviews. These histories include attitudes toward birth spacing and family size as well as facts about birth intervals, contraception, and fecundity. It is left to a second set of substantive chapters, Chapters X through XIX, to relate selected fertility indices to a broad range of social and psychological variables.

Because the context is present-day, metropolitan America, a convenient starting point is the following very obvious proposition. The number of births happening to a couple and the spacing between these births are only loosely determined by the couple's fertility preferences. The major reasons for this looseness, when it is not the couple's own vagueness or disagreement over what they want, are failures of pregnancy postponement and problems of fecundity.

As a way of building on this proposition, it is convenient to distinguish six dimensions of fertility which may be roughly designated as follows:

> number of births
> birth intervals
> desired family size
> preferred birth intervals
> birth postponement
> fecundity

By "number of births" is meant the live issue ever born to the couple. "Birth intervals" is taken to include the interval between marriage and first birth as well as intervals between successive births. The corresponding two classes of fertility preference are "desired family size" and "preferred birth intervals," the latter including preferred timing of the first-born in relation to marriage as well as preferred intervals between successive children. Naturally these preferences vary from couple to couple in such respects as explicitness and strength, spouse consensus, and stability through time.

The agreement between actual fertility and fertility preferences is rarely perfect and two facets of the imperfect correspondence may be distinguished. The first aspect, denoted "birth postponement," is the degree to which couples are able to achieve desired delays in their pregnancies and births. Potentially available for this purpose are such means of fertility regulation as contraception, induced abortion, and sterilization. The second aspect, "fecundity," is the degree to which couples are able to hasten pregnancy and birth when and if they are desired. The factors involved, such as ease of conception, pregnancy wastage, and military separation, are primarily involuntary.

The interconnections among these six fertility dimensions have received very unequal emphasis in the literature. The bulk of research has pertained to relationships among number of births, desired family size, contraception, and fecundity.[1] The published studies of birth spacing are few and, with the exception of a British study, narrow in scope.[2] To the writers' knowledge, no intensive study has been made of birth spacing preferences. The Indianapolis Study is a partial exception; but Kiser and Whelpton only relate "most desirable" birth intervals to a classification of family-planning status.[3] Accordingly, the chance to investigate the interrelations of all six fertility aspects, even if only for a specialized sample, is regarded as one of the special opportunities afforded by the current study.

The first chapter of this section, Chapter IV, and its accompanying Appendix A deal with fecundity. The topic of birth postponement is addressed in Chapter V and Appendix B. Birth intervals, preferred birth spacing, and desired family size are the respective focuses of Chapters VI through VIII. Chapter IX summarizes results.

The reader who does not have a specialist's interest in fertility is well advised to turn to Chapter IX. The intervening chapters are relatively detailed and technical, with considerable emphasis placed upon measurement problems. This is especially true of Chapters IV and V, concerned with fecundity and contraception, inasmuch as these chapters and their appendices concentrate on new procedures of classification and analysis.

[1] Four classic Western studies of contraception that also pay some attention to fecundity and number of births are Raymond Pearl, "Contraception and Fertility in 2,000 Women," *Human Biology*, 4 (1932), 365–407; R. K. Stix and Frank W. Notestein, *Controlled Fertility*, Williams and Wilkins, Baltimore, 1940; Gilbert W. Beebe, *Contraception and Fertility in the Southern Appalachians*, Williams and Wilkins, Baltimore, 1942; and E. Lewis-Faning, "Report on an Enquiry into Family Limitation and Its Influence on Human Fertility During the Past Fifty Years," *Papers of the Royal Commission on Population*, I, H.M.S.O. London, 1949. Two surveys which have given relatively great stress to desired or expected family size in relation to other fertility aspects are the Indianapolis Study reported in P. K. Whelpton and C. V. Kiser, eds., *Social and Psychological Factors Affecting Fertility*, Milbank Memorial Fund, New York, 5 vols. 1946–1958, and Ronald Freedman, P. K. Whelpton and Arthur A. Campbell, *Family Planning, Sterility and Population Growth*, McGraw–Hill, New York, 1959.

[2] D. V. Glass and E. Grebenik, *The Trend and Pattern of Fertility in Great Britain: A Report on the Family Census of 1946*, H.M.S.O., London, 1954, especially Chapter VII of Part I.

[3] Whelpton and Kiser, *Social and Psychological Factors Affecting Fertility*, II, p. 255.

44

Chapter IV. Fecundity

DEFINITION OF FECUNDITY

The couple who want another child as rapidly as possible cannot be certain either that conception will be immediate or that pregnancy will eventuate in a live birth. After stopping contraception, they have to wait, sometimes many months, for conception. Because of post-partum sterility, the wait tends to be longer if they have just had a birth and are seeking another pregnancy without an interlude of contraception. Then also, given pregnancy, the couple faces a risk of pregnancy wastage, which defers the next birth until after another wait for conception and approximately nine months of pregnancy. Thus, any couple is subject to involuntary factors of fertility regulation expressed in the twin possibilities of conception delay and pregnancy wastage.

A couple is absolutely sterile either if their monthly probability of conception is zero, or if their chances are zero that pregnancy will lead to a live birth. In one case, there is an indefinite wait for pregnancy; in the other, there is habitual abortion. If both these probabilities are greater than zero, then the couple is fecund. But fecundity is a matter of degree, varying over a wide range, and to give it precision it is necessary to consider both the couple's monthly chance of conception and their risk of pregnancy wastage.

RISK OF PREGNANCY WASTAGE[1]

It is commonly supposed that most women are subject to a uniform, low risk of pregnancy wastage which acts as though determined by a host of small factors, with little correlation obtaining between presence and absence of wastage in consecutive birth intervals.[2] For a

---

[1] At issue here is recognized pregnancy wastage, because, as Rock and Hertig stress, many early abortions go undetected. From their operations on 150 multipara, the authors estimate that as high as 30 to 40 per cent of all menstrual cycles may be associated with defective ova or early abortions. See A. T. Hertig and J. Rock, "A Series of Potentially Abortive Ova Recovered from Fertile Women Prior to Their First Missed Menstrual Period," *American Journal of Obstetrics and Gynecology*, 58 (1949), 968–993. Hertig comments further on this pioneering research project in E. T. Engle, ed., *Pregnancy Wastage*, Charles C. Thomas, Springfield, Ill., 1953, p. 18. This finding of Hertig and Rock does not so much invalidate existing statistics on pregnancy wastage as it redefines them. These statistics measure merely that part of pregnancy wastage which is recognized as such by informants.

[2] One attempt to demonstrate this generalization directly is F. J. Schoeneck's analysis of pregnancy wastage among 776 women having 5 or more pregnancies, "Pregnancy Patterns and Fetal Salvage," *Obstetrics and Gynecology*, 1 (1953), 610–614.

minority of women, the risk of pregnancy wastage is definitely increased by a specific condition such as measles, syphilis, diabetes, former Caesarean section, etc.[3] Finally, there is a group of habitual aborters in which some condition inimical to the growth of the ovum recurs in each pregnancy. According to fragmentary evidence, habitual aborters may contribute from 4 to 10 per cent of all spontaneous abortions.[4]

If women whose risk of pregnancy wastage is well above average do play a secondary role in pregnancy wastage statistics, then it becomes permissible to estimate the average risk of the remainder by relating total wastage to total pregnancies. It is useful to distinguish stillbirths from miscarriages, the latter including all noninduced abortions following pregnancies of 7 months duration or less. Statistics on spontaneous abortion converge on 10 per cent of all pregnancies for unselected Western populations.[5] The modal lengths of pregnancy preceding these miscarriages are two and three months, with the average being closer to three than two.[6] Risk of stillbirth has proven responsive to environmental factors,[7] as well as biological ones, and 2 per cent of all pregnancies gives a reasonable order of magnitude for contemporary metropolitan America.[8] Pregnancies ending in stillbirths average a little under 9 months.[9]

Delay Caused by Pregnancy Wastage

As interesting as the incidence of pregnancy wastage is the average amount of delay it causes per birth interval. A miscarriage or a stillbirth entails an added conception wait, an extra period of pregnancy, as well as the time needed to recover fecundity after that

[3] J. J. Rommer lists several such conditions, together with some statistics, in his *Sterility: Its Causes and Its Treatment*, Charles C. Thomas, Springfield, Ill., 1952, pp. 42–46.

[4] N. J. Eastman, (*Williams Obstetrics*, Tenth Edition, Appleton-Century-Croft, New York, 1950, p. 490) discusses the fragmentary statistics on habitual abortion. The most frequently cited source on incidence of habitual abortion is A. T. Hertig and R. G. Livingstone, "Spontaneous, Threatened, and Habitual Abortion: Their Pathogenesis and Treatment," *New England Journal of Medicine*, 230 (1944), 797–806.

[5] A table summarizing 20 studies and emerging with a grand average of 9.5 unintentional abortions per 100 pregnancies is contained in *Foetal, Infant, and Early Childhood Mortality*, United Nations, ST/SOA/Series A/13, New York, 1954, I, p. 15. Another brief review is furnished by "Reports of the Biological and Medical Committee, *Royal Commission on Population*, H.M.S.O., London, 1950, Vol. IV, p. 4.

[6] See *Foetal, Infant, and Early Childhood Mortality*, I, p. 16, and Eastman, *Williams Obstetrics*, p. 477.

[7] One of the many references here is Ian Sutherland, *Stillbirths, Their Epidemiology and Social Significance*, Oxford University Press, London, 1949.

[8] *Foetal, Infant, and Early Childhood Mortality*, I, p. 98.

[9] Paul, Vincent, "Donneés biometriques sur la conception et la grossesse," *Population*, II (1956).

additional pregnancy. A ceiling estimate of the average delay occasioned by a stillbirth is $11+9+3=23$ months, where the 11, 9 and 3 months represent generous allowances for average conception wait, average pregnancy length, and average postpartum period of amenorrhea and consecutive anovulatory cycles.[10] The corresponding ceiling estimate of the average delay occasioned by a spontaneous miscarriage is $11+3+1=15$ months. Now suppose that in metropolitan America every 100 pregnancies average 88 live births, 10 spontaneous abortions, and 2 stillbirths. Using the estimates above, the average delay per birth interval caused by pregnancy wastage may be approximated by the equation:

$$.88(0)+.10(15)+.02(23)=2 \text{ months}$$

Thus when averaged for all birth intervals, the delay caused by pregnancy wastage is not large, being of the order of 2 months. The average delay is even less in the present study owing to the elimination of couples with stillbirths or more than one miscarriage between marriage and second birth.

FECUNDABILITY

In addition to their risk of pregnancy wastage, a couple's fecundity depends on their monthly probability of conception during certain periods.

For a fecund couple, the monthly chance of conception is zero during pregnancy, usually zero during separation of the spouses, and essentially zero for periods of postpartum amenorrhea. It is reduced by contraception. It is reduced by the higher frequency of anovulatory cycles immediately following postpartum amenorrhea.

When these various periods are excluded, one has left the period during which the wife is most fully exposed to the risk of conception. It is convenient to have a term for a couple's average monthly chance of conception during this type of exposure and Louis Henry has already popularized the term "fecundability."[11]

[10] An authoritative article here is A. Sharman, "Ovulation After Pregnancy," *Fertility and Sterility*, 2 (1951), 371–393.

[11] Actually, as L. Henry uses the term "fecundability," average monthly chance of conception is multiplied by 12 in order to shift the time unit from one month to one year. It is not clear what is gained by this extra step. See Louis Henry, "Analysis and Calculation of the Fertility of Populations of Under-developed Countries," *Population Bulletin of the United Nations, No. 5*, (July 1956) for a discussion in English of fertility including the concept of fecundability. A more mathematical statement is presented in his "Fondements Théoriques des Mesures de la Fecondité Naturelle," *Revue de l'Institute International de Statistique*, 21 (1953), 135–151. The concept of fecundability was originated by Corrado Gini, "Prime ricerche sulla 'fecondabilitá' della donna," *Atti del Reale Instituto Venito di Scienze*, 83 (1923–1924).

By definition, fecund couples have a fecundability greater than zero, but for many reasons it falls short of unity. In any menstrual cycle, the fertile period, during which coitus has a tangible chance of leading to conception, is relatively short—probably well under 72 hours.[12] Hence, there exists a chance that in a given month no coitus will coincide with the fertile period. A particular menstrual cycle may be anovulatory with the occurrence of menstrual flow but not ovulation. The incidence of these cycles is usually put at 5 per cent for seemingly pathology-free women aged 20 to 35 years, and of course is higher for subfecund women[13]. Then also, ovulation may produce an ovum incapable of fertilization or failing to implant in the uterus or aborting so early that pregnancy is not recognized. Finally, the quality of the husband's sexual product may be deficient with the degree of deficiency not wholly constant from month to month.[14]

Conception Delay as a Waiting-Time Problem

Fecundability can be estimated only indirectly through information about conception delays and such estimation presupposes a model explicitly relating fecundability to conception delay experience. A particularly simple model becomes available when one views conception delays as a waiting time problem, in which the monthly conception chance of any couple remains fixed throughout a single pregnancy interval, though it may change in the next pregnancy interval. Of course, during any pregnancy interval this monthly conception chance varies among couples.

[12] According to A. F. Guttmacher, estimates of the fertilizing life-span of sperms in the female range from 14 to 36 hours while, for the ovum estimates of its period of fertilizability range from 2 to 24 hours: "Artificial Insemination" in J. V. Meigs and S. H. Sturgis, eds., *Progress in Gynecology*, Grune and Stratton, New York, 1950, II, p. 352. See also the review article by E. B. Rubenstein, H. Strauss, M. L. Lazarus, and H. Hankins, "Sperm Survival in Women," *Fertility and Sterility*, 2 (1951), p. 15.

[13] For three fairly recent studies of this incidence, see A. S. H. Wong, E. T. Engle, and C. L. Buxton, "Anovulatory Menstruation in Women," *American Journal of Obstetrics and Gynecology*, 60 (1950), 790–795; P. Topkins, "Endometrial Biopsy Determination of Incidence of Ovulation in 402 Regularly Menstruating Women," *Fertility and Sterility*, 4 (1953), 76–79; and M. E. Collett, G. E. Wertenberger, and V. M. Fiske, "The Effect of Age Upon the Pattern of the Menstrual Cycle," *Fertility and Sterility*, 5 (1954), 437–448. See also J. Rock, M. K. Bartlett, and D. D. Mattson, "The Incidence of Anovulatory Menstruation Among Patients of Low Fertility," *American Journal of Obstetrics and Gynecology*, 37 (1939), 3–12.

[14] John MacLeod and Ruth Z. Gold have published a long series of papers dealing with human semen in *Fertility and Sterility*, two particularly relevant ones being: "Semen Quality and Certain Other Factors in Relation to Ease of Conception," 4 (1953), 10–33, and (with C. M. McLane) "Correlation of the Male and Female Factors in Human Infertility," 6 (1955), 112–143.

Although fecundability varies from couple to couple, one may think of a large population as divided into many subsamples, each homogeneous with respect to fecundability. Consider a subsample of couples whose common fecundability is p. In the first month of waiting, one expects a proportion of p to become pregnant; in the second month, a proportion of pq; in the third month, a proportion of pq^2; and more generally in the ith month, a proportion of pq^{i-1}. Furthermore, these expected proportions yield a mean wait of $1/p$ and a variance of q/p^2.[15]

Little is known about the distribution of p in human populations. Later in this chapter a point-estimate of .18 is derived as the mean fecundability of couples in the present sample, whose ease of conception is presumably somewhat above the average of urban Americans. Of course, this single statistic does not provide a basis for confident generalizing, but for what it is worth, it suggests that possibly half the couples in urban America have monthly conception chances averaging below .2.

This provisional finding, combined with the waiting-time model presented above, has two main implications. First of all, it serves to rationalize the very considerable variation in conception waits repeatedly encountered in human samples. Obviousuly as p decreases below .2, $1/p$ increases rapidly, and q/p^2 even more rapidly. For instance, if p equals .2, the expected mean and variance of conception waits is 5 and 20; if p equals .10, these expected values increase to 10 and 90; while if p equals .05, they become 20 and 380. Thus, a few subfecund couples can greatly increase the variance of conception delays.

Though substantial, this variability in conception waits does not measure the full variability of birth delays when included in the latter are the additional delays accruing from pregnancy wastage. Besides entailing a wasted gestation, pregnancy wastage requires waiting for a second conception. In Chapter VI the birth delays of couples in this study will be shown to be sufficiently variable that these delays usually account for more than half the variance of birth intervals. Of course, this means that birth delays, most of them presumably involuntary, constitute a larger source of variation than do the voluntary postponements of pregnancy achieved by contraception.

A second implication which follows from the waiting-time model, in conjunction with a mean fecundability of .2, is the impossibility of a close association between fecundability and length of conception

---

[15] This simple model can tolerate a certain amount of variation of monthly conception chances around p, especially if the deviations from p vary independently of each other.

wait. Couples homogeneous in fecundability may be expected to exhibit variant conception delays, all the more so if they share a low fecundability. This means that single conception delays do not furnish an efficient basis for ranking couples according to fecundability. Furthermore, a classification based on the conception waits of a single pregnancy interval contains such a large random component that a rather low ceiling is imposed upon the correlations which may realistically be expected to accrue from the classification.

Measuring Fecundability

Given a random sample of fecund couples, their average fecundability may be estimated either by the percentage of noncontraceptors becoming pregnant in the first month of marriage, or by the percentage of successful contraceptors becoming pregnant the first month after deliberately stopping contraception. In either procedure, the maximum amount of experience contributed by a single couple is one month.

An alternative measure of the sample's conception ease is their average conception delay. For noncontraceptors, this means calculating the average period elapsing between marriage and first pregnancy; and for successful contraceptors, the average period reported as elapsing between deliberately stopping contraception and pregnancy. Here the couples are contributing unequal lengths of experience instead of a maximum of one month as in the first measure. For this reason, the sample's average conception wait is not necessarily the reciprocal of the sample's average fecundability, and indeed is usually substantially larger, so that one measure is not directly derivable from the other.

Unfortunately, although several distributions of conception waits have been published, these distributions do not permit precise or confident statements about either average fecundability or average conception delay. In virtually all instances, conception waits are classified in a manner which leads to gross overestimates of average fecundability. Many of the supposed "one-month" waits include a second ovulation and therefore overstate the percentage of couples conceiving during their first menstrual cycle without contraception. Hitherto no one has tried to design a classification which would minimize this problem.

The chief problem in estimating average conception delay is that the two main sources of data, namely, the conception waits inferred for noncontraceptors by subtracting pregnancy time from birth intervals and the conception waits recalled by successful contraceptors, yield discrepant results. For example, in the samples coming closest to a claim of being unspecialized, waits for first pregnancy average in the neighborhood of 11 months for noncontraceptors and 6 to 9 months for successful contraceptors. (See Table 4). This lack of agreement has not gone unnoticed; but discussions of it have been fragmentary and superficial. Yet until the sources of the discrepancy are better understood, it remains uncertain which of the two types of data furnishes the more appropriate standard against which to measure the accomplishments of contraception.

In the remainder of this chapter the most useful of the existing distributions of conception waits are compared. New data from the present study are presented and compared with data from the Indianapolis Study. Several reasons are advanced to help explain why conception waits inferred for noncontraceptors tend to be longer than the waits reported by successful contraceptors. Finally, a measure of fecundability is outlined and then applied to data from the present study.

Previous Research

The conception delays of noncontraceptors are tangibly longer after first pregnancy than before it because of postpartum amenorrhea and a closer association between nonuse of contraception and subfecundity after the initial pregnancy than before it. Thus to compare the conception waits of interruptors and nonusers of contraception after a first pregnancy is merely to rehearse a well-known, well-understood contrast. Much more interesting, because much more controversial, is the discrepancy between inferred and reported waits before first pregnancy. Actually it is not critical to restrict the waits following interruption of contraception to the period preceding first pregnancy since this type of conception delay differs little before and after first pregnancy; at least the differences are minor as compared with those prevailing between reported and inferred waits.

In Table 4 are assembled the most useful of the published distributions of conception waits. Samples representing obviously subfecund gynecological patients are omitted. The assembled series are of three classes: distributions of reported waits (top third of the table); distributions of inferred waits (bottom third); and "mixed" distributions in which the above two types of conception waits are scrambled together for lack of information to separate them. Lack of information also explains why many column entries stand empty.

A cursory glance at Table 4 shows that the series representing reported waits imply a quicker course of conception than do the

51

series representing inferred waits. In line with this result, the mixed series indicate an intermediate ease of conception. This is most clearly seen by glancing down the columns that give percentages of couples conceiving within 3 and 6 months.

TABLE 4

Per Cent Conceiving within a Specified Number of Months, in absence of Contraception

Type of Conception Wait and Source	Number of pregnancies	Per Cent Conceiving within a Specified Number of Months					Mean length of wait (mos.)
		1 mo.	2 mos.	3 mos.	6 mos.	12 mos.	
Reported conception waits							
Stix and Notestein: first pregnancy	206	59%	67%	84%	92%	–%	2.6%
: subsequent pregnancies	391	52	62	77	88	–	2.8
Beebe: all pregnancies[a]	239	(50)	–	(80)	(90)	–	–
Whelpton and Kiser: first pregnancy	453	39	53	63	77	87	8.8
Tietze et al.: subsequent pregnancies	935	33	–	64	82	93 ⎫	6.0
: first pregnancy	792	28	–	58	76	90 ⎭	
Mixed conception waits[b]							
Llewellyn-Jones: age 15–19	87	–	–	62	92	100	–
Bender: age under 20	135	–	–	67	81	90	–
Russell	197	35	–	65	–	85	–
Llewellyn-Jones: age 20–24	496	–	–	53	76	98	–
Diddle et al.	261	–	–	–	73	87	–
Bender: age 20–24	280	–	–	51	66	80	–
Inferred conception waits							
Stix and Notestein	468	–	–	–	–	–	4.0
Beebe: Rural Kentucky and West Virginia	1,452	30	–	51	65	82	–
Whelpton and Kiser	482	29	39	48	61	80	11.4
Beebe: Watauga County, N.C.	481	26	–	42	56	73	–

[a] The percentages of this row are placed in parentheses because, read from a graph, they are only approximate.
[b] The series of Diddle et al., Llewellyn-Jones, and Russell include both reported and inferred waits. Presumably this is true also of Bender's series, though his report is not explicit about the matter.

The six distributions of waits following deliberate interruption of contraception present a considerable range of values. Almost certainly the data of Stix and Notestein,[16] based on a sample of patients attending a birth control clinic in New York City, over-estimate quickness of conception in the general population. The authors themselves acknowledge a possible selection toward higher than average fecundability.[17] Beebe offers reasons (to be discussed

[16] Regine K. Stix and Frank W. Notestein, *Controlled Fertility*, Williams and Wilkins, Baltimore, 1940, p. 68.
[17] *Ibid.*, pp. 11, 13.

later) for believing that long conception waits are discriminated against in his data for 239 private patients.[18] The series which deserve closest attention, because they come closer than the others to representing general populations, are the Indianapolis data analyzed by Whelpton and Kiser[19] and two series published by Tietze *et al* representing an unselected sample of obstetric patients.[20] In all three of these last series, the median wait is three months; however, the mean wait varies, being 9 months in the Indianapolis sample and 6 months in the combined series of Tietze *et al*. This difference occurs because a higher incidence of long conception waits among Indianapolis couples more than compensates for a slightly higher frequency of one-month waits.

The series of Bender,[21] Diddle *et al*,[22] Llewellyn-Jones,[23] and Russell,[24] which confound the conception experience of noncontraceptors and successful contraceptors, are interesting chiefly because they imply a quickness of conception intermediate between the eases of conception implied by series composed wholly of reported or inferred waits. Incidentally, the age-specific data of Bender and Llewellyn-Jones (corroborated by uncited data from MacLeod and Gold)[25] demonstrate the powerful selective force of age on fecundability.[26]

Regarding the waits of noncontraceptors, the data of Stix and Notestein again imply such extreme ease of conception[27] that one must suspect the selected character of their sample. The two series of Beebe, though also representing patients from contraceptive clinics,

[18] Gilbert W. Beebe, *Contraception and Fertility in the Southern Appalachians*, Williams and Wilkins, Baltimore, 1942, p. 66.

[19] P. K. Whelpton and C. V. Kiser, "The Comparative Influence on Fertility of Contraception and Impairments of Fecundity," in Kiser and Whelpton, eds., *Social and Psychological Factors Affecting Fertility*, 5 vols., Milbank Memorial Fund, New York (1950) II, pp. 303–357.

[20] C. Tietze, A. F. Guttmacher, and S. Rubin, "Time Required for Conception in 1727 Planned Pregnancies," *Fertility and Sterility*, 1 (1950), pp. 338–346.

[21] S. Bender, "End Results in Treatment of Primary Sterility," *Fertility and Sterility*, 4 (1953), p. 34.

[22] A. W. Diddle, R. W. Jack, and R. L. Pearse, "Fertility in Women: The Length of Time Required to Conceive," *American Journal of Obstetrics and Gynecology*, 54 (1947), pp. 57–61.

[23] D. Llewellyn-Jones, "Female Fertility," *British Medical Journal*, 2 (1953), pp. 180–182.

[24] C. S. Russell, "Human Fertility," *Lancet*, 250 (1946), pp. 300–303.

[25] J. MacLeod and R. Z. Gold, "The Male Factor in Fertility and Infertility," *Fertility and Sterility*, 4 (1953), pp. 15, 16.

[26] This is not to say that during the reproductive period fecundability lessens sharply with advancing age, but rather that when American women recently having a first pregnancy are classified by current age, they will inevitably be sharply differentiated with respect to conception ease because so many of them married in their early twenties.

[27] Stix and Notestein, *Controlled Fertility*, p. 69.

are apparently less selective toward high fecundability.[28] At least his two series agree fairly well together and with comparable Indianapolis data.[29] In these last three series the median waits cluster around 4 months, the mean waits around 11 months, both these averages being greater than the corresponding ones estimated for successful contraceptors. Less than two-thirds of the noncontraceptors conceive within 6 months, as compared to three-quarters or more among interrupters of contraception. The proportion of first-month conceptions is also somewhat lower among noncontraceptors—26 to 30 per cent in contrast to 28 to 39 per cent.

The tendency for inferred waits to exceed reported waits is most rigorously demonstrated by those studies which publish both types of data. Table 4 furnishes two examples. The data of Stix and Notestein show mean waits of 2.6 and 4.0 months respectively for interruptors and nonusers of contraception; the Indianapolis data show corresponding mean waits of 8.8 and 11.4 months. Enough information is available to test the statistical significance of this last difference and it appears that under the null hypothesis a difference as large as this one would not occur by chance once in a thousand times.[30]

Results from the Present Study

Enough information has been collected in the current study to estimate conception delays both for noncontraceptors and successful contraceptors. For couples not using contraception before first pregnancy there is available a marriage date and the date when first pregnancy terminated. From the difference (in days) between these two dates, 90 or 270 days are subtracted, depending whether the first pregnancy ends in miscarriage or a live birth, to yield an estimated conception delay. Couples who had their first pregnancy after deliberately stopping contraception in order to conceive are asked how long they waited, and the number of months they report is accepted as their conception delay. In either instance, couples suspected of premarital conception, or whose situations are complicated by separations, are excluded.

[28] Beebe's Series for Watauga County and for rural Kentucky and West Virginia are cited in C. Tietze, "Statistical Contributions to the Study of Human Fertility," *Fertility and Sterility*, 7, (1956), p. 92.

[29] Whelpton and Kiser, "The Comparative Influence on Fertility of Contraception and Impairments of Fecundity," p. 343.

[30] Being tested here is whether one set of conception waits is statistically greater than the other set. The statistic used is $4D^2 \, N_1 N_2/(N_1+N_2)$, approximately distributed as chi-square with 2 degrees of freedom, where D is the maximum difference between corresponding cumulative percentages. See Section I of Appendix A for a discussion of significance tests appropriate to conception wait data.

Before inquiring whether these data exhibit the familiar pattern of inferred conception waits exceeding those reported, it is appropriate to consider how far the present distributions of conception waits deviate from data of less specialized samples. One anticipates less subfecundity among couples of this sample as a result of the eligibility requirements of two live births and a maximum pregnancy wastage of one miscarriage.

More detailed comparisons are feasible with the Indianapolis data than with other series, and these comparisons are summarized in Table 5. Care is taken to duplicate the classification procedures of

TABLE 5

Present and Indianapolis Studies Compared with Respect to Conception Waits prior to First Pregnancy

LENGTH OF CON-CEPTION WAIT (in months)	PERCENTAGES					
	Reported conception waits			*Inferred conception waits*		
	FGMA S.	Indianapolis S.	Difference	FGMA S.	Indianapolis S.	Difference
1	40.0%	39.1%	0.9%	28.2%	29.0%	−0.8%
2	17.1	13.9	3.2	12.4	10.0	2.4
3	7.9	9.9	−2.0	11.6	8.7	2.9
4	2.9	4.6	−1.7	5.7	5.4	.3
5 to 6	12.1	9.7	2.3	5.9	8.3	−2.4
7 to 9	5.3	4.0	1.3	10.0	8.3	1.7
10 to 12	4.7	6.0	−1.3	6.3	10.8	−4.5
13 to 24	7.6	3.8	3.8	9.0	7.3	1.7
25 to 48	2.1	4.9	−2.8	5.7	7.5	−1.8
49 to 84	.3	1.8	−1.5	4.4	1.5	2.9
85 or more	.0	2.4	−2.4	0.9	3.3	−2.4
Per cent total	100.0	100.1	–	100.1	100.1	–
Number of wives	340	453	–	458	482	–
Mean wait (months)	5.2	8.8	–	10.8	11.4	–

Whelpton and Kiser. In the case of conception waits following interruption of contraception, this duplication means simply accepting the reported waits unless a premarital conception is suspected. In the case of conception delays inferred for noncontraceptors, the equating of classification procedures requires the following allocation: waits estimated to be −30 days or less eliminated as cases of premarital conception; waits of −29 to 44 days treated as first-month conception waits of 45 to 74 days as second-month conceptions; waits of 75 to

104 days as third month conceptions; and so on, continuing in this manner with 30-day intervals.[31]

Examination of the last three columns of Table 5 reveals good agreement between the two distributions of inferred conception waits. The percentages of first-month conceptions is virtually the same in the two studies, 29 and 28 per cent; the means of the two distributions are only one month apart, 11.4 months versus 10.0; and the signs of the percentage differences (last column) tend to alternate. Moreover, neither the chi-square test (10 degrees of freedom) nor the Kolmogorov-Smirnov tests (using the same intervals) indicate statistically significant differences.

When the comparison is shifted to the reported conception delays of successful contraceptors, more contrast is found between the two studies. Examining the first three columns of Table 5, one again observes essentially identical percentages of first-month conceptions (39 and 40 per cent); but this time the mean delay for Indianapolis couples is 8.8 months as opposed to 5.2 months for couples of the present study. This difference is mainly attributable to an unequal incidence of long conception waits. Waits exceeding 24 months comprise 9.1 per cent of all waits of Indianapolis couples, but only 2.4 per cent among the other couples. Broadly speaking, the two series of cumulative percentages develop in rather similar fashion until the upper ends of the distributions, when differences become sharp. The chi-square test proves more sensitive to this localized contrast, interpreting its probability as between .01 and .001 under the null hypothesis, whereas the two-tailed Kolmogorov-Smirnov test indicates a probability in excess of .10.

It is not clear why there should be such a marked deficit of long conception waits among successful contraceptors in the present sample. The 2.4 per cent of waits longer than 24 months compares with 11.0 per cent for noncontraceptors, and this ratio of 2.4 to 11.0 per cent is strikingly different from the corresponding ratio of 9.1 to 12.3 per cent among Indianapolis couples. The selected nature of the present sample is not a full explanation because the marked deficit of long waits does not apply to noncontraceptors as well as successful contraceptors. Whether biases or a large chance deviation deserve the blame is not clear. But whatever the explanation for this discrepancy, the over-all correspondence of Indianapolis and present distributions appears close enough that the latter need not be discarded as too highly selected.

---

[31] For details of the Indianapolis coding, see Whelpton and Kiser, "The Comparative Influence on Fertility of Contraception and Impairments of Fecundity," p. 343, fns. 2 and 4.

Consistent with the Stix and Notestein and the Indianapolis data, the present data reveal a highly significant difference between inferred and reported conception waits.[32] Indeed, the disagreement is more extreme than in the other two series, with inferred waits averaging 4.8 months longer than reported ones.

SUGGESTED CAUSES

The fact that the conception waits inferred for noncontraceptors tend to be longer than those reported by successful contraceptors has not gone unnoticed. Beebe, Stix and Notestein, Tietze, and Whelpton and Kiser have all speculated about the bases of this disagreement. Their explanations, together with two additional ones, are worth reviewing; and for this purpose it is convenient to distinguish two types of hypothesis. First are explanations attributing part or all of the discrepancy to measurement errors. Second are hypotheses in terms of selective factors, which posit that differences would remain even granting perfect measurement.

Several kinds of measurement error may contribute to the contrast. As one type of measurement error, Tietze has suggested that in any sample, "It appears likely that . . . there will be at least a few couples who practice contraception half-heartedly and who plan to have a child or another child at some future time. If conception occurs by accident, the temptation is great to claim it as planned. The exposure period reported in such cases would, of course, be brief."[33]

Obviously this kind of misreporting inflates the number of quick conceptions attributed to successful contraceptors. Unfortunately, little is known about the frequency of such misreporting.

G. Beebe cites another type of error in connection with his analysis of 239 patients claiming to have interrupted contraception in order to conceive: "The facts about planned conceptions are most readily obtainable for patients who conceive most easily. The patients who conceive with greater than average difficulty are not adequately represented."[34] That is, the longer the conception wait the more likely is the respondent to lack confidence in her recall of it and to beg off giving an answer. Although sound, Beebe's point acquires importance only when the percentage of rejected histories becomes appreciable. This percentage, varying from study to study, is likely to be low, even spuriously low, in such surveys as the Indianapolis

---

[32] According to the one-tailed Kolmogorov-Smirnov test, as large or larger differences would be expected under the null hypothesis less than once in a thousand times.

[33] C. Tietze, "Statistical Contributions to the Study of Human Fertility," *Fertility and Sterility*, 7 (1956), p. 94.

[34] Beebe, *Contraception and Fertility in the Southern Appalachians*, p. 66.

and present studies where the interviewers are under pressure to obtain answers to all questions, even when the respondent plainly lacks confidence in her replies. For instance, in the present study, excluding cases of suspected premarital conception, only five histories of successful contraceptors have been rejected as contradictory, although it is admitted that, in line with Beebe's expectation, these five histories contain longer than average birth intervals.[35]

Beebe might have extended his point by noting that the same factor, elimination of unusable histories, probably produces the opposite bias in the conception waits of noncontraceptors. These conception waits are rejected only when they assume negative values and become identified as premarital conceptions. This sets the stage for an association between nonusability of history and brevity of conception delay.[36]

A final type of measurement error, tending to exaggerate the length of inferred conception waits, is feigned nonuse of contraception. Such dissimulations may be guileless, as when respondents neglect to mention one or two months of contraception because they do not see

[35] Had it been possible to retain these five cases, with correct conception delays reported, the percentage of reported waits exceeding 24 months in the period preceding first pregnancy might have increased from 2.4 per cent (representing 8 cases) to nearly 4 per cent, thereby reducing the sharp contrast with Indianapolis data at this end of the distribution.

[36] A third type of measurement error is mentioned by Whelpton and Kiser who suggest that successful contraceptors may tend to underestimate their conception waits. This hypothesis is plausible. The fallibility of recalled conception waits is demonstrated by the gross heaping of reported waits at 3 months and every multiple of 6 months. For example, in the present study, among interruptors of contraception, the percentage of conception waits reported to be multiples of 6 months is 68 per cent of all waits reported as 10 months or longer instead of the approximately 20 per cent that might be expected with more reliable reporting.

This hypothesis of Whelpton and Kiser also fits with the fact that long conception waits are so much more numerous among successful contraceptors in the Indianapolis sample than in the present sample. If a tendency to understate conception waits exists, then one would expect it to be minimized in an interview situation where very detailed pregnancy and contraceptive histories are being collected, with the respondents given time and encouragement to make as careful estimates of their conception waits as possible, even when, as in the case of prolonged conception delays, this requires some calculating. Particularly detailed histories were collected in the Indianapolis study.

Unfortunately, despite its plausibility, this hypothesis fails to find support from the one direct test that is available. If the tendency to underestimate conception waits were a strong one, then one would expect to find an inverse association between durations of contraceptive practice and reported conception delays. This follows, because an underestimated conception delay necessarily means an overestimated period of contraception, since periods of contraceptive practice are estimated by subtracting reported conception waits and pregnancy times from total pregnancy intervals. Yet, as will be documented in Chapter VI, such an association does not emerge either in the first or second birth interval. Thus it is hard to believe that a tendency to underestimate conception waits offers a primary explanation either for the disagreement between the two measures of conception delay or for the anomalous contrast between Indianapolis and present distributions of reported conception waits.

how such information could interest the interviewer. But other couples may deliberately mask tangible periods of contraceptive practice. The only clue concerning the frequency of such concealments comes from Freedman, Whelpton, and Campbell who, on the basis of a number of indirect checks, conclude that these deliberate misrepresentations are rare.[37] But even a few such concealments could exercise an appreciable effect upon the mean conception delay estimated for noncontraceptors.

In addition to measurement error, several selective factors have been proposed as contributing to differences between inferred and reported conception waits. For example, Whelpton and Kiser hypothesize that at marriage some couples are aware of reproductive difficulties and this knowledge prompts them to postpone contraception at least until after their first pregnancy. Thus the association between nonuse of contraception and subfecundity, so well documented for the period after first pregnancy, may apply, albeit in attenuated form, to the earlier period. In support of this view, they point to a higher percentage of "relatively sterile" couples among noncontraceptors as compared to successful contraceptors prior to first pregnancy.[38] However, the difference is not statistically significant and, besides this, the evidence is somewhat circular inasmuch as the classification of "relatively fecund" and "relatively sterile" depends upon a conception-wait criterion. Data from the present study permit a somewhat less circular test, in which noncontraceptors and successful contraceptors are compared with respect to percentages ever doubting their fecundity. Here, also, the percentage difference is not statistically significant. Although it is true that the hypothesis has not yet been proven, it is also true that the negative verdicts of such weak tests do little to disprove it. A few seriously subfecund couples behaving according to the hypothesis could appreciably increase the mean conception delay estimated for non-contraceptors while at the same time not materially changing the percentage of fecundity doubters among noncontraceptors.

Stix and Notestein have suggested as a special factor operating to reduce fecundability at the beginning of marriage: ". . . that in many marriages a month or more may have elapsed before complete entry took place. Such periods were part of the noncontraceptive exposure of women who had never used contraception, while, for women who

[37] Ronald Freedman, P. K. Whelpton and Arthur Campbell, *Family Planning, Sterility and Population Growth*, McGraw–Hill, New York, 1959, pp. 469–477.

[38] Whelpton and Kiser, "The Comparative Influence on Fertility of Contraception and Impairments of Fecundity," p. 344.

first used contraception and then planned pregnancies, they were part of the exposure during which contraception was used."[39] An alternative hypothesis, postulating the same result, holds that the bride's emotionality during the initial adjustment to marriage may temporarily raise her incidence of anovulatory cycles. These two hypotheses imply a lower conception chance among noncontraceptors during the first month of marriage than the second. All evidence in the form of percentages of one- and two-month conception delays from published distributions of inferred conception waits (see Table 7) would seem to contradict this expectation. However, it will be shown later that the pertinence of this evidence may be doubted, so that the matter cannot be regarded as settled.

Because of the uncertain amounts of exposure preceding premarital conception, it is conventional to exclude any conception waits suspected of being associated with premarital pregnancy. While accepting this precaution as necessary, Whelpton and Kiser, and also Tietze, believe it upwardly biases the conception waits of noncontraceptors.[40] Among couples having premarital sexual relations unaccompanied by contraception, those who do not become pregnant premaritally tend to be less fecund than those who do. Moreover, since they do not practice contraception before marriage, few of this selectedly subfecund group are likely to begin contraception at marriage. Hence, they contribute mostly inferred conception waits. Moreover, there is no compensation from couples who become premaritally pregnant because their experience is excluded.

Of course, there are also couples who practice contraception during periods of premarital exposure and many of these will continue their contraception into marriage. But since contraception greatly weakens the association between fecundability and premarital pregnancy or nonpregnancy, it matters little how their marital conception experience is apportioned between reported and inferred waits.

The present data provide a certain amount of support for this hypothesis (reviewed in Section 2.e. of Appendix A), but do not permit a quantitative estimate of the bias. Whether this bias accounts for half a month, a full month, or even more in a total discrepancy of five months remains unknown.

[39] Stix and Notestein, *Controlled Fertility*, pp. 69, 70.
[40] Whelpton and Kiser, "The Comparative Influence on Fertility of Contraception and Impairments of Fecundity" pp. 342, 343; see also Tietze, "Statistical Contributions to the Study of Human Fertility", p. 95, and "Differential Fecundity and Effectiveness of Contraception," *Eugenics Review*, 50 (1959), p. 235.

A final hypothesis, advanced by G. W. Beebe,[41] states that a larger percentage of successful contraceptors than habitual nonusers know about the the positioning of the fertile period within the menstrual cycle and also are motivated to use this knowledge to minimize their conception wait.[42] This hypothesis, like so many of the others listed, has not yet been tested. Testing it would require information from each respondent concerning her knowledge of the menstrual cycle and its fertile period, plus any practical uses made of this knowledge. No such information has been collected from the present couples, though there are plans to correct this omission in the second set of interviews.

What conclusions are to be drawn from this lengthy review of possible explanations for inferred conception waits exceeding reported ones? It seems likely that noncontraceptors and successful contraceptors are not exactly equal in their fecundability, even before first pregnancy. Involuntary, and perhaps voluntary, factors engender shorter delays of conception following interruption of contraception than in its complete absence. Quite likely also, measurement errors enhance the inequality. But this is not to deny the existence of other selective factors and measurement errors working to reverse the observed direction of contrast, that is, working to make inferred conception waits shorter than reported waits. Doubtless some couples misreport their marriage dates in order to conceal premarital pregnancies, with the need for this subterfuge rising more often among noncontraceptors. Then too, couples who interrupt contraception in order to conceive tend to be less fecund than couples who fail in their contraception and to this extent are selected toward subfecundity.[43] (Indeed, one suspects that an agile mind, misinformed about the direction of contrast between inferred and reported conception waits, could concoct a list of "suggested causes" as long as the one reviewed.) Thus, the differences observed between the two types of conception wait must always be regarded as a net balance of opposing measurement biases and opposing selective factors. Moreover, it is obvious that particular measurement errors and selective factors are shifting in relative importance from study to study.

[41] Beebe, *Conception and Fertility in the Southern Appalachians*, p. 65.

[42] There may even be an obverse to this hypothesis. Among noncontraceptors the women who have ambivalent feelings about a first pregnancy may express these negative attitudes in reduced coital frequency or perhaps unacknowledged use of periodic abstinence. Of course, the successful contraceptors include women having similar ambivalences. Among these women, as long as negative feelings dominate, contraception is continued; but when contraception is deliberately stopped, this may mark the successful repression of such feelings in many cases.

[43] However, Table 24 contains evidence to show that differences with respect to fecundability between successful and unsuccessful contraceptors are probably slight.

An Operational Definition of Fecundability

Attention now shifts from conception waits to fecundability which, it may be recalled, is broadly defined as a couple's monthly probability of conception during periods of maximum risk. Until more direct ways are found to measure it, fecundability must be measured indirectly on the basis of conception waits. Because chance plays so important a part in the lengths of conception delays, one or two such waits do not provide a useful estimate of a couple's fecundability. Only estimates of the mean fecundability of a sample are feasible and in the remainder of this chapter fecundability is used in this sense. It is to be expected that inferred and reported conception waits will generate different estimates of fecundability.

Actually few persons have tried to derive estimates of fecundability. An exception is Louis Henry who cites Indianapolis data as the source of an estimate of .19, though without stating how he derived this figure.[44] The obvious approach, namely, to scrutinize published distributions of conception waits for the percentages of couples conceiving the first month, proves unsound. It will be shown later that these percentages overestimate fecundability, probably grossly. A more precise classification of conception waits is needed than those used in compiling distributions of conception waits. In an attempt to meet this need, an operational definition of fecundability will now be outlined and then applied to data from the present study.

Careful estimating of fecundability requires allowance for the cyclical nature of conception chances. During the normal menstrual cycle, chances of conception are tangible only during a relatively short period, almost certainly under 72 hours, occurring usually in the middle of the cycle. A minority of menstrual cycles are anovulatory, terminating in menstruation even though ovulation has not taken place. If conception takes place but the fertilized ovum fails to implant, the next menstruation may come on time, or be delayed only a few days. The delays tend to be longer when implantation occurs but the fetus aborts too soon for recognition. When pregnancy endures long enough for recognition, a moderate or scant menstrual flow occasionally follows two weeks or so after conception. These several contingencies mean the possibility of defining fecundability in a number of different ways.

However, the choice of operationally feasible definitions is much narrower. As a practical matter, any estimate of fecundability must be in terms of recognized pregnancies. Then, also, respondents can

---

[44] L. Henry, *Fécondité des Marriages: Nouvelle Methode de Mésure*, Press Univ. France, Paris, 1953, p. 95.

recognize and report about menstruations but not ovulations. Finally, it seems necessary to exclude premarital conceptions, even if this exclusion produces bias, because information regarding exposure to the risk of premarital pregnancy is so uncertain.

Because of these limiting conditions, it does no good to define the fecundability of noncontraceptors as the percentage of couples who, not having become pregnant prior to marriage, become pregnant their first ovulation after marriage. Difficult enough in the medical laboratory, it is quite impossible in the field to distinguish anovulatory menstrual cycles from ovulatory ones. However, advantage may be taken of the generalization that the brief fertile period usually occurs near the middle of the cycle. Thus, a reasonable definition of the number of conception "opportunities" that a couple has required for pregnancy is the number of menstrual mid-periods elapsing before pregnancy. One need only determine the number of menstruations intervening between marriage and pregnancy, and then add one to this figure if the period between marriage and first menstruation after marriage is deemed to include a menstrual mid-period.

Thus, one is led to define the fecundability of noncontraceptors as follows: the percentage of couples who, not having become pregnant prior to marriage, become pregnant during their first menstrual mid-period after marriage. Moreover, comparing this percentage with the percentage of noncontraceptors exposed to, and becoming pregnant during, the second menstrual mid-period after marriage presumably offers the most powerful test of the hypothesis that factors are operating to reduce fecundability during the beginning of marriage. Obviously this definition of fecundability may be adapted to successful contraceptors by taking interruption of contraception, rather than marriage, as the point of origin.

CLASSIFYING THE CONCEPTION WAITS OF NONCONTRACEPTORS

Even when there is no direct information about numbers of menstruations from which to infer the numbers of menstrual mid-periods, and only estimates of conception waits (in days) are available, the definition of fecundability just outlined remains applicable. The operational problem then becomes one of classifying these estimated conception waits into 28-day intervals so centered that the numbers of pregnancies defined by these intervals furnish reasonably unbiased estimates of the numbers of pregnancies occurring during the second and first menstrual mid-periods before marriage and the first, second, third . . . mid-periods after marriage. Once obtaining these pregnancy frequencies, it is simple enough to relate them to the numbers of couples exposed to risk of pregnancy, and so derive a series of pregnancy rates.

A width of 28 days is chosen because this is the figure most often cited as the average length of menstrual cycles. The intervals are advantageously centered on days . . ., $-42, -14, 14, 42, \ldots$ for reasons readily understood if one thinks about the distribution of conception waits that might be estimated for couples conceiving during the first mid-period after marriage. Conception waits are being estimated by subtracting an allowance for pregnancy time from the measured interval between marriage and termination of first pregnancy. Now if the allowance for pregnancy time is unbiased, then in a large sample the average length of the estimated conception waits will be close to the average length of the interval between marriage and first menstrual mid-period after marriage, which as far as known is approximately 14 days.[45] Likewise for couples conceiving during the second menstrual mid-period after marriage, the expected mean of their estimated conception waits is the expected interval between marriage and second menstrual mid-period, or approximately $14+28=42$ days. Thus, the preferred set of 28-day intervals becomes . . ., $(-56, -29)$, $(-28, -1)$, $(1, 28)$, $(29, 56)$, . . . days.

But even if properly centered, is this set of intervals likely to do a good job in the sense of generating numbers of pregnancies which will closely correspond to the numbers of pregnancies occurring during menstrual mid-periods . . . $-2, -1, 1, 2, \ldots$ after marriage? The answer depends on how variable are the conception waits estimated for couples actually becoming pregnant during a particular menstrual mid-period. If the scatter of estimated conception waits is small enough so that most of them are assigned to the appropriate interval, and very few to the adjacent intervals, then biases will be small. But if their scatter is greater, with tangible percentages extending into adjacent intervals, then serious biases become likely, even inevitable. In general, the more complete the information collected about such things as length of gestation, or days elapsing between marriage and first menstruation, the narrower the scatters of estimated conception waits.

APPLICATION

For various reasons the information collected in the present study is minimal and, as a result, a substantial scatter of conception waits is

[45] The rationale for this inference is given in Section 3 of Appendix A. It is, of course, not likely that the interval between marriage and first menstrual mid-period is exactly 14 days, and indeed there are speculative grounds for believing that it may be a few days shorter than 14.

coded for couples becoming pregnant during a particular mid-period. Actually, the observed scatters are smallest for pregnancies conceived during the last mid-period before or the first mid-period after marriage (Section 3 of Appendix A) and these scatters gradually increase as one proceeds to pregnancies more remote from the marriage date.

Perhaps the best point-estimate of the number of mid-period 1 pregnancies is derived by adding together the conception waits of intervals (−28, −1) and (1, 28). According to the calculations of Appendix A, this broader interval encompasses perhaps three-quarters of mid-period 1 pregnancies, as well as three-quarters of mid-period −1 and a quarter or more of mid-period 2 pregnancies to compensate for the quarter of mid-period 1 pregnancies lost to interval (29, 56). Thus the extended interval (−28, 28) should yield a reasonably close estimate, perhaps even an overestimate, of the pregnancies occurring during the first mid-period after marriage.

By widening the interval still further, to (−28, 42) days, one obtains a gross upper bound for the number of pregnancies of mid-period 1. Included now presumably are nearly all of mid-period 1 pregnancies but, in addition, perhaps three-quarters of mid-period −1 pregnancies, as well as half of mid-period 2 pregnancies. Theoretically the overestimate here might be as much as 50 per cent.

Nevertheless the interval used by Whelpton and Kiser to define the number of one-month conception delays (see Table 5) is still wider yet, being (−30, 45) days. It may be recalled that following their classification system, waits estimated as less than −30 days are excluded as premarital conceptions; the interval (−30, 45) days defines the number of one-month conception delays; while a series of 30-day intervals, (46, 75), (76, 105), . . . define the frequencies of longer waits.[46]

In Table 6, the conception waits of noncontraceptors in the present sample are classified according to the recommended set of 28-day intervals, with the interval (−28, 28) defining mid-period

---

[46] It will also be noted that the intervals used by Whelpton and Kiser are "off-center." For example, the mean conception waits of couples conceiving during the second and third mid-periods after marriage are in the neighborhoods of 42 and 70 days, but these days nearly match the ends of one of their intervals, namely (46, 75) days. These remarks are not meant to imply that Whelpton and Kiser's classification fails its original purpose, namely, to estimate the average delay of first pregnancies among noncontraceptors. For this objective, their definition of conception wait as the interval between marriage and first conception is entirely appropriate and no great bias is introduced by coding waits to the nearest month and somewhat overestimating one-month waits. However, the same classification yields very dubious results when it comes to estimating fecundability because here the definition of conception wait is no longer appropriate and a minor downward bias has become a serious upward one.

1 pregnancies, while conception waits coded as less than −28 days are eliminated as premarital conceptions. Using this classification, the numbers of pregnancies, exposures, and corresponding pregnancy rates (pregnancies divided by exposures) are tabulated for menstrual mid-periods 1, 2, 3, 4–6, 7–12, 13–24, 25–48, and 49 or more.

TABLE 6

Present Study Noncontraceptors: Time Waited for First Pregnancy and First Pregnancy Rates, Predicated on Menstrual Mid-Periods

Estimated Menstrual Mid-Period	Months/Days Waited after Marriage	Number of Pregnancies	Number of Exposures	Pregnancy rate (Pregnancies ÷ Exposures)
−2 or less	−2/28 or less	56		
−1	−1/1 to −1/28	28 ⎫ 80	453	.18
1	0/1 to 0/28	52 ⎭		
2	1/1 to 1/28	81	373	.22
3	2/1 to 2/28	41	292	.14
4 to 6	3/1 to 5/28	77	646	.12
7 to 12	6/1 to 11/28	77	824	.09
13 to 24	12/1 to 23/28	45	843	.05
25 to 48	24/1 to 47/28	27	855	.03
49 or more	48/1 or more	25	504	.05
Total	−	509	−	−

A .18 pregnancy rate is obtained for the first menstrual mid-period after marriage. This is .10 below the frequency of one-month conception delays obtained in Table 5. Interestingly enough, this rate also falls short of the .22 pregnancy rate for the second menstrual mid-period after marriage, though of course the difference is not statistically significant.[47] Though this result cannot be construed as decisive evidence for the existence of factors lowering fecundability at the start of marriage, it does keep the issue alive.

Thus, the present data yield an approximate estimate of .2 as the fecundability of noncontraceptors at marriage. It seems likely that if the procedures of Table 6 were applied to Indianapolis data, they might also yield an estimate of fecundability closer to .2 than .3. Unfortunately, it is impossible to speculate about Beebe's two series of noncontraceptors since not enough is known about the way he classified his data.

[47] This difference, .18 to .22, is somewhat underestimated if, as seems possible, the interval between marriage and first menstrual mid-period is actually less than the 14 days estimated.

66

Fecundability of Successful Contraceptors

From earlier discussion in this chapter, one expects to estimate a higher fecundability for successful contraceptors than for non-contraceptors. Most of the explanations advanced for the differences between inferred and reported conception waits imply a relatively higher frequency of one-month waits among interruptors of contraception. However, it must be feared that published proportions of one-month waits grossly overestimate the fecundability of successful contraceptors. Presumably these percentages encompass nearly all of the pregnancies occurring during the first mid-period after interruption of contraception, but also perhaps half of the second mid-period pregnancies as well.

The basis of this inference is made clear by a few examples. Consider first the women who decide not to resume contraception after menses and then conceive during the second menstrual mid-period following this menstruation. Their objective wait is of the order of 6 weeks. When asked how many months they waited, they are placed in a dilemma. Do they answer two months, meaning that they did not become pregnant until exposure to a second mid-period? Or do they answer, as seems more likely, one month, meaning that they had to wait through one unwanted menstruation? Another group of women decide to stop contraception just before the middle of the month and conceive during the second mid-period thereafter. Since their objective waits are not much longer than four weeks, these women are even more likely to answer one month, even though they required exposure to two menstrual mid-periods in order to become pregnant. A third group of women, interrupting contraception shortly after a mid-period and conceiving during the second mid-period thereafter, are unlikely to say one month because they experience two unwanted menstruations in combination with objective waits nearer 8 weeks than 6. But virtually all the women conceiving during the first mid-period after stopping contraception may be expected to answer one month—unless they answer 0 months or "immediately"—since their objective waits are usually less than 4 weeks and no more than one unwanted menstruation is experienced.

Thus, when the only data available are answers to the question: "How many months did you have to wait after interrupting contraception?", the calculated percentage of one-month waits can be expected to include most first mid-period pregnancies as well as an appreciable fraction of second mid-period pregnancies. On this basis, the estimated percentage of one-month waits is 39 per cent for successful contraceptors in the Indianapolis Study and 40 per cent in the

present study. The percentages are lower in the data of Tietze *et al*—
28 per cent among waits for first pregnancy and 33 per cent among
the waits for subsequent pregnancies. Why the frequency of one-
month waits is lower in the last study is not clear, unless possibly
the patients were asked about numbers of unwanted menstruations
rather than lengths of conception delay.

In summary, one may confidently conclude that the successful
contraceptors in this and the Indianapolis studies have fecund-
abilities below .4; while for the Tietze *et al* sample, a crude approximation is .3, though to what extent this latter figure is subject to
upward biases is unknown.

SUMMARY

In this chapter, concerned with conception delays, most of the
useful distributions of conception waits have been collected together
and compared. These distributions comprise three types: (1) the first
pregnancy waits of noncontraceptors, inferred by subtracting
pregnancy time from the interval between marriage and termination
of first pregnancy; (2) waits reported by successful contraceptors as
following deliberate interruption of contraception; and (3) "mixed"
distributions in which the two types above are scrambled together
for lack of information to separate them. Although each set of
distributions reveal a scatter of values, the previously observed
tendency emerges for waits of noncontraceptors to be longer than
those reported by successful contraceptors, while the mixed distributions assume an intermediate position.

New data are presented from the current study and compared in
detail with data from the Indianapolis study. Despite differences in
the samples, the distributions of conception waits prove quite
similar. The principal anomaly is an unexplained deficit of long
conception waits among couples of the present study who deliberately interrupted contraception before their first pregnancy.

In the literature several reasons have been advanced to explain the
tendency of conception waits inferred for noncontraceptors to exceed
those reported by successful contraceptors. These explanations are
explored as far as data permit. Seemingly both measurement errors
and selective factors contribute to the differences between the two
measures of conception delay. The biggest unknown is the role of
voluntary factors which may operate through a tendency for successful contraceptors to know more about the positioning of the fertile
period in the menstrual cycle and to use this knowledge to hasten
conception. Being researchable and potentially important, these

voluntary factors deserve study which they have not yet received.

With careful classification, data pertaining to conception waits can be made to yield useful estimates of fecundability, by which is meant a sample's average monthly chance of pregnancy when each couple contributes one month of experience. Unfortunately, the classifications used in most published distributions of conception waits are not adapted to this purpose and presumably lead to rather gross overestimates. By means of a special analysis, a point-estimate of .2 is derived for noncontraceptors in the present sample. No attempt is made to estimate the fecundability of interruptors of contraception because of insufficient information.

Chapter V. Contraception

Controlling the time of a birth presents a double problem: pregnancy must be postponed as long as desired; but once desired, conception delay must be minimized and pregnancy wastage avoided. Couples have little or no control over spontaneous abortion, and the previous chapter has shown that many couples suffer substantial conception delays. This chapter considers how successful couples are at voluntarily postponing pregnancy.

The voluntary means of birth deferment include contraception, induced abortion, and sterilization. However, for couples in metropolitan America, especially if they are in an early stage of marriage, contraception is the predominant means of postponing births. Sterilization is not an appropriate means until after desired family size is attained and even then strong legal and medical barriers sharply limit its use.[1] Moreover, many of the same barriers inhibit use of induced abortion.[2]

Since the present sample acknowledges little use of induced abortion or sterilization, the attention of this chapter will be restricted to contraception. The analysis is organized into three main sections: availability of contraception, choice of method, and contraceptive effectiveness. Even if a couple wish to postpone pregnancy, contraception is not always available for one reason or another. If contraception is available, then usually there is a problem of choosing among alternative methods and the decision about which method is most acceptable often rests on how high a priority the couple give to reliability considerations as opposed to religious or asethetic ones. Finally, there is a question of how effective is the chosen method as it is being used by the couple. Additional analyses, comparing methods of contraception, are contained in Appendix B.

Besides presenting results for the entire sample, limited comparisons will be conducted among class-religious groups, though these divisions do not move into the foreground of attention until Chapters X to XIX. For reasons discussed elsewhere,[3] four religious groups are distinguished: Jews, Protestants, Catholics, and Mixed Catholics (Catholic–non-Catholic marriages performed by a priest). When

[1] A 9 per cent incidence of sterilization is found in the study Growth of American Families (hereafter abbreviated to GAF). The authors find that the frequency of these operations correlate directly with age of wife and number of births, but inversely with education. See Ronald Freedman, P. K. Whelpton, and Arthur Campbell, *Family Planning, Sterility and Population Growth*, McGraw–Hill, New York, 1959, pp. 26–31.

[2] For a lively discussion of these barriers, see Mary S. Calderone, *Abortion in the United States*, Hoeber–Harper, New York, 1958.

[3] See Chapter XI.

appropriate, each religious group is stratified into white-collar and blue-collar classes on the basis of husband's usual occupation.

The results of this chapter, like the others, are qualified by the special nature of the sample. Broadly speaking, the effect of the eligibility criteria is to yield a group of couples relatively well informed about contraception, together with a possibility that some of them are not yet fully motivated to use this knowledge. Several factors operate to insure that the couples are relatively knowledgeable about contraception. They are urban. They are young enough so that their schooling represents the educational standards of the 1940's and 1950's. In addition, most husbands have gone through the service, and so have been exposed to military publicity about condoms. Finally, nonwhites and persons born outside of the continental United States are excluded.

On the other hand, contraceptive data are restricted to the period between marriage and second birth and, as far as is known, few couples want one or no children. Thus to date their contraceptive problem has been one of child-spacing rather than preventing unwanted children. Accordingly, if timing of births is less important than number, one suspects that many of these couples are not yet making a full effort to achieve efficient contraception.

Availability of Contraception

Unless contraception is used, obviously it cannot aid in postponing pregnancy. Hence, in any survey of contraceptive behavior, interest attaches to the proportion of couples who eventually avail themselves of contraception, as well as the stage of marriage when first use occurs.

Usage may be delayed for two sorts of reason. First, couples may not feel a need for contraception, the two most common situations being: (a) when the couple desire a pregnancy as soon as physically possible; and (b) when they doubt their fecundity and are seeking to minimize chances of a prolonged birth delay. In both instances, the couples, by foregoing contraception, are behaving rationally with respect to their birth-spacing preferences. Ordinarily as marriage duration increases, the incidence of suspected subfecundity also increases; while among couples retaining confidence in their fecundity, indifference about delaying pregnancy may be expected to decline sharply after a child is born.

A second and quite different sort of reason for not using contraception is needing it but finding it unavailable. Obstacles to contraceptive use may derive from such diverse sources as religious principle, ignorance about trustworthy methods, or finding known methods of contraception aesthetically unacceptable. Other studies have shown that in urban America these barriers lose their power when the need for fertility control grows stronger, as it often does after a birth, and more surely does after attaining desired family size.

Distinguishing nonusers who do not need contraception from nonusers who do but find it unavailable means that one has asked for reasons why contraception is not being used. These reports, like any subjective data, are liable to bias, one possible form of which is a hesitation to acknowledge ignorance or dislike of contraception, with a consequent tendency to mask real motives under a reported desire for prompt pregnancy. If such a bias exists, it means underestimating the percentage of couples for whom contraception is not available.

First Use of Contraception

As they pertain to the present study, the statistics on first use of contraception can be quickly reviewed. As Table 7 shows, just over

TABLE 7

First Use of Contraception, by Religion and Class

| Religion and Class | Number | First Use of Contraception | | | | Per Cent Total |
		Before First Birth	Between Two Births	After Second Birth	Still not Using	
Protestant						
White-collar	230	71	22	4	4	101
Blue-collar	243	51	34	9	6	100
Mixed Catholic						
White-collar	35	46	43	3	9	101
Blue-collar	51	45	37	4	14	100
Catholic						
White-collar	200	35	37	8	22	102
Blue-collar	281	39	36	7	17	99
Jewish						
White-collar	103	89	8	2	1	100
Blue-collar	22	86	5	5	5	101
Total	1,165	53	30	6	11	100

half of the couples start their contraception prior to first birth. Another 30 per cent commence between first and second births, while 6 per cent wait until after the second birth. Only 11 per cent report having never used contraception by time of interview (henceforth these 127 couples are called Never Users, to distinguish them from the 1,038 Ever Users.)

Religious differences are marked. A large majority of Jews initiate

72

contraception before their first births. Next most prompt are Protestants, followed by Mixed Catholics. Slowest to begin are Catholics who represent nearly three-quarters of the Never Users. Within the four religious groups, class fails to differentiate time of first use except among Protestants, among whom white-collar couples tend to start sooner than blue-collar couples. The relevant chi-square value here is 19.8, significant at beyond the .001 level for 3 degrees of freedom. In the other three religious groups, occupation fails to yield significant chi-squares.

Reasons for Nonuse of Contraception

Each respondent who does not practice contraception during a pregnancy interval is asked the reason why in an open-ended question. The exceptions are the 127 Never Users who are asked just once in an open-ended question why they have never used contraception.

The distribution of reasons given by the 127 Never Users are tabulated in the last column of Table 8. Only 15 respondents state

TABLE 8

Reasons Given for Not Starting Contraception

Reasons	Not Starting Contraception until		Never User
	After First Pregnancy	After Second or Third Pregnancy	
Wanted children as soon as possible	55%	52%	12%
Doubts concerning fecundity	2	7	14
Religious reasons	5	8	51
Ignorance or fear of contraception	9	3	5
Interfered with sexual enjoyment, etc.	10	8	9
Have not cared when children came	19	6	7
Didn't think would become pregnant so soon	1	13	–
Don't know	1	1	2
Not reported	–	2	–
Per cent total	102	100	100
Number	429	88	127

wanting three children as quickly as possible as their sole reason for nonuse, demonstrating that the overwhelming majority of fecund women want to reproduce at a rate slower than physically possible. Another 18 respondents report subfecundity. Presumably most of these failed to use contraception before their first pregnancy for whatever reason, discovered their subfecundity, and have felt no need

73

to use contraceptives since. Thus, altogether 33 of the 127 Never Users profess no need for contraception to date.

This leaves 94 couples, or about 8 per cent of the total sample, for whom contraception is still not available, though needed, after a second birth. The principal obstacle is religious conviction, cited by 65 respondents. Twelve wives dislike contraception for aesthetic reasons. Perhaps these wives, like the 9 who report not caring when their children come, do not strongly oppose the idea of three children spaced closely together.

The Never Users are drawn primarily from the Catholic group (72 per cent) and secondarily from the Protestant group (18 per cent), but show little selectivity with respect to class. Of the 65 respondents who cite religious objections as a reason for never using contraception, 61 are Catholics.

Reasons for Delayed Use

Almost half the sample (517 of 1,165 couples) delay their start of contraception and it is interesting to consider to what extent these delayed starts represent belated availability of contraception. The reasons reported for delaying contraception until after first pregnancy (first column of Table 8) exhibit a fairly equal division between wanting the first pregnancy right away and temporary nonavailability of contraception. The reasons cited for longer postponements of contraception indicate about the same percentage division, although only one-fifth as many couples are involved. Thus, as expected, far more mothers are willing to have a first pregnancy right away than to have two pregnancies following each other as closely as physically possible. Also as anticipated, the percentage of couples for whom contraception becomes available after first pregnancy swiftly climbs. The two barriers which lose importance most rapidly are "ignorance or fear of contraception" and "have not cared when children come." One reason actually increases in frequency, namely, "I didn't think I would become pregnant so soon," possibly because some couples overestimate the term of protection afforded by breast-feeding.

Discontinuation of Contraception

A total of 121 couples discontinue contraception at some point in their history, but apparently only in a minority of instances does such discontinuation reflect a disenchantment with contraception. Frequently the failure to resume contraception occurs after a miscarriage. For example, among couples practicing contraception before first pregnancy, 39 per cent discontinue it after that pregnancy when it ends in an abortion, as opposed to 5 per cent when it ends in a live birth. Percentages discontinuing after the second pregnancy are 27 per cent following a miscarriage and 8 per cent following a live birth. Furthermore, desire for another pregnancy right away is the predominant reason given for discontinuing contraception. (Together with fecundity doubts, this reason accounts for two-thirds of all reasons given.) Obviously many couples regret the time lost by miscarriage and, in order to minimize further delay, do not resume contraception.

Class–Religious Differentials

Reasons for delaying or discontinuing contraception are differentiated by class as well as religion. In order to have enough cases in most class-religious groups, it is necessary to merge data from all pregnancy intervals, as well as to combine reasons for discontinuing contraception with reasons for delaying its initial use. This aggregating is done in Table 9, which gives percentage distributions for the 8 class-religious groups and the total sample. The only obvious religious difference is the mention of religious objections by Catholics

TABLE 9

Reasons for Nonuse of Contraception, by Religion and Class

| REASONS | PER CENT CITING SPECIFIED REASON | | | | | | | |
| | Protestant | | Mixed Catholic | | Catholic | | Jewish | |
	White-Collar	Blue-Collar	White-Collar	Blue-Collar	White-Collar	Blue-Collar	White-Collar	Blue-Collar
Wanted children as soon as possible	63%	54%	33%	32%	53%	55%	80%	17%
Doubts concerning fecundity	8	7	–	–	3	3	8	33
Religious reasons	–	–	33	13	9	4	–	–
Ignorance or fear of contraception	4	11	4	16	2	5	4	17
Interfered with sexual enjoyment, etc.	6	11	8	19	10	14	4	33
Have not cared when children came	17	16	21	10	17	15	4	–
Didn't think would become pregnant so soon	2	2	–	10	5	4	–	–
Don't know	1	–	–	–	–	–	–	–
Per cent total	101	101	100	100	99	100	100	100
Number of wives	91	153	24	31	128	172	25	6

and Mixed Catholics, but not by Protestants or Jews. Within the four religious groups, there is a consistent tendency for blue-collar couples to explain their nonuse more frequently in terms of "ignorance or fear of contraception" or "contraception interferes with sexual enjoyment." On the other hand, white-collar wives more often say that they "have not cared when the children come." Few of these class differences are large, but they are consistent for the four religious groups.

Relation to Other Studies

The foregoing results are in general accord with two other studies. In agreement with the Indianapolis Study, over 90 per cent of the fecund Protestant couples find their way to contraception, with the percentage of users increasing sharply after first pregnancy. As reasons for this sharp increase, Westoff *et al* suggest "the gain in knowledge of contraception which frequently accompanies obstetrical service," but even more important, "an intensified determination to control reproduction."[4] This last explanation, finding support in the large percentage of present couples who report delaying contraception because they wanted a first pregnancy as soon as possible, finds further support in Chapter VII where it is shown that nearly all mothers believe that some degree of spacing between consecutive births is desirable.

The differences encountered between religious groups agree for the most part with those obtained in GAF.[5] In all three religious groups— Catholic, Jewish, and Protestant—large majorities eventually come to use contraception, but the fraction is lower among Catholics than Jews or Protestants. Moreover, Catholic users start contraception at later stages in their family building; Protestant users begin earlier; while Jewish users begin earliest. Socio-economic differentials are found among Protestants, but in contrast to GAF experience, not found among Catholics. However, this may be partly a function of using a crude occupational dichotomy instead of multiple categories of income or educational attainment.

METHOD CHOICE

In this section the distribution of contraceptive methods employed is shown to correspond with the GAF estimates. However, in contrast

[4] Westoff *et al.*, "The Use, Effectiveness, and Acceptability of Methods of Fertility Control," in Clyde V. Kiser and P. K. Whelpton, eds., *Social and Psychological Factors Affecting Fertility*, 5 Vols., Milbank Memorial Fund, New York, IV, pp. 893–898.

[5] Freedman, Whelpton and Campbell, *Family Planning, Sterility and Population Growth*, pp. 103–115.

to the experience of GAF and Indianapolis Studies, there is no sign of a tendency to gravitate toward the more effective methods as marriage duration increases. This anomaly raises a question about how many of the present couples are yet fully motivated to achieve efficient contraception.

Classification of Methods

The sample of couples utilize a wide variety of methods. Ten categories of method are distinguished on the basis of a classification discussed in Appendix B. Six of the categories represent use of a single method: safe period, douche, withdrawal, condom, diaphragm and jelly, or "other." The residual category "other" comprises mainly jelly used without the diaphragm. The remaining four categories represent use of multiple methods. A distinction is made between "combinations" (two, or rarely three, methods combined with this combination of methods used throughout a pregnancy interval) and "alternations" (two or more sets of methods used at different times during the pregnancy interval). Somewhat arbitrarily the safe period united with another method (no method used on "safe days" and the second method on "unsafe days") is defined as a combination and denoted as "combined-safe period." Because nearly all the other combinations represent adding a douche to a second method, they are designated "combination-douche." Alternations are divided into two groups: "alternation-douche" when the douche is alternated with another method, and "alternation-other" representing mainly paired alternations of withdrawal, condom, and diaphragm and jelly.

It is shown in Appendix B (Table B–2) that as used by the present couples, the most effective method categories are diaphragm and jelly, condom, alternation-other, and withdrawal; the least effective are safe period, douche, and other; while intermediate are combined-safe period, combination-douche, and alternation-douche. Effectiveness refers here to pregnancy rate during use of a method. Thus, an effective method is one yielding a small number of pregnancies per 100 years of exposure with that method. Generally speaking, the effectiveness of alternations and combinations is consistent with the effectiveness of the component methods being alternated or combined. That is, there is no evidence, with the possible exception of combined-safe period, that couples in contraceptive difficulty are drawn to the use of multiple methods. Appendix B also furnishes evidence (Table B–11) that diaphragm and jelly, and to a less extent condom, enjoy a reputation for reliability which goes beyond personal experience with them, while rhythm and douche bear a negative reputation in this regard.

77

Methods Used

The distributions of methods used in each pregnancy interval are tabulated in Table 10. These distributions are much the same from one interval to another. As the most popular method, condom

TABLE 10

Distribution of Methods of Contraception Used, by Pregnancy Interval

Method of Contraception	Before First Pregnancy[a]	Before Second Pregnancy	Before Third Pregnancy	Current Usage
Safe period	14%	19%	19%	19%
Douche	6	5	4	4
Withdrawal	4	5	4	5
Condom	35	29	41	31
Diaphragm and jelly	17	18	15	18
Other	4	3	3	3
Combined-safe period	5	7	4	8
Combination-douche	3	3	3	5
Alternation-douche	3	3	4	2
Alternation-other	8	6	4	5
Per cent total	100	100	100	100
Number of couples	607	914	113	983

[a] Includes 28 couples whose first pregnancy conceived premaritally.

accounts for about one third of all use. The safe period and diaphragm and jelly, each account for a fifth. The remaining seven categories each claim from 3 to 7 per cent of total use. About 80 per cent of the time a single method is used throughout the pregnancy interval; otherwise two or more methods are combined or alternated.

If no attention is paid to use of multiple methods as such, but merely to the frequency with which each single method is cited, then the following order from most to least popular among the five most frequently mentioned methods is obtained: condom, diaphragm and jelly, rhythm, douche, and withdrawal. This order happens to conform exactly with the one derived from GAF data; and as Freedman *et al* point out, this order indicates a change toward much greater use of rhythm, somewhat greater use of condom, diaphragm, and withdrawal, and much less use of the douche since 1940. The reader is referred to their discussion of the causes of these changes.[6]

[6] Freedman, Whelpton and Campbell, *Family Planning, Sterility and Population Growth*, pp. 174–178.

TABLE 11

Distribution of Methods of Contraception Used for All Pregnancy Intervals Combined, by Religion and Class[a]

Method of Contraception	Protestants		Mixed Catholics		Catholics		Jews		Total
	White-Collar	Blue-Collar	White-Collar	Blue-Collar	White-Collar	Blue-Collar	White-Collar	Blue-Collar	
Safe period	9%	4%	27%	19%	49%	29%	1%	–%	18%
Douche	3	7	7	13	3	7	1	–	5
Withdrawal	2	8	–	3	4	9	2	–	5
Condom	25	36	25	30	24	26	52	63	32
Diaphragm and jelly	30	19	16	8	6	8	27	26	18
Other	5	4	–	4	3	5	2	–	4
Combined-safe period	9	6	19	8	9	6	–	–	7
Combination-douche	6	6	1	4	1	4	3	–	4
Alternation-douche	2	4	1	6	1	3	1	5	3
Alternation-other	9	6	3	6	1	4	11	7	6
Per cent total	100	100	99	101	101	101	100	101	102
Number of pregnancy intervals	596	557	73	113	363	552	301	62	2,617

[a] Includes methods used before first, second, and third pregnancies as well as current interval. In the first 8 columns of figures, a per cent is italicized whenever it is more than one and a half times as large as the corresponding per cent in the last column, denoting total sample experience.

In further agreement with GAF experience, the main religious groups exhibit markedly different method preferences (Table 11). The experience of all·pregnancy intervals is pooled in order to obtain more stable percentages. Most striking is the reliance of Jews upon condom, diaphragm and jelly, and alternation-other—the three most effective method categories as used by all couples. Avoiding ineffective methods typifies blue-collar as well as white-collar Jews, so that the class differences are not statistically significant.

White-collar Protestants favor diaphragm and jelly but also exhibit a disproportionately high emphasis upon other (mostly jelly), combined-safe period (mostly diaphragm and jelly combined with the safe period) and alternation-other (mostly diaphragm and jelly alternated with condom or withdrawal). In contrast, blue-collar Protestants, whose methods differ significantly from those of their white-collar counterparts, make less use of diaphragm and jelly and more use of condoms and all methods involving a douche (i.e., douche alone, combination-douche, or alternation-douche).

Catholics favor the safe period method. To a statistically significant degree, white-collar Catholics concentrate more on the safe period than do blue-collar Catholics. The latter rely disproportionately upon withdrawal.

As compared to Catholics, Mixed Catholics rely less on safe period but more on combined-safe period. This pattern of reliance is more pronounced among white-collar than blue-collar members, who also rely heavily on douche and alternation-douche.

In general, religion is a more significant differentiator of methods than is class, but class yields significant differences in all religious groups except Jews.

Thus the four religious groups take very unequal advantage of the most effective methods. This differential is dramatized by computing the percentages of times that the four most effective method categories are mentioned—i.e., diaphragm and jelly, condom, alternation-other, and withdrawal. Among white-collar couples, these percentages are 92 per cent for Jews, 66 per cent for Protestants, 44 per cent for Mixed Catholics, and 35 per cent for Catholics. Corresponding percentages among blue-collar couples are 95, 70, 47, and 46 per cent. Notice too that consistently in all four religious groups, blue-collar couples make slightly more use of these effective methods than do white-collar couples.

Method Changes

Surprisingly enough, couples in the present sample show very little tendency to gravitate toward the more effective methods with increasing marriage duration. This lack of trend is demonstrated by Table 12, which, separately for couples practicing 2, 3, and 4 intervals of contraception, tabulates percentage differences between methods initially and last used. Aside from some tendency for the importance of douches to decline, no shifts are revealed. This resutl persists within religious groups, where no statistically significant differences are found between distributions of initial and last methods used. Of course, a significant shift toward more effective methods can hardly take place among Jews, who rely so exclusively upon effective methods from the start. However, more room for improvement exists among Protestants, and more room yet among Mixed Catholics and Catholics.

The failure of Protestants to increase their emphasis upon the more effective methods conflicts with Indianapolis experience, where such a trend proves strong during marriage durations of 12–15 years.[7]

[7] Westoff *et al*, "The Use, Effectiveness and Acceptability of Methods of Fertility Control," pp. 939–941.

TABLE 12

Percentage Differences between Distributions of Methods Initially and Last Used by
Couples Having Two, Three, or Four Intervals of Contraceptive Use

| Method | Percentage differences[a] | | |
	Two Intervals of Use	Three Intervals of Use	Four Intervals of Use
Safe period	−2%	−2%	0%
Douche	0	−3	−9
Withdrawal	0	1	5
Condom	0	2	0
Diaphragm and jelly	2	3	0
Other	1	−2	0
Combined-safe period	0	1	0
Combination-douche	1	1	3
Alternation-douche	−2	−1	0
Alternation-other	0	−1	0
Total	0	−1	−1

[a] Derived by subtracting the percentage using initially from the percentage using most recently.

The conflict with GAF data is less definite for two reasons. First, when discussing method changes in relation to marriage duration, Freedman, Whelpton, and Campbell confine their classification of methods to rhythm, withdrawal, and appliance methods. Secondly, as the authors caution: "Differences in the type of family limitation with duration of marriage may reflect the effects of either historical change in choice of methods or longer marital experience."[8] Nevertheless, both among Protestants and Catholics in the GAF sample, the reductions in the proportion using rhythm with increasing marriage duration are such as to suggest that more couples abandon rhythm for other methods than vice versa.

The most obvious hypothesis for why Protestants and Catholics in the present sample fail to increase their reliance upon the more effective methods is that many of these couples are not yet fully motivated to achieve efficient contraception. In Chapter VIII, it is shown that a minority of Protestants, and even fewer Catholics, express preference for as few as two children. Thus, the majority, desiring three or more children, have faced only a problem of spacing wanted births. Without the risk of an unwanted birth to spur their

[8] Freedman, Whelpton and Campbell, *Family Planning, Sterility and Population Growth*, p. 188.

efforts, many of these couples may be unable to force themselves to practice a method consistently or to substitute a less congenial though more effective method for one which has given them indifferent protection in the past.

Low Motivation

The possibility of low motivation finds some support in data linking past experience with a method to the likelihood of persisting with it. Seventy per cent of the couples use the same method in consecutive intervals. Following an interval of successful usage, this likelihood of repetition increases to 80 per cent. Contrariwise, after a failure while taking a chance, the frequency of repeating falls to 63 per cent and, after a failure while actually practicing the method, to 59 per cent. As Appendix B shows (Table B–7), the extent to which past experience differentiates shifting and not shifting varies with the method. Apparently past experience is least heeded by rhythm users and most attended by douchers. However, these differences according to method do not alter the fact that many couples cling to a method oblivious of its failures, which indicates that considerations other than reliability frequently dictate choice of method.

This inference is borne out by the fact that barely half the wives report reliability as a reason for preferring their current method (Table B–3). Moreover, less than half the wives express themselves as "very confident" about their present method, the majority indicating less confidence (Table B–8).

Adherence to Method Despite Failures

The types of couples who remain loyal to a method despite multiple failures with it are best glimpsed through the 50 couples who are currently using methods that have already failed them at least twice. Three ideal types may be distinguished, each characterized by a distinctive set of attitudes.

First are 17 devout Catholic couples. Despite repeated failure with safe period or combined-safe period, they are still using the same method, and all but two insist that they will not change in the future. Not one of the couples is highly confident of the method, and all of them give church prescription as their reason for using it. However, with one exception, both spouses want three or more children, so that the stark choice between unwanted children and church disapproval has not yet presented itself.

A second type comprises 11 couples who have failed twice with their method as the result of omissions. They blame themselves, not the method. The wives report they are very confident in their method and that they do not expect to change in the future. This method is typically condom, diaphragm and jelly, or jelly used alone or combined with a second method.

The remaining 22 couples admit they have a problem. Usually one or both of their failures occurred while practicing the method. Their confidence in the method is incomplete. Moreover, the reasons they give for using it are typically unrelated to reliability. Examples are "only method I know," "don't know any other method that is safe," "husband wants it that way," "simplest and most convenient."

This group of couples may be divided into two subgroups, the "procrastinators" and the "nonplussed," according to the definiteness of their future plans. The 10 nonplussed wives are quite vague about future method changes, or else say they do not expect to shift from their present method, which is usually safe period, douche, or withdrawal. The 12 procrastinators know of more reliable methods and express an interest in using them eventually. In nearly every case the reference is to diaphragm and jelly.

CONTRACEPTIVE EFFECTIVENESS

It remains to consider what kind of protection couples are receiving from their contraception. This protection may be measured either relatively, by comparing pregnancy rates when contraception is or is not practiced, or it may be measured absolutely by calculating numbers of pregnancies per time unit of contraceptive exposure. Generally speaking, the absolute measures are less complicated than the relative ones and for that reason furnish the more convenient means of conducting detailed comparisons. The absolute rates are discussed first.

Absolute Effectiveness of Contraception

Perhaps the simplest absolute measure of contraceptive effectiveness is the per cent of couples who postpone pregnancy as long as desired and then deliberately stop contraception in order to conceive, rather than having their contraception interrupted by an unintentional pregnancy. Unfortunately this percentage of successful contraceptors is much affected by whether long or short delays of pregnancy are being sought, because, other things equal, the shorter the desired postponement, the easier it is to attain contraceptive success.

A more refined measure of contraceptive effectiveness is the number of failures over 100 years of contraceptive exposure, with contraceptive exposure measuring as closely as possible the number of months of contraceptive practice during which there exists a chance of contraceptive failure. Although more laborious to compute, this failure rate is usually preferred to the per cent of successful contraceptors because it is less affected by contrasting lengths of intended pregnancy postponement. However, contrary to common supposition, a failure rate based on exposure time *is* affected by intended length of pregnancy postponement. When intended birth intervals are long, the more efficient contraceptors of a sample have opportunity to dilute the high failure rates of the accident-prone members. When intended intervals are short, they do not have this opportunity in the same degree. Thus two samples may be equal in their contraceptive effectiveness but that sample seeking the shorter intervals will register the higher failure rate. This problem, previously neglected in the literature, has been briefly discussed in a recent paper.[9]

Unfortunately, when comparing the contraceptive effectiveness of two samples, it is not possible to estimate exactly the extent to which the difference in failure rates is being exaggerated or underestimated as a result of differing pregnancy postponements. The size of the bias depends not only on the degree to which the two sets of desired postponements are dissimilar, but also on the extent to which the samples are heterogeneous with respect to monthly chance of contraceptive failure, as well as any correlations between these monthly chances of contraceptive failure and desired periods of pregnancy postponement.

However, certain steps can be taken to obtain very approximate estimates of the bias. Consider some data from the present survey, summarized in Table 13.[10] In the interval following marriage, couples exhibit a contraceptive failure rate of 25.5 pregnancies per 100 years of exposure; after first birth the rate is 20.4; while after miscarriage it is 48.3 pregnancies per 100 years exposure. Differences among these failure rates are statistically significant.[11]

[9] Robert G. Potter, Jr., "Contraceptive Practice and Birth Intervals Among Two-Child White Couples in Metropolitan America," in *Thirty Years of Research in Human Fertility: Retrospect and Prospect*, Milbank Memorial Fund, New York, 1959, pp. 74–92.

[10] This table and, unless the contrary is indicated, all subsequent tables pertaining to contraceptive effectiveness exclude the experience of birth intervals in which separations are reported. Contraceptive failure rates are lower for such intervals, presumably because respondents tend to exclude periods of partial separation from their reports of separation. (See Section 2b of Appendix A.). Regarding couples suspected of premarital pregnancy, only experience after first pregnancy is utilized.

[11] Significance tests are based on the formula:

$$\left(p_1 - p_2\right) \Big/ \sqrt{p\,q\left(\frac{1}{N_1} + \frac{1}{N_2}\right)}$$

where p_1 and N_1 denote the number of contraceptive failures per month and the total months of contraceptive exposure respectively in group 1; p_2 and N_2 have the same meanings for group 2; $p = (p_1 N_1 + p_2 N_2)/(N_1 + N_2)$; and $q = 1 - p$. This formula represents

These differences depend partly on biases. With only one month allowed for postpartum amenorrhea, the 20.4 rate for contraception after first birth is probably too low by at least two pregnancies.[12]

Differences among the three failure rates are also magnified by the unequal delays of pregnancy sought after marriage, first birth, and miscarriage. To gauge the effect of this bias even approximately, one needs, initially, to have some idea of the sensitivity of the three failure rates to specified changes in average length of intended pregnancy postponement and, secondly, to have a way of estimating the average postponements sought in each of the three periods.

TABLE 13

Effectiveness of Contraception following Marriage, First Birth, and Miscarriage

Period of Contraception	Months of Contraceptive Exposure	Intended Interval[a]	Per Cent of Successful Contraceptors[b]	Failure Rate[c]	Standard Error[d]
After marriage	8,758	18.3	65%	25.5	1.8
After first birth	19,121	24.3	64	20.4	1.1
After miscarriage	795	7.4	65	48.3	8.4

[a] Average number of exposure months per successful contraceptor.
[b] Per cent of contraceptors deliberately stopping contraception in order to conceive.
[c] Total failures divided by total contraceptive exposure, all multiplied by 1,200.
[d] Based on the crudely approximate formula 1200 (pq/n), where p is the number of contraceptive failures per month; q is $1-p$; and n is the total months of contraceptive exposure.

To gauge the sensitivity of a failure rate, one may take an interval of contraceptive use (e.g., the interval between marriage and first pregnancy) and successively truncate the longest contraceptive exposures at 48, 24, 12, 6, and 1 months, with failure rates then computed for each of these truncated bodies of contraceptive experience. Thus, in the case of cutting off exposures at 6 months, if a couple fails in the fourth month, they are coded as contributing 4 months of exposure and one failure. If they fail in the 7th, or any later month, they are coded as contributing 6 months of exposure and no failure. As the cut-off point is made earlier, the failure rate tends to

a highly simplified approximation. A partial justification of it is contained in a paper presently being prepared. There is some reason to believe that it is optimistic, that is, values greater than 1.96 or less than -1.96 are to be expected more than 5 per cent of the time under the null hypothesis. Therefore it is advisable to require a critical ratio of somewhat in excess of 2 before postulating significance at the 95 per cent level of confidence. According to the formula, the failure rates after marriage and first birth are 2.4 standard deviations apart; those after marriage and miscarriage 3.0; and those after miscarriage and first birth 3.9 standard deviations apart.

[12] If instead of one month, three months is substituted as a more reasonable allowance for postpartum amenorrhea, the failure rate increases from 20.4 pregnancies to 22.5.

increase because the higher failure rates of the earlier months are receiving greater and greater weight proportionally.

Subsample sizes are large enough to apply this procedure to contraception following marriage and first birth, but not to contraception following miscarriage. The results, given in Table 14, show that as the

TABLE 14

Failures per 100 Years of Contraceptive Exposure when Observation is Terminated at Specified Intervals

| Span of Observation Period | Interval from Marriage to First Pregnancy | | Interval from First Birth to Next Pregnancy [a] | |
	Number of Exposure Months	Failure Rate	Number of Exposure Months	Failure Rate
Zero to 1 (months)	1,006	42.4	1,488	14.5
Zero to 6	3,025	37.1	4,870	25.1
Zero to 12	4,782	35.7	8,171	24.7
Zero to 18	6,012	30.8	10,534	23.8
Zero to 24	6,871	29.4	12,135	22.3
Zero to 36	7,925	27.3	13,994	20.8
Zero to 48	8,389	26.2	15,046	19.9
Total interval	8,758	25.5	16,655	19.5

[a] Includes only couples without miscarriages.

cut-off point is made earlier, failure rates increase more slowly after a birth than after marriage. In part, this is attributable to the inadequate allowance for postpartum amenorrhea. The inadequate one-month allowance means that contraceptive exposure is being defined in such a way that each couple enjoys a few months of low risk immediately after birth and this reduces heterogeneity of failure risk during this period. As a consequence, in the period after first birth, even a six-month change in average length of desired pregnancy postponement is not likely to change the calculated failure rate by more than 1 or 2 pregnancies per 100 years of exposure, certainly a minor effect. But in the interval following marriage, corresponding effects tend to be larger, so that more caution is necessary.

To estimate the average delay of pregnancy sought by a group, one may use the average exposure lengths of successful contraceptors in that group. For example, applied to the present data, this procedure yields an estimate of 24 months as the average postponement sought after first birth, in contrast to 18 months after marriage and only 7 months after a miscarriage. These estimates somewhat exaggerate the contrast in postponements sought during the three periods, since the less effective a group's contraception, the more underestimated will their average intended delays be. This is made clear by an extreme example. Suppose a sample is split 50-50 between wanting to delay pregnancy 2 months and 50 months. If they practice very inefficient contraception, then only those aiming for two months have much chance to succeed and the average exposure time of successful contraceptors comes out close to two months. But if all couples are practicing nearly perfect contraception, then virtually all achieve their spacing objectives and the average exposure of successful contraceptors approaches 26 months. Thus, the more inefficient is a group's contraception, the more its average intended pregnancy postponement is underestimated. Undoubtedly then the delays of pregnancy intended after marriage, first birth, and miscarriage are more similar than appears in Table 13.

However an easy check that the postponements sought after first birth somewhat exceed those intended after marriage, and greatly exceed those intended after miscarriage, is provided by juxtaposing success rates and failure rates. Despite the disparate failure rates— 20, 25, and 48 pregnancies per 100 years of exposure—the percentages of couples successful in their contraception are virtually the same in the three periods, varying from 64 per cent successful after first birth to 65 per cent successful after marriage or miscarriage.

Combining the results of Table 13 and Table 14, one concludes that if the postponements desired after first birth had been as short as those desired after marriage—very roughly, 18 months instead of 24— the 20.4 failure rate for contraception after first birth might have been 1 or 2 pregnancies higher. Conversely if the desired postponements of first pregnancy had averaged 24 months instead of 18, the 25.5 failure rate might have been reduced by somewhat more than 1 or 2 pregnancies. Thus, although the failure rates after marriage and first birth are significantly different, statistically speaking, the difference, 20.4 as opposed to 25.5 pregnancies per 100 years exposure, is in large part attributable to biases resulting both from an inadequate allowance for postpartum amenorrhea and from dissimilar lengths of intended pregnancy postponement.

No evidence, then, has been found that contraception after first birth is more effective than contraception during the earlier period, though of course the remote possibility exists that an extreme sampling fluctuation is masking a real difference. Finally, regarding contraception after miscarriage, if desired pregnancy delays had averaged 18 or 24 months instead of somewhat more than 7 months, then the failure rate would have been well below 48 pregnancies, though remaining above the rates of the other two periods.

Comparison with the Indianapolis Study

The contraceptive failure rates just reviewed are so much higher than those obtained in the Indianapolis Study that it is important to investigate the reasons why. When the experience of "relatively fecund" Indianapolis couples is divided into contraception before and after first pregnancy, the respective failure rates are 12 and 10 pregnancies per 100 years of contraceptive exposure,[13] as compared to 25 and 21 pregnancies in the present study.

Two explanations may be dismissed at once. First, the inclusion of Catholics and Jews in the present study has not operated to increase failure rates. As will be shown in Tables 17 and 18, the failure rates calculated for the entire sample are slightly below those for Protestants alone. Secondly, the differences in methods used by Indianapolis and the present Protestant couples are such that the latter ought to have lower, not higher, failure rates than the Indianapolis couples. Although couples in the current study fail to increase their reliance upon the more effective methods as marriage duration increases, their initial emphasis upon these methods is tangibly greater.

Harder to evaluate is the possibility that the present couples are more weakly motivated to achieve effective contraception. The previous section on method choice has revealed that in choosing a method many of these couples place other values ahead of reliability. But the two samples differ in this respect only as a matter of degree, since an appreciable proportion of Indianapolis couples also cite non-reliability reasons and others acknowledge practicing their method irregularly.

More basic are sample differences with respect to fecundity and desired postponements of pregnancy. In the case of couples in the current study, contraceptive experience is confined to the period between marriage and second birth. Since contraception always precedes a pregnancy, there is a fecund condition during nearly all of this exposure. Then too, it is believed that most of these couples have wanted at least two children, so that few of them have yet sought to delay pregnancy much longer than the two or three years desirable for spacing consecutive births.

In contrast, Indianapolis couples, married from 12 to 15 years were not restricted to a particular number of births and they desired fewer children on the average. Wanting so few children, many of these Indianapolis couples attained their desired family sizes long before the interview. Therefore, their contraceptive histories include attempts to delay pregnancy for long periods. Moreover, since contraception

[13] Westoff *et al*, "The Use, Effectiveness, and Acceptability of Methods of Fertility Control," p. 926.

was not always followed by a pregnancy, there is no assurance that all couples practicing contraception were fecund. For example, the failure rate for contraception before first pregnancy is spuriously low if several of the voluntarily childless couples were unknowingly sterile from marriage.

No satisfactory way exists to test the effects of these sample contrasts. The best that can be done is to examine the failure rate of Indianapolis couples who have at least two pregnancies, well recognizing that this subsample may be selective with respect to contraceptive effectiveness. To permit this test, data pertaining to "relatively fecund" Indianapolis couples who had at least two pregnancies, the first of which ended in a live birth, have been utilized. The results, summarized in Table 15, show a failure rate of

TABLE 15

Effectiveness of Contraception before and after First Pregnancy as Practiced by "Relatively Fecund" Indianapolis Couples Having at Least Two Pregnancies [a]

Period of Contraception	Months of Contra- ceptive Exposure	Percentage of Successful Contra- ceptors	Failure Rate	Standard Error
Before first pregnancy	10,202	36%	37.5	2.1
After first pregnancy	23.496	33%	23.0	1.1

[a] With first pregnancies ending in live births.

37.5 for contraception prior to first pregnancy and 23.0 for contraception prior to second pregnancy. The first rate is substantially above, the second rate barely above, corresponding rates in the present study.[14] This, of course, amounts to a reversal in relative sizes of failure rate between the two studies.

Interestingly enough, differences in intended length of pregnancy postponement are operating to reduce, rather than enlarge, this reversal in failure rates. That the subsample of Indianapolis couples sought to delay their second pregnancies longer than did the present couples is indicated by a much lower percentage successful (33 per cent instead of 64 per cent) in conjunction with a nearly identical failure rate (23 pregnancies per 100 years compared to 21). In lesser degree, the Indianapolis subsample also tried to delay their first pregnancies longer than did the present couples. This fact is indicated

[14] On the basis of the significance test cited earlier, the interstudy difference in failure rates before first pregnancy is highly significant (4.3 standard deviations) but the difference is not statistically significant after first pregnancy (1.2 standard deviations).

by a success rate of only 36 per cent in combination with a failure rate of 37 pregnancies per 100 years. In comparison, as Table 17 will show, two class-religious groups from the current study combine equally high or higher failure rates with success percentages in excess of 50. Thus, were it not for the Indianapolis subsample seeking longer pregnancy postponements, the reversal in failure rates would be even more extreme.

Presumably what lies behind this unexpected reversal of failure rates is that with so many Indianapolis couples wanting only one child or none, a subsample restricted to couples having at least two pregnancies is necessarily selected toward ineffective contraception. Of course, the same selection is operating in the present sample, but not to the same extent because urban Americans today seek larger families than did the marriage cohort represented by Indianapolis couples.

Previous Performance

A good predictor of contraceptive effectiveness is contraceptive performance in a previous interval. Table 16 documents this association for 807 couples having no miscarriages and practicing contraception before their second pregnancy. Couples who initially succeed by deliberately interrupting their first interval of contraception in order to conceive achieve a failure rate of 8.6 pregnancies

TABLE 16

Contraceptive Effectiveness as Related to Past Contraceptive Performance [a]

Contraceptive Performance during First Pregnancy Interval	*Contraceptive Performance during Second Pregnancy Interval*				
	Months of Contra- ceptive Exposure	Intended Interval	Per Cent of Successful Contra- ceptors	Failure Rate	Standard Error
Successful contraception	7,505	24.6	83%	8.6	1.2
Nonuse for reasons relevant to child-spacing	2,994	20.6	65	23.2	3.0
Failure while taking a chance	2,624	26.2	46	28.8	3.6
Failure while practicing contraception	1,614	27.1	46	31.2	4.7
Nonuse for reasons irrelevant to child-spacing	2,321	24.8	45	37.7	4.3
Total	17,058	24.1	64	20.4	1.2

[a] Restricted to couples having but two pregnancies and reporting contraception before the second one.

90

per 100 years in the next interval, much the lowest failure rate in the table.[15] The next lowest failure rate is contributed by couples who explain their initial nonuse of contraception in terms of subfecundity or wanting a first child as soon as possible. Their failure rate of 20.6 is as high as it is partly because they sought relatively shorter delays of second pregnancy. Partly for the same reason, their failure rate is not significantly below the 28.8 and 31.2 failure rates of couples initially failing either while taking a chance or while using a method; on the other hand, it is significantly lower than the 37.7 failure rate of couples ascribing their initial nonuse of contraception to reasons irrelevant to child-spacing.[16]

Past performance appears more impressive as a predictor when success rates are inspected, instead of failure rates. Among couples initially successful, over 80 per cent repeat their success in the next interval. This compares with 65 per cent for couples explaining their initial nonuse of contraception in terms of subfecundity or wanting a child as soon as possible, and the difference would be larger except for the shorter pregnancy delays sought by the latter group. Couples representing the other three categories of past performance exhibit success rates of 45 or 46 per cent.

These results have relevance for an index of fertility planning success, which figures prominently in Chapters X–XIX. This index seeks to summarize, for entire marriage durations, the success of individual couples in postponing pregnancy as long as desired. Each pregnancy interval is classified as representing either successful or unsuccessful contraception: successful if contraception is deliberately stopped in order to conceive, or if contraception is not used for child-spacing reasons, and unsuccessful if pregnancy occurs while taking a chance or using a method, or if contraception is not used for reasons unconnected with child-spacing preferences. This classification derives some justification from Table 16 which has shown that delayed availability and initially ineffective contraception carry a poor prognosis for subsequent contraceptive success, while initially successful contraception, and to a less extent nonuse for reasons relevant to spacing objectives, carry a favorable prognosis.

Couples having a record of consistent success are labelled "highly successful," while the label "highly unsuccessful" is attached to couples having a record of consistent failure. Couples having one success and one failure are classified either as "semi-successful" or "semi-unsuccessful" depending whether the success pertains to the

---

[15] For example, this rate and the next lowest rate are estimated to be 5 standard deviations apart.

[16] This last difference is estimated to represent 2.8 standard deviations.

last or the first interval.[17] The allocation of couples having three pregnancies to these four categories of planning success is more difficult and arbitrary. The details are given in Appendix B.

Class-Religious Differentials

Commanding interest are class-religious differences with respect to contraceptive effectiveness. The data for contraception before first pregnancy are assembled in Table 17. The Jewish failure rate, 9.8

TABLE 17

Effectiveness of Contraception before First Pregnancy, by Class and Religion

Religion and Class	Months of Contraceptive Exposure	Intended Interval	Per Cent of Successful Contraceptors	Failure Rate	Standard Error
Protestant	4,224	20.1	58%	27.3	2.7
White-collar	2,574	21.5	59	26.6	3.5
Blue-collar	1,650	18.2	58	28.4	4.5
Mixed Catholic	606	21.2	50	29.7	7.6
Catholic	1,968	13.4	61	35.4	4.6
White-collar	752	14.3	51	46.3	8.4
Blue-collar	1,216	13.0	68	28.6	5.2
Jewish	1,960	20.6	81	9.8	2.4
Total	8,758	18.3	65	25.5	1.8

failures per 100 years of exposure, is much lower than any other; and the difference between Jews and non-Jews is highly significant statistically. The only other significant religious difference, holding constant class, is between the 46.3 failure rate of white-collar Catholics and the 26.6 failure rate of white-collar Protestants.[18] Virtually no difference exists between blue-collar Catholics and blue-collar Protestants. Like the Jews, the Mixed Catholics are too few to divide by class. Ignoring class, Mixed Catholics have a failure rate intermediate between Protestants and Catholics.

[17] Obviously a rather heterogeneous variable is being measured here. For instance, a successful interval of contraception depends on several factors: (1) intended period of pregnancy postponement; (2) fecundability, as defined in the previous chapter; (3) degree to which contraception is reducing the monthly risk of pregnancy below fecundability level; and (4) chance factors. Moreover, reporting accuracy is also involved, because an interval of contraception is not classified as successful unless the respondent reports that she deliberately stopped contraception in order to conceive. Clearly then the above index of planning success does not have a simple meaning even for contraceptors.

[18] The failure rates of Jews and non-Jews are 5.3 standard deviations apart; those of white-collar Catholics and white-collar Protestants are 2.5 standard deviations apart. No other comparison yields a value as high as 2.0.

With regard to average lengths of intended pregnancy postponement, as measured by average exposure time of successful contraceptors, little variation appears between Jews, Mixed Catholics, and Protestants. The Jews may have sought slightly shorter intervals than the Mixed Catholics in view of a slightly shorter exposure despite a much lower failure rate. However, the distinctive group are the Catholics, who apparently sought shorter delays of first pregnancy than did the other religious groups. For example, the blue-collar Catholics, despite a failure rate as low as the Protestants' or Mixed Catholics', show any average exposure length among their successful contraceptors which is 5 to 7 months shorter. Apparently the white-collar Catholics sought barely longer postponements than the blue-collar Catholics, though of course the small difference may be a product of sampling fluctuations. At any rate, if the intended postponements of first pregnancy are shorter for Catholics, the effect on failure rates is to exaggerate somewhat the substantial contrast between white-collar Catholics and white-collar Protestants, and also to conceal what may be a slightly higher efficiency by blue-collar Catholics than blue-collar Protestants.

Comparable data for contraception after first pregnancy are assembled in Table 18. Again the Jewish failure rate is significantly

TABLE 18

Effectiveness of Contraception after First Pregnancy, by Class and Religion[a]

Religion and Class	Months of Contraceptive Exposure	Intended Interval	Per Cent of Successful Contraceptors	Failure Rate	Standard Error
Protestant	7,901	20.6	60%	24.6	1.9
White-collar	4,070	20.9	65	21.5	2.5
Blue-collar	3,831	20.2	55	27.9	2.9
Mixed Catholic	1,434	22.9	58	25.9	4.6
Catholic	7,640	24.7	62	21.7	1.8
White-collar	2,981	24.0	59	23.8	3.1
Blue-collar	4,659	25.2	63	20.3	2.3
Jewish	2,941	22.2	85	7.8	1.8
Total	19,916	22.6	64	21.1	1.2

[a] Includes contraception following both first birth and miscarriage.

lower than any other. As before, white-collar Protestants have a lower failure rate than white-collar Catholics, though not significantly so. Only one other difference is statistically significant,[19] namely, the

[19] The Jewish-Gentile difference represents 5.9 standard deviations; the blue-collar Catholic versus blue-collar Protestant, 2.1; no other difference yields a value as large as 2.0.

lower failure rate of blue-collar Catholics as compared to blue-collar Protestants. This differential is surprising because blue-collar Catholics rely on somewhat less effective methods (Table 20). However, it should be kept in mind that groups of contraceptors are being compared, not total groups. Possibly, among blue-collared Catholics, contraceptors are a more selected group than among blue-collar Protestants. Forty-six per cent of the blue-collar Catholics practice withdrawal, condom, diaphragm and jelly, or paired alternations of these methods. One assumes that these couples must be highly anxious about their child-spacing in order to use methods disapproved by their church. To practice efficient methods of contraception, Protestants do not have to overcome the same religious inhibitions.

With respect to intended intervals after first pregnancy, that the Jews' average exposure is two months longer than for Protestants is attributable partly to their much lower failure rate. Again the Catholics are the distinctive group, though this time they appear to have sought a wider spacing between births than did the others. Though their failure rates are not tangibly lower than the Protestants, Catholic contraceptors who are successful average 4 or 5 months more exposure. However, in previous discussion it has been noted that differing intended intervals have only weak effects upon failure rates computed for contraception after a birth and, therefore, it is doubtful whether these differences in intended interval seriously affect the comparisons among religious groups.[20]

The above comparisons are incomplete in one respect: they do not register the fact that class-religious groups differ in the percentages of couples who need contraception but find it unavailable for one reason or another. This omission is serious if one views nonavailability of contraception as equivalent to practicing contraception with zero efficiency. In such cases the risk of pregnancy remains at fecundability levels, with a "failure rate," if one uses the experience of noncontraceptors waiting for first conception, of approximately one pregnancy per 10 months, or 120 pregnancies per 100 years of exposure.

These considerations suggest a way of constructing failure rates which will be responsive to levels of contraceptive availability. Suppose that in a particular class-religious group, there are N_1

[20] Only one class-religious group shows a statistically significant drop in failure rate before and after first pregnancy. The failure rate of white-collar Catholics drops from 46.3 to 23.8 failures per 100 years, a difference representing 3 standard deviations. There is no obvious substantive reason why white-collar Catholics have so much higher a failure rate before first pregnancy than any other class-religious group when such is not the case after first pregnancy. Possibly an extreme sampling deviation is reponsible.

contraceptors contributing a total of e_1 months of contraceptive exposure, during which exposure pregnancies occur at a rate of f_1 pregnancies per 100 years. Suppose that also belonging to the group are N_2 couples who need contraception but find it unavailable. These N_2 couples may be regarded as contributing $10N_2$ months of exposure, during which "exposure" pregnancies occur at a rate of 120 pregnancies per 100 years. An adjusted failure rate is derived by weighting the two failure rates according to the amounts of "exposure" associated with them, that is,

$$\frac{e_1 f_1 + 10N_2 \cdot 120}{e_1 + 10N_2}$$

Failure rates adjusted in this fashion are given in Table 19. Before first pregnancy, when contraception commonly is not available, the

TABLE 19

Contraceptive Failure Rates Corrected for Nonavailability of Contraception, by Class and Religion

Religion and Class	*Failures per* 100 *Years of Contraceptive "Exposure"*	
	Before First Pregnancy	After First Pregnancy
Protestant		
White-collar	36.1	23.2
Blue-Collar	51.9	32.7
Mixed Catholic	59.6	32.1
Catholic		
White-collar	81.6	38.3
Blue-collar	68.2	31.2
Jewish	12.0	8.5
All couples	48.5	28.0

modified failure rates are much higher than conventional ones for all class-religious groups except Jews. The rise in failure rate is most marked for Catholics, especially white-collar Catholics, who have a failure rate two thirds that predicted upon no contraception at all. A similar pattern of contrasts between adjusted and conventional failure rates prevails after first pregnancy, though in much attenuated form because of the higher availability of contraception in this later period.

The class-religious comparisons contained in Tables 17 and 18 may be refined in another way. Table 11 has shown that class-religious

95

groups differ markedly in the methods they use, while, as Table B–2 demonstrates, the methods themselves are correlated with widely contrasting percentages of successful users. Hence it is interesting to see to what extent dissimilarities in methods used account for class-religious differences with respect to contraceptive success rates.

An analysis, utilizing Westergaard's method of expected cases,[21] is summarized in Table 20. Experience before and after first pregnancy is merged in order to obtain more stable success proportions. Though not ideal, success proportions are used in place of failure rates because no satisfactory way of estimating standard errors is known for the case of failure rates in conjunction with the Westergaard method.

TABLE 20

Observed Rates of Contraceptive Success Compared with Those Expected on the Basis of Methods Used, by Class and Religion

Religion and Class	Proportion of Times Contraception Interrupted Deliberately [a]		
	Observed	Expected	Difference
Protestant			
White-collar	.64	.64	.00
Blue-collar	.56	.65	−.09**
Mixed Catholic			
White-collar	.52	.58	−.06
Blue-collar	.61	.58	+.03
Catholic			
White-collar	.58	.56	+.02
Blue-collar	.65	.59	+.06*
Jewish			
White-collar	.84	.72	+.12**
Blue-collar	.77	.73	+.04
All couples	.63	.63	.00

NOTE: A single asterisk indicates the figure is significant at .05 level of confidence; a double asterisk at .001 level.

[a] These rates of contraceptive success are based on experience before and after first pregnancy, including birth intervals in which separations are reported.

The first column of figures represents success proportions actually observed for the eight class-religious groups. The second column of figures gives success proportions expected if each class-religious group had the distribution of methods that they do but used each method with the level of success that the entire sample exhibits with that

[21] S. A. Stouffer and C. Tibbetts, "Tests of Significance in Applying Westergaard's Method of Expected Cases to Sociological Data," in A. J. Jaffe, ed., *Handbook of Statistical Methods for Demographers*, U.S. G.P.O., Washington, 1951, 65–70.

method. The last column furnishes differences in the form: observed proportions successful minus expected proportions successful. If the difference is positive, the members of the particular class-religious group are using their methods with above average success. A negative difference implies that the members of the group are less successful with their methods than is average for the sample.

It may be seen that a substantial part, though not all, of the Jewish superiority is ascribable to the methods they use. Especially the white-collar Jews appear to employ their methods with unusual efficiency. According to the methods they use, Protestants ought to produce a better record than the two Catholic groups. The fact that the blue-collar Protestants do not is due to their relatively unsuccessful use of adopted methods. Among Mixed Catholics, the methods used offer no reason for expecting white-collar and blue-collar couples to differ in their success proportions. Nor is it very clear from the final column of figures that they do, though here the weak power of the significance test may be a factor. It is not definite either that the proportions of successful Catholics are significantly higher than expected.

Relative Effectiveness of Contraception

Attention now shifts from absolute measures of contraceptive effectiveness to relative ones. During the period before first pregnancy the present couples experienced a rate of 25.5 pregnancies per 100 years of contraceptive exposure, and after first birth a rate of 20.4 pregnancies. How large a reduction from fecundability levels do these rates represent? The measure conventionally employed to answer this kind of question is the effectiveness ratio. Initiated by Stix and Notestein, this ratio expresses the number of pregnancies prevented during a unit period of contraceptive exposure as a percentage of the number expected, without use of contraception, during the same period.[22]

To measure the relative effectiveness of contraception practiced in this sample before first pregnancy, one needs, besides the rate of 25.5 pregnancies per 100 years of contraceptive exposure, an estimate of the number of first pregnancies that might occur in 100 years of exposure without contraception. Chapter IV furnishes two estimates. The couples not using contraception before their first pregnancy waited on the average 10 months for their first conception, this being equivalent to a rate of 120 pregnancies per 100 years of exposure. In contrast, the couples deliberately stopping contraception in order to conceive

[22] R. K. Stix and F. W. Notestein, *Controlled Fertility*, Williams and Wilkins, Baltimore, 1940, pp. 58–64.

waited only an average of 5.2 months, which represents a rate of 230.8 pregnancies per 100 years. Depending on which estimate is used, one obtains:

$$(120.0-25.5)/120.0=.79, \text{ or}$$

$$(230.8-25.5)/230.8=.89$$

as the relative effectiveness of contraception practiced before first pregnancy.

Estimating the relative effectiveness of contraception after a birth is complicated by the matter of postpartum amenorrhea. Seemingly the best course is to exclude postpartum amenorrhea both from contraceptive exposure and noncontraceptive exposure, and to define the numerator and denominator of the effectiveness ratio accordingly. This means using, once again, 120.0 and 230.8 as the numbers of pregnancies expected when no contraception is practiced. It also means subtracting a generous allowance for postpartum amenorrhea from time spent in contraception before computing the number of pregnancies per 100 years of contraceptive exposure. A problem arises here because mean length of postpartum amenorrhea is never known precisely. Certainly the single month allowed in deriving the rate of 20.4 pregnancies per 100 years of contraceptive exposure is inadequate. From what little is known, three months is more reasonable, and substituting this allowance leads to a corrected rate of 22.5 pregnancies. On the basis of this corrected rate, one estimates that, following first birth, the present couples practiced contraception with a relative effectiveness of

$$(120.0-22.5)/120.0=.81, \text{ to}$$

$$(230.8-22.5)/230.8=.90$$

This range of .81 to .90 is barely higher than the range of .79 to .89 estimated for contraception preceding first pregnancy; and as indicated earlier, this small difference may depend upon the longer pregnancy delays sought after first birth.

Most of the published criticism of the effectiveness ratio has focused on the term representing number of pregnancies expected in the absence of contraception. The estimate of this number varies depending upon whether the conception wait experience of non-contraceptors or successful contraceptors is used. Because of measurement errors and selectivities, the experience of successful contraceptors presumably leads to too high an estimate while the experience of noncontraceptors leads to too low an estimate. More specifically, the experience of successful contraceptors may exaggerate ease of conception in part because these couples are making deliberate efforts to shorten their conception waits, and presumably the same efforts are not made during periods of contraceptive practice. On this account, the estimate based on noncontraceptor experience is sometimes favored over the experience of successful contraceptors. Another reason for favoring the experience of noncontraceptors is in the interest of conservatism: underestimating the number of pregnancies to be expected without contraception produces a conservative rather than an optimistic estimate of relative contraceptive effectiveness.[23]

Actually a more serious defect of the effectiveness ratio is its partial dependence upon the lengths of pregnancy postponement being sought. Thus, it is the second term which appears in the effectiveness ratio, namely, the number of pregnancies per 100 years of contraceptive exposure, which may cause the greatest trouble. Because this number of pregnancies is not independent of the lengths of pregnancy postponements being sought, neither is the effectiveness ratio. When these desired postponements differ as grossly as they do between the present study and the Indianapolis Study, any comparison concerning contraceptive effectiveness, absolute or relative, is invalidated. Hence, for cases like this, it is desirable to redefine the effectiveness ratio in such a way that it becomes more independent of desired lengths of pregnancy postponement.

The dependence upon intended lengths of pregnancy delay operates through the differential weighting of effective and ineffective contraceptors. A contraceptive failure rate is simply a weighted average of the failure rates of individual couples, with the weight received by any couple being the number of months of contraceptive exposure which they contribute. By virtue of their longer contraceptive exposures, the effective contraceptors receive heavier weights than do the ineffective ones, whose exposures are cut short by unintentional pregnancy. Moreover, weighting differentials become more extreme as longer pregnancy delays are sought. Hence, to eliminate the dependence, one must find a way of weighting all couples equally.

Ideally this is done by utilizing only the contraceptive experience of the initial month—or more exactly, the initial menstrual mid-cycle—since in any subsequent month a selected group of couples have already been removed by pregnancy. It has been estimated elsewhere that following marriage, during the first month of contra-

[23] Still another alternative, proposed by Westoff *et al*, involves pooling the experiences of nonusers and successful users of contraception and proceeding from there. See Westoff *et al*, "The Use, Effectiveness, and Acceptibility of Methods of Fertility Control," pp. 948–951.

ception, the couples of this study experienced a rate of 37 pregnancies per 100 years of exposure.[24] Naturally it is desirable to define analogously the rate of pregnancies during absence of contraception. Useful for this purpose is an estimate of .2 pregnancies per month derived in Chapter IV for noncontraceptors, which rate is equivalent to 216 pregnancies per 100 years. (A corresponding estimate for successful contraceptors is not available.) Using these estimates, one obtains

$$(216-37)/216=.83$$

as the relative effectiveness of contraception practiced during the first month of marriage.

Of course, one must regard this estimate skeptically because during the first month of marriage special factors are apparently operating to lower both fecundability and contraceptive assiduousness. Hence, supplementary estimates are desirable. An alternative effectiveness ratio may be built on the experience of the second month of marriage, which month, incidentally, generates both the highest contraceptive failure rate (50 pregnancies per 100 years) as well as the highest pregnancy rate for noncontraceptors (265 pregnancies per 100 years). These data yield an estimate of

$$(265-50)/265=.81$$

Still another estimate may be derived by utilizing the experience of the first three months of marriage. This rate does not eliminate differential weighting, but greatly minimizes it, at the gains of greater freedom from the special factors operating in the first month of marriage, as well as having a greater amount of exposure. The estimate resulting from this procedure is

$$(217-40)/217=.81$$

Thus, it turns out to be of minor significance whether the estimates of relative contraceptive effectiveness are based on the first month of marriage, the second, or the first three. In all cases the effectiveness ratio barely exceeds .8, which corresponds closely to the estimate of .79 obtained with the conventional effectiveness ratio when an expected rate of 120 pregnancies per 100 years is used in the denominator. Algebraically this correspondence means that in the conventional effectiveness ratio generating the .79 estimate, effective and ineffective contraceptors are being differentially weighted to approximately the same extent as are highly fecund and subfecund couples.

[24] Potter, "Contraceptive Practice and Birth Intervals Among Two-Child White Couples in Metropolitan America," p. 76.

Such an equivalence is quite accidental. Ordinarily effectiveness ratios which weight couples equally, or nearly equally, may be expected to yield results different from those based on conventional effectiveness ratios. Presumably the Indianapolis Study is a case in point. It is quite possible that weighting the experience of individual Indianapolis contraceptors equally would have produced results conforming closely to those obtained in the present study; while the pursuit of conventional methodology, as in Westoff *et al*, produces estimates of relative effectiveness mostly in the .90's.[25]

SUMMARY

This chapter has directed attention to three aspects of contraception: availability, choice of method, and effectiveness.

The data pertaining to availability of contraception have produced no surprises. As might be expected of a sample of contemporary, urban, native-born, white Americans, the use of contraception is the rule rather than the exception. Only 11 per cent of the couples are still not using contraception after a second birth. Use of contraception increases sharply after the first pregnancy. It varies with religion, being most frequently and earliest used by Jews; somewhat less so by Protestants; and least frequently and latest used by Mixed Catholics and Catholics. White-collar Protestants start their contraception earlier than do blue-collar Protestants; otherwise class (as crudely measured in this chapter) fails to differentiate contraceptive use within religion. The comparative influence of religion and class on fertility planning is examined more systematically in Chapter XI.

A distinction is made between couples not using contraception because they profess no need for it and those who acknowledge a need for it but find it unavailable for religious or other reasons. In general, the three factors of parity, class, and religion differentiate availability and nonavailability of contraception in the same manner as they do contraceptive use and nonuse. In addition, discontinuations of contraception, which frequently follow a miscarriage, usually reflect a temporary lack of need for contraception rather than disenchantment with it.

With regard to method choice, the distribution found in this study accords well with that observed in the GAF Study. Condom is the most popular method, followed in order by diaphragm and jelly, rhythm, douche, and withdrawal. Jews utilize efficient methods almost exclusively; Catholics and Mixed Catholics take advantage of them less

[25] Westoff *et al*, "The Use, Effectiveness, and Acceptability of Methods of Fertility Control," p. 950.

than half the time; while Protestants occupy an intermediate position.

Surprisingly enough, these couples do not increase their use of the more effective methods as marriage duration increases. It is hypothesized that many couples are not yet fully motivated to achieve efficient contraception because their problem of birth control has been confined to spacing wanted births. Some evidence for this conjecture is found in: (1) a low association between past experience with a method and shifting from it; (2) the fact that barely half of the wives report reliability as a reason for preferring their current method; and (3) an analysis of 50 couples persisting with a method despite at least two failures with it in the past.

Couples in the present study do not take any honors for contraceptive effectiveness. Prior to first pregnancy their failure rate is 26 pregnancies per 100 years of contraception; after first pregnancy, it is 20 pregnancies. These rates are twice as high as those encountered in the Indianapolis Study. Contributing factors are: (1) since contraception in this sample is always followed by pregnancy, there is a fecund condition during most of this exposure; and (2) since most of the couples have been spacing wanted births, they have rarely aspired to pregnancy postponements much longer than two or three years. Substantial space is devoted to the methodological considerations whereby these two factors spell considerably heightened failure rates.

A good predictor of contraceptive effectiveness is contraceptive performance in a previous interval.

The degree to which Jewish couples practice more effective contraception than either Protestants or Catholics both in the periods preceding and following first pregnancy strains credulity. Not only do the Jewish couples of this sample rely more exclusively on the most effective methods, but they apparently manage these methods with unusual efficiency.

In a methodological vein, the final pages of this chapter attempt to translate failure rates of 20 and 26 pregnancies per 100 years of contraception into estimated reductions of pregnancy risk from fecundability levels. Readers of the literature have become accustomed to reductions of the order of 90 per cent and higher. But in the present study, where care has been taken to weight the experience of each contraceptor equally or nearly equally, the results approach nearer to 80 per cent. It may be regarded as a fault of the conventional estimates of relative contraceptive effectiveness that the most efficient contraceptors in a sample receive disproportionately heavy weight, which contributes to an exaggerated view of the protection received from contraception.

Chapter VI. Birth Intervals

Birth intervals are not precisely determined by birth spacing preferences except when the couple agrees on what spacing they want and achieves complete "interval control." Such control presupposes delaying pregnancy as long as desired, achieving conception quickly once it is wanted, and escaping pregnancy wastage. Preceding chapters have shown that such control is infrequently achieved. When contraception fails, pregnancy occurs sooner than desired. Nor does successful contraception insure that the birth will not be delayed by tardy conception, pregnancy wastage, or an involuntary separation.

Thus, only a limited understanding of birth intervals is reached by treating them as simple expressions of spacing preferences. More is learned by partitioning each birth interval into an "intended component," representing length of contraceptive practice, and a "residual component," comprising the remainder of the birth interval. Essentially the intended component measures the postponement of pregnancy achieved by contraception, while the residual component encompasses the various types of birth delay.

The objectives of this chapter are three. First, it will be shown that the variance of the residual component often exceeds that of the intended component, and that the two components are only weakly correlated. Second, having demonstrated the composite nature of birth intervals, the possibility is tested that attitudinal variables correlate better with intended components than with total birth intervals. Third, the first birth interval and its components are analyzed as predictors of spacing intent and achievement in the next interval.

A report in which this procedure of partitioning birth intervals is applied to the present data has already been published.[1] The present chapter differs from the original article mainly in placing more emphasis upon the substantive and less upon the methodological aspect.

METHOD

Definitions

The division of birth intervals into intended and residual components is straightforward when there is neither pregnancy wastage

[1] Philip C. Sagi, "A Component Analysis of Birth Intervals Among Two-Child White Couples in Metropolitan America," in *Thirty Years of Research in Human Fertility: Retrospect and Prospect*, Milbank Memorial Fund, New York, 1959, pp. 135–148.

nor separations. Every month of the birth interval is classified as belonging to one of the following categories of time: contraception, conception wait, or pregnancy. (Periods of postpartum amenorrhea are not distinguished.) The intended component is taken as the time spent in practice of contraception; the remainder of the interval defines the residual component.

Temporary separations of husbands and wives add complications which are solved rather arbitrarily. Each wife is asked to report the initial and terminal dates of separations lasting three months or longer. That portion of a separation which overlaps with pregnancy time remains as pregnancy time; the remainder is classified as separation time. When practice of contraception immediately precedes this separation time, the latter is added to the intended component on the rationale that since separations are usually foreseen, the couple have indicated their intent to defer pregnancy until after the separation by continuing to practice contraception up to the separation. When nonpractice of contraception precedes the separation, separation time is added to the residual component.

Birth intervals including a miscarriage potentially encompass two periods of contraception, two pregnancies, and two conception waits. In such cases, the intended component is made equal to the first period of contraception, while the entire remainder is assigned to the residual component.

Sample

Defined in the manner indicated above, the two components have their simplest meaning for couples successfully planning their pregnancies either in the sense of deliberately stopping contraception in order to conceive or foregoing contraception in order to conceive as soon as physically possible. For these couples, the intended component is essentially equivalent to intended length of pregnancy postponement, while the residual component, less nine months, measures the period of birth delay. Altogether there are 596 couples reporting successful planning in the first birth interval; 656 in the second interval; and 429 couples reporting successful planning in both intervals.

The procedure of distinguishing intended and residual components may be extended to birth intervals in which contraception is not successful or else is not used for reasons other than wanting pregnancy as soon as physically possible. In this extension the intended component loses its simplicity of meaning since its variation comes to reflect not only desired postponements of pregnancy, but also such elements as nonavailability of contraception, fecundity doubts, and contraceptive effectiveness. In the first birth interval, 100 couples suspected of premarital conception must be excluded, reducing to 1,065 the number of couples to whom the analysis can be applied. However, in the second birth interval, the analysis is applicable to all 1,165 couples.[2]

Religion will be ignored in this chapter because subclassification by religious groups does not seem to alter conclusions. While the four principal religious groups vary markedly in their distributions of intended components, the interrelations among intended components, residual components, and total birth intervals appear quite similar in the four religious groups.

RELATIVE VARIABILITY OF THE TWO COMPONENTS

To what extent does variation in birth intervals depend on the different lengths of time that contracption is used? Theoretically, the variance of intended components could be quite small if couples agreed about the ideal spacing of children and at the same time practiced highly effective contraception. On the other hand, given more erratic contraception and a diversity of opinions about ideal birth intervals, the variation in intended components would become much larger.

A simple measure is derived by expressing the variance of intended components as a percentage of the variance of total birth intervals. However, this measure is hard to interpret whenever residual and intended components correlate strongly. The variances of residual and intended components sum exactly to the variance of the total birth interval only when the two components have a zero correlation. An alternative measure, avoiding this problem, is the relative variability of the intended component as compared to the residual component. When this ratio of variances falls short of 1, then birth delays are making a larger contribution to the variability of birth intervals than the postponements of pregnancy achieved by contraception.

The variances of first and second birth intervals and their components are furnished in Table 21, separately for successful planners

[2] The classification of planning success used in this chapter differs in one respect from that utilized in the index of fertility-planning success, discussed in the latter part of Appendix B. Couples not using contraception because of assumed subfecundity are not considered as planning successfully since they are not realizing their desired pregnancy postponements through contraception. But in the index of fertility-planning success, the same behavior is treated as successful planning, on the grounds that such nonuse, given the perception of subfecundity, represents rational behavior with respect to spacing objectives and therefore is to be distinguished from cases of nonuse in which contraception is needed but not available.

and the larger sample. In three out of four instances, birth delays prove more variable than achieved postponements of pregnancy, and as a consequence the variances of these achieved postponements amount to less than half those of the total intervals. The one exception occurs in the first interval of successful planners, when the intended components are 62 per cent as variable as the total intervals. One might have expected to find the opposite result, namely a greater relative importance attaching to periods of contraception in the second interval than in the first.

TABLE 21

Variances of Birth Intervals and Birth Interval Components,
by Interval and Planning Success

Sample and Birth Interval	Number of Couples	Variances (months)			Ratio of Variances Intended/Total Residual
		Intended Com- ponents	Residual Com- ponents	Total Intervals	
Successful planners					
First interval	596	205	145	330	.62
Second interval	656	230	252	520	.44
Total sample					
First interval	1,065	128	147	288	.44
Second interval	1,165	256	346	546	.47

Actually this apparent increase in the relative importance of birth delays, from first to second birth interval, is somewhat spurious, depending partly as it does upon an abnormally low incidence of miscarriages in the first interval and a more normal frequency in the second. For instance, in the total sample of 1,165 couples, there are only 50 miscarriages in the first birth interval, but 91 miscarriages in the next one. The lesser figure represents a subnormal rate of 4 per cent; the larger figure, a rate much nearer the typical level of 10 per cent. This differential is important because some of the longest birth delays follow miscarriages. As a result, residual components are much more variable in the second interval, thereby depressing the variance ratio of intended components to residual components.[3]

[3] The decline in the ratio of intended component to residual component variances from first to second birth interval is much more precipitous among successful planners because, while the variance of their residual components increases, the variance of their intended components remains essentially constant. This constancy reflects a balance of factors. In the second interval, successful contraceptors are seeking longer and more varied postponements of pregnancy, but there is a much smaller percentage of couples who, as noncontraceptors seeking to become pregnant as soon as physically possible, are assigned zero intended components.

Regarding the total sample, no decline in the ratio of intended component to residual component variances occurs because the variance of the intended component increases as

Thus, the birth intervals of couples in this study vary as much from unintentional birth delays as from voluntary postponements of pregnancy.

Birth Intervals as Dependent Variables

A Hypothesis

Finding that birth delays figure as prominently in the variability of birth intervals as do pregnancy postponements achieved by contraception raises some pointed questions about the composite nature of birth intervals. Suppose that achieved postponements of pregnancy reflect mainly voluntary factors and birth delays mainly involuntary ones. Then residual components will be less predictable by many social and psychological variables than intended components. Perhaps it often happens that an attitudinal variable is moderately associated with the intended component of an interval, but is scarcely correlated at all with the residual component, and, as a result, exhibits only a weak correlation with the total interval. In other words, given a battery of background and attitudinal variables (such as those covered in Chapters X to XIX), one might appreciably raise correlations by substituting intended components for total birth intervals.

This hypothesis may be formalized. Let the total birth interval be designated as T, its residual component as R, and its intended component as I. Assume that R has a zero correlation with I as well as with the attitudinal predictor Y. However, Y correlates significantly with I. Given these simplifying assumptions, then r_{IY}, the correlation between I and Y, is related to r_{TY}, the correlations between T and Y, by the formula

$$r_{IY} = r_{TY}\sqrt{1 + \sigma_R^2/\sigma_I^2}$$

That is, under the conditions being assumed, r_{IY} will be *relatively* larger than r_{TY} by a factor of 1.4 to 1.7 when the ratio of the variance of residual components is one to two times the variance of intended components. Of course, a large relative gain means little predictively if r_{TY} is small to start with. For instance, it accomplishes little, predictively, to lift an .06 correlation to .09.

rapidly as the variance of the residual component. Intended components manifest such a small variance in the first interval mainly because the unsuccessful contraceptors are contributing spans of contraception which are longer than the zero lengths contributed by the numerous noncontraceptors, but usually shorter than the pregnancy postponements achieved by successful contraceptors. But in the next interval, noncontraceptors are no longer numerous, so that intended components shortened by contraceptive failure tend to enhance, rather than reduce, the total variation of intended components.

At first glance the conditions necessary for the relevance and practical interest of this formula seem fairly well met by the data. Correlations between intended and residual components remain below .10 for successful planners and all couples, both in the first and second birth intervals. Furthermore, from the previous section, the variance of the residual component exceeds that of the intended component and, according to the formula, this should mean correlations 50 per cent higher when intended components are substituted for total intervals. Then also, among the attitudinal and background variables examined,[4] correlations with residual components of birth intervals are typically, though not always substantially, lower than correlations with intended components.

However the real test is whether, for these background and attitudinal variables, the predicted increases are realized. A negative result emerges. Though typically increases do take place, they seldom approach the magnitudes predicted by the formula as indicated by the results for wife's total fertility desires, summarized in Table 22.

TABLE 22

Observed and Predicted Correlations between Wife's Total Fertility Desires
and Intended Components of First and Second Birth Intervals

Sample and Birth Interval	Number of Couples	Observed Correlation with Total Interval	Observed Correlation with Intended Component	Expected Correlation with Intended Component
(1)	(2)	(3)	(4)	(5)
First birth interval				
Successful planners	596	−.21	−.22	−.27
All couples	1,065	−.19	−.21	−.28
Second birth interval				
Successful planners	656	−.26	−.30	−.38
All couples	1,165	−.32	−.35	−.49

When intended components are substituted for total birth intervals, correlations with wife's total fertility desires increase, but only by fractions of the amounts promised by the formula.

Thus the hypothesis does not appear to have general validity for these data. However, an extenuating circumstance should be noted. The very fact that the residual component accounts for so much of the

[4] Correlations were examined for the following variables: liking for children, age at which children become most enjoyable, preferred interval between second and third births, hedonic tone of childhood, marital adjustment score, adjustment to mother role, patterns of help available to wife, future work intentions of wife, and numbers of siblings of husband, of wife, and of both husband and wife.

total variation of birth intervals makes it difficult to obtain even a moderate correlation with the total birth interval unless the predictor correlates in some degree with the residual component as well as the intended. Therefore, to test the hypothesis mainly on the basis of variables showing some association with total birth intervals is to select the cases in which the correlations with the residual component, be it for reasons of sampling fluctuations or genuine association, are not negligible.

The negative results leave little incentive to substitute intended components for total birth intervals in the analyses of subsequent chapters. However, these results do not gainsay the composite character of birth intervals within which variation is fairly equally divided between two components which hardly correlate with each other. Why the correlation between components should be so low merits brief consideration.

Association of the Two Components

As already noted, the correlations between residual and intended components remain below an absolute value of .10, both in the first and the second birth intervals. Among successful planners, the correlations are —.06 and .08; and in the enlarged samples, they are .05 and —.09. The question is whether such low associations are peculiar to this sample or reflect tendencies which might be expected to operate in many samples.

On the basis of differential fecundability one would expect a direct relationship between the two components. Long postponements of pregnancy are more easily achieved by subfecund couples who in turn experience longer birth delays. In contrast, the highly fecund are more apt to fail in their contraception, which in turn leads both to shorter postponements of pregnancy and minimal birth delays. However, these forces toward a direct relationship are not necessarily strong. Table 23 demonstrates that, among couples successful in their contraception, the association between length of contraceptive practice and time waited for conception is very weak indeed. Moreover, according to the incomplete data of Table 24, the association between contraceptive success or failure and length of conception wait is probably not strong either.

Furthermore, there are factors working to produce an inverse relationship between intended and residual components. Non-contraceptors have zero intended components and, from Chapter IV, they average longer conception waits than do the successful contraceptors. The waits are especially longer for couples who dispense with contraception because they doubt their fecundity. Since these latter couples are not classified as successful planners and are more numerous in the second birth interval than the first, they may be partly responsible for the negative correlation of −.09 observed in the second interval for the total sample.

TABLE 23

Conception Waits of Successful Contraceptors, by Length of
Time Contraception Practiced

Months of Contraceptive Exposure	Before First Pregnancy[a]		After First Birth[b]	
	Number of Couples	Mean Conception Wait (months)	Number of Couples	Mean Conception Wait (months)
0 to 6 (months)	86	5.15	39	4.08
7 to 12	58	4.98	76	4.00
13 to 24	98	5.44	201	4.94
25 to 48	76	5.35	117	5.97
49 or more	19	4.83	45	5.64
Total	337	5.23	478	5.04

[a] Cases involving separations excluded.
[b] Cases involving separations or miscarriages excluded.

Thus in the present sample there is some justification for viewing the weak correlations between intended and residual components as growing out of an opposition of weak tendencies. Moreover, as far as

TABLE 24

Conception Waits of Couples Twice Successful in their Contraception
and Couples Successful Once and Failing Once[a]

Contraceptive performance in First and Second Birth Interval	Number of Couples	Mean Conception Waits	
		First Interval (months)	Second Interval (months)
Success–success	242	4.82	
Success–failure	46	4.37	
Success–success	242		5.86
Failure–success	84		5.31

[a] Confined to couples having no miscarriages or separations and practicing contraception before both pregnancies.

can be judged, this feature is not just a peculiarity of the present birth intervals. Although it is not realistic to suppose that in other studies of American fertility the correlation between components would always prove negligible, it still seems likely that the same opposition of tendencies would operate to keep the association moderate if not low. The factors tending to produce an inverse relationship between the two components can be expected to exist. For instance, other research besides the Indianapolis and GAF studies, has shown that contraception is commonly delayed until after first pregnancy and that nonuse of contraception in later intervals tends to go together with subfecundity. Then also, it is hard to visualize differential fecundability generating a strong correlation between lengths of contraceptive practice and lengths of conception delay because these two variables are subject to such large random fluctuations.

BIRTH INTERVALS AS INDEPENDENT VARIABLES

Hypotheses

Birth intervals and their components may also be viewed as independent variables predicting the events of the next birth interval. There are several reasons for thinking that the components of the first birth interval might correlate more highly with the components of the second birth interval than, say, the first and second total intervals correlate with each other. Presumably the factors governing fecundability in the first interval are much the same as those governing fecundability in the second, so that the correlation between residual components should be appreciable notwithstanding the presence of large random elements. The correlation between intended components may not be as high, despite the continuity of factors determining contraceptive efficiency, because different deferments of pregnancy are usually sought in the two intervals. Finally, lengthy delays of first birth may prompt couples to plan relatively shorter postponements of their next pregnancy.

The subsample which offers the most critical test of these ideas are the 429 couples who claim to have planned successfully in both intervals.[5]

Results

It has been hypothesized that a lengthy delay of first birth might prompt couples to plan relatively short postponements of their next pregnancy, and so lead to an inverse correlation between the residual component of the first interval and the intended component

---

[5] There are few birth intervals in which these couples fail to use contraception. Partly for this reason, their intended components have variances which are only 50 and 35 per cent as large respectively as the variances of their first and second birth intervals. Also, for obscure reasons, the correlation between intended and residual components is below .10 in the first interval, but .16 in the second interval. The latter coefficient is highly significant statistically.

of the second. A barely significant —.10 correlation weakly corroborates this conjecture. Possibly one reason why the association is not stronger is that some of the couples who suffer the longest delays of first birth come to doubt their fecundity and therefore forego contraception in the next interval and hence exclude themselves from the category of successful planners.[6]

As Table 25 shows, the residual component of the first interval correlates .21 with the residual component of the second interval,

TABLE 25

Correlations between First and Second Birth Intervals and
Their Respective Components, for 429 Successful Planners of both intervals

Birth Intervals and Components	Correlation[a]
First interval and second interval	.10
First interval and second residual	.05
First interval and second intended	.04
First residual and second residual	.21
First intended and second intended	.16
First residual and second intended	−.10
First intended and second residual	.04

[a] Needed for significance at the .05 level is an absolute value of .09.

while the two sets of intended components correlate .16. Both correlations exceed the .10 value found between first and second birth intervals, not to speak of the nonsignificant .04 and .05 correlations observed between first birth interval and the intended and residual components respectively of the second birth interval. These results indicate, at least for these data, that components of birth intervals are better predictors of future spacing intents and achievement than is the composite variable of total birth interval. However, it is also true that the correlations involved are all too small to have practical significance predictively.

Fecundability in Successive Intervals

The .21 correlation between birth delays in the first and second intervals has interest in its own right, especially when set beside a similar correlation of .14 obtained by Tietze for a group of Hutterites

[6] There is no reason to expect an association between the converse pair of components, namely, the achieved postponements of first pregnancy and the involuntary delays of second birth. This supposition is borne out by a nonsignificant correlation of .04.

112

supposedly using little or no contraception.[7] At least two reasons may be adduced for the rather modest sizes of these two correlations. First, with many couples having monthly conception chances of .2 or less, fecundability only loosely determines length of conception waits. Hence, the correlation between successive conception waits would be moderate or low even if the fecundability of each couple remained constant from month to month and from birth interval to birth interval, which it certainly does not. Secondly, pregnancy wastage serves to weaken the correlations between successive birth delays still further, because for the majority the risk of pregnancy wastage is low enough so that wastage in a birth interval is infrequently followed by wastage in the next interval. That the correlation is higher in the present sample, .21 to .14, may depend on the artificially low incidence of pregnancy wastage in the present sample. Another possible reason for Tietze's correlation being lower is that Hutterite mothers, not using contraception, have the variability of their birth delays increased by differentials of postpartum amenorrhea—a source of variability which is almost absent in a sample predominantly composed of successful contraceptors.

Marriage Duration

In the present sample, the combined length of the first and second birth interval defines the couple's marriage duration and this variable will serve as one of four main dependent variables in many of the chapters from X through XIX. The original decision to emphasize marriage duration was made in the belief that by pooling first and second birth intervals, chance components would be reduced relative to systematic ones and, as a result, marriage duration would produce higher correlations than either first or second birth interval taken singly.

This expectation has been only partially fulfilled. Most of the attitudinal and background variables included in this study correlate higher with second interval than first interval. But first interval variation comprises a considerable part of the variation of marriage duration. Perhaps mainly for this reason, marriage duration yields about the same level of correlation as does second interval. Thus, to favor marriage duration over second interval is arbitrary. But the pairs of correlations produced by the two variables are usually too similar to justify consideration of both. Moreover, the higher priority assigned to marriage duration is not rigid. Whenever second interval yields a sensibly higher correlation or is more germane to the topic

[7] C. Tietze, "Reproductive Span and Rate of Reproduction among Hutterite Women," *Fertility and Sterility*, 8 (1957), p. 94.

under analysis, second interval is substituted for marriage duration without hesitation.

SUMMARY

In this chapter birth intervals are partitioned into "intended components," representing lengths of contraceptive practice, and "residual components," comprising the remainders of the intervals. These two divisions are essentially equivalent to the pregnancy postponements achieved by contraception and birth delays.

In the present sample, birth delays usually contribute somewhat more to the variation of birth intervals than do periods of contraceptive practice. The two components, residual and intended, exhibit a weak, inverse correlation. These results indicate the composite nature of the present set of birth intervals. Moreover, as far as can be judged, this compositeness is a fairly general property of birth intervals.

Contrary to expectation, the background and attitudinal variables included in this study show hardly any more association with intended components than with total birth intervals.

The two components of first birth interval appear to predict their counterparts in the next birth interval better than does the aggregate first interval predict the second. However, the highest correlation involved between the two sets of birth delays is only .21.

Chapter VII. Preferred Birth Intervals

The discussion, which thus far has dealt with means and barriers to fertility control, now turns to a major category of fertility preference, namely, desired spacing of children. The relationship between spacing preferences and birth intervals is looser than one might first believe, though still strong enough to invest spacing preferences with a practical interest. The couples in the present study exercise only partial control over their birth intervals, which, as the previous chapter shows, are as much a product of involuntary birth delays as voluntary postponements of pregnancy. Spacing preferences significantly influence only these latter periods of contraceptive practice, and even then the correspondence is not always close. For example, contraception may be interrupted by an unintentional pregnancy. If the couple doubt their fecundity, they may dispense with contraception rather than risk an excessive pregnancy delay. Finally, in cases where contraception is unavailable for such reasons as ignorance or religious scruple, spacing preferences become irrelevant.

PREVIOUS RESEARCH

Previous research has tended to pass over the study of birth spacing attitudes, though the Indianapolis Study provides an exception. A partial synopsis of Kiser and Whelpton's results is worth quoting:

"Opinions as to the spacing of children are quite uniform. Between 68 and 76 per cent of the couples in each (fertility planning) group said the 'most desirable' time for the first child is two to three years after marriage. Between 81 and 89 per cent said the 'most desirable' time between subsequent children is two to three years. The actual spacing of children, in contrast, varied widely from group to group and from the reported 'most desirable' spacing."[1]

However, no questions were asked in the Indianapolis Study inquiring why respondents considered one time more desirable than another. Nor was any attempt made to differentiate couples desiring long or short birth intervals beyond noting contrasts with respect to a classification of fertility planning status.

Thus spacing preferences have remained a relatively unexplored topic and it seems well worthwhile to scrutinize them in detail for the first time. The analysis is organized into three sections, each corresponding to a different time reference. The first set of spacing

[1] P. K. Whelpton and C. V. Kiser, "The Planning of Fertility," in Kiser and Whelpton, eds., *Social and Psychological Factors Affecting Fertility*, 5 vols., Milbank Memorial Fund, New York, 1946–1958, II, p. 255.

preferences are retrospective, being the respondents' current opinions of their first and second birth intervals. The second are the originally preferred first and second intervals, available for a subsample of successful contraceptors in the form of lengths of contraceptive practice immediately following marriage or first birth. The third set of spacing preferences, having a future reference, concern the preferred spacing between second and third children.

Appraisals of First and Second Birth Intervals

Data

All 1,165 mothers in this study were asked to evaluate the timing of their first two children in terms of "too soon," "it didn't matter," "just right" or "waited too long." With respect both to the first child and to the second, only 3 per cent say "it didn't matter," thereby failing to express a definite opinion. Of course, these evaluations come after the fact and many of them may disagree with earlier preferences. The most likely bias is a tendency to report one's intervals as just right unless they are very extreme. Of interest in this connection is the manner in which appraisals of interval length vary depending on whether a particular pregnancy is successfully planned or not. By successful planning is meant either nonuse of contraception in order to have the pregnancy as soon as possible, or else deliberately stopping contraception for pregnancy purposes. In Table 26 the evaluations of couples consistently successful in their contraception are compared with those of couples consistently failing in their contraception.[2] Less than 10 per cent of the successful planners rate their intervals as too short and from 15 to 26 per cent rate their intervals as too long. As might be expected, the unsuccessful planners regard a smaller proportion of their intervals as too long and a substantially higher proportion as too short. However, more than 50 per cent of these unsuccessful planners view their intervals as just right, indicating a fairly strong tendency to accept whatever intervals occur unless they be extreme.

[2] In terms of the classification of fertility planning control, discussed in more detail elsewhere, these two groups represent the "highly successful" and the "highly unsuccessful" planners. There remains 205 "semi-successful" planners who successfully planned their last pregnancy but failed to plan an earlier pregnancy and 172 "semi-unsuccessful" planners most of whom planned at least one pregnancy but failed to plan their last one. The interval judgments of these last two groups conform very precisely to what would be expected on the basis of the appraisals of the first two. Thus, for example, with reference to the first interval the semi-successful planners exhibit a distribution of ratings almost identical with that of the highly unsuccessful while their distribution of second interval ratings virtually duplicates that of the highly successful planners. An analogous fit holds for the semi-unsuccessful.

TABLE 26

Evaluation of First and Second Intervals, by Success with Contraception

| Planning Status | Number of Wives | Per Cent Evaluating Interval as | | | | Total |
		Too Short	Just Right	Too Long	Didn't Matter	
Marriage to first birth:						
Successful planners	482	8%	75%	15%	2%	100%
Unsuccessful planners	306	35	57	5	4	101
First to second birth:						
Successful planners	482	3	70	26	1	100
Unsuccessful planners	306	25	56	12	7	100

Preferred Timing of the First Child

Asked to evaluate the timing of their first child, 66 per cent of the wives appraise their timing as "just right," 22 per cent say their first baby came too soon, 10 per cent say it came too late, while 3 per cent claim the timing didn't matter.

Intervals deemed just right cover a wide range of lengths. This is clear from Table 27, which first subdivides the sample of mothers into nine classes according to length of first interval and then subdivides each class into percentages appraising their interval as too short, just right, too long, or didn't matter. Responses of just right predominate in six classes, which together embrace interval lengths of 8 to 53 months. Indeed, these approved first intervals have a standard

TABLE 27

Per Cent of Wives Considering Their First Child as Coming "Too Soon," "Just Right," "Too Late," or "It Didn't Matter," by Length of Interval between Marriage and First Birth

Length of Interval Marriage to First Birth	Number of Wives	Timing Too Soon	Timing Just Right	Timing Too Late	It Didn't Matter	Total
Under 8 months	62	55%	40%	–%	5%	100%
8 to 11	281	38	57	–	5	100
12 to 17	258	28	70	1	2	101
18 to 23	149	17	77	5	2	101
24 to 29	99	8	87	4	1	100
30 to 41	135	3	86	11	–	100
42 to 53	84	–	65	31	4	100
54 to 71	66	–	35	64	2	101
72 and over	31	–	26	74	–	100
Total	1,165	21	66	10	3	100

deviation of 15 months, which is not much less than the standard deviation of 17 months for the entire sample of first intervals. Appraisals of the interval as too short predominate only among intervals shorter than 8 months, presumably cases of premarital conception. At the other extreme, regrets about excessive length predominate only among intervals $4\frac{1}{2}$ years or longer.

These results suggest that many mothers do not perceive a narrow range of first interval length as just right and all other lengths as too short or too long. Rather they perceive a broad span of interval length as not causing serious inconvenience. When their actual interval falls anywhere in this range, they tend to rate it as just right.

Considerations in Timing First Children

Mothers who say their first child came too soon are apt to complain that they lacked time for marital adjustment, to ready their finances, or to enjoy things with their husband before the responsibilities of motherhood.

In answer to the question:

> "Do you think it's best for a couple to have their first child
> as soon as possible after marriage or wait a while?"

only one-fourth of the mothers checked "as soon as possible," the remainder favoring replies of "wait a while" or "depends." A similar result was obtained in the pretest of 100 Camden mothers. Moreover, when asked why a couple should wait, the Camden mothers repeatedly mentioned the importance of having time to adjust to marriage, to improve one's financial status, and to enjoy things with one's husband before the responsibilities of children. Accordingly, three questions were included in the final questionnaire to represent these themes:

> "Did you and your husband have enough time really to
> get to know each other and become adjusted to marriage
> before your first child came?"
> "Have you ever wished that you and your husband would
> have had more time to enjoy things together before your
> first child came?"
> "Do you think you and your husband had enough time to
> get ready financially before your first child?"

The percentage of wives reporting dissatisfaction on these three scores ranges from 19 to 41 per cent. The smallest proportion feels that they lacked time to adjust to marriage; the largest proportion that they had insufficient time to prepare their finances. As shown by

TABLE 28

Per Cent of Wives Considering Their First Child as Coming "Too Soon" from the Standpoints of Becoming Adjusted to Marriage, Enjoying Things with Husband, or Readying Finances

Interval Marriage to First Birth	Number of Wives	Per Cent Considering Their First Child as Coming Too Soon from Standpoint of		
		Marital Adjustment	Enjoying Things	Readying Finances
Under 8 months	62	37%	52%	76%
8 to 11	281	35	38	49
12 to 17	258	24	35	54
18 to 23	149	12	22	41
24 to 29	99	9	17	33
30 to 41	135	6	10	23
42 to 53	84	–	7	15
54 to 71	66	1	3	12
72 and over	31	–	3	16
Total	1,165	19	26	41

Table 28, nearly all those who report having had insufficient time to adjust to marriage, or to enjoy things with their husband before the arrival of children, have first intervals of less than two years. The mothers agree much less about the manner in which the timing of the first child affects finances. In fact, one suspects that some of the mothers might have been prepared to say that any timing of their first child would have complicated their finances.

Answers to the three questions are highly correlated. They yield a Guttman scale with only 58 per cent as many imperfect scale types as expected by chance. This is not too surprising since it is usually short intervals which are regarded as complicating marital adjustment or prematurely truncating the period of childlessness, and these same intervals yield the highest rate of reportedly embarrassed finances. Correlations among answers to the three questions largely disappear when computed for subsamples of mothers having similar first intervals.

Relation to Desired Family Size

Are first interval preferences affected by the number of children a mother wants? Suppose that the three considerations just studied (time for marital adjustment, time to enjoy things with husband, and time to ready finances) are the dominant considerations for many women. Presumably the implications which these considerations have for the best timing of the first-born remain unchanged whether the mother wants 2, 3 or 4 children. On this basis, then, one might

119

anticipate very little association between first interval preferences and desired family size.

Taking the sample as a whole, this seems to be the case. No tendency is found for wives wanting larger families to approve shorter first intervals or for small-family advocates to approve longer intervals. A crude measure is used here: mothers who rate their first interval as just right are subdivided into three groups according to whether they prefer 2, 3, or 4 or more children, and then chi-square is used to test whether the three groups differ in their distributions of first interval lengths. The chi-square value falls short of statistical significance.

Insufficient cases preclude this chi-square analysis for each religious group separately. This is perhaps unfortunate because, among Catholics, responses to the question:

> "Do you think it's best for a couple to have their first child
> as soon as possible after marriage or wait a while?"

do correlate significantly $(r=-.20)$ with size of family desired, while among Protestants there is no association $(r=.01)$. This contrast between Catholics and Protestants applies to preferred third intervals as well, as will be shown later in this chapter.

Preferred Spacing of First and Second Children

Mothers in the present study also rate a wide diversity of intervals between first and second children as just right. According to Table 29,

TABLE 29

Per Cent of Wives Considering Timing of Second Child as "Too Soon," "Just Right," "Too Late," or "It Didn't Matter," by Length of Interval between First and Second Births

Length of Interval First to Second Birth	Number of Wives	Timing Too Soon	Timing Just Right	Timing Too Late	It Didn't Matter	Total
12 months or less	57	58%	37%	2%	4%	101%
13 to 18	222	40	55	0	5	100
19 to 24	205	12	81	1	4	98
25 to 30	155	5	90	5	1	101
31 to 36	131	2	82	15	1	100
37 to 48	149	–	68	31	1	100
49 to 60	94	1	38	59	2	100
61 to 84	77	–	19	78	3	100
85 and over	75	–	9	89	1	99
Total	1,165	13	61	22	3	99

over 85 per cent of the wives having second intervals 19 to 36 months long now appraise them as just right. Even among wives experiencing second intervals of 13 to 18 months, or 37 to 48 months, a majority now view them as just right. Thus a considerable span of second intervals is deemed acceptable.

Nevertheless the mothers are slightly more specific about what constitutes a satisfactory interval between first and second children than what constitutes a satisfactory timing of the first child. The range of second intervals evoking majority responses of just right, namely 13 to 48 months, is narrower than the corresponding range of 8 to 53 months applying to first intervals. The standard deviation of second intervals judged just right is less than that for first intervals so judged (13 months to 15), despite the fact that second intervals are more variable than first intervals (standard deviation of 23 months instead of 17). The greater consensus regarding preferable second intervals is also recorded in a closer association between evaluation (too short, just right, etc.) and length of interval being evaluated, the coefficient of contingency being .64, as opposed to .58 for first intervals.

A slightly smaller proportion is satisfied with their second interval —61 per cent compared to 66 per cent satisfied with their first interval. Moreover, almost twice as many regard their second interval as too long (22 per cent) as deem it too short (13 per cent). This constitutes an interesting reversal from the first interval, about which more mothers regret excessive brevity than length.

Considerations in Spacing First Two Children

In the pretest, many of the Camden mothers indicated that ideal child-spacing involves a balancing of two considerations: having the children far enough apart to limit the burden of infant care, while keeping them close enough together so that they become playmates. Accordingly, two questions of the multiple choice type were designed to represent these two considerations:

"Thinking of your children becoming good playmates, do you think they are too close together in age, just right, or too far apart?"

"As far as taking care of your children goes, do you think the difference in their ages is just right or do you think things might be easier if they were farther apart or closer together in age?"

The mothers substantially agree about what length of second interval encourages their children to become playmates, but are in much less accord about the interval length which facilitates child care.

According to data contained in Table 30, most of the mothers judge intervals longer than 4 years as jeopardizing chances that their

Table 30

Per Cent of Wives Considering the Spacing of Their First and Second Children as Just Right from the Standpoints of Their Becoming Playmates or Facilitating Child Care, by Length of Second Interval

Interval First to Second Birth	Number of Wives	Per Cent Approving Their Second Intervals from Standpoint of	
		Children as Playmates	Ease of Child Care
12 months or less	57	98%	43%
13 to 18	222	96	52
19 to 24	205	97	64
25 to 30	155	93	71
31 to 36	131	65	84
37 to 48	149	44	82
49 to 60	94	18	84
61 to 84	77	8	73
85 months or more	75	7	60
Total	1,165	68	68

two children will become playmates; intervals shorter than $2\frac{1}{2}$ years are generally regarded as quite safe in this regard; while intervals $2\frac{1}{2}$ to 4 years leave room for argument. Incidentally, these attitudes fit with the data of Table 29, which reveal 4 years as the dividing point between usually being satisfied with one's second interval and typically viewing it as too long.

The mothers are much less agreed about the effect of birth-spacing upon ease of child care. Turning back to Table 30, one finds that for nearly all lengths of second interval there is divided opinion as to whether child care is being facilitated or not. This lack of consensus is affirmed by a coefficient of contingency of .41 between perceived effect upon child care and length of second interval, which is much lower than the .60 coefficient between perceived effect on children becoming playmates and length of second interval. Less than 20 per cent of the mothers having $2\frac{1}{2}$ to 5 years between children disapprove of their interval from the standpoint of child care. But this proportion doubles when the interval is longer than 7 years or shorter than 2 years.

Relation to Desired Family Size

There is no apparent association between second interval preferences and desired family size. A chi-square test based on a sample of

711 mothers judging their second intervals as just right fails to demonstrate dependence between three categories of desired family size and nine categories of second interval length.

This result duplicates the one obtained for preferred first intervals, and the same hypothesis may be advanced by way of explanation. Seemingly the main spacing considerations involved here, such as insuring companionship or facilitating child care, have meanings which are unaffected by the number of additional children desired by the wife.

ORIGINAL VERSUS RETROSPECTIVE PREFERENCES

Scope of Analysis

Some mothers now saying that their past intervals were just right wanted quite different intervals at the time they were making their spacing decisions. Thus, intervals retrospectively judged just right do not always correspond with original spacing preferences. Strictly speaking, original spacing preferences are definable only for successful contraceptors who had no reason to doubt their fecundity. Despite this limitation, it is interesting, first, to compare the variability of these original preferences with that of retrospective preferences and, secondly, to consider whether original spacing preferences correlate at all with total fertility desires.

Data

Original spacing preferences are best estimated for successful contraceptors. With regard to the interval between marriage and first birth, there are 596 couples either who stopped contraception deliberately in order to conceive or else who did not use contraception in this interval because of a desire to become pregnant as soon as possible after marriage. The periods of contraceptive practice plus a constant may be taken as useful estimates of originally preferred first intervals; and since the concern here is solely with variability, this constant may be left undefined. Applying the same conventions to the second interval, there are 656 couples whose contraception may be considered as successful.[3]

Undoubtedly the spacing preferences of these successful contraceptors are not representative of the total sample. Most likely, preferences for short intervals are overrepresented because intending

---

[3] These lengths of contraceptive practice, together with the remaining portions of the birth intervals, are synonymous with the division of birth intervals into "intended" and "residual components," discussed in Chapter VI. For procedural details the reader should turn back to that chapter.

a short postponement of pregnancy increases chances of contraceptive success. If this bias exists, and the longer preferred intervals are underrepresented, then the standard deviation of original preferences is being underestimated; and perhaps too, the correlation with wife's total fertility desires is being underestimated, though this is less certain.

Comparative Variabilities

Despite probable underestimation, the measured variability of original spacing preferences proves nearly as large as that for retrospective preferences. With respect to the first interval, the standard deviation for original preferences is 14 months, which is very close to the 15 months calculated for first intervals retrospectively rated as just right. For the second interval, corresponding standard deviations are 12 months for original preferences and 13 months for retrospective ones.

Presumably two tendencies underlie this result. Some couples who originally preferred intervals of intermediate length actually experienced, and subsequently rationalized as just right, intervals shortened by contraceptive failure or lengthened by some combination of military separation, pregnancy wastage, or conception wait. On the other hand, the couples who are most apt to perceive their birth intervals as disadvantageous (and therefore not to be appraised as "just right") are precisely those who originally preferred and achieved the most extreme interval lengths. In any case, the appreciable standard deviations of 12 months or more indicate that the mothers, both currently and earlier at the time of decision, fail to agree upon any narrow span of interval length as peculiarly advantageous for child spacing.

Relation to Desired Family Size

If the two types of spacing preference are loosely enough associated, then there exists a possibility that original spacing preferences will correlate with total fertility desires, even though it has been demonstrated that retrospective spacing preferences do not. Interestingly enough this contrast does obtain. Despite crude estimation, original spacing preferences yield statistically significant correlations with wife's total fertility desires. The correlations are $-.19$ for originally preferred first intervals, and $-.35$ for originally preferred second intervals. Thus, it would seem that spacing decisions are responsive to factors which correlate with total fertility desires, but which tend to get excluded from retrospective spacing preferences. Gaining some insight into the nature of these factors constitutes one of the objectives of the many analyses of Chapters X through XIX, which include marriage duration and desired family size among their dependent variables.

Implications for the Glass-Grebenik Finding

These last results have implications for the persistent inverse association between length of birth intervals and completed family size, observed by Glass and Grebenik in their analysis of British data.[4] Presumably differential fecundity and differential contraceptive effectiveness both contribute to this association. In addition, that first and second birth intervals originally preferred by the present couples correlate inversely with desired family size suggests that spacing preferences also operate in a minor way to reinforce the association. This follows because preferred and actual birth intervals are positively correlated and it seems likely that family sizes presently desired by the couples and their final family sizes will be positively correlated.

PREFERRED INTERVAL BETWEEN SECOND AND THIRD BIRTHS

Data

Attention is now turned from preferences concerning past intervals to preferences concerning a future one, the interval between second and third births. The basic data depend on replies to:

"If you should decide to go on to a third child, how long from now would be the best time for it to be born?"

This question is asked of all mothers, including those who say they want only two children. Forty-seven respondents, or about 4 per cent, find the question too hypothetical; the other 1,118, pressed for a numerical answer, report preferences in multiples of 6 months, though with a considerable heaping on multiples of 12 months.[5] Since the interview took place 4 to 7 months after the birth of the second child, 6 months was added to each answer as an estimate of the mother's preferred spacing between second and third children.

[4] On the basis of the British Family Census of 1946, D. V. Glass and E. Grebenik demonstrated a consistent inverse association between completed family size and (a) median lengths of interval between marriage and any order of birth, or (b) median lengths of interval between adjacent births, up to the fourth parity when analysis stops. See their *The Trend and Pattern of Fertility in Great Britain: A Report on the Family Census of 1946*, H.M.S.O., London, 1954, especially Chapter VII of Part I.

[5] Wives having confidence in their fecundity and desiring three or more children were asked a second time about their preferred third interval: "How long from now would you personally like your next child to be born?" The two sets of answers correlate .91, based on a sample of 753 women. This correlation is high enough so that the second set of responses need not be analyzed separately.

Preferred Spacing of Second and Third Child

The distribution of preferred third intervals is given in Table 31. There appears to be heaping on lengths ending in half years, but this

TABLE 31

Preferred Spacing between Second and Third Child

Preferred spacing[a]	Number of Wives	Per Cent
Under 2 years	118	11%
2 years	155	14
2 1/2 years	368	33
3 years	109	10
3 1/2 years	178	16
4 years	30	3
4 1/2 years	71	6
5 years	11	1
5 1/2 years	66	6
6 or more	12	1
	1,118	101
Too hypothetical—respondent wants only 2 children	26	–
Too hypothetical—respondent sterile	12	–
Noncommittal answers (don't care when it comes, etc.)	9	–
	47	–
Total	1,165	–

[a] Wives were asked: "If you should decide to go on to a third child, how long from now would be the *best* time for it to be born?" Six months were added to their answer to obtain "preferred spacing."

is a result of adding 6 months to all replies, which actually heap on multiples of 12 months.

Three-quarters of the respondents prefer intervals 24 to 48 months long. Nevertheless for the total sample the standard deviation is 12 months, which conforms closely to the variability found for preferred second intervals. It will now be shown that the same two considerations, companionship and facilitation of child care, figuring so prominently in the mother's appraisals of second intervals also represent the most frequently mentioned considerations with regard to preferred third intervals.

Considerations in Timing the Third Child

Limiting the load of child care and insuring that the children will become playmates emerge as the two most salient considerations in defining the best spacing of second and third children. The 1,118 mothers who report preferring a specific third interval are asked why in an open-ended question. All but a small minority give at least one reason.

The largest subgroup of 503 respondents speak of limiting the load of child care. Illustrative phrasings are "easier to take care of the children"; "oldest will be out of diapers" or "will be trained," "in school," "able to take care of or amuse himself"; "two infants at one time would be too much work." Another 30 respondents allude to giving the mother time to rest between children so that "she can catch her breath or have some time to herself." Eighty-seven would lighten their maternal duties for the sake of their children: "I would be able to give more care and attention to the children." Thus, more than half view their preferred interval as a means of controlling the burden of child care, whether for their own sake or their children's.

Next in frequency are answers about children being better companions or playmates, getting along better, being less jealous of one another. Altogether 172 respondents answer along this line.

As might be expected, the reasons given to justify preferences vary depending on the length of the intervals preferred. Preference for a longer than average interval is usually justified in terms of limiting the burden of child care, though sometimes it is explained in terms of an inability to afford another child just now (93 cases) or else in terms of protecting the mother's health (62 cases). As justification of preferences for a short interval, the playmate consideration is most often mentioned. But age is a consideration for 59 respondents. Some sample responses here are: "like to have them while still young," "want to be able to grow up with them before we get too old to enjoy them"; "if we wait too long, we won't want any more." Two additional reasons for wanting a short interval are first: "want to get through the childbearing as soon as possible," "want to finish with baby routines so we can travel and do other things" (23 cases); and second, "like babies; want another as soon as possible" (22 cases).

Wives' Expected Third Intervals

When mothers are asked to state their preferred spacing between second and third children so soon after the birth of their second child, how often are these stated preferences firm commitments to future spacing behavior? This important question cannot be effectively answered until at least after the second interview. However, some insight is gained by comparing the respondents' expected third intervals with their desired ones.

The necessary data are not available for mothers who fail to report a preferred third interval or who, reporting themselves as subfecund, are not questioned about expected third intervals. This leaves two groups for study; 751 mothers believing themselves fecund and wanting three or more children, and 303 mothers believing themselves fecund but wanting only two children.

The former group who want three or more children were asked:

> "Do you really expect that your next child will be born at about that time (i.e., preferred time) or do you expect it to be sooner or later than that time?"

Significantly enough, barely over half expect their next birth about the time they would like it. Another 20 per cent are uncertain. The 16 per cent who expect it sooner than desired usually cite nonuse or inefficiency with contraception. Less numerous are the wives who expect the child later than desired, and who give such reasons as possibility of economic or housing changes for the worse, difficulty conceiving, and the possible risks to their health of becoming pregnant too soon again.

The proportion expecting to realize their preferred spacing between second and third children remains fairly constant irrespective of the length of interval preferred. Of course the proportion anticipating intervals longer than desired increases as preferred interval decreases; and conversely, shorter spacing than desired is more frequently predicted when a longer interval is preferred. As a result, the coefficient of contingency is .30, significant at the .005 level.

A moderate tendency also exists for mothers to be more confident about realizing their preferred third intervals when they perceive their husbands as agreeing with them. The relevant coefficient of contingency here is .29, also significant at beyond the .005 level.

Turning now to the 303 wives who are confident of their fecundity but want only two children, one finds 32, or about 11 per cent, who expect to have, or are uncertain about having, a third child within the next two or three years. A majority of these 32 mothers express doubts about their contraception, while a few are hoping that an altered economic or housing situation will permit a change of mind in favor of having another child.

Clearly then, many of the mothers perceive a discrepancy between the third interval they would like to have and the third interval they will probably get. Inadequate contraception is often stressed as a problem. Accordingly, one might expect the four religious groups to display different levels of confidence about realizing their spacing preferences, with Jewish mothers expressing the most confidence and

Catholic mothers the least. These contrasts obtain. Among mothers wanting a third child, the percentages who expect their next intervals to conform to desires are: Jews 77 per cent, Protestants 58, Catholics 46, and Mixed Catholics 43, based on subsamples of 66, 279, 366, and 64 women. Among mothers wanting only two children, the proportions replying "uncertain" or "yes" about having a third child in the next two or three years are 19 and 17 per cent for Catholics and Mixed Catholics (based on 94 and 18 cases), but only 5 and 6 per cent for Protestants and Jews (based on 172 and 51 cases).

Husband's Expected Third Interval

Another indication that the wife's preferred third interval will prove a poor predictor of actual third interval is the low correlation between her preference and her husband's expected spacing of second and third children.

All husbands were asked:

> "If you expect to have another child, how long from now would you like to have it born?"

Answers to this question yield only a .28 correlation with preferred third intervals of wives. This low correlation stands in striking contrast to the .67 correlation between total fertility desires of husband and wife. At least four explanations for the low correlation are relevant. First of all, approximately one third of the husbands do not expect a third child, and these husbands are arbitrarily assigned to the category representing longest expected intervals. Secondly, it is clear from the immediately preceding section that even the wives' expected third intervals correlate only moderately with their preferred ones. Thirdly, undoubtedly the questions asked force both spouses to report their spacing preferences in terms of a much greater precision than they actually feel. Finally, holding the interview so soon after the second birth may mean that relatively few couples have yet started to discuss in any serious way the timing of their third child. Whatever the relative importance of these four explanations, a correlation of .28 with husband's expected interval offers additional evidence that the wives' preferred third intervals will not do an efficient job of predicting actual third intervals.

Review of Hypotheses

A final task of this chapter is to consider the relationships of preferred third intervals to a variety of social and psychological factors. Can any factors be uncovered which differentiate preferences for long or short intervals between second and third children? Before

129

undertaking this correlational analysis it is useful to review some hypotheses.

Is it realistic to expect any substantial correlations between preferred third intervals and selected social and psychological variables? The answer to this question may depend on how early in a birth interval mothers typically start thinking seriously about when they want their next child. If 4 to 7 months after a second birth, most mothers have gotten no farther than "I certainly do not want to become pregnant yet," then they are in a poor position to offer considered spacing preferences. In this case, enough arbitrariness may attach to their replies so as to impose a rather low ceiling on the correlations that may realistically be expected. On the other hand, the experience gained in spacing the first two children may be enough so that, even soon after the second birth, most mothers have fairly definite ideas about a delimited range of interval length as preferable to anything longer or shorter. In this case, the correlational potentialities are not necessarily so bleak. Unfortunately, the fact that wife's preferred third interval correlates only .28 with husband's expected third interval makes the first possibility more credible than the second. This impression will be strengthened if a number of correlations are found between wife's preferred third intervals and selected social and psychological factors, but all these correlations prove low.

As for more specific hypotheses, a close spacing of the first two children means the temporarily heavy burden of two diapered babies in the household at once; but two consecutive, close spacings mean risking the even heavier burden of three diapered children in the household at once. Thus the mother who has narrowly spaced her first two children has special incentives to avoid a short third interval. On this basis, one expects an inverse relationship between second intervals and preferred third intervals. On flimsier grounds, it is also hypothesized that the more poorly adjusted a wife is to marriage or motherhood the more anxious she will be to avoid adding to her burden of child care by a close spacing of children. It might appear that these hypotheses are somewhat weakened by the finding that the present mothers disagree whether a close spacing of the first two children makes it harder or easier to take care of them. However, other evidence suggests that the same mothers are much more agreed that when it is a question of three children, it is advisable from the standpoint of child care to delay the arrival of the third until the oldest reaches some specified stage of development (out of diapers, in nursery school, etc.). Furthermore with the interview taking place 4 to 7 months after the birth of the second child, the period a mother must wait before her oldest reaches the specified stage of development depends mainly on the interval between first and second children. The longer the second interval, the shorter the period she has to wait. Here then is a very definite reason for expecting an inverse association between second interval and preferred third interval.

Two reasons mentioned by a number of mothers to justify average or short third intervals are, first, their advancing age and, second, a desire to abridge the total child-rearing period. Enough mothers feeling this way would insure inverse correlations between preferred third interval and current age of wife or marriage duration.

It is not clear whether a correlation should be expected between preferred third intervals and desired family size. One reason for not expecting an association is that none of the mothers mention spacing considerations that are explicitly contingent upon number of children wanted. Also, no associations have been found between wife's total fertility desires and her retrospective spacing preferences. On the other hand, family size preferences do correlate with originally intended intervals and therefore may correlate with spacing preferences currently in the process of formation.

Correlates of Preferred Intervals between Second and Third Births

Altogether 69 variables, derived from the interview or the wife's questionnaire (but not the husband's questionnaire), have been correlated with preferred third intervals, producing 25 correlations significant at the .05 level, of which 16 are also significant at the .001 level. However, none of these correlations reaches a .3 value. Thus, while it may be supposed that preferred third intervals contain some information, it is obvious that they have yielded disappointingly low correlations.

Ten variables represent personality measures, available for 938 mothers on the basis of the wife's questionnaire. Only one of the ten measures produces a correlation significant at the .05 level, so that little justification exists for positing a connection between preferred third intervals and personality factors, at least as the latter are measured in this study.

Another 59 variables, covering a variety of topics, are available for the entire sample of 1,165 mothers. Among these are 5 measures of wife's adjustment to marriage or mother role.[6] All 5 measures fail to correlate significantly with preferred third intervals. Thus, no basis has been found for believing that maladjusted mothers seek to reduce their

---

[6] These measures will be discussed in greater detail in Chapter XVII. Here it suffices merely to name them: adjustment to mother role, age at which children become enjoyable, liking for children, pattern of help available to wife, and wife's marital adjustment.

problems of child care through longer than average birth intervals.

Because the number of hypotheses is so much smaller than the number of correlations examined, the risk of accepting as real a relationship caused by chance is much inflated. Accordingly, notice will be taken only of the 16 correlations significant at the .001 level.[7]

The ten most interesting of these correlations are listed in Table 32.[8] They include two relationships not anticipated. Perhaps not too surprisingly, mothers who believe that having another child would jeopardize chances of getting ahead prefer longer intervals. The same is true of mothers who consider finances relevant in deciding whether or not to have another child.

The other eight relations in Table 32 appear to operate differently among Protestants than among Catholics. Hence, it is essential to analyze results within religion. Because of the low level of correlations, considerations of the Jews and Mixed Catholics adds little to

TABLE 32

Relationships of Wife's Preferred Third Intervals to Selected Variables, for Total Sample and Separately for Protestants, Catholics, and Catholics Holding Constant Number of Children Desired

Variables		Product-Moment Correlations		
	Total Sample	Catholics	Catholics Controlled	Protestants
Wife's total fertility desires	−.16	−.24		.02
Marriage duration	−.15	−.04	−.16	−.28
Interval first to second birth	−.13	−.01	−.13	−.24
Best spacing of first child	−.12	−.20	−.15	.01
Current age of wife	−.18	−.10	−.18	−.25
Availability of contraception	−.12	−.13	−.07	−.01
Church attendance of wife	.14	.11	.06	.03
Wife's religious-mindedness	.09	.11	.08	.08
Relation of another child to chances of getting ahead	.19	.19	.17	.23
Relevance of finances to having another child	−.13	−.20	−.13	−.01
Number of wives	1,165	481	481	473

[7] The large number of variables correlated with preferred third intervals is a by-product of the computational program designed for the analyses in Chapters XI through XIX.

[8] The following six correlations with values over .09 are omitted from Table 37: husband's total fertility desires (yielding a r of −.13, but highly correlated with wife's total fertility desires; husband's church attendance as reported by wife (r of −.12 and highly correlated with wife's church attendance); wife's satisfaction with husband's job (r of −.09); wife's duration of employment during marriage (r of −.12, but explainable largely in terms of its correlation with marriage duration); and finally, husband's current age and wife's marriage age (r's of −.15 and −.13 respectively, but both highly correlated with wife's current age).

the picture, and the analysis will be confined to comparing Catholics and Protestants. Generally speaking, the correlations exhibited by Jews, and less so the correlations exhibited by Mixed Catholics, resemble those of the Protestants.

Results for the Protestants accord well with the hypotheses reviewed earlier in this chapter. Preferred third intervals correlate inversely with marriage duration ($-.28$), with current age of wife ($-.25$), and with length of second interval ($-.24$); while no association is found with total number of children desired ($.02$) or with best spacing of first child ($.01$). In sharp contrast, among Catholic mothers, preferred third intervals are significantly correlated with desired family size ($-.24$) and with best spacing of first child ($-.20$); but only weakly correlated with current age of wife ($-.10$) and uncorrelated with marriage duration ($-.04$) or second interval ($-.01$). Moreover, only among Catholics do unanticipated correlations emerge between preferred third intervals and such measures as availability of contraception ($-.13$), frequency of wife's church attendance ($.11$), and degree to which wife reports herself as religious-minded ($.09$). More interesting yet, when wife's desired size of family is held constant, nearly all the correlations for Catholics change in ways which bring them much closer to the values found among Protestants. This result strongly suggests that operating among Catholics, but not among Protestants, is a factor which links spacing preferences to total number of children desired. However, all efforts to explain this factor have failed.[9]

---

[9] Two hypotheses have been tested and found wanting. First, it was supposed that a minority of Catholics wanting only two or three children but feeling themselves committed to an inefficient method of contraception might view long birth intervals as an auxiliary means of limiting final family size. This granted, one would expect the correlation between desired family size and spacing preferences to be stronger among Catholics when contraception is least available or past contraception least successful. That is, one would expect the correlations between desired family size and spacing preferences to decrease when one holds constant such factors as availability of contraception, fertility-planning control, frequency of church attendance, and reported degree of religious-mindedness. But these expectations are not borne out. Partial correlation shows that the association between preferred third intervals and total fertility desires is only trivially reduced by any of these controls. On the other hand, when desired family size is held constant, all the correlations of these controls with preferred third intervals are much reduced.

Secondly, it was hypothesized that mothers desiring large families, say 5 or more children, might feel they could not afford long birth intervals without unduly extending the childbearing period; while mothers desiring 2, 3, or even 4 children might not feel the same pressure to avoid long intervals. Moreover, because almost all the mothers desiring 5 children or more belong to the Catholic group, this would help to explain the presence of a significant correlation between spacing preferences and total fertility desires among Catholics and its absence among Protestants. The plausibility of this argument rests on finding a curvilinear regression between desired family size and preferred third intervals among Catholics. An analysis of variance indicates that more extreme departures from linearity than found in the Catholic group could occur by chance approximately 10 per cent of the time.

Summary

Two thirds of the mothers in this study judge their first intervals as just right, and these approved intervals have a standard deviation of fifteen months. Such a large variation suggests that many mothers do not perceive a narrow range of first interval length as just right and all other lengths as too short or too long. Rather they perceive a broad span of interval length as not causing serious inconvenience, and when their actual interval falls anywhere in this range, they tend to rate it as just right. Most of the mothers believe that a couple should wait a while before having their first child, three reasons being: (1) to furnish time to become adjusted to marriage; (2) to ready finances; and (3) to enjoy things with one's husband before the responsibilities of parenthood.

A large standard deviation (13 months) also characterizes the second birth intervals deemed just right. Here also presumably, most mothers do not perceive a narrow range of interval length as peculiarly advantageous and all other lengths as inconvenient. The respondents agree fairly well that spacing children more than 4 years apart reduces chances of their becoming playmates; but the respondents are less agreed about the relation between spacing of children and ease of rearing them.

Length of contraceptive practice after marriage and after first birth offers a way of measuring the originally intended first and second intervals of successful contraceptors. Estimated in this manner, original spacing preferences prove just as variable as the first and second intervals retrospectively judged as just right. Furthermore, originally intended first and second intervals correlate —.19 and —.35 respectively with wife's total fertility desires, while first and second intervals deemed just right show no correlation. Apparently there are factors linking spacing decisions and total fertility desires, but these factors tend to get excluded from retrospective spacing preferences. Gaining some insight into these common factors constitutes one of the challenges to be faced in Chapters X to XIX.

Preferred third intervals have a standard deviation of 12 months, making them almost as variable as the other spacing preferences studied. A third interval long enough to permit adequate care of three children without unreasonable strain upon the mother proves the most salient consideration, with nearly half of the mothers indicating a desire to delay their third birth until the oldest child reaches a specified stage of development. Spacing the second and third children closely enough to insure their companionship emerges as the second most frequently mentioned consideration. Only half the mothers desiring a third child expect their third intervals to conform even approximately to their preferences, which indicates that these preferences are not always firm commitments to future spacing behavior. A lower correlation of .28 is obtained with husband's expected third interval, which shows again that preferred third intervals do not offer an efficient device for predicting future third intervals.

Out of 69 additional correlations with wife's preferred third intervals, 16 are highly significant statistically, including inverse relationships with marriage duration, second interval, and current age of wife. But none of the correlations reach the .3 level and the 16 correlates are, of course, not independent. The speculative interpretation placed on this result is that at time of interview, only 4 to 7 months after birth of the second child, few mothers have started to think seriously about spacing their next child and hence have only the vaguest ideas about what interval they will eventually seek.

Preferred third intervals do not correlate with total fertility desires among Protestants but for unexplained reasons they do correlate —.24 with total fertility desires among Catholics.

Chapter VIII. Desired Family Size

Desired family size, the focus of this chapter, represents a second main category of fertility preference. The family-size preferences reported separately by husband and wife play a central role in subsequent analyses. They comprise two of four main dependent variables in Chapters X to XIX, as well as being the dependent variables for which the greatest wealth of hypotheses exist. (See especially Chapter X.)

Information secured from the wife includes not only the number of children she desires, but her confidence in the stability of her preference, perception of her husband's preference, and recency of family discussion about the matter. Husbands were also directly queried about their total fertility desires. The interrelations among these data are examined in a later section of this chapter. Subsequent divisions analyze the manner in which desired family size is related to other fertility aspects, such as fecundity, contraception, birth intervals, and completed fertility. The previous chapter has already touched upon ties with birth-spacing preferences.

MEASUREMENT

The wives were asked three questions regarding their preferred family size:

> "How many children do you want to have *altogether*, counting the two you have now?"
>
> "Do you feel sure that is the number you want or do you feel that you might want more or that you might want fewer children?"[1]
>
> "Many husbands and wives really have different ideas even though they talk it over and reach an agreement. How many children do you think your husband really wants to have *altogether*, counting the two you have now?"

A single question was asked of husbands:

> "Your wife was interviewed on her feelings about children and family life. How many children do *you* want to have *altogether*, counting those you have now?"

---

[1] This question was not asked of 66 respondents expressing doubts about their current fecundity. The preceding question was also rephrased for these couples as follows: "If you were able to have more children, how many would you yourself want to have altogether, counting those you now have?"

The first two questions are combined to form an index of wife's total fertility desires. For example, wives who say they want four children but "may want less" are ranked lower on total fertility desires than wives who are sure they want four, who in turn are ranked below those preferring at least four and perhaps more. The third and fourth questions measure respectively the wife's perception of her husband's preference and his own perception of it. Based on single questions, these two measures are not strictly comparable with the index of wife's total fertility desires.

SIZE OF FAMILY DESIRED

Two, three, and four children prove equally popular sizes, while only a small minority of respondents report wanting five or more children. For example, an identical 30 per cent of the wives want two, three, or four children; while only 7 per cent prefer five children or more; and the remaining 2 per cent respond in terms of ranges— 2 to 3, 3 to 4, 3 to 5 . . . children. None expressed desire for no children or only one child but admittedly the phrasing of the question all but excluded such answers.

Three quarters of the wives were certain about their preferences. Those who were uncertain usually believed they might want more children in the future than they do now. Uncertainty is found most often among those desiring large families, indicating that many of these mothers know they want more children but not how many more.

Husbands present a distribution of family-size preferences similar to their wives'. Family sizes of two, three, and four children command roughly equal popularity, and together they account for 90 per cent of the preferences reported.

SPOUSE CONSENSUS

Hill, Stycos, and Back have argued that scope of communication between spouses basically influences the couple's chances of achieving effective fertility control or agreeing about the number of children they want. In addition, the authors maintain that an authoritarian relationship of husband to wife militates against favorable communication patterns.[2] Herbst also has argued for an inverse relationship between authoritarianism and ability to communicate about fertility matters or to achieve successful fertility control. However, Herbst is unable to demonstrate an association between a classification of

[2] Reuben Hill, J. Mayone Stycos, Kurt W. Back, *The Family and Population Control*, University of North Carolina Press, Chapel Hill, 1959, pp. 156–161, 216–217.

family dominance-patterns and fertility;[3] and even the evidence of Hill *et al* is not as decisive as the authors might wish.[4]

Applying the above thesis to the present study, one expects to find that couples who agree about their desired family size and who are realistic about each other's preferences also tend to be successful contraceptors, and that these characteristics associate with an egalitarian family structure. The first set of relationships are examined now; connections with dominance patterns are deferred until Chapter XVII.

In the present study, husbands and wives appear to agree substantially about their family-size preferences. Their fertility desires correlate .65. Two thirds of the time the same number of children is mentioned by both spouses. However, in unknown degree, this apparent agreement between spouses is the product of collusions. Presumably in the course of filling out their mail questionnaires, some of the husbands discussed their answers with their wives. Hence, the correlation between fertility desires of the husband and wife is probably exaggerated, but there is little reason to believe that this bias distorts the comparison of degrees of consensus found among subgroups.

Degree of consensus varies among the four religious groups, being strongest among Jews and weakest among Mixed Catholics (Table 33). Catholics and Protestants are intermediate and the slightly higher correlation found among the Catholics may be entirely owing to greater variability in desired family size.

With the same possibility of exaggeration as mentioned above, the degree of realism about spouse's desired family size also appears high. Information is available only for the wife's perception of her husband's preference, but the correlation between this perception and the preference reported by her husband is .71. This correlation varies among the four religious groups, once again being strongest for Jews and weakest for Mixed Catholics, with Catholics and Protestants intermediate and much alike in their degree of realism. Thus, it seems that the four religious groups differ not only with respect to number of children desired, a topic discussed at length in Chapter XI, but also in the amount of agreement existing between spouses and in knowledge of each other's desires. Moreover, fullest agreement and knowledge is found in the group practicing the most

[3] P. G. Herbst, "Family Living-Patterns of Interaction" in O. A. Oeser and S. B. Hammond, *Social Structure and Personality in a City*, Macmillan, New York, 1954, p. 176.

[4] Hill, Stycos, and Back, *The Family and Population Control*, p. 228. Both "communication on general issues" and "communication on birth control" correlate significantly with "ever use of birth control" and "length of use," but do not significantly correlate with "success rate" of birth control.

TABLE 33

Correlations among the Number of Children Desired by the Wife, the Number of Children Desired by the Husband, and the Wife's Perception of the Number of Children Desired by Her Husband

Variables Correlated	Protestant	Mixed Catholic	Catholic	Jewish	Total
Number of children desired by wife and husband	.55	.39	.64	.76	.65**
Number of children desired by wife and number she perceives her husband to desire	.66	.42	.71	.71	.71*
Number of children wife perceives her husband to desire and number husband desires	.66	.58	.67	.88	.71*

NOTE:
Correlations with a single asterisk are heterogeneous among religious groups at the .05 level of significance; correlations with a double asterisk at the .01 level.

effective contraception, namely, Jews. However, it is not true that Mixed Catholics, showing least agreement and knowledge, practice contraception inferior to that of Catholics and Protestants.

These results, then, only partially substantiate the thesis of Hill *et al* and Herbst. Further evidence comes from a question asking the wife how recently she and her husband discussed the subject of family size. Was it recently, not for a while, or never? Two thirds report recent discussions; few admit never discussing the subject. Three quarters of the Jewish wives claim recent discussion, while this proportion ranges from 56 to 64 per cent among the other three religious groups.[5] This small differential persists when the sample is divided between mothers wanting two children and wanting three or more, so that the greater frequency of recent discussion reported by Jewish wives is not a function of desiring smaller families. Thus, communication about fertility matters may be more complete in Jewish households, though of course the evidence cited is far from decisive.

Surprisingly enough, the wife is slightly more likely to report recent discussion when she perceives her preference as disagreeing with her husband's. This suggests that perceived disagreement stimulates discussion, or perhaps that arguments about family size are more often remembered as discussion than mutual assurances of unanimity. Recency of discussion shows no relationship with wife's certainty about the number of children she desires. One possible

[5] Under the null hypothesis, the likelihood of a chi-square at least as large as the one observed is less than .005.

reason for such low correlations is that the terms "recent" and "discussion" are vague and subjective enough so that answers about recency of discussion have little reliability. In this connection, it is interesting that Hill, Stycos, and Back found considerable inconsistency in the reports of husbands and wives about degrees of communication.[6]

Finally worth noting is a very weak, though statistically significant relationship between the wife's certainty about her family size preference and her perception of agreement or disagreement with her husband. If she perceives herself as wanting fewer children than her spouse, she is slightly less apt to be certain about her preference.

RELATIONS WITH OTHER FERTILITY ASPECTS

Attention now turns to the relationships of desired family size to other fertility components: fecundity, birth intervals, contraceptive practice, and completed fertility. The fertility preferences of husbands and wives exhibit similar enough correlations so that it would be redundant to present both sets of relationships. Those involving wives' total fertility desires are preferred because they average somewhat higher, at least in connection with birth intervals and contraceptive behavior than those for husbands.[7]

Relation to Fecundity

The more children desired, the more likely that subfecundity will play a restrictive role. On the average, this restrictive role is less when the mother marries at a younger age. But the relationship between fecundity and desired family size is two-sided. To the extent that a woman doubts her fecundity, the addition of more children becomes hypothetical. This circumstance may favor exaggerated statements about the number of children desired, since these women need never contemplate seriously the implications of a large family.

However, data from the present study fail to reveal a tendency for subfecund women to report wanting more children than average. Nonsignificant differences are found between 66 mothers uncertain

---

[6] Hill, Stycos, and Back, *The Family and Population Control*, p. 150.

[7] A test, outlined in Palmer O. Johnson's *Statistical Methods in Research*, Prentice-Hall, New York, 1949, p. 87, is used to compare correlations involving husbands' and wives' fertility desires. The results suggest that wives' fertility desires are somewhat more closely related to birth intervals and contraceptive variables than are husbands' fertility preferences. However, it does not follow from this that wives exercise greater control over the couple's reproductive behavior, since any such inference is compromised by differences in the ways desired family size is measured for husbands and wives.

about, or doubting, their present fecundity and 1,099 mothers retaining confidence in their fecundity.[8]

Relation to Birth Intervals

Desired family size correlates moderately with birth intervals. The correlations, classified by religion, are assembled in Table 34. With

TABLE 34

Correlations between Number of Children Desired by Wife and Birth Intervals, by Religion

Intervals	Protestant	Mixed Catholic	Catholic	Jewish	Total
Marriage to second birth	−.27	−.24	−.45	−.17	−.36
First to second birth	−.22	−.12	−.44	−.21	−.31**
Marriage to first birth	−.19	−.24	−.24	.03	−.22**

NOTE: Correlations marked with a double asterisk are heterogeneous among religious groups at the .01 level of significance.

one exception, which is not statistically significant, the correlations are negative. Furthermore, the correlations with first and second birth intervals are significantly heterogeneous among religious groups, being highest for Catholics and lowest for Jews. Correlations with marriage duration do not exhibit this heterogeneity.

Presumably, the primary basis of this association between wife's fertility desires and birth intervals is a tendency for wives wanting fewer children to seek longer intervals. It is shown later that mothers desiring small families tend to start contraception earlier, except among Jews, nearly all of whom start contraception at marriage. Also, it may be recalled from the previous chapter that the "originally intended" birth intervals of successful contraceptors tended to be longer when fewer children are desired.

The association between total fertility desires and birth intervals appears to be strongest among Catholics. It is shown below that a contributing factor is the fact that family-size preferences and contraceptive behavior correlate most closely in the Catholic group, and, of course, contraceptive practice substantially influences interval length.

Relation to Contraceptive Practice

Total fertility desires also correlate with measures of contraceptive practice. For example, Table 35 indicates that mothers

[8] Mean sizes of family desired by the two groups are 3.21 and 3.17 children. Distributional differences are nonsignificant according to chi-square.

TABLE 35

Correlations among Number of Children Desired by Wife, Availability of
Contraception, and Fertility-Planning Success, by Religion

Variables Correlated	Protestant	Mixed Catholic	Catholic	Jewish	Total
Wife's desired family size and fertility-planning success	−.14	−.10	−.27	.09	−.22**
Wife's desired family size and availability of contraception	−.27	−.10	−.35	−.04	−.35*
Availability of contraception and fertility-planning success	.42	.44	.64	.65	.55***

NOTE:
A single, double, or triple asterisk indicates that the correlation is heterogeneous
amongst religious groups at the .05, .01, or .001 levels of significance respectively.

desiring larger families tend to plan their pregnancies less successfully
and to find contraception less available than mothers preferring
smaller families. It should be noted that the two measures of contraceptive behavior are highly associated.[9] Also, the correlations are
heterogeneous among religious groups, the correlational values being
highest for Catholics and lowest for Jews.

Two quite different arguments may be advanced to explain this
inverse association between desired family size and contraceptive
efficiency, though the available data do not permit testing the
relevance of either hypothesis. First, couples who have attained
desired family size must prevent further births, while couples still
short of their goal use contraception to space births. In a very real
sense, the "preventers" have more to lose by a contraceptive failure
than the "spacers," and as a consequence may tend to practice
contraception more zealously and effectively. But in the present
sample the measures of "fertility-planning success" and "availability
of contraception" refer primarily to behavior preceding the second
birth, and presumably most of the present couples want at least two
children. Therefore it becomes necessary to argue, with reduced
plausibility, that a closer approach to desired family size is enough

[9] The measure of contraceptive availability distinguishes couples for whom contraception becomes available before first birth, between first and second, and not until
after second birth. Contraception is considered available whenever the couple use it
in some form, including withdrawal or rhythm, or else explain its nonuse in terms of not
needing it, either because of subfecundity or wanting pregnancy as soon as physically
possible. The four-category index of fertility-planning success registers whether the
couple's contraception has failed them in neither birth interval, in the first interval only,
in the second only, or in both intervals. This index correlates strongly with availability
of contraception partly because its definition of contraceptive failure includes nonavailability of contraception as well as unintentional pregnancy while practicing contraception or omitting it to take a chance.

to inspire more conscientious contraception. That is, couples one child short of desired family size will practice contraception less perfunctorily than couples short by two children or more.

Only in the current interval, following second birth, is there opportunity to test the hypothesis in its more plausible form. In the current interval roughly one third of the mothers have attained their desired family size. It is expected that these mothers desiring two children are more inclined to mention reliability as a primary consideration in choosing their present method and that more often this present method is an effective one, such as condom, diaphragm and jelly, withdrawal, or some combination or alternation involving these methods. Actually, a tendency is found for wives desiring two children to mention reliability reasons more often than wives desiring three children or more: Protestants, 65 to 54 per cent; Mixed Catholics, 44 to 41 per cent; Catholics, 53 to 38 per cent; and Jews, 83 to 58 per cent; with three out of four of these differences statistically significant according to chi-square. Contrarily, statistically significant differences fail to emerge for type of method. Thus, the available evidence works both for and against the hypothesis.

Thus far it has been argued that total fertility desires influence contraceptive practice, but one may also adopt as a second hypothesis that contraceptive practice conditions preferred family size. Thus, couples diffident about their contraception and anticipating large families may adjust to this prospect by persuading themselves that they really want numerous children.

Table 35 also reveals that the correlations between total fertility desires and two measures of contraceptive practice are heterogeneous among religious groups, being strongest among Catholics and weakest among Jews. One reason for this heterogeneity is that Catholics are more varied both with respect to family-size preferences and their contraceptive behavior. On the other hand, Jews are the most uniform, usually preferring two or three children, and starting contraception at marriage and using it efficiently.[10]

Less support is found for a second hypothesis concerning why total fertility desires correlate more strongly with contraceptive practice among Catholics than non-Catholics. In the Catholic group, religious devoutness, by selecting for low availability of contraception and reported desire for larger families, may increase the apparent association between size of family desired and contraceptive behavior.

[10] Variances for availability of contraception are .35, .64, .69, and .13 respectively for Protestants, Mixed Catholics, Catholics, and Jews. Corresponding variances for fertility planning success are 1.51, 1.39, 1.61, and .83; and for wife's desired family size, they are 3.06, 2.61, 4.95, and 2.27. Thus, variances for Jews are consistently lowest.

143

It is not expected that religious devoutness plays the same role among Protestants or Jews, for whom religious doctrine and fertility matters are less directly connected. However, evidence to support this hypothesis is lacking. When frequency of church attendance or informal religious orientation (defined in Chapter XII) is held constant by means of partial correlation, appreciable reductions in the zero-order correlations for Catholics fail to materialize.

Incidentally, this heterogeneity of correlation between total fertility desires and contraception fits with, though does not prove, a hypothesis mentioned earlier, namely that couples diffident about their contraception adjust to the inevitability of a large family by persuading themselves that they really want numerous children. According to this view, Jews are rarely impelled to an interest in large families, while Catholics, so much more variable in their contraceptive efficiency, more frequently have incentive to consider the desirability of large families.

Relation to Completed Family Size

Whether or not the desired family sizes reported in this study will correlate closely with actual completed fertility is a crucial question for this report. Obviously these family-size preferences, which serve as two of four main dependent variables in Chapter X through XIX, forfeit much of their interest unless they associate at least moderately with subsequent fertility. Such association presupposes that total fertility desires are fairly stable through time and that couples wanting many children will have more children than those wanting few. Unfortunately, there are no comparable fertility surveys by which to check conclusively the plausibility of these assumptions. But indirect evidence from three other studies, together with certain material culled from the present survey, do provide, it is believed, a basis for optimism.

Coming closest to the status of direct evidence are data from a study by E. L. Kelly, in which a group of 300 engaged couples were intensively interviewed and, then almost twenty years later, recontacted by mail. A reduced sample of 145 couples met the following criteria: (a) eventually married each other with both spouses still living together; (b) no problems of sterility and no foster or adopted children reported; and (c) sufficient information returned by both spouses. For these 145 couples the correlations between original fertility preferences and number of births at time of second contact are .26 for husbands, .27 for wives. These represent rather weak associations, which the authors explain as follows:

"In summary, the most plausible hypothesis accounting for the low correlations observed are, in the first place, that people just before marriage have had little experience against which to test their plans. Thus their preferences are unrealistic. Secondly, even assuming a high degree of realism and perfect control of fertility (an impossible assumption for any general population), events and circumstances intervene unpredictably to modify and change feelings about having another child at a given time."[11]

It will be surprising if these correlations of .26 and .27 are not exceeded in the present study. With the experience of two children, these present mothers are likely to be far more realistic about their family-size preferences than the fiancées in Kelly's sample. Moreover, with several years of marriage behind them, the present respondents have already done much of their mind changing about preferred family size.

Goldberg, Sharp, and Freedman provide information about the stability of family-size expectations over a three-year period.[12] Their data are based on a 1955 cross-sectional survey of married Detroit women aged 18 to 44, followed by a telephone reinterview with as many of these women (56 per cent of the original sample) as could be contacted three years later. Eighty-four of the recontacted women had two births in 1955, and of these, 70 per cent reported the same expected family size in 1958 as they did in 1955. Another 18 per cent reported higher expectations and 11 per cent lower expectations in 1958 than in 1955. The stability of family size expectations are shown to increase with increasing marriage duration. Also, these 1955 expectations correlate strongly with number of births during the 1955–1958 period.

Using materials from the Indianapolis Study, Muhsam and Kiser have correlated number of children desired at marriage with family size after 12 to 15 years of marriage.[13] The family size preferences are retrospective, and the authors stress the likelihood that these recollections are influenced by subsequent experience. The correlations prove quite low. For the total sample of 1,376 couples, the correlations with actual fertility are 30 for husband's recollected preferences

[11] Charles F. Westoff, Elliot G. Mishler, and E. Lowell Kelly, "Preferences in Size of Family and Eventual Fertility Twenty Years After," *American Journal of Sociology*, 62 (1957), p. 495. See also Charles F. Westoff, Philip C. Sagi, and E. Lowell Kelly, "Fertility Through Twenty Years of Marriage: A Study in Predictive Possibilities," *American Sociological Review*, 23 (1958), pp. 549–556.

[12] David Goldberg, Harry Sharp, and Ronald Freedman, "The Stability and Reliability of Expected Family Size Data," paper presented at the 1959 meetings of the Population Association of America.

[13] H. V. Muhsam, and C. V. Kiser, "Number of Children Desired at the Time of Marriage," Milbank Memorial Fund *Quarterly*, 34 (1956), pp. 287–312.

at marriage and .32 for wife's. Restricted to 379 Number and Spacing Planners, the correlations increase to .38 and .40. These values are not a great deal higher than those encountered in the Kelly study and, as the authors note, they may be "unduly high because of the *ex post facto* nature of the data on fertility desires."[14]

The Indianapolis Study also provides a comparison between desired and attained family size at time of interview. The number of births thwarted by subfecundity are estimated to compensate approximately for the number of unintended births resulting from admitted failures of birth control.[15] Among the "relatively fecund" couples, who by definition have not had a subfecundity problem, only 30 per cent admit to having more children than they want. This 30 per cent constitutes an underestimate if, as seems likely, there exists a tendency to adjust stated preferences to the facts of accomplished family size.

The GAF study, based on a national cross section of white, married women between the ages of 18 and 39, focuses attention upon the correspondence between the additional children wanted and additional children expected by wives at the time of interview. Here also, one finds similarity between the percentage doubting that they will be able to produce all the births wanted (23 per cent) and the percentage anticipating more births than desired as a result of fallible birth control (15 per cent).[16] It seems likely that the latter statistic underestimates, perhaps grossly, the percentage who will eventually have their family sizes inflated by lapses of fertility regulation.

What implications do these results have for the current fertility study? First of all, it is clear that subfecundity played a larger role in the Indianapolis and GAF Studies than it will in the present one because of the eligibility criteria requiring two live births and no serious pregnancy wastage. On the other hand, the Indianapolis and GAF experiences suggest that a tangible fraction, almost certainly more than 15 per cent and perhaps more than 30 per cent, of the present couples will find their family size objectives exceeded. Stability of total fertility desires through time remains the biggest unknown, although encouragement may be drawn from the data of Goldberg *et al* that showed fertility expectations to be quite stable over a three-year period, at least among mothers of two children. It

[14] *Ibid.*, p. 312.

[15] P. K. Whelpton, and C. V. Kiser, "The Comparative Influence on Fertility of Contraception and Impairments of Fecundity," in Kiser and Whelpton, eds., *Social and Psychological Factors Affecting Fertility*, 5 Vols., Milbank Memorial Fund, New York, 1946–1958, II, pp. 331, 341.

[16] Ronald Freedman, P. K. Whelpton, and Arthur Campbell, *Family Planning, Sterility and Population Growth*, McGraw–Hill, New York, 1959, p. 264.

seems probable that fertility desires will be stable enough to yield correlations with completed fertility higher than the coefficients met in the Kelly study, but, of course, there is no way of proving this at the moment.

Certain results may be gleaned from the present fertility study itself to increase confidence that the total fertility desires of its members will correlate substantially with completed fertility. The first is the small percentage of couples who report any serious doubts about their fecundity, which confirms the relatively small role to be played by subfecundity. The second is the moderately strong correlations between total fertility desires and past birth intervals, which indicate that total fertility desires associate with variables known to correlate with completed family size. The last is the .65 correlation between the family-size preferences reported separately by husband and wife, which indicates that the total fertility desires of many of these couples are mutually reinforcing.

Summary

This chapter has furnished an analysis of family-size preferences. Two, three, and four children prove the most popular family sizes, accounting for more than 90 per cent of the preferences reported by wives. Husbands exhibit a similar distribution of total fertility desires. Spouse consensus is substantial, the correlation being .65, despite non-comparabilities of measurement. Wives perceive slightly more consensus than exists, their perceptions of husbands' desires correlating .71 with their own. Surprisingly, perceived agreement with husband's preference has little bearing on whether the wife is confident about the stability of her preference or has recently discussed the subject with her spouse. Jewish couples exhibit the most agreement and the most realism about each other's preferences, while Mixed Catholics manifest the least. Also Jewish wives more frequently report recent discussion with their husbands about family size than do wives in the other three religious groups.

The 66 wives who currently doubt their fecundity do not differ from the others in their family-size preferences.

In the present sample, wives desiring larger families have shorter birth intervals, this inverse association being strongest among Catholics. As expected, these relations depend, at least partly, on a tendency for couples desiring large families to seek shorter than average birth intervals.

Larger sizes of desired family also associates with lower availability of contraception and less successful planning of pregnancies. The

147

associations are strongest among Catholics, weakest for Jews. Contributing to this result is the fact that Catholics are the most varied both with respect to desired family size and contraceptive behavior, while Jews are the most homogeneous. Though other hypotheses are advanced, no way has been found to test their pertinence.

Family-size preferences, which play such a central role in subsequent analyses, forfeit much of their interest unless it may be assumed that they will correlate at least moderately with completed fertility. Several reasons are advanced to justify optimism in this regard.

Chapter IX. Summary of the Fertility Variables

In the preceding five chapters, the fertility behavior of the present sample has been studied from several angles. Chapter IV (supplemented by Appendix A) dealt with the couples' fecundity; Chapter V (supplemented by Appendix B) with their efforts to delay pregnancy by means of contraception. Chapter VI furnished an analysis of birth intervals. Chapter VII followed with an investigation of birth-spacing preferences. Finally, Chapter VIII considered family-size preferences. This chapter undertakes to summarize the substantive highlights of these five chapters, with a deliberate slighting of methodological issues, so heavily stressed in the chapters themselves.

For the present discussion, number of births is not problematical because all couples have exactly two children, the second birth occurring in September of 1956, a few months before the interviewing. Of course by the time of the reinterviews, scheduled for early 1960, family size will vary and therefore will have central importance for the analyses of those reinterviews.

The 1,165 couples under study are specialized in ways other than all having two children. They all reside in the eight largest Standard Metropolitan Areas, exclusive of Boston; both spouses are once-married and born in continental United States; and their marriage, up to time of interview, had not been complicated by death, extensive pregnancy wastage, adoption, or plural birth. Given so specialized a sample, little interest attaches to the details of fertility performance. Precisely computed means or proportions are superfluous and even more so are frequency distributions. Stress is properly reserved for directions and rough magnitudes of association. Indeed, many of the eligibility restrictions were applied so as to simplify, and thereby facilitate the analysis of, these associations. The one section of this chapter which indulges in some descriptive detail relates to birth-spacing preferences, the justification being that these preferences have received virtually no past study.

Many of the fertility interrelationships acquire added interest when their values are compared from one religious group to another. For reasons elaborated in Chapter XI, marriages are divided into four religious divisions: Catholic, Jewish, Protestant, and Mixed Catholic (Catholic—non-Catholic marriages officiated by a priest). Many of the religious contrasts mentioned in this chapter are explored in greater detail in Chapter XI.

Fecundity

Involuntary birth delays are one reason why actual and preferred birth intervals frequently deviate from each other. In the present sample, the principal sources of these delays are: (a) slowness to conceive; (b) temporary separations, especially in connection with military service; and (c) pregnancy wastage.

Of the three factors, pregnancy wastage is the least important. Pregnancy wastage is such a minor factor in the present sample in part because couples experiencing a stillbirth or more than one miscarriage are excluded. Less than 10 per cent of the birth intervals include a miscarriage and these intervals are prolonged slightly more than one year on the average. When all birth intervals are used as the base, the mean delay ensuing from pregnancy wastage does not quite reach one month. Even in a more general sample of American couples, the expected time added by pregnancy wastage per birth interval is only of the order of 2 months.

In the present sample, a somewhat larger minority of birth intervals are prolonged by separations. Most of these separations relate to military service and average longer than a year.

By far the most important source of involuntary birth delay in the present sample is slowness to conceive, even though the effects of this factor are also slightly weakened by the eligibility criteria imposed. After deliberately interrupting contraception in order to conceive, couples in this sample wait on the average 5 months for pregnancy, in contrast to six months waited by a large sample of obstetric patients studied by Tietze, Guttmacher, and Rubin, and 8 months waited by the Indianapolis couples studied by Whelpton, Kiser, and associates.

Conception delays before starting contraception prove longer than those after deliberately interrupting contraception. Before contraception, the present couples waited an average of 10 months for first pregnancy and an average of 20 months for subsequent pregnancies. The explanation why waits for subsequent pregnancies are so much longer before starting contraception than after deliberately interrupting it is usually offered in terms of (a) postpartum amenorrhea and anovulatory menstrual cycles; and (b) a tendency for nonuse of contraception after an initial pregnancy to associate with subfecundity.

It is much harder to explain why deliberate interrupters of contraception conceive their first pregnancies so much more promptly than noncontraceptors. Postpartum amenorrhea and anovulatory cycles are not a factor here. At marriage many subfecund couples are not aware of their fertility problem and so are not specially motivated against contraception. Nevertheless, the relative slowness of non-contraceptors to conceive first pregnancies has been documented in other studies. Several pages of Chapter IV are devoted to a discussion of possible causes, including both measurement biases and selections with respect to fecundity. Possibly of importance is a tendency for successful contraceptors to know more about the positioning of the brief fertile period within the menstrual cycle and to be more inclined to use such knowledge to hasten conception. This hypothesis is testable since mothers can be questioned regarding their knowledge of the fertile period and also about any use made of this knowledge. We plan to include questions of this nature in the reinterviews.

CONTRACEPTION

Failure to postpone pregnancies as long as desired is a second major reason why actual and preferred birth intervals frequently diverge from one another. The voluntary means of birth deferment include contraception, induced abortion, and sterilization. Typical of urban Americans early in marriage, the present couples report little use of sterilization or induced abortion and have relied almost exclusively upon contraception.

The analyses of Chapter V dealing with contraception are organized around three topics: availability of contraception, choice of method, and effectiveness of contraception. A simple rationale lies behind this division. Barriers such as ignorance or religious scruple may debar a couple from contraception even though they wish to postpone pregnancy, so that the availability of contraception can never be taken for granted. If contraception is available, usually more than one method is known, which means a problem of method choice. Finally, there is a question of how effective is the chosen method as it is being used by the couple.

Broadly speaking, the characteristics of the present couples are such as to render them relatively knowledgeable about contraception, but not always motivated to use this knowledge to full advantage. Several circumstances increase the likelihood that the couples know something about contraception. They are native-born whites residing in highly urbanized areas; they are young enough so that their schooling represents the high educational standards of the 1940's and 1950's; and most of the husbands have had a term of military duty. On the other hand, most of these couples have desired at least two children. Accordingly, their contraceptive problem has been one of spacing desired births rather than preventing unwanted

151

ones. Quite possibly this circumstance has weakened the will of many to put their contraceptive knowledge to full use.

About half the couples wait until after their first pregnancy before starting contraception. Only about 10 per cent have yet to start contraception after a second birth. For the great majority, then, contraception is available rather early in marriage. This varies by religion, with virtually all Jews starting contraception before first pregnancy and Catholics and Mixed Catholics delaying longer than Protestants. Social class appears to be a weaker differentiator of contraceptive use than religion.

To tighten the concept of contraception not being available, reasons for not using contraception have been classified into two categories: (a) temporarily not needing contraception, and (b) needing contraception but finding it unavailable. The principal reasons for not needing contraception are subfecundity and wanting a pregnancy as soon as physically possible. Some of the reasons for contraception not being available despite need for it are: religious principle, interference with sexual pleasure, and ignorance of methods. Refined in this manner, nonavailability of contraception shows the same pattern of contrasts by parity and religion as does contraceptive nonuse, though of course fewer couples are involved.

Regarding choice of method, the results of this study coincide closely with those from a national survey recently conducted by Freedman, Whelpton, and Campbell. The order of popularity runs: condom, diaphragm and jelly, rhythm, douche, and withdrawal. Again, religious differences are marked, with very different proportions in these groups found using effective methods (i.e., diaphragm and jelly, condom, and withdrawal). Jews utilize effective methods almost exclusively—condom primarily and diaphragm and jelly secondarily. Because of their heavy reliance upon the rhythm method used either alone or combined with another method, less than half the Catholic couples are using effective methods; and the same is true of Mixed Catholics. Protestants are intermediate in their reliance upon effective methods. Class differences are generally weaker than religious differences. The strongest class differences are found among Protestants, with white-collar Protestants distinctive for their emphasis upon diaphragm and jelly, while blue-collar Protestants place relatively more emphasis upon condoms as well as douches used either alone or paired with other methods.

In contrast to other samples, the present couples are not seen gravitating to the more effective methods as marriage duration increases. The distribution of methods used at marriage resembles closely those being used after second birth. This makes sense for the

152

Jewish group who use effective methods from the start. It is more surprising in the other three religious groups and is a main reason for suspecting that many of the couples are not yet fully motivated to achieve efficient contraception. Many Catholic and Protestant couples have not yet reached their desired family sizes and may delay switching to an effective method of contraception until they do so.

Contraceptors in the present sample have not distinguished themselves for effectiveness. Prior to first pregnancy their rate of unplanned pregnancies is 26 pregnancies per 100 years of contraception; after first pregnancy, it is 20 pregnancies. These are relatively high rates of unplanned pregnancy. For instance, they are twice as high as those met in the Indianapolis Study. Inclusion of Catholic and Jewish couples in the present study is not an explanation since the total sample shows a slightly lower failure rate than the Protestant segment by itself. Lower motivation to achieve efficient contraception may be a factor, though this cannot be proven. One factor has more certainly contributed: all couples have had at least two pregnancies. This means that since contraception is either interrupted by unplanned pregnancy or eventually followed by a planned pregnancy, a fecund condition during virtually all of the contraceptive exposure may be inferred. Also, most of the couples have been spacing wanted births so that they have rarely aspired to pregnancy postponements much longer than two or three years. This last circumstance can be shown to heighten failure rates.

Once again, religious differences are larger than class differences. Much the largest difference appears between Jews and non-Jews. The Jewish rates of contraceptive failure are less than half those of the other religious groups both before and after first birth. This superiority reflects not only more reliance upon the most effective methods but also more consistent and skilful use. However, it should be emphasized that even if one group has twice the failure rate of the other, both failure rates are low as compared to the pregnancy rates that might occur in the absence of contraception.

No consistent, statistically significant differences in failure rates are found within each class (white-collar or blue-collar) between Catholics and Protestants. This is surprising in view of the Catholics' preference for the relatively ineffective rhythm method. However, it should be kept in mind that groups of contraceptors are being compared, not total groups. Perhaps as a result of some Catholics misconstruing the position of their church as condemning all contraception, contraceptors in the Catholic group are more selected for an active concern about spacing children than are Protestant contraceptors.

However, the contraception of Catholics emerges as definitely inferior to that of Protestants if nonavailable contraception is treated as contraception of zero efficiency and contraceptive failure rates adjusted accordingly.

BIRTH INTERVALS

Birth intervals are not precisely determined by birth spacing preferences except when the couple agree on what spacing they want and achieve complete "interval control." Such control presupposes delaying pregnancy as long as desired, achieving conception quickly once it is wanted, and escaping pregnancy wastage. Thus only a limited understanding of birth intervals is reached by treating them as simple expressions of spacing preferences. Additional knowledge is gained by partitioning each birth interval into an "intended component," representing length of contraceptive practice, and a "residual component," comprising the remainder of the birth interval. Essentially the intended component measures the postponement of pregnancy achieved by contraception, while the residual component encompasses the various types of birth delay.

Interestingly enough, in the present sample, birth delays usually contribute somewhat more to the variation of birth intervals than do periods of contraceptive practice. The two components, residual and intended, are only barely correlated These results indicate the composite nature of the present set of birth intervals and, as far as can be judged, this compositeness is a fairly general property of birth intervals.

It was expected that most social and psychological variables would correlate more closely with the intended component of birth intervals than with total birth intervals. Presumably birth delays are mainly involuntary (though this has never been formally tested), while postponements of pregnancy achieved by contraception are subject to a substantial measure of voluntary control. If this were so, most social and psychological variables should correlate more closely with the intended component of birth intervals than with the residual component, and since the residual component contributes such a large part of the variation of total birth intervals, the correlations with the intended component should tend to exceed those with total intervals. Yet this expectation was not borne out. The test was conducted on the basis of a few social and psychological variables exhibiting appreciable correlations with total birth intervals. Quite possibly this choice of variables is part of the reason for the negative result. Because the residual component is such an important part of the total birth interval, it is difficult to find a variable which will at once correlate substantially with the total birth interval but negligibly with its residual component.

The intended and residual components of the first birth interval appear to predict their counterparts in the next birth interval better than does the aggregate first interval predict the second. However, the highest correlation, which is only .21 between the two sets of birth delays, is too low for practical significance.

Preferred Birth Intervals

Thus far something has been said about means and barriers to fertility control and about birth intervals, but nothing yet has been said about fertility preferences. Two categories of fertility preference will be considered: preferred birth intervals and preferred family sizes. While the latter have been intensively studied in a number of surveys, the former, birth spacing preferences, have received practically no attention.

Because the relationship between preferred and actual birth intervals is so loose, the practical significance of spacing preferences is easily exaggerated. As the previous section has indicated, birth intervals are as much a product of involuntary birth delays as voluntary postponements of pregnancy. Spacing preferences significantly influence only these latter periods of contraceptive practice and even then the correspondence is not always close. For example, contraception may be interrupted by unintentional pregnancy. If the couple doubt their fecundity, they may dispense with contraception rather than risk an excessive pregnancy delay. In cases where contraception is unavailable for such reasons as ignorance or religious scruple, spacing preferences for all intents and purposes become irrelevant.

Nevertheless, birth-spacing preferences constitute an integral part of the fertility variable. Being so little studied in the past, they are worth describing even for so specialized a sample as the present one.

Asked to evaluate their first birth intervals (marriage to first birth) in terms of too short, just right, or too long, two thirds of the mothers deemed them just right, with the approved intervals proving highly variable. Such a large variation suggests that many mothers do not perceive a narrow range of first interval length as just right and all other lengths as too short or too long. Rather, they perceive a broad span of interval length as not causing serious inconvenience, and when their actual interval falls anywhere in this range, they tend to rate it as just right. Most of the mothers believe that a couple should wait a while before having their first child. Mothers who say

155

their first child came too soon are apt to complain that they lacked time for marital adjustment, to ready their finances, or to enjoy things with their husband before the responsibilities of motherhood.

A majority of second birth intervals (first to second birth) are also approved retrospectively and, as with approved first intervals, their lengths show considerable variation. Presumably here also, most mothers do not perceive a narrow range of interval length as peculiarly advantageous and all other lengths as inconvenient. The respondents agree fairly well that spacing children more than four years apart reduces chances of their becoming playmates; but the respondents are less agreed about the manner in which spacing of children affects the ease of rearing them.

For successful contraceptors, lengths of contraceptive practice after marriage and after first birth offer a way of measuring originally intended first and second birth intervals. Included as "successful contraceptors" are couples who forego contraception because they want a pregnancy as soon as physically possible. Estimated in this manner, original spacing preferences prove just as variable as intervals retrospectively judged to be just right. Furthermore, originally intended first and second birth intervals correlate $-.19$ and $-.35$ with wife's desired family size, while first and second intervals deemed just right show no such correlations. Apparently there are factors linking spacing decisions to total fertility desires, but these factors tend to get excluded from retrospective spacing preferences.

Respondents were also asked about their preferred spacing between second and third children, a somewhat hypothetical question for those intending only two children. Inasmuch as these preferred third intervals are almost as variable as the other intervals discussed, again the evidence is that the majority fail to perceive a narrow range of interval length as peculiarly advantageous. Two considerations dominate among the reasons given for preferring particular intervals between second and third children. An interval long enough to permit adequate care of three children without unreasonable strain upon the mother proves the most salient consideration, with nearly half the mothers indicating a desire to delay their third birth until the oldest child reaches a specified stage of development. Spacing the second and third children close enough to ensure their companionship emerges as the second most frequently mentioned consideration.

Apparently mothers recognize the weak relationship between spacing preferences and actual birth intervals. Only half the mothers desiring a third child expect their third intervals to conform even approximately with their preferences. Another reason for suspecting

156

that wife's preferred third interval has little predictive value is that it correlates only .28 with her husband's expected third interval.

Correlating wife's preferred third interval with a wide variety of social and psychological variables produced several statistically significant relationships, but none of these correlations reached a value of .3. The reader is referred to Chapter VII for details. The speculative interpretation placed on this set of consistently low associations is that many mothers had not started to think seriously about spacing their next child so soon after the birth of their second and therefore had only vague ideas about what interval they would eventually seek.

DESIRED FAMILY SIZE

A second major category of fertility preference is desired family size, measured separately for husbands and wives on the basis of the question: "How many children do you want to have altogether, counting the two you have now?" Two, three, and four children have roughly equal popularity and account for more than 90 per cent of the preferences reported by wives. Husbands exhibit a similar distribution of total fertility desires.

Some investigators have argued that the nature and extent of communication between spouses basically influences the couple's chances of achieving effective fertility control and agreeing about the number of children they want. Not enough information was collected in the present study to test this hypothesis conclusively. The present husbands and wives agree substantially about their family-size preferences. Despite differences in measurement, their total fertility desires correlate .65. Two-thirds of the time, the same number of children is mentioned by both spouses. Degree of consensus varies among the four religious groups, being strongest among Jews and weakest among Mixed Catholics.

The degree of realism about spouse's desired family size also appears high. Information is available only for the wife's perception of her husband's preference, but the correlation between this perception and the preference reported by her husband is .71. This correlation varies among the four religious groups, once again being strongest for Jews and weakest for Mixed Catholics. Thus, fullest agreement and knowledge is found in the group practicing the most effective contraception, namely, Jews. In addition, the Jewish wife most frequently reports that she and her husband have recently discussed the subject of family size. However, the direct association between recency of discussion and level of agreement operates only at the group level among the four religious groups. Within each of these groups, the direction of association reverses. A wife is slightly more likely to report recent discussion when she perceives her preference as disagreeing with her husband's. This suggests that perceived disagreement stimulates discussion, or perhaps that arguments about family size are more often remembered as discussion than mutual assurances of unanimity.

The 66 wives who currently doubt their fecundity do not seem to differ from the more fecund majority with respect to their family-size preferences. No evidence has been found, then, that subfecund respondents tend to think so wishfully about family size that they report larger than average numbers of children desired.

In the present sample, wives desiring larger families have shorter birth intervals, this inverse association being strongest among Catholics. Contributing to this result is a tendency for couples desiring large families to seek shorter than average birth intervals.

Larger size of desired family also associates with lower availability of contraception and less successful planning of pregnancies. These relationships fit with, but do not prove, the hypothesis that couples diffident about their contraception and anticipating large families adjust to this prospect by persuading themselves that they really want numerous children. The associations between desired family size and contraceptive behavior are strongest among Catholics, weakest for Jews. In part, this results from Catholics being the most varied both with respect to desired family size and contraceptive behavior, while Jews are most homogeneous. Data fail to support the hypothesis that in the Catholic groups religious devoutness, by selecting for low availability of contraception and reported desire for large families, increases the association between size of family wanted and contraceptive performance.

Family-size preferences, which play such a central role in the analyses of subsequent chapters, forfeit much of their interest unless it may be assumed that they will correlate at least moderately with completed fertility. There are several reasons, discussed in Chapter VIII, for being optimistic about this association. In another study, low but statistically significant correlations were obtained between the family-size preferences reported by engaged couples and their actual family sizes ascertained twenty years later. Almost certainly the family-size preferences of couples well along in their family building will correlate much higher with eventual fertility. In support of this premise, another study of urban couples has shown that fertility desires are quite stable over a three-year period, especially when there are children already born. One further reason for believing that this stability will prevail in the present sample is the high level of agreement exhibited by the spouses regarding number of children desired.

Two factors always operating to loosen the correlation between the desired family sizes of individual couples and their completed fertilities are subfecundity and contraceptive failure. The characteristics of the present sample are well chosen to minimize the importance of subfecundity. A final source of encouragement is the fact that the respondents' desired family sizes correlate with their birth intervals and birth intervals are known to correlate with completed fertility.

Chapter IX completes analysis of the fertility variables and their relationships. The rest of this report is devoted to an analysis of social and psychological factors correlating with a selective group of fertility variables, namely, desired family size, lengths of birth intervals, and fertility-planning success.

PART III

SOCIAL AND PSYCHOLOGICAL DETERMINANTS

Chapter X. Concepts and Hypotheses

Four classes of variables are included in the study. First, there is the group of dependent variables to be predicted. These denote different aspects of the fertility process described in the preceding section. The main dependent variable for present purposes is regarded as the total number of children or size of family desired. Other dependent variables of interest are the pattern of past fertility planning and the spacing of the two children. The second interview, and the analysis of its results, will focus more specifically on the occurrence and spacing of the third pregnancy. The latter, of course, obviously cannot be included in this first report.

In this section, there are three broad classes of independent variables to be analyzed in search of explanations of variations in these dependent variables. The first is concerned with the *socio-cultural environment* of the respondents, both as an historical and contemporary setting for their values, attitudes, and behavior. The second is concerned with those social-psychological variables that determine the respondents' *personal orientations* toward various aspects of their life situations. The third class of variables is a group of selected *personality characteristics*. The purpose of this chapter is to describe the major assumptions and hypotheses that guided the selection of specific independent variables for inclusion in the study.

The Conceptual Structure

Except for the group of personality characteristics, all of the components of the independent variables are located within one of four major substantive areas: religion, socio-economic status, family, and residence. In other words, each specific independent variable, whether an aspect of the respondents' socio-cultural environment or of their personal orientations, refers directly to one of these four dimensions of social life. Socio-economic status and residence have been subdivided further for organizational convenience. A brief characterization of all independent variables in the study except for the personality characteristics may be found in Table 36. Each variable has been placed in the most appropriate of the eight cells that result from cross-classifying the four content areas by the two classes of variables.

A reading of this chart shows that arbitrary decisions of classification had to be made in a few instances. For example, "wife's work history" might with some justification have been placed in a socio-economic status rather than a family category. In addition, there are

163

TABLE 36

Conceptual Organization of Independent Variables

Content Areas	Socio-Cultural Environment	Personal Orientations
Religion	Affiliational preference Type of (mixed) marriage ceremony Religious education Ethnic origin	Frequency of church attendance Informal religious orientation Commitment to religious values

Socio-Economic Status	Occupation and Job:
	  Current occupation and
	    occupational prestige
	  Occupation at marriage
	  Occupation of parents
	  Inter- and intra-generational
	    occupational mobility
	  Number of job changes
	  Owner-employee status
	  Size of firm
	  Employment history
	Education:
	  Formal education of wife and
	    husband
	  Verbal ability test score of wife
	Income:
	  Husband's earnings in 1956
	  Family income in 1956
	  Changes in income since marriage
	  Extent of credit buying
	Housing:
	  Type of tenure
	  Value of housing: operating costs
	Neighborhood:
	  Type of land use
	  Value of housing in immediate
	    vicinity
		Achievement of life goals
		Feelings of economic security
		Relevance of finances in fertility
		  decisions
		Job satisfaction
		Perception of opportunities
		Commitment to work values
		Status satisfaction
		Social class identification
		Importance of "getting ahead"
		Drive to "get ahead"
		Aspirations for children's
		  education

Residence	Community:
	  Region of birth
	  Size and type of community
	    lived in as child
	  Types of moves since marriage
	  Metropolitan area of current
	    residence
	  Type of community of
	            current residence
	Housing:
	  Number of moves since marriage
	  Length of residence in present
	    home
	  Type of dwelling unit
	  Number of bedrooms
	  Type of dwelling units in
	    vicinity
		Expectations of moving
		Perceptions of space adequacy
		Reasons moved from previous
		  residence

(continued)

Content Areas	Socio-Cultural Environment	Personal Orientations
Family	Age of parents Number of siblings Age at marriage Wife's work history Future work intentions Marriage duration Birth intervals Sex of children	Preferences for babies or older children Level of enjoyment of children Adjustment to mother role Patterns of help available to mother Patterns of husband-wife dominance Marital adjustment Childhood happiness

also a number of variables included here that serve both as independent and dependent variables. For example, the lengths of the intervals between marriage and the birth of the first child and between the first and second child were hypothesized to influence the total number of children desired and the preferred spacing of the third child. In this connection, they were viewed as independent variables. We are, though, interested in the relationships between, let us say, family income in the first year of marriage and the interval between marriage and the first child. From this perspective, the interval becomes a dependent variable. Most of the variables, however, fall naturally into one or another part of the classification scheme without undue violence to their ordinary meaning or traditional usage. More importantly, it should be clear that this arrangement of variables is intended only as a device to facilitate presentation and discussion rather than as a systematic theoretical framework.

It is apparent from the content areas of the conceptual organization that although they are quite broad and inclusive, some principle of selection was operative. Other possible areas, such as politics, community associations, and nonfamilial social relations, have been excluded from consideration. The basic rationale for concentrating on these four particular areas is the obvious one that there is either a body of accumulated evidence or strong plausible speculation that variations within each of them are relevant for differences in fertility. Thus, there is evidence that Catholics have larger families than Protestants, that the economic situation of the family affects fertility, that those who marry early have larger families, that rural migrants have a different fertility history from that of indigenous urbanites, and so on. To state that these relationships are "known" is both an

165

overstatement and a simplification of our current state of knowledge. What is known is that within each of these content areas there is a variable or cluster of variables operating that is sufficiently strong so that comparisons between gross categories reveal significant differences among a wide range of fertility-connected variables. To take intelligence as an example, there is a considerable body of evidence that family size and intelligence are negatively correlated.[1] What is not known, however, is whether this relationship is an effect of an intervening correlation between intelligence and the efficiency of contraceptive practice or whether the less generously endowed segments of the population actually want more children.

Numerous other illustrations could be offered of instances where significant associations have been observed between fertility and such gross environmental variables as religion, occupation, and income. One of the primary objectives of the study and of the selection of particular variables has been that of attempting to trace the influence on completed family size of these socio-environmental variables, and to elucidate the social-psychological variables that mediate between an environmental factor and fertility performance (for example, level of income and feelings of economic security). Or put another way, although existing empirical evidence links fertility to variables that we have grouped into a category termed the socio-cultural environment, a more meaningful explanation of these fertility differentials requires an intervening set of psychological concepts which show how these large-scale social facts are translated into individual fertility events. The category of personal orientations is intended primarily to serve this function.

In summary, the variables within the socio-cultural environment category provide a description of the major characteristics of the social milieu within which individuals must act. They are the conditions to which they react and to which they adjust in one form or another. The personal orientation variables are conceived as the resultants of this reaction and adjustment process. It is these orientations that are viewed as impinging directly on the fertility process although clearly, in terms of action potential, they are filtered through and no doubt partly determined by the personalities of wife and husband.

SUBSTANTIVE QUESTIONS AND HYPOTHESES

The general hypotheses constituting the basic framework for the study are heuristic rather than systematic.[2] They flow from a variety

[1] For a summary of the evidence and a representative bibliography, see Ann Anastasi "Intelligence and Family Size," *Psychological Bulletin*, 53 (1956), pp. 187–209

[2] The present formulation derives from but is different in several respects from an earlier statement which formed the basis for the development of the study. (Cf. Elliot G.,

of empirical and theoretical sources rather than from one unified theory and they serve the function of opening up the problem for exploration in terms of a wide range of variables rather than of providing a test of a restricted number of hypotheses.

Foremost among the general assumptions influencing the choice of variables for study is what may be called the "assumption of compatibility." This states that a particular pattern of fertility performance and control depends on the extent to which having another child (or a certain number of children) is compatible with other life values and interests. Although at the level of a truism, this serves to bring into prominence the notion that a fertility choice (whether implicit or explicit) involves a "cost" for the individual and for the family, that is, certain desires and interests are either yielded or compromised in preference to others.[3] This assumption underlies most of the broad "theme" hypotheses and specific variables discussed below.

In general, the socio-cultural environment is viewed as setting limits on the range of other values and behavior with which different family-size preferences may be compatible; that is, as the set of social conditions within which and to which the individual must react, they determine the nature and the magnitude of the "costs" involved if the individuals select the option of a larger family rather than a small family. From this it follows that the basic questions asked about the variables of the socio-cultural environment are: what are the limits and how flexible are they with reference to the "adequate" satisfaction of competing values?

It is convenient to discuss the different content areas separately.

RELIGION

The hypothesized relationship of fertility to religious variables is direct and empirically founded.[4] Catholics are known to have higher

Mishler, and Charles F. Westoff, "A Proposal for Research on Social Psychological Factors Affecting Fertility: Concepts and Hypotheses," *Current Research in Human Fertility*, Milbank Memorial Fund, New York, 1954). In addition to changes resulting from the development of our thinking about the problems, the major differences result from the fact that the study reported on here is concerned with a preference variable rather than fertility itself, and our focus is toward the third rather than the first child. In these two respects the actual study differs from the assumptions that entered into the earlier model. On the other hand, it is easily seen on comparison that many of the leading hypotheses developed in the earlier article have figured prominently in the variables and hypotheses included in the study.

[3] Mishler and Westoff, "A Proposal for Research on Social Psychological Factors Affecting Fertility," p. 132.

[4] The most recent evidence is reported both in Ronald Freedman, P. K. Whelpton, and Arthur Campbell, *Family Planning, Sterility and Population Growth*, McGraw–Hill, New York, 1959, and in the *Statistical Abstract of the United States*, 1958, U.S. Department of Commerce, Bureau of the Census, p. 41.

rates of fertility than non-Catholics. Once married, they are restricted by theological doctrine to use the operationally less efficient methods of family limitation and, as initially evidenced from pretest results, they indicate preferences for substantially larger families than do non-Catholics. At first glance, such a relationship might seem obvious. It is common knowledge that Catholics have more children because of the Church's injunctions against the use of birth control. However, the dependent variable in this case is the number of children desired and there is no simple explanation of why family-size preferences should be strongly correlated with religion. The Catholic Church has traditionally emphasized the family as the basis of society, a position that may be translated into positive attitudes toward larger families. Another plausible explanation is that this may be a rationalization in advance of the inevitable biological consequences of not using contraception or of using less reliable methods. Other hypotheses derive from the evidence of internal differential fertility among Catholics and from theories of social change which stress an increasing homogeneity of values in American culture accompanied by an initial lag in the adjustment of subcultural groups further removed from the dominant ideologies of the time. The available evidence indicates that fertility varies by different measures of socio-economic status in approximately the same pattern among Catholics as among Protestants, although class by class comparisons reveal significantly larger families among Catholics.[5] A similar pattern of assimilation of values as inferred from fertility rates has been observed for racial and residential comparisons.[6]

One avenue of investigation to be pursued in attempting to shed further light on the reasons for family-size differences by religion deriving from these considerations is the pattern of authority relationships within the family. Does the Catholic family system conform to the image of the traditional patriarchal structure presumably characteristic of some other minority groups (including the rural farm family which can now be regarded at least statistically, if not sociologically, as a minority)?

Other lines of analysis will seek to probe the possible differences in family-size values that might stem from the atmosphere of the home in which Catholic parents were raised, as reflected in the number of their siblings, childhood happiness, and the marital adjustment of their parents. The relationship between family-size desires and

[5] P. K. Whelpton, and Clyde V. Kiser, eds., *Social and Psychological Factors Affecting Fertility*, 5 Vols., Milbank Memorial Fund, New York, 1946–1958, Vol. I.

[6] Charles F. Westoff, "Differential Fertility in the United States: 1900 to 1952," *American Sociological Review*, 19 (1954), pp. 549–561.

religion will also be examined in the light of differences in ethnic origin, intensity of religious practices and attitudes, and the whole range of socio-economic variables.

There is some evidence from the pretest of the current study that degree of religiosity, regardless of religious preference, is related to family-size preferences. Returning to our assumption of compatibility, it would appear that a commitment to "other worldly" or spiritual values is quite compatible with large family preferences. Either these values preclude (or interfere with) the maintenance of other values that might compete with fertility or the very nature of these values, since they do not involve costs in the usual sense, permits them to exist side by side with large family-size ideals.

And finally, questions relating to different levels of mobility aspirations and the importance of the work life may be especially pertinent. In effect, religion will be employed as a major control factor throughout the analyses.

SOCIO-ECONOMIC STATUS

The hypotheses relating to the influence of socio-economic status on fertility are in some respects more complicated than those about religion. This is partly because the variable itself is more heterogeneous as we have used it (it includes a number of different measures of occupation and income as well as other variables), but also because the variable may operate differently for men and women, because past experience may be as important as current position, and numerous other complications. Nevertheless, within all this complexity there are a few general notions that have tended to dominate our approach in this direction.

The first broad hypothesis is that a high level of security in the area of socio-economic status is associated with desires for larger families. This includes actual level of current income as well as the pattern of income changes over the course of the marriage.

In addition to the level of "objective" security, we are very much interested in the respondent's level of "subjective" security. For the variable labeled feelings of economic security, defined by the extent to which the respondent is worried about her present and future financial situation, we have developed a scale calling for responses to a number of different situations of possible financial loss or uncertainty. A number of other items focus more on consumption patterns and the extent to which financial considerations enter into decisions regarding family size. Finally, a noneconomic variable has been included that deals with the level of general confidence felt by the respondent that the course of her own life over the past years of marriage and the immediate future is both dependable and desirable. This measure appears in Table 36 as "achievement of life goals."

The most meaningful analyses of relations between the fertility variables and these variables of "subjective" security will require the use of some measure of "objective" security as a control. This assumes that the type of economic insecurity reported by a respondent at a high level of income is qualitatively different than that reported by a respondent at a subsistence level, a factor to be taken into account in the analysis and interpretation of relationships.

A second broad hypothesis is that high aspirations for social mobility will be associated with smaller family-size desires. In other words, it is expected that large families are perceived as incompatible with successful social mobility and therefore respondents for whom the latter is important are likely to show a preference for small families.

This hypothesis is based in part on the assumption that the particularly rapid decline in the fertility of the white-collar class through the nineteenth and early years of the twentieth centuries resulted to some extent from the significance attached by members of this class to social mobility and to their view of work as a primary focus of meaningful activity. The major substantive assumptions and hypotheses contained in earlier theoretical formulations[7] developed for this study can be outlined as follows:

1. One traditional ideology in American socio-economic history has been the work-success-mobility ethos. As internalized, this has meant to the individual a devotion of a major part of his life to work and work-related goals. Nonwork time is used as a means of self-improvement and self-promotion. There is no clear separation between work and nonwork; leisure-time activities are seen as an extension of work. Patterns of association reflect this orientation. Stylized consumption, luxury, and recreation are devalued as such; savings are encouraged, and consumption expenditures apart from necessities are viewed as wasteful.

2. After the early religious emphasis and sanctions on these values are diminished, the large family is seen as an impediment to mobility-oriented aspirations. The time, money, and energies involved in the care of a large family are viewed as distractions from the path of achieving the major goal. Family size is sharply limited among

[7] Joseph Bensman and Charles F. Westoff, "A Theoretical Model for Research on Social and Psychological Factors Affecting Fertility," January 15, 1954, (mimeo. in possession of authors); Charles F. Westoff and Joseph Bensman, "The Social Mobility Model Restated with Some Research Implications and Suggestions," March 20 1954 (mimeo. in possession of authors).

adherents of the mobility ideology. Considerable ambivalence is expressed toward one's children.

3. This mobility ethos was accompanied by a favorable social and economic environment. The rapid rates of economic expansion provided by industrialization offered numerous channels and opportunities for mobility corresponding to those expressed in the ideology.

4. The bureaucratization of large-scale economic organization and the concomitant stabilization of administration and recruitment have given rise to perceptions of mobility ceilings among increasingly larger segments of both the industrial and middle classes.

5. The perception of structured (in some classes assured, in others lessened) mobility plus increasing routinization of work gives rise to an increased recognition of the negative aspects of the work life.

6. Those groups that perceive lower ceilings on their mobility are less likely to be influenced by the injunctions of the mobility ethic. Specifically, those elements of the mobility ethic which act as deterrents to family size are weakened.

7. As work is devalued as the major system of meaning among these groups, alternative life plans develop.

8. One such major life plan centers around the stylization and enrichment of the private life. The job and work life becomes redefined as sources of income and security. This reorientation focuses on the home and home life and on the use of resources for private consumption ends. Children become more a source of enjoyment in themselves and an increasing amount of time and energies are devoted to their development.

As summarized here, this theory is obviously a gross oversimplification particularly in ignoring the different responses of various occupational classes. Particularly, it is not sufficient to account for the fact that the blue-collar classes experienced a later but nevertheless sharp decline in their fertility prior to the postwar period. It is probable that the state of high fertility which characterized this class was not an altogether happy one and that part of the decline stemmed primarily from the rapid reduction in infant mortality along with the general dissemination and popularization of methods of effective contraception. Further, it is clear that a desire to live a better life was not restricted to the white-collar class. As aspirations for themselves and their children came gradually to be more realistic for members of the working class, they presumably came to be guided by motivations for family size similar to those that were present in the more privileged group.

These broad speculations on the historical changes in orientations

171

of the various social classes cannot be validated directly in the current study. However, a number of variables have been included that permit testing related and derivative hypotheses. Among these are measures of occupational prestige, status satisfaction, size of firm, perceptions of opportunities for future mobility, the importance of and the intensity of the drive for "getting ahead," and inter- and intragenerational occupational mobility. As with the variables of "subjective" economic security, these mobility variables are also to be analyzed within an "objective" measure of socio-economic status.

RESIDENCE

As revealed in Table 36, certain aspects of the community and housing are included under socio-economic status and others under residence. Although this allocation is to some extent arbitrary, the purpose is to distinguish those aspects of the two which imply a status dimension (such as the value of housing and type of land use) from those relating to nonstratified characteristics (such as size of community, and length of residence).

The first set of variables included with the residence classification relate to the community environment both in terms of the respondent's past (region of birth, size and type of community lived in during childhood) and the present (the city they live in now and whether resident in a suburban area or in the city proper). Two general considerations determined the inclusion of these variables. First, the literature abounds with research and generalizations about the differences in family-size values of rural and urban residents. Although by design our sample is confined to residents of large metropolitan areas, a significant proportion of the respondents at one time or another in their lives lived in smaller communities. Thus, there is the natural question of whether couples who have migrated to cities from less populous areas or who themselves were raised in a nonurban atmosphere have imported with them any of the traditional fertility values presumably associated with such a background.

A more interesting aspect of this general variable is the question of the significance for fertility of city-suburban residence. Observers of postwar American society have speculated extensively about the modern social revolution reflected by the mass exodus to the suburbs. Many have regarded the new dormitory suburbs as the breeding grounds of America. What is less clear, however, is whether the suburbs are a result of the need for more space because of larger families or whether suburban life and its "return to the earth" ideologies and the presumed pressure for conformity actually fosters larger families. Our study design is uniquely suited for supplying at least a partial answer to this question since the respondents have all had their second child at the same time, and it will be possible to compare the family-size preferences of two groups differentiated at least by some crude index of urban-suburban residence. The question of whether suburban areas attract a selective familistic group as opposed to fostering familism, however, cannot be assessed in this study.

The second group of variables under "residence," both environmental and attitudinal, relate mainly to the capacity of the respondents' present housing to accommodate an additional child. Other aspects of this variable are concerned with the frequency of past residential mobility and expectations of future moving. The general rationale for securing data on this subject is the hypothesis that residential stability as opposed to frequent mobility will be associated with larger family-size preferences. All such hypotheses, of course, can only be intelligently tested within the framework of numerous controls.

The Family

There are three types of variables included within the area of the family. The first of these are the demographic characteristics such as age, age at marriage, child-spacing intervals, and the like, which are conceived to set vague limits to family-size desires. Thus, considerations of the mother's age (perhaps perceived in health terms) or the interval between the two children were evident in many replies to direct motivational questions about the reasons for wanting a certain number of children. The sex of the two existing children is also considered relevant to future fertility intentions, and it is expected, on the basis of pretest results, that couples whose first two children are both of the same sex, particularly if they are both girls, will be more inclined to want additional children than couples who already have a child of each sex.

The second type of variable related to the family pertains to the wife's "adjustment" to the mother role. One hypothesis—that personal involvement in or identification with an extrafamilial social role will be incompatible with desires for larger families—refers obviously to the extent that the wife has found alternative sources of personal and social satisfaction in activities besides those involved in motherhood, particularly in a job or career.

One of the general notions underlying the development of the area of adjustment to the mother role, as well as the third group of variables to be discussed below, is the question of the extent to which the

173

structure of the family is equipped to absorb adequately the strains resulting from the addition of another child. Thus, we are interested in seeing whether mothers who have available help and relief from the daily burdens of child care and housekeeping are inclined to view an additional child with less concern than mothers who cannot depend upon such help.

Since fertility involves both wife and husband, and the number of children desired represents either explicitly or implicitly the process of adjustment between the spouses, a number of variables have been included which describe the pattern of social interaction between spouses as perceived by the wife. These constitute the last group of variables within the family classification.

There has been considerable speculation and some inconclusive research that couples whose marriage has been successful (another aspect of husband-wife interaction) have larger families. The traditional image, probably deriving from rural culture, pictures the large happy family (although the mass communications industry over the past few years has probably changed this image), with the implication that well-adjusted, happily married couples have larger families. Previous research has not confirmed this relationship. On the contrary, the Indianapolis Study revealed that less happily married couples had more children, although this was seen to be primarily a function of the more well-adjusted couple's greater success in preventing unwanted pregnancies. The inclusion of the variable in this study results from an interest in determining whether family-size desires, rather than the total number of pregnancies, is affected by marital adjustment. No direction of hypothesized relationship has been stated because there are a number of controls that have to be exercised in the analysis. For example, the Indianapolis Study indicated that some unhappily married couples had additional children in order to keep the marriage going, "to bring husband and wife closer together." Since this type of fertility motivation would seem to be a rather neurotic solution to the problem, it is possible that certain personality characteristics might refine the analysis and make the results more meaningful.

Patterns of husband-wife dominance in selected areas of decision-making have also been incorporated in the study. The rationale for studying this variable reflects mainly two points. The sociological literature on the family has emphasized the patriarchal family as a type in which the wife's role is confined primarily to that of mother and housekeeper. Since the father presumably does not become involved in the child-rearing routines in this type of family as much as within the modern egalitarian structure, he is less exposed to the immediate concerns of the large family and because of the authority relationships both spouses are more inclined to let nature take its course. The fact that this type of family structure has been most prevalent in peasant and agrarian societies where large families were not an economic handicap is no sociological accident. The second point is the consideration that the modern family structure, with its greater equality between the sexes and its consequent obfuscation of traditional roles, produces social relationships which permit communication between the spouses; a consideration of some importance in the matter of family-size goals and contraceptive practice. Another recent large-scale study[8] of fertility has placed great emphasis on this aspect of the family, an approach which seems more promising for the type of society studied than it does in modern American society.

As in the case of marital adjustment, no direct hypothesis is stated but rather the significance of the variable for fertility is regarded as an exploratory question. Although our expectation is that fertility will be higher in families where the husband is the dominant figure of authority, a similar consequence may result within the egalitarian family structure from the problems created by legitimizing family limitation as a subject for mutual decision.

PERSONALITY CHARACTERISTICS

The class of variables labeled "personality characteristics" constitutes the fourth major group of variables in the study as distinct from the dependent variables, the socio-cultural environment, and its related personal orientation variables.

The inclusion of personality variables in the study is, in large measure, unique in investigations of factors affecting fertility. There are a number of general considerations which prompted such inclusion. First, there is some scattered research evidence that at least one trait (neuroticism) has shown a relationship with fertility. Secondly, the study, as its broad objectives are conceived, is regarded as research into the motivations determining family size and we were naturally interested in determining whether certain types of personality characteristics are associated with family-size orientations and with the practice of contraception. And thirdly, students of population quality have for a long time expressed an interest in the selectivity of certain traits, although it is clear that they have been more occupied with the dysgenic results of perpetuating hereditary mental defects.

[8] Reuben Hill, J. Mayone Stycos, and Kurt Back, *The Family and Population Control*, University of North Carolina Press, Chapel Hill, 1959.

The specific personality characteristics included are listed in Table 37. They are conceived as relatively stable dispositions to

TABLE 37

Personality Characteristics Included in the Study

1. Generalized manifest anxiety
2. Nurturance needs
3. Ability to delay gratification of impulses
4. Self-awareness
5. Compulsiveness
6. Ambiguity tolerance
7. Cooperativeness
8. Need achievement

behave in a characteristic way in social situations. Like other variables in the study, the personality variables have not been drawn from any single theory but rather have been selected from a few basic hypotheses. The specific variables listed in Table 37 represent only those which have successfully passed an intensive series of preliminary screening tests. The hypotheses, however, since they were used to select the original group, refer to the original set and some of the differences in emphasis results from the fact that it was not always possible to develop adequate measuring instruments.[9]

In connection with fertility preferences, the most important hypothesis is that marked unsatisfied dependency needs and an immature concern for one's self and one's personal problems would reduce desires for additional children. Another way of describing this is that if the wife has strong needs for continual emotional support, this would presumably interfere with her capacity to give this kind of necessary support to children, motherhood would be less satisfying and more demanding than for other women, and therefore she would not wish to have a large family. The two specific variables related to this general concept that were retained for the final study are what we have termed "generalized manifest anxiety" (this is quite similar in content to the usual "neuroticism" scales found in many standard personality inventories) and "needs for nurturance."

In the area of contraception it was hypothesized that the practice of effective contraception would be affected by the adequacy of the impulse-control balance established within the personality. That is, if there is not a satisfactory pattern both for expressing and controlling inner impulses without undue strain, anxiety, or guilt, then it was

[9] The measurement problem for this and other sets of variables is taken up in detail in a series of methodological appendices.

176

believed that it would be difficult to maintain regular and effective use of contraception. Two of the variables here were also expected to be relevant to fertility preference: the "ability to delay the gratification of impulses" and "self-awareness." In addition, there are measures of "compulsiveness" and the "ability to tolerate ambiguity." Finally, inasmuch as effective contraception depends on the ability of the partners to work out together their problems of adjustment, a measure of "cooperativeness" was included.

It is necessary to reiterate here a consideration mentioned several times in earlier chapters. The study design by confining the sample to couples with two children automatically excludes couples who remain childless or who have only one child. It may be that such low fertility couples would be selective also with respect to certain personality characteristics, social mobility patterns, or other variables included in the study. The various hypotheses being tested, therefore, must be viewed in the context of the type of couples and experience studied.

The following chapters are ordered according to the organization of variables presented in this chapter. The next two chapters will examine the influence on fertility of religion and religiousness. These will be followed by two chapters on socio-economic status and social mobility, two chapters on the family, one chapter each on residence and the personality variables, and a summary multivariate analysis.

Chapter XI. Religion, Class, and Fertility[1]

The two dimensions of the socio-cultural environment of greatest presumed significance for fertility are religion and social class. The concept of religious affiliation implies a system of values which can affect family size via several routes: (a) by imposing sanctions on the practice of birth control or legitimizing the practice of less effective methods only; or, (b) by indoctrinating its members with a moral and social philosophy of marriage and family which emphasizes the virtues of reproduction. To these effects can be added others of a more subtle nature, such as the greater solidarity of the family which characterizes certain religious cultures more than others and the degree of "other worldliness" associated with the particular religion.

Social class, although perhaps even more subtle in its relation to fertility than is religion, also presents greater problems of definition. While there is a lack of consensus among sociologists on a standard definition, there seems to be little disagreement about what components are involved. Most would agree, for example, that "social class" incorporates income, occupation, and education as a minimum. Although there may be merit in other types of research in conceiving class as a sociological reality transcending the various combinations of these individual characteristics, a survey of the present type could easily sidestep the whole issue, confine the analysis to relationships involving the specific components and omit use of the term "class" altogether. However, for reasons that will be evident as we proceed, it is convenient to summarize this dimension in occupational terms and refer to the white-collar and blue-collar classes. This admittedly crude dichotomy does not preclude a subsequently more refined analysis of occupation, income, and education but is intended simply to index the phenomenon of differential life chances.

In view of the theoretical importance of religion and class and the body of supporting evidence from previous research,[2] a decision was reached to use these two dimensions as statistical controls throughout most of the analysis. Each religious group, subdivided into white- and blue-collar classes, can be viewed as a particular subculture of American society. However crude a distinction it may be, the class dichotomy to some extent separates the population into two groups

[1] Part of the contents of this chapter were described in an earlier publication: Charles F. Westoff, "Religion and Fertility in Metropolitan America," in *Thirty Years of Research in Human Fertility: Retrospect and Prospect*, Milbank Memorial Fund, New York, 1959.
[2] See especially Ronald Freedman, P. K. Whelpton, and Arthur Campbell, *Family Planning, Sterility and Population Growth*, McGraw-Hill, New York, 1959; and P. K. Whelpton and Clyde V. Kiser, eds., *Social and Psychological Factors Affecting Fertility*, 5 Vols., Milbank Memorial Fund, New York, 1946–1958, i, Nos. I and II.

presumed to differ significantly in modal styles of life and resources which, in turn, are conceived to set limits on the compatibility of children with other values and interests.

RELIGION

The association between religion and fertility can be subdivided into two specific aspects, one the effects of religious preference or affiliation, and two, the effects of the degree of religious interest independent of church preference. The latter aspect is reserved for the next chapter. In connection with the former, our expectations are that Catholics, in general, would be characterized by a high fertility pattern—that is, preferences for larger families, a record of shorter birth intervals, and a history of unsuccessful fertility planning resulting partly from ineffective contraceptive practice but mostly from a low psychological availability of contraception. Jewish couples, in contrast, are expected to be at the opposite end of this scale and Protestants intermediate between the two. This general hypothesis is consistent, in part, with findings reported in several previous studies.[3]

CLASSIFICATION BY RELIGION AND NUMBER OF CHILDREN DESIRED

The sample divides into over a third Protestant, nearly a half Catholic, a tenth Jewish, and the remaining four or five per cent who report some other or no religious preference. The proportion of Catholics and Jews is considerably higher than in the national population[4] because the sample is confined to the white population of the largest metropolitan areas. One effect of this restriction is that the more fundamentalist Protestant sects found in the southern and rural parts of the country are not represented in the sample.

Although the distributions by religion are the same for wives and husbands, there is a significant proportion of marriages involving

[3] See, for example: Freedman, Whelpton, and Campbell, *Family Planning, Sterility and Population Growth*; Whelpton and Kiser, *Social and Psychological Factors Affecting Fertility*, Nos. I and II; Ronald Freedman and Harry Sharp, "Correlates of Values about Ideal Family Size in the Detroit Metropolitan Area," *Population Studies*, VIII, (1954), pp. 35–45; Ben B. Seligman and Aaron Antonovsky, "Some Aspects of Jewish Demography," in Marshall Sklare, ed., *The Jews: Social Patterns of an American Group*, Free Press, Glencoe, Ill., 1958, pp. 45–93; David Goldberg and Harry Sharp, "Some Characteristics of Detroit Area Jewish and Non-Jewish Adults," *ibid.*, pp. 107–118; Bernard Mulvaney, "How Catholics and Non-Catholics Differ in Fertility," *American Catholic Sociological Review*, VII, (June 1946), pp. 124–127; Erwin S. Solomon, "Social Characteristics and Fertility: A Study of Two Religious Groups in Metropolitan New York," *Eugenics Quarterly*, 3 (June 1956) pp. 100–103; Dudley Kirk, "Recent Trends of Catholic Fertility in the United States," in *Current Research in Human Fertility*, Milbank Memorial Fund, New York, 1955, pp. 93–105.

[4] U.S. Bureau of the Census, *Current Population Reports—Population Characteristics*, Series P-20, No. 79 (February 2, 1958).

different religions. Restricting the comparisons to the three major religious preferences, approximately 13 per cent of the respondents had married across religious lines. This proportion was highest for the Protestants (14 per cent) and lowest for the Jews (4 per cent) while the Catholic rate of exogamous marriages fell just below the Protestant (13 per cent). This incidence of mixed marriage argues for an analysis of fertility variations by a classification of the religion of the couple rather than that of the individual parent.

The average total number of children desired by the wife is presented in Table 38 for each of the various major religious classifications. In this classification the Protestant-Catholic marriages

TABLE 38

Number of Children Desired by Wives, by Religious Preference of Couple

Religious Preference	Mean Number of Children Desired	Number of Wives
Both Protestant	3.0	369
Both Catholic	3.6	480
Both Jewish	2.7	116
Wife Protestant, Husband Catholic	3.1	58
Wife Catholic, Husband Protestant	3.2	54
Other	2.9	88
All couples	3.3	1,165

(constituting 86 per cent of all mixed marriages) have been sub-divided by the religion of each spouse. Two conclusions emerge from analyses of the differences among the means of the five groupings. A comparison of the three major religious categories confirms the hypothesis that in Catholic marriages the wives want the largest families (3.6 children) and in Jewish families the average family-size preference is the lowest (2.7), with the Protestant couples intermediate (3.0). The differences between the three pairs of means are statistically significant.[5] The husband's family-size preferences follow a similar pattern except that the Protestant and Jewish averages are slightly closer together.[6]

[5] An application of the *t* test for the significance of difference between means of independent samples reveals *p* values of less than .001 for the Catholic–Protestant and Catholic–Jewish comparisons and of .02 for the Protestant–Jewish comparison.

[6] The measure of number of children desired by the wife includes an adjustment for the intensity of her preferences. Thus, a woman who replied that she wanted at least 3 children but perhaps 4 was scored as 3.5. A woman who was definitely sure that she wanted 3 children, no more and no less, was given a score of 3.0. Data secured from the husband did not include this qualification, so that in a rigorous statistical sense the measures for wives and husbands are not strictly comparable.

The second conclusion is that the two types of Protestant-Catholic marriages are virtually indistinguishable with respect to number of children desired.[7] In anticipation of this possibility, the following question was asked in all cases of mixed marriages where either the wife or the husband was Catholic: "Were you married by a Catholic priest?" By the response to this question we hoped to be able to classify the marriage as Catholic or non-Catholic on the assumption that marriage in the Church reflects the dominance of the values of the Catholic partner. Of the total 140 Catholic individuals married to a non-Catholic, 86 reported having been married by a priest, including one woman who was initially married in a civil ceremony and was subsequently remarried in the Church. Marriage by a priest was almost twice as frequent among couples where the wife was the Catholic.

Although a persuasive argument could be advanced on *a priori* grounds for grouping mixed marriages involving a Catholic married in the Church with the Catholic marriages and, conversely, grouping the other mixed marriage category with the Protestant marriages, more empirical evidence was sought. The average family-size preferences of wives in the two types of mixed marriages were compared (see Table 39) and found to be significantly different. Further

TABLE 39

Number of Children Desired by Wives in Catholic–non-Catholic
Marriages, by Type of Marriage Ceremony

Type of Marriage Ceremony	Mean Number of Children Desired	Number of Wives
Married by a priest	3.3	86
Not married by a priest	3.0	54

analysis revealed no significant difference between the family size preferred by wives in mixed marriages not performed by a priest and the exclusively Protestant marriages. The final comparison, however, did indicate average family-size preferences for the mixed marriages performed by a priest to be significantly lower than the exclusively Catholic marriages.

One further question remained before developing a final classification of religion: do the various Protestant denominations differ with respect to family-size preferences?[8] If so, the logic of an

[7] The difference between these two means is not statistically significant.

[8] For a similar analysis, see Ronald Freedman, and P. K. Whelpton, "Fertility Planning and Fertility Rates by Religious Interest and Denomination", Whelpton and Kiser, *Social and Psychological Factors Affecting Fertility*, II, pp. 417–466.

all-Protestant classification could be seriously questioned. There are five denominations of sufficient frequency to be analyzed separately: Baptists, Episcopalians, Lutherans, Methodists, and Presbyterians. A sixth grouping was formed by combining Unitarians, Congregationalists, and Evangelical sects, and a residual category represented the seventh grouping.[9] The mean family-size preferences of all seven of these groupings ranged only between 2.8 and 3.1 children desired, with the result that the hypothesis of heterogeneity was rejected.

The net result of these findings was to classify the total sample into four religious subgroups: (1) Protestant marriages, including marriages of Protestants with Catholics not performed by a priest (41 per cent); (2) Catholic–non-Catholic marriages performed by a priest (7 per cent); (3) Catholic marriages (41 per cent); and (4) Jewish marriages (11 per cent).[10]

FERTILITY PLANNING AND BIRTH INTERVALS

Thus far in the analysis, the only dependent variable considered has been the total number of children desired by the parents. Of equal if not greater significance is the extent to which the couple has evidenced control over conception. This variable is represented in this analysis by a measure labeled "fertility-planning success," an index ordering couples from those whose pregnancies were both unintentionally conceived to couples who reported both pregnancies as planned. Couples who planned the second but not the first pregnancy were ranked higher on this scale than those whose history revealed the opposite pattern.

Of more immediate demographic interest than either family-size preferences or fertility-planning control is the actual time taken to have a given number of children—an index of some predictive value for completed family size. The interval between births reflects at least both the number of children desired and the effectiveness of contraceptive control. The two other major components are fecundity

---

[9] The proportion of Protestant marriages with wife and husband of the same denomination is 78 per cent.

[10] These four categories were not sufficient to classify all 1,165 couples in the sample, leaving 74 couples unassigned who belonged to other religions, stated no religious preference, or were in other types of mixed marriages. Rather than eliminating these couples from subsequent analyses or grouping them in a single residual category, they were assigned to one of the above four groupings according to various criteria: couples with a religious preference other than the major three were assigned with Protestants; couples expressing no religious preference were assigned on the basis of their responses to a question on their religious background; and couples in other mixed marriages were generally assigned by the religion of the wife.

and preferences for child-spacing. Since all couples in this sample have two children, the data relate to the interval between marriage and the first birth and the interval between the first and second births. The sum of the two intervals constitutes marriage duration for these couples.

Collectively, these variables of family-size preferences of both wife and husband, their past record of fertility-planning success, and the length of time taken to have their two children presumably constitute the best information available at this stage regarding these couples' probable future fertility performance.

The general hypothesis is the same as stated previously for family-size preferences: Catholics are expected to exhibit the highest fertility pattern (less successful planning and shorter intervals), Protestants intermediate, and Jews the lowest, with the mixed Catholic marriages between Catholics and Protestants.

One of the causes and perhaps the main factor accounting for higher levels of Catholic fertility in general is the unavailability of the more effective methods of family limitation to Catholics. This is not to deny the potential effectiveness of periodic continence but simply that, as currently practiced, this method results in more unplanned pregnancies than many chemical and mechanical methods. The result of a doctrine which proscribes the use of more effective contraception is evident from the proportions of couples planning fertility successfully (Table 40). The Catholic groups exhibit the least and the Jews

TABLE 40

Number of Children Desired, Fertility-Planning Success, and Number of Months from Marriage to Second Birth, by Religious Preference

Religious Preference	*Mean Number of Children Desired*		*Per Cent Successful Planners*[b]	*Mean Number of Months from Marriage to Second Birth*	Number of Couples
	Wives[a]	Husbands			
Protestant	3.0	2.8	60%	60	388
Mixed Catholic	3.3	3.4	53	61	70
Catholic	3.6	3.6	52	57	370
Jewish	2.8	2.9	84	72	110
All couples	3.2	3.2	59	60	938

[a] The means vary slightly from those in Table 38 because of the difference in the sample, being based on the 938 couples returning mail questionnaires. The evidence for regarding this subsample as representative of the total is presented in Chapter II.

[b] "Successful planning" is defined as planning either the second or both pregnancies successfully.

the most successful planning (the very high proportion of 84 per cent classified as successful) with Protestants again generally intermediate, although tending to approximate Catholics more closely than Jews. The mixed Catholic group shows the same proportion as the Catholic subsample.

The analysis of birth intervals by religion also confirms the general fertility hypothesis. The extremes are again Catholics and Jews, with averages of 57 and 72 months respectively taken to have two children (Table 40). And, again, Protestants are much closer to the typical Catholic than to the Jewish experience.

OCCUPATION

The second dimension of the socio-cultural environment of traditional interest in the analysis of differential fertility is social class. As noted earlier, this dimension is indexed in the present study by a classification of the sample into white-collar and blue-collar occupational classes. Before this classification system was decided upon, the more refined occupational groupings were examined to determine whether such a crude dichotomy would be obscuring variations in family-size preferences. The general expectation was that couples with the husband in a higher occupational category would prefer larger families. This hypothesis was derived from the observations of the changing relationship between class and actual fertility that has characterized the postwar baby boom. It was further expected that this type of association would prevail independently of religious preference. This is equivalent to expecting a cumulative increase in the explanation of the variation in family-size preferences from a knowledge of occupation over and above that accounted for by religion alone.

The average number of children desired by the wife, classified by her husband's usual occupation, is presented in Table 41, for each religious group. There is hardly any variation among the eight occupational classes in the total sample. Analyses of variance reveal no significant association between desired family size, except within the Catholic group. Here there does seem to be a pattern of larger family orientations in white-collar classes, particularly for wives whose husbands are in the three highest occupational categories. It is clear from an examination of the means in Table 41, where frequencies permit comparisons, that the variations among the religious groupings present the same pattern within occupational class as for the total sample.

Although the comparable statistics for fertility-planning success and interval between marriage and the second birth are not repro-

TABLE 41

Mean Number of Children Desired by Wives, by Husband's Usual
Occupation within Each Religious Grouping

Occupational Class	Total Sample	Religious Preference			
		Protestant	Mixed Catholic	Catholic	Jewish
Professional	3.4	3.1	*	4.0	3.0
Managerial, Official, and Proprietary	3.3	3.0	*	4.0	2.6
Sales	3.3	3.0	*	4.0	2.9
Clerical	3.4	2.9	*	3.7	*
Skilled	3.3	2.9	3.6	3.6	*
Semiskilled	3.1	2.9	*	3.4	*
Service	3.2	*	*	3.6	*
Unskilled	3.4	*	*	3.4	–
White-Collar total	3.3	3.0	3.3	3.8	2.8
Blue-Collar total	3.2	2.9	3.4	3.5	2.7
All couples	3.3	3.0	3.3	3.6	2.8

NOTE:
    Asterisk indicates frequency of under 20. The frequencies on which means have been computed in this table can be inferred from Table 42.

duced in the tables for reasons of economy, the same generalization applies. There is some slight evidence of association for Protestants but this is a matter mostly of the occupational extremes, that is, the professional class compared to the semiskilled class reveals a higher proportion of planners and a longer (ten months) interval. The intermediate occupational classes exhibit no significant differences. Among Catholics, the various occupational categories might just as well be random subsamples of the total Catholic sample in so far as these two fertility indicators are concerned. The same conclusion holds for the Jewish sample.

In view of the lack of any systematic and convincing fertility differences by occupation, the decision to simplify the subsequent analyses by dichotomizing occupational class into white-collar and blue-collar categories does not imply loss of information. The following section deals with the relationship of this dimension with religion and fertility.

CLASS, RELIGION, AND FERTILITY

The association between occupation and religion is the logical point of departure in this analysis. As the distributions of occupational

TABLE 42

Class of Husband's Usual Occupation, by Couple's Religion

Occupational Class	Per Cent Distribution				
	Total Sample	Protestant	Mixed Catholic	Catholic	Jewish
Professional	19%	23%	14%	13%	34%
Managerial, Official and Proprietary	10	9	9	7	25
Sales	10	10	8	9	18
Clerical	9	7	9	13	5
Skilled	26	27	29	29	9
Semiskilled	18	19	21	19	7
Service	4	2	5	5	2
Unskilled	4	3	5	5	–
Per cent total	100	100	100	100	100
Number	1,165	473	86	481	125
White-collar class proportion	49	49	41	42	82
Blue-collar class proportion	51	51	59	58	18

class by religion (Table 42) reveal, there are a number of clearly evident variations among the religious groupings. The outstanding contrast is the concentration of Jews in the white-collar classes, especially in the professional and managerial–official–proprietary classes. And although less pronounced, there are higher proportions of Catholics in the blue-collar occupations.

The following analysis poses two questions: (1) how much of the variance of the dependent variables can be accounted for by religion and class together; and (2) which of the two is the better predictor, religion or class? The general hypothesis is the same as stated previously: Catholics are expected to exhibit a high fertility pattern, Protestants intermediate, Jews the lowest, with the Mixed Catholic marriages averaging between Catholics and Protestants. Within each of these four religious groupings, the white-collar class is expected to reveal slightly higher fertility indications. The comparative influence of religion and class was not developed as a hypothesis but was left as an open question.

Turning first to desired family size, the same general pattern of association with religion and class is evident for both wives and husbands (Table 43). It is apparent that both Catholic wives and husbands express preferences for the largest families, while Protestant

TABLE 43

Number of Children Desired by Wives and Husbands, by Religion and Class

Religious Preference	Wives			Husbands		
	White-Collar	Blue-Collar	Total	White-Collar	Blue-Collar	Total
Protestant	3.0	2.9	3.0	2.9	2.8	2.8
Mixed Catholic	3.2	3.4	3.3	3.4	3.4	3.4
Catholic	3.8	3.5	3.6	3.7	3.5	3.6
Jewish	2.8	2.7	2.8	2.9	2.9	2.9
All couples	3.3	3.2	3.2	3.2	3.2	3.2

and Jewish spouses desire equally small families. Analysis of variance reveals highly significant differences among the eight independent subgroups for both wives and husbands, with correlation ratios indicating 11 and 12 per cent of the variances of family-size preferences (for wives and husbands respectively) accounted for by the joint classification of religion and class. However, it is clear even from these averages that the variation among the four religious groupings is greater than that between the two classes.

As noted earlier, the Catholic groups exhibit the least, and the Jews the most, effective planning, while the Protestants are generally intermediate, although tending to approximate Catholics more than Jews (Table 44). The Jewish group shows a very high proportion (two-thirds) of couples who have planned both pregnancies. Comparing these proportions by class within religious preference groupings again reveals smaller differences, with couples in the white-

TABLE 44

Fertility-Planning Success and Number of Months from Marriage to Second Birth, by Religion and Class

Religious Preference	Per Cent Successful Planners			Mean Number of Months from Marriage to Second Birth		
	White-Collar	Blue-Collar	Total	White-Collar	Blue-Collar	Total
Protestant	66	54	60	63	57	60
Mixed Catholic	57	50	53	63	59	61
Catholic	49	54	52	54	59	57
Jewish	85	76	84	71	76	72
All couples	64	55	59	62	59	60

collar classes tending to plan more successfully. The magnitude of this association is very low, however, and among Catholics the tendency is reversed. Together, religion and class account for 5 per cent of the variance in fertility planning.

The final fertility variable to be examined in the context of both class and religion is the time taken to have two births. As the averages in the second half of Table 44 indicate, the same pattern of association obtains as for family-size preferences and fertility-planning success. That the Jewish couples take the longest time to have children and that Catholics tend to have births earlier and closer together is to be expected from the group differences in number of children desired and fertility-planning success. Again the class difference is less than the variations among religious groups; the two factors together account for 3 per cent of the total variance of the interval.

Thus far the generalization which emerges from analyzing the variations of these fertility indicators with religion and class is that religion is by far the more important factor. In order to evaluate this more precisely, a series of chi-square tests for significance of differences were conducted in which religion and class are respectively varied and held constant. The results are presented (Table 45) in the

TABLE 45

Association[a] of Religion and Class with Number of Children Desired, Fertility-Planning Success, and Birth Intervals

Religion and Class	Number of Children Desired		Fertility Planning Success	Birth Interval		
	Wives	Husbands		First	Second	Total
Varying religion:						
Total	.37	.39	.26	.26	.19	.24
Within white-collar class	.45	.42	.33	.31	.24	.32
Within blue-collar class	.31	.39	NS	NS	NS	NS
Varying class:						
Total	NS	NS	.12	NS	NS	.12
Among Protestants	NS	NS	NS	NS	NS	NS
Among Mixed Catholics	NS	NS	NS	NS	NS	NS
Among Catholics	.20	NS	NS	NS	NS	NS
Among Jews	NS	NS	NS	NS	NS	NS

[a] Pearson's coefficient of contingency adjusted to a scale varying from zero to one. The chi-squares for religion are based on 4×4 classifications; for class, on 2×4 classifications. In the latter instance, the correction of the contingency coefficient is based on the arbitrary assumption of the ceiling for a 3×3 classification. The designation NS means not statistically significant at the .05 level. All values for religion are significant beyond the .001 level except the four designated NS and the two for the second interval which are significant at the .01 level. The three contingency coefficients appearing for class are significant between the .01 and .05 levels.

form of coefficients of contingency computed only where significant differences exist. The results appear to be very clear-cut. Of the 10 independent[11] tests with religion varied, 7 produce chi-square values significant at the .001 level. In contrast only 1 of the 20 tests in which class is varied reveals a significant association.

The Organization Man and the Entrepreneur

Another type of analysis performed relates to occupational class, except that interest lies primarily in the effect on fertility of type of employment rather than occupation itself. Type of employment can be classified crudely into: (1) self-employed; (2) employee in a large organization; (3) employee in a smaller organization. Each of these types, in turn, can be subclassified by occupation, but this is mainly for purposes of control.

The theoretical connection of type of employment with fertility derives from assumptions about the nature of security differentiating self-employment from employment with a large corporation. For a man to go into business today, or if a professional, into private practice, requires at least initially a great deal more effort, sacrifice, and risk than enlisting in the salaried ranks of the big firm or government with its visible ladder of advancement, salary increments, insurance provisions, and all the other miscellaneous fringe benefits. Individualistic competition still exists in certain respects, but it is dulled by the group psychology which characterizes so many activities[12] and is certainly far weaker than in the competitive milieu of small business.

If this is a reasonably valid characterization, and if fertility behavior responds to differences in perceptions of security, then we should expect smaller family preferences, more effective fertility planning, and longer birth intervals for couples where the husband is self-employed. At the opposite end of the scale would be families in which the husband works for a large-scale organization, and intermediate, those connected with smaller organizations.

As revealed in Table 46, such a pattern does prevail for the white-collar classes but the differences are slight. The same differences

[11] Excluding totals.

[12] See William H. Whyte, Jr., *The Organization Man*, Simon and Schuster, New York, 1957, for provocative speculations about the changing ideological climate from an individualistic to a group ethos accompanying the development and spread of the large corporation, and Reinhard Bendix, *Work and Authority in Industry*, Wiley, New York, 1956, for a systematic review of the history of managerial ideologies. See also Daniel R. Miller and Guy E. Swanson, *The Changing American Parent*, Wiley, New York, Chapman and Hall, London, 1958.

TABLE 46

Number of Children Desired, Extent of Successful Fertility-Planning, and Number of Months from Marriage to Second Birth, by Type of Employment and Occupational Class

Type of employment[a] and Occupational Class	Mean Number of Children Desired		Per Cent Successful Planners	Mean Number of Months from Marriage to Second Birth	Number of Couples
	Wives	Husbands			
White-collar class:					
Self-employed	3.1	3.1	83%	67	65
Small organization employees	3.3	3.2	61	64	179
Large organization employees	3.3	3.3	60	59	204
Blue-collar class:					
Self-employed	3.2	3.4	61	60	33
Small organization employees	3.2	3.1	52	59	249
Large organization employees	3.3	3.2	58	60	179

[a] Large organizations defined as those with at least 1,000 employees. Data were derived from husbands' reports.

obtain when occupation is held constant in more detail, with comparisons made between salaried and free professionals, as well as between the self-employed and the managerial executives, salesmen, and other white-collar workers. The most extreme comparison is between the self-employed and the managers in large-scale organizations. The wives of the self-employed desire 2.9 children on the average as compared to the 3.5 children preferred by the wives of executives. For husbands themselves, the averages are 2.8 and 3.3 respectively. The most striking contrast lies in the extent of successful fertility planning, with 88 per cent of couples in the self-employed group reporting that either their last or both births were planned compared to 56 per cent among the executive group. The interval between marriage and the second birth is in the same direction, with the self-employed group averaging 69 months and the executive class 59 months to have two births. Similarly, the fertility indices are intermediate for the smaller organization occupational classes.

At first glance, the hypothesis would seem to be confirmed (in direction if not impressive magnitude) among the white-collar class at least. Partly as a routine check and partly in order to understand the absence of similar differences within the blue-collar class, the religious composition of these categories was examined. The tabulation revealed a very high concentration of Jews (43 per cent) in the self-employed, white-collar class, and a low proportion of Catholics (22 per cent). White-collar employees, however, were distributed by religion in about the same proportions as in the total sample. This factor could easily account for the slight fertility differences noted, an observation strengthened by the fact that the religious composition of type of employment categories within the blue-collar class showed no differences.

Summary and Evaluation

In summary, the conclusion seems inescapable that religion exerts a strong influence on fertility. Moreover, the comparative influence of class appears negligible. However, the association between religion and these fertility variables is consistently higher within the white-collar class. This phenomenon was thought to arise partly from the fact that the Jewish couples, whose fertility experience deviates so radically from the rest of the sample, are predominantly (82 per cent) in the white-collar class. This hypothesis was rejected when a comparison of the contributions of the Jewish group to the statistical association revealed no class difference for any of the fertility variables. The comparison did confirm the observation, however, that the Jews are primarily responsible for the association of religion with fertility-planning success and marriage duration (contributing about 60 per cent of the association in each case) and that the Catholics, particularly white-collar class Catholics, are mainly responsible for the association of religion with the wives' and husbands' family-size preferences (slightly over 60 per cent in each case).

The following generalizations can be advanced at this stage about the associations among religion, class, and the fertility indices:

1. The family-size preferences of the most common form of mixed marriage—the Protestant-Catholic marriage—cannot be determined from a knowledge of which spouse is Catholic. However, whether the marriage was performed by a Catholic priest does provide a basis for differentiation. Such marriages if not performed by a priest cannot be distinguished in the fertility sense from marriage in which both spouses are Protestant. Conversely, in mixed marriages performed by a Catholic priest, the wife's family-size orientations were significantly higher than Protestants, but were lower than in the purely Catholic marriages.

2. Religion is clearly a better predictor than class.[13] For all

[13] On the whole, a similar generalization emerges from the analyses reported in Freedman, Whelpton, and Campbell.

comparisons, the hypothesis of a rank ordering of Catholics, Protestants, and Jews in that order with preferences for larger families, less success in planning, and shorter intervals is confirmed. The hypothesis of class differences is rejected with only minor qualifications.

3. The Jews deviate from the total sample norm of fertility-planning success and marriage duration more than any other religious group and they account for most of the observed associations.

4. Although Catholics and Protestants behave more similarly in their fertility planning and the length of interval between marriage and the second child, Protestants and Jews are more alike in the number of children they desire. For this variable, the Catholics deviate more from the norm in their desires for larger families. This observation, however, obtains only for the white-collar classes.

5. Thus, although religion accounts for more of the variation in the fertility variables than does class, the magnitude of the association is consistently higher in the white-collar class (Table 45), a phenomenon which cannot be dismissed as an artifact of the class composition of the different religions.

6. In view of the increasing proportion of persons employed by large-scale organizations, and in line with recent speculations about the social-psychological character of the large organization, a number of hypotheses about fertility were derived and tested. As hypothesized, patterns of lower fertility appeared in the self-employed class and higher fertility among employees of larger organizations, but only among white-collar occupational groups. Even this conclusion, however, appears to be at least partly a function of religious composition.

The apparently negligible influence of occupational class on fertility as compared with the effects of religion raises a question about the continued use of the class factor in subsequent correlational analyses. All of the correlations in this study were originally computed within each of the eight independent subsamples defined by cross-classification of the four religious groupings with the occupational class dichotomy. The decision was reached to retain the class division in spite of the above findings because: (1) class has traditionally been regarded as substantively important in fertility studies; (2) the absence of differences in univariate distributions carries no necessary implications for covariation or correlation; and (3) although, for the most part, a theory of the social and psychological bases of fertility is not sufficiently developed from which to derive hypotheses about differences in correlations among substrata of the population, the analysis is conceived to have a hypothesis-producing as well as a hypothesis-testing function. The longitudinal design of the study is especially well suited for further exploration of such hypotheses that are suggested.

The question actually reduces to whether the detailed correlational values for the class subdivisions of the religious groupings should be reproduced in the tables. In the following chapters, such detail is not usually included, primarily because consideration of the class factor does not change interpretation. This conclusion is based on the results of systematic statistical tests of the homogeneity of correlational values throughout the subsamples. This generalization does not, of course, preclude subsequent consideration of this factor in other contexts.

Chapter XII. Religiousness

Thus far the analysis of religion has focused on the ways in which identification with a major religious affiliation affects fertility. Within any religious grouping, however, there is considerable individual variation in the degree of formal and informal religious observances and in the level of psychological commitment to the ideologies and values associated with the particular religion. In short, people vary in degree of religiousness whether they be Catholic, Protestant, or Jewish. Some Catholics attend religious service more than others, some Protestants take religion more seriously than others, and for some Jews religion imposes a powerful focus on their daily activities while for others it is only a weak cultural identification. The main implication of this consideration is that some part of the variation of fertility *within* each major religious category may be associated with degree of religiousness.

MEASURES OF RELIGIOUSNESS

An immediate problem of conceptualization and measurement arises when the question is posed about the meaning of religion to persons of different religious persuasions. For example, frequency of church attendance is relevant for Catholics and measures, as a minimum, their adherence to the formal requirements of the Catholic church. For non-Catholics, however, church attendance may have quite a different meaning. Two thirds of the Catholics in this sample report attending religious services outside the home at least once a week, whereas less than a quarter of the Protestants and under 2 per cent of the Jews claim weekly attendance.[1] Certainly it cannot be inferred directly from these marked differences in frequency of church attendance that Protestants and Jews are less religious than Catholics. A more plausible conclusion is that the institutional requirements of the three religions are different.

This problem requires additional measures of religious orientation. Two other scales have been developed. The first, labelled "informal religious orientation," combines information from two questions, one on the extent to which religion is included in the home activities of the family and the other the self-rating of the wife on a scale of religious-mindedness apart from attendance at religious services.[2]

[1] Women report more frequent attendance for themselves than for their husbands except among the Jewish group.

[2] Although this index correlates with the frequency of church attendance, the magnitude is .45, which means that other factors certainly are being tapped as well.

194

In addition to this index of informal religious orientation, the wife was asked another series of questions that attempt to measure her perception of the importance of spiritual and religious values in comparison to secular values. The questions, in an abbreviated form of paired comparisons, asked her to choose between religious values and such competing values as politics, literary interests, and economic security, admiration, romantic themes, and others.

Altogether, therefore, there are three different though overlapping[3] measures of religious values: formal practice or attendance at religious services outside the home; informal observances within the home; and a measure of personal commitment to religious values.

RELIGIOUSNESS AND THE FERTILITY INDICES

The hypotheses originally formulated are that religious couples would desire larger families, and that their fertility history would be characterized by less successful fertility planning and shorter birth intervals. These relationships were hypothesized to persist for each church preference.

Correlations of the number of children desired by wives and husbands with frequency of church attendance, informal religious orientation, and religiosity all reveal a positive association (see Table 47). However, the correlations within each religious group

TABLE 47

Correlations between Measures of Religiousness and Number of Children Desired, by Religion[a]

Religious Preference	Correlations between Number of Children Desired by Wife and:			Correlations between Number of Children Desired by Husband and:	
	Frequency of Church Attendance	Informal Religious Orientation	Religiosity	Frequency of Church Attendance	Informal Religious Orientation
Protestant total	.05	.04	.02	.06	−.03
Mixed Catholic total	.18	.20	.28	.16	.14
Catholic total	.30	.22	.27	.19	.19
Jewish total	−.13	.14	.08	.04	.17
All couples	.29	.19	.20	.27	.15

[a] The correlations among the four independent subsamples differ significantly for wife's church attendance, wife's religiosity score, and husband's informal religious orientation.

[3] The correlation between wife's frequency of church attendance and the index of religiosity is .36 for the total sample.

fail to support the hypothesis that the relationship is equally relevant for all religions. There is no association at all among Protestants, while the highest values emerge among Catholics and Mixed Catholics for all measures of religiousness. The relationship between the wife's regularity of church attendance and the number of children she wants to have is inversely related for Jewish women, although other measures of religiosity indicate a positive association. This may reflect the selection of women with stronger extrafamilial interests in church activities.[4] All values for the Jewish group, however, fall short of being significantly different from zero.

Findings of previous research tend to be consistent with these findings, although the studies differ in important respects. Freedman, Whelpton, and Campbell report that the Catholic wives in their national sample who attend church regularly expect more births than those who seldom go to church. The "most likely expected total births" for the regular church-goers among the youngest Catholic wives—those 18 to 24 years old when interviewed—is 50 per cent higher than for those reporting infrequent church attendance.[5] Less pronounced differences were observed among older Catholic wives. They report no differences in expected fertility by church attendance among Protestants. Freedman and Whelpton, in an earlier analysis, report only negligible associations between religious interest and fertility among the Protestant Indianapolis sample.[6] Coogan, in his study of Catholic fertility in Florida,[7] reports a positive though only slight association between regularity of church attendance and actual fertility, but finds the magnitude of the association increases when the regularity of reception of communion is used as an index of religiousness. And Brooks and Henry, in a more recent analysis of Catholic fertility,[8] report a correlation of .15 between a scale on Catholic practice and fertility with some diminution following the introduction of controls. It is important to reemphasize that the comparatively strong correlations evidenced for religiousness among Catholics (Table

[4] This interpretation is advanced by Maria Davidson in an unpublished doctoral dissertation, "Predictors of Fertility," submitted to New York University in 1960.

[5] The actual values are 4.2 as compared to 2.8 "most likely" expected total births. See Ronald Freedman, P. K. Whelpton, and Arthur Campbell, *Family Planning, Sterility and PopulationGrowth*, McGraw-Hill, New York, 1959, pp. 281–283.

[6] Ronald Freedman and P. K. Whelpton, "Fertility Planning and Fertility Rates by Religious Interest and Denominations," in Kiser and Whelpton, eds., *Social and Psychological Factors Affecting Fertility*, 5 vols., Milbank Memorial Fund, New York (1950) II, pp. 417–466.

[7] Thomas Francis Coogan, *Catholic Fertility in Florida. Differential Fertility Among 4,891 Florida Catholic Families*, Catholic University of America Press, Washington, 1946.

[8] Hugh E. Brooks and Franklin J. Henry, "An Empirical Study of the Relationships of Catholic Practice and Occupational Mobility to Fertility," Milbank Memorial Fund *Quarterly*, XXXVI, No. 3, (July 1958), pp. 222–277.

TABLE 48

Correlations between Measures of Religiousness and Fertility-Planning
Success, by Religion[a]

RELIGIOUS PREFERENCE	CORRELATIONS BETWEEN FERTILITY-PLANNING SUCCESS AND:			
	Church Attendance		Informal Religious Orientation	Index of Religiosity
	Wife	Husband		
Protestant total	.15	.14	.11	.02
Mixed Catholic total	−.09	−.07	−.12	−.07
Catholic total	−.09	−.14	.11	−.10
Jewish total	.23	.17	.35	.09
All couples	−.07	−.07	−.01	−.09

[a] The correlations among the four independent subsamples vary significantly for wife's and husband's church attendance and informal religious orientation.

47) refer to number of children reported as *desired* and not actual fertility.

In summary, the more general part of the hypothesis is unsupported. Even with measures of religiousness other than church attendance, the hypothesized direct association with family-size desires is evident only for the Catholic families.

The same type of analysis is repeated for fertility-planning success (Table 48) and the interval between marriage and the birth of the second child (Table 49). With regard to interval, no correlations of magnitudes worth mentioning are evident. Nor do any of the measures of religiousness correlate with fertility-planning success for the total

TABLE 49

Correlations between Measures of Religiousness and Number of Months
from Marriage to Second Birth, by Religion[a]

Religious Preference	Church Attendance		Informal Religious Orientation	Index of Religiosity
	Wife	Husband		
Protestant total	.07	.05	.13	.00
Mixed Catholic total	.06	−.07	−.02	−.04
Catholic total	.03	−.05	−.02	−.18
Jewish total	−.06	−.11	−.04	.08
All couples	−.04	−.07	.01	−.11

[a] The correlations among the four independent subsamples vary significantly for the index of religiosity.

sample. However, when the religious groupings are examined separately (Table 48), it is clear that the absence of association for the total sample is due to opposite types of relationships among Protestants and Jews in contrast to the Catholic groups. Although the values differ in magnitude, the more religious Protestants and Jews tend to be successful planners, while for the Catholic groups religiousness is negatively associated with fertility-planning success.

Freedman, Whelpton, and Campbell report a similar type of association between regularity of church attendance and the use of contraception. Among Protestant wives the association is positive while among Catholic wives regularity of church attendance is associated with lesser use of contraception.[9] They observe a similar pattern of association with attitude toward family limitation[10] and report considerably greater use of the less effective rhythm method among the more devout Catholics.[11] Their data did not permit analysis of internal differences among Jews.

That religious Catholics should tend to be less successful planners is a plausible extension of the implications of the Catholic position on family planning. But why the obverse for Protestants and Jews? (Actually, the positive correlations are much higher for Jews than for Protestants.)

One possible explanation is that the more religious Protestants and Jews tend to be more highly educated and it is this component which explains the observed direct association of religiousness and fertility-planning success. In the process of testing this hypothesis, positive correlations were found for both Jews and Protestants between education and both religiousness and fertility-planning success. However, these values were not high enough to explain the initial correlations; partial correlations revealed hardly any diminution of the original associations between religiousness and fertility-planning success.[12]

One explanation that could account for the general Catholic–non-Catholic pattern is that the type of religious ideology stressed in non-Catholic religions emphasizes social responsibility in parenthood, that is, correct behavior being defined more in terms of ethical standards of conduct. Catholicism, on the other hand, tends to define morality as adherence to a set of absolute standards with social and economic consequences as secondary considerations.

[9] Freedman, Whelpton, and Campbell, "Family Planning Sterility and Population growth." pp. 107–108.

[10] *Ibid.*, pp. 159–160.

[11] *Ibid.*, pp. 183–184.

[12] The greatest drop is among Jews where the .35 correlation between informal religious orientation and fertility-planning success drops to .33 with wife's education held constant.

Although clearly an oversimplification, this interpretation gains support from a comparison of answers to the question: "To what extent should couples consider their finances in deciding whether or not to have another child?" Among Protestants and Jewish wives, 35 per cent answered "very much" as compared to only 19 per cent of the wives in the Catholic and Mixed Catholic groups.

Religious Education

The extent of commitment to any value system can be profoundly influenced by the degree of exposure to the system in the formative years. The amount of religious education constitutes one index of such exposure. As expected, religious education is reported primarily by Catholics, about 50 per cent reporting that some or all of their own, or their husband's, education was in Catholic schools and colleges. Only 10 per cent of the Protestants and less than 5 per cent of the Jews report that some of their education was in religious schools. The following discussion, therefore, is limited to the Catholic population.

There is strong indication that religiously educated Catholics are more faithful adherents to the formal requirements of the church than Catholics whose education was secular. Of the latter, 50 per cent report weekly church attendance, while over 90 per cent of Catholics whose education was exclusively in church schools report such faithful attendance. Thus, it would seem plausible to assume that attendance at schools under church auspices has reinforced the practice of Catholicism. In brief, it can be regarded as an experience strengthening the position of the Catholic church that opposes many techniques of family limitation.

For these reasons, the theoretical expectation is that education under church auspices is associated with a high fertility configuration. This hypothesis is clearly confirmed as indicated in Table 50. As the amount of such school attendance increases, the proportion of couples successfully planning fertility decreases, and the length of time between marriage and the birth of the second child also decreases. For the most part, this pattern of association exists for both wives and husbands but tends to be somewhat stronger among wives.

Similarly, Coogan found that "wives who received a complete Catholic education are 15 per cent more fertile than wives who have received no Catholic education."[13] The factor of education in religious schools was one of the strongest single predictors in his study of differentials in Catholic fertility.

[13] Coogan, *Catholic Fertility in Florida*, p. 46.

199

TABLE 50

Number of Children Desired, Fertility-Planning Success, and Number of Months from Marriage to Second Birth for Catholics, by extent of Catholic School Education

Extent of Catholic School Education	Mean Number of Children Desired	Per Cent Successful Planners	Mean Number of Months from Marriage to Second Birth	Number of Respondents
Wives				
None	3.4	59%	59	208
Some	3.7	50	57	148
All	4.2	42	48	122
Husbands				
None	3.4	59	59	228
Some	3.8	50	54	156
All	3.8	39	52	93

In interpreting the association with fertility-planning status, it is important to reiterate the criteria of fertility-planning success. "Success" is defined as either interrupting contraception (which includes periodic continence) deliberately in order to conceive or not having practiced any contraception at all because of an avowed desire to have a child as soon as possible. In a certain sense, therefore, the whole concept of planning might be considered alien to very religious Catholics and the legitimacy of placing them on a single scale of planning success along with other religious groups can be questioned. For this reason, a scale labeled the "psychological availability of contraception" had been devised to incorporate other dimensions such as moral objections to the practice of contraception. However, although the distinction between the two concepts of planning is logical, the measures as developed tend to order individuals in about the same way, so that little additional information is contributed by using both scales.

In any event, the strong probability emerges that Catholics educated in denominational schools are likely to be a very high fertility group. These significant effects of exposure to the Catholic value system through its education program seem to influence the fertility behavior of the wife somewhat more than that of the husband. There is a tendency for Catholic men and women who have attended denominational schools to marry those who have similarly attended denominational schools,[14] but the presumed reinforcement of values

[14] The correlation between the proportion of total education received in Catholic schools by wives and husbands is .38.

through such a selection does not enhance the relationships observed for wives alone.

The broader social implications of these findings are significant certainly to those interested in social and demographic change, as well as to the Catholic church, which is concerned with the effects of its educational system on the development and reinforcement of Catholic values. It seems likely that women who have been exposed to Catholic teachings throughout all their years of education will go on to have appreciably larger families than Catholic women who have either not been exposed at all or for a lesser period of time. As a matter of fact, Catholics who did not go to Catholic schools behave more like Protestants with respect to fertility (and possibly other types of behavior as well) than like the more indoctrinated members of their own faith. As noted above, 59 per cent of the secularly educated Catholics planned their first two births, while the proportion among Protestants is 60 per cent. The lower incidence of 42 per cent characterizes Catholics who went to church-related schools. The same generalization applies with respect to number of children desired, with secularly educated Catholic wives wanting an average of 3.4 children, Protestants 3.0 children, but Catholics educated in Catholic schools 4.2 children. Also, secularly educated Catholic women take the same time on the average to have two children (59 months) as do Protestant women (60 months), while the religiously educated Catholic wives take a year less (48 months).

It is impossible to tell whether the larger family orientations of religiously educated Catholics are simply a rationalization in advance of the probable biological consequences of the teachings of the Church on fertility control, or whether Catholic education, particularly Catholic secondary school and higher education, also develops a strong favorable attitude toward the large family. From a sociological point of view this distinction is significant. If the latter is correct, the inference would be that these Catholic couples will have large families because they want to have children and for reasons other than only conformity to the Church's interpretation of natural law. Probably the two motivations are so subtly interwoven, however, that in most cases it would be impossible to separate them. Strictly in terms of demographic consequences, the distinction is irrelevant: the likelihood is that religiously educated Catholics will have more children.

Sociological interpretations are obscured by the probable process of selection. We noted that Catholics educated in Catholic schools were better practicing Catholics (as indexed by their regularity of church attendance) than those with a background of secular education. At

201

the same time, it is plausible to assume that more religious parents will make a greater effort to send their children to church-related schools. So it is likely that these products of the Catholic educational system are, to some extent, reflecting the religious values fostered by the parents. It is reasonable to assume, though, that Catholic education at least reinforces these values.

One last caution on interpretation must be added. It costs money to send children to Catholic high schools and colleges, a consideration that necessitates separating out the class factor. Analysis of this type, however, has shown that the interpretation would not be significantly changed.

CATHOLIC PRACTICE AND NATIONALITY BACKGROUND

There are a number of possible theoretical frameworks within which to study the effects of national descent on fertility. For example, it could be conceptualized in terms of an underlying socio-economic status dimension, acculturation to the dominant American ethos, the family structures characteristic of different ethnic groups, or other possible theoretical foci. Without implying invidious comparisons, the subject is explored here within the general topic of religion. The main reason that data were secured on nationality background was on the assumption that some of the variation of fertility among Catholics might be associated with differences in the practice of religion by Irish, Italian, Polish, German, and other Catholic groups. No such assumption was entertained for Protestants or Jews.

The ethnic composition of the present Catholic population in the United States was initially determined by immigration, at first from Ireland and Germany and later from southern and central Europe, the Americas, and more recently from Puerto Rico. These immigrants brought with them their own cultural approximations of the Catholic ideal of marriage and the family.[15] The Italian-Catholic family, for example, has been noted for its evident departure from this ideal— "their indifference to the practice of religion has long been a subject of concern to American churchmen."[16] The Irish-Catholic family, in contrast, is regarded as the most faithful adherent to the Catholic value system. It was therefore hypothesized that Italian Catholics would be characterized by the lowest fertility pattern and Irish

[15] John L. Thomas, *The American Catholic Family*, Prentice-Hall, Englewood Cliffs, N.J., 1956, p. 100.
[16] Henry J. Browne, "The 'Italian Problem' in the Catholic Church of the United States, 1880–1900," *Historical Records and Studies, United States Catholic Historical Society*, xxxv (1946), 46–75, quoted in Thomas, *The American Catholic Family*, p. 110.

couples the highest, with the other Catholic ethnic groups in an intermediate position.

Although the hypothesis is relatively straightforward, the test of it presents some difficulties. The Irish are of an earlier immigrant wave; the Italian migration occurred in the early part of this century. Thus, the comparison is complicated by recency of exposure to a foreign culture as well as differences in class composition.

By definition, all couples interviewed in the sample were born in the United States. This eligibility requirement was imposed in order to minimize whatever implications for fertility that values of a foreign culture might have. However, such a restriction only reduces the influence; it does not necessarily eliminate it. Since the sample was confined to the large metropolitan areas, it was expected that a sizable proportion of the couples would be children of foreign-born parents. The proportion of the total sample reporting at least one of their parents as foreign born[17] is 38 per cent for the wives and 41 per cent for the husbands. For Catholics, the comparable proportion is 49 and 52 per cent for wives and husbands respectively. As expected, most Protestants in the sample are of native parentage (80 per cent), and most Jews of foreign parentage (76 per cent) and mainly of Slavic origin.[18] Although no hypotheses had been developed relating fertility to the ethnic origin of non-Catholics, analyses were routinely completed. But no particular differences were observed. Among Catholics, however, the picture is considerably different (Table 51).

TABLE 51

Number of Children Desired, Per Cent of Successful Planners, and the Number of Months from Marriage to the Second Birth for Catholic Wives and Husbands, by Nationality Background

Nationality Background	*Mean Number of Children Desired*		*Per Cent Successful Planners*		*Mean Number of Months from Marriage to Second Birth*	
	Wives	Husbands	Wives	Husbands	Wives	Husbands
Irish	4.1	4.0	47%	36%	53	50
German	3.7	3.6	49	53	51	50
Slavic	3.6	3.3	50	48	58	65
Italian	3.3	3.5	62	66	63	61
Catholic total[a]	3.7	3.6	52	52	56	56

[a] Includes nationalities such as Spanish, English, French, Scandinavian, Greek, and others in addition to those specified in the tables. Those specified account for over 85 per cent of the total Catholic sample.

[17] The data are derived from the question: "Was either of your parents born outside the United States?"

[18] These proportions are for wives; the comparable statistics for husbands are 78 per cent of native parentage for Protestants and 74 per cent of foreign parentage for Jews.

The Irish exhibit the highest fertility indications and Italians the lowest, with German and Slavic Catholics generally intermediate.[19] With only few exceptions, the same pattern prevails irrespective of whether the individual spouse is a first or earlier generation American, the only difference being that the fertility measures tend to be slightly lower in the foreign-parentage category for all ethnic groups.

This same Irish-Italian fertility difference has been evidenced also in another recent analysis of some factors affecting Catholic fertility. Although the authors were concerned with ethnic origin as an index of social status only, their data from a sample of 3,202 Catholic respondents of nine national origins indicate that Italians have the lowest fertility and Irish the highest.[20]

Our analysis of fertility has been guided by the assumption that the Irish and Italian cultural backgrounds differ radically in interpretation of Catholicism. In brief, ethnic origin has been conceived as associated with religiousness. To what extent is this assumption justified? Do these two groups actually differ in their practice of Catholicism? If they do, would this account entirely for the fertility variations or are there other aspects of ethnic origin relevant to fertility in addition to religiousness? There is, for example, presumably a socio-economic status dimension underlying ethnic origin (at least partly a function of the period of immigration).

As to the question of the association between ethnic origin and religiousness, the proportion of wives attending church at least weekly is much higher for Irish than for Italian Catholics regardless of foreign-born parentage (Table 52). Since the analysis reveals the same results for both wives and husbands, details for the former only are presented. With respect to the nativity of parentage, the range tends to diminish in the older generation. Also as expected, the Irish Catholics tend to be of somewhat higher socio-economic status judging both from the proportion in white-collar occupations and from average income. The other ethnic groups are in an intermediate position. Since the theoretical interest relates most clearly to the Irish-Italian comparison, however, the following intensive analyses are presented for these two groups only.

The Irish-Italian fertility differences are clearly not a function of the differences in class composition (Table 53). Within both the white-collar and blue-collar class, the women of Irish descent express desires for larger families than do women of Italian background, are

---

[19] All differences between the Irish and the Italians are statistically significant except for marriage duration.

[20] Brooks and Henry, "An Empirical Study of the Relationships of Catholic Practice and Occupational Mobility to Fertility," p. 245.

TABLE 52

Religious and Socio-Economic Characteristics of Catholics,
by Ethnic Origin

Nationality Background	Per Cent Attending Church at Least Once a Week	Mean Earnings of Husband in 1956 (dollars)	Per Cent White-Collar
All Catholic Wives	69	5300	42
Irish	81	5600	51
Other	69	5400	41
Italian	56	5000	35
Native Parentage	73	5500	47
Irish	82	5700	51
Other	69	5400	44
Italian	67	5200	44
Foreign Parentage	64	5200	36
Irish	81	5500	53
Other	69	5300	36
Italian	52	5000	31

less successful planners, and have taken less time to have their two children. This rules out class as the intervening factor.

The more plausible hypothesis is that the difference relates to religiousness—that is, that the Irish Catholics reveal higher fertility

TABLE 53

Relationship of the Fertility Variables to Irish and Italian Background,
by Occupational Class

Occupational Class and Nationality Background	Mean Number of Children Desired	Per Cent Successful Planners	Mean Number of Months from Marriage to Second Birth	Number of Wives
White-collar class				
Irish	4.6	46	47	63
Italian	3.5	64	59	47
Blue-collar class				
Irish	3.6	48	61	60
Italian	3.2	61	65	89

patterns because they are more religious than Italian Catholics. The differences in religiousness are clearly inferable from the Irish-Italian differences in church attendance. If the variance of fertility associated with ethnic origin can be accounted for exclusively by religiousness, then among Catholic women who attend church faithfully (once a week at least), there should be no fertility differences by ethnic origin. An absence of association should prevail also among the less religious group, that is, among those who attend church with less regularity. On the other hand, if ethnic origin has some connection with fertility other than its joint association with religiousness, then we should expect to find differences with homogeneous categories of church attendance. These comparisons appear in Table 54.

TABLE 54

Relationship of the Fertility Variables to Irish and Italian Background,
by Regularity of Church Attendance

Church attendance and Nationality Background	Mean Number of Children Desired	Per Cent Successful Planners	Mean Number of Months from Marriage to Second Birth	Number of Wives
Attend church at least weekly				
Irish	4.3	42	51	100
Italian	3.6	63	64	76
Attend church less than weekly				
Irish	3.0	70	64	23
Italian	3.1	60	61	60

The results confirm neither expectation. Among regular churchgoers, the same differences between Irish and Italians prevail as was observed for the total Catholic sample. But among the less regular churchgoers, the Irish-Italian difference does disappear and there is even some indication, though probably not significant, of a reversal of the pattern.

Thus, no simple generalization is possible even when the comparison is confined to the Irish and the Italian. Nor does holding both class and church attendance constant and relating ethnic origin to fertility reveal any possibly concealed interactional effects except that the differences are sharper within the white-collar class. Since the difference persists only among Catholics attending church regularly, the thought occurred that perhaps a difference in religiousness exists which is simply beyond that reflected by regular church attendance. In other words, perhaps regularity of church attendance is not discriminating sufficiently at the most religious end of the scale.

In order to test this possibility, Catholic women who reported attending church regularly were further subdivided into two categories based on their score on the measure of "informal religious orientation." Of the 330 women attending church regularly, 172 also reported themselves as religious-minded and as practicing religious observances in their home as well. The other 158 women, although they also reported regular church attendance, scored in the lower half of this additional scale.

Within each of these two groups, the fertility variables were again tabulated by ethnic origin (Table 55). It is clear, however, that this

TABLE 55

Relationship of the Fertility Variables to Irish and Italian Background for Women Who Attend Church Regularly, by an Additional Measure of Religiousness.

Informal Religious Orientation and Nationality Background	Mean Number of Children Desired	Per Cent Successful Planners	Mean Number of Months from Marriage to Second Birth	Number of Wives
Religiously oriented				
Irish	4.5	44	48	61
Italian	3.7	60	69	35
Not religiously oriented				
Irish	4.0	38	56	39
Italian	3.4	66	60	41

further refinement of religiousness does not account for the differences. Even among the most religious third of the Catholic sample, Irish women still locate on the high and Italians at the low end of the fertility scale.

Are there any characteristics measured in this study which might "explain" this association? Let us restrict the comparison to Irish and Italian-Catholic wives in the white-collar class who attend church regularly. This reduces the sample to a total of only 90 individuals but offers the advantage of theoretical refinement. A number of hunches were tested and the following profile emerges: although women both of Irish and Italian descent average the same age (27.5 at interview), the former married a year older (23 compared to 22 for Italian women). Both groups of women themselves came from families of about the same size: the Irish averaged 2.8 siblings and Italians 2.6.

With respect to familial structure and interaction, the families with wife of Irish descent tend to be dominated more by the wife at least as far as running the home is concerned. They also score significantly higher on indices of marital adjustment and feelings of economic security and lower on an index measuring "drive to get ahead." A more critical difference, aside from the higher level of satisfaction with life in general, is suggested by the difference in education. Even though the comparison is confined to the homogeneous group of white-collar Catholic women who are regular churchgoers, the proportion of Irish descent who attended college is 46 per cent compared with only 19 per cent of the wives with an Italian background. We know from other analyses (reported in the following chapter) that higher education for Catholics implies more religious schooling.

This hypothesis is clearly borne out—92 per cent of the women of Irish descent attended church-related schools during the course of their education compared with 43 per cent of the women from an Italian background. If the ethnic difference can be accounted for by this difference in composition of religious education, no fertility difference should emerge if religious education is held constant. If, however, both religious training and ethnic origin are operating then we would expect the highest fertility to characterize Catholic women of Irish descent all of whose education was in Catholic schools. In terms of this expectation, the lowest fertility group should be found among the women of Italian descent all of whose education was secular. Since the comparison is still confined to the homogeneous white-collar class of regular churchgoers, the number of observations is very small. The rates are computed only because of the theoretical interest and no great reliability can be assumed.

There are two inferences to be drawn from the statistics in Table 56: (1) the hypothesis that the women of Irish descent, educated

TABLE 56

Relationship of the Fertility Variables to Nationality Background by Extent of Education in Catholic Schools, for White-Collar Class Catholic Wives Who Attend Church at Least Weekly

Nationality Background and Extent of Catholic Education	Mean Number of Children Desired	Per Cent Successful Planners	Mean Number of Months from Marriage to Second Birth	Number of Wives
Irish, all Catholic education	5.0	32	40	34
Irish, some Catholic education	4.4	40	52	20
Italian, all or some Catholic education	4.1	41	50	14
Italian, no Catholic education	3.3	77	66	17

exclusively in church-related schools, would be the highest fertility group is confirmed. Also, the women of Italian descent who were educated in public schools are at the lowest end of this fertility scale. There are extremely wide fertility differences (about 50 per cent) between these two groups. (2) The more theoretically significant comparison is that of the two intermediate categories—the Irish and Italian groups with extent of Catholic school education at least crudely held constant. It is only for the category "some" education in Catholic schools that numbers permit comparison. Hardly any difference is visible in these fertility indicators, an observation that suggests differences in Catholic education as the explanation of the Irish-Italian difference. We do not know whether the ethnic differences would disappear in the groups educated exclusively in the Catholic school system or in those whose education was all in non-sectarian schools.

In order to examine this broader aspect of the question and also to increase the sample size, a final tabulation was made for all Catholic wives. Sacrificing the homogeneity of occupational class and religiousness as indexed by regularity of church attendance implies that the questions just raised cannot be answered with any degree of finality. However, the over-all comparisons for the total Catholic sample seem worthwhile (Table 57).

There is a definite tendency for fertility to vary in the expected direction with extent of Catholic education for all nationality backgrounds. Moreover, confining our attention primarily to the Irish-Italian comparison, differences in fertility (at least with number of children desired and fertility-planning success) disappear in the category with no Catholic education. But when the comparison moves to the category of "all" education in Catholic schools, the Irish still appear to be the high fertility group.

Admittedly, this analysis lacks conclusiveness. It would seem that most of the differences in fertility between the Irish and the Italian can be explained by differences in religiousness, particularly as indexed by church-connected education. However, there is still some variance in fertility associated with ethnic background that cannot be attributed to religiousness.

Summary

This chapter has presented the findings on the association between religiousness and fertility. Religiousness has been indexed by (a) regularity of attendance at religious services outside the home, (b) a measure of informal orientation combining the frequency of religious observances within the home with a self-rating on degree of religious-mindedness, (c) an index of religiosity reflecting the importance of religious symbols compared with a number of secular values, and (d) extent of education in schools and colleges under formal church auspices. This last variable has been analyzed only for

TABLE 57

Fertility Variables by Extent of Catholic School Education and Nationality Background of All Catholic Wives

Extent of Catholic School Education	Mean Number of Children Desired			Per Cent Successful Planners[a]			Mean Number of Months from Marriage to Second Birth[a]			Number of Wives[a]		
	Irish	Other[a]	Italian	Irish	Other[a]	Italian	Irish	Other[a]	Italian	Irish	Other[a]	Italian
None	3.7	4.0	3.7	65	53	64	60	52	67	20	99	89
Some	4.3	4.1	4.1	52	44	63	59	55	57	46	73	32
All	5.0	4.6	4.0	37	46	47	46	50	53	57	50	15

[a] "Other" includes all nationality backgrounds other than Irish or Italian.

210

Catholics, since Protestants and Jews did not report religious education in numbers sufficient for statistical purposes. In line with this special analysis of factors affecting the fertility of Catholics, nationality background was also investigated with the general hypothesis that different cultural approximations of Catholicism would have implications for differential fertility. Particular attention was paid to Irish and Italian background differences.

The results of these analyses may be summarized as follows:

1. The expected direct association of religiousness with number of children desired prevails only for Catholics. Although no correlation with fertility-planning success is evident for the total sample, this is a result of positive associations among Jews and Protestants and negative relationships among the Catholic groups. Only negligible relationships are observed with interval between marriage and the second birth.

2. Religious education was seen to exert a strong influence both on the number of children desired by Catholics as well as on the success of their fertility-planning and the length of time taken to have two children. In general, Catholics educated in secular schools and colleges behave more like Protestants in their fertility behavior than they do like Catholics with religious education.

3. The expectation of significant fertility differences among Catholics of different ethnic origins was confirmed with Catholics of Irish background revealing the highest fertility pattern and Catholics of Italian background the lowest.

4. The hypothesis that this association with ethnic origin could be attributed to differences in recency of immigration and/or social class was tested and rejected.

5. The hypothesis that the association could be explained in terms of differences in religiousness was tested and partly confirmed. Such indices as the regularity of church attendance and the degree of informal religious orientation proved insufficient to account for the fertility differences of Catholics of Irish and Italian background. However, a large part of the association appears to be a function of differences in the extent of education in church-related schools.

Chapter XIII. Socio-Economic Status

The dimensions of socio-economic status have been considered of prime importance in studies of differential fertility.[1] In the past, the inverse relationship between measures of socio-economic status and fertility was frequently viewed with anxiety because of its possible implications for long term decline in the quality of the population. This reaction was especially typical in studies revealing a negative relationship between education or intelligence and family size.

Recent postwar changes in fertility have not supported this pessimistic view. On the contrary, trends have revealed a partial reversal in the pattern, with the greatest upswing in fertility manifested among the more highly educated and financially higher segments of the population. Part of this reversal, as the Indianapolis Study findings imply, is no doubt due to increased control in preventing unwanted pregnancies among the lower status families. However, the fertility increases among the higher socio-economic categories can probably be attributed to changing circumstances which favor a desire for more children or, at least, that reduce the anxieties previously associated with the possibility of unplanned pregnancies.

From these points of view, it is relevant to investigate the relation of socio-economic status to the size of family desired and to the pattern of past success in planning fertility. In general, higher socio-economic status is expected to associate with a desire for more children and with greater past success in controlling conception. At the same time, within the category which has evidenced the least success, the incidence of unsuccessful control due to "taking a chance" with irregular practice of contraception is expected to vary directly with socio-economic status. Conversely, ineffective as opposed to irregular practice is viewed as more characteristic of the lower socio-economic groupings. This hypothesis derives from the theory advanced above, that the recent greater fertility of the better educated and higher income groups may be partly because of increased economic security that results in a relaxation of contraceptive vigilance, rather than exclusively because of conscious desires for larger families.

Socio-economic status is divided for analytical convenience as well as conceptual refinement into three components: (1) education;

---

[1] The research literature on this subject has proliferated rapidly in recent years. For useful bibliographies on the subject, *see*: Wilson H. Grabill, Clyde V. Kiser, and P. K. Whelpton, *The Fertility of American Women*, Wiley, New York, 1958, pp. 393–399; United Nations, *The Determinants and Consequences of Population Trends*, New York, 1953, Chapter V and Bibliography.

(2) social status as reflected in occupational prestige and other indices; and (3) economic status, indexed by income and related measures.

EDUCATION

So∴e 26 per cent of the wives and 39 per cent of the husbands in the sample had attended college.[2] Educational attainment differs sharply by religion, however, as well as by occupational class, with Jews and Protestants having had the most education and the Catholic groups the least. Half the Jewish women in the sample and two thirds of the Jewish men reported having attended college compared to only 15 per cent and 26 per cent of Catholic wives and husbands respectively. Although somewhat narrowed, these differences by religion persist within the white-collar and blue-collar classes. The association of educational level with class is, of course, much stronger than its relationship with religion.

In view of the correlation between the wife's vocabulary test score[3] and her education (.51), it is appropriate to discuss the two variables together. The chief expectation was that education and intelligence test score would associate with successful fertility planning and preferences for additional children. The appropriate correlations are presented in Table 58. Fertility-planning success reveals only very slight positive correlations with education and verbal intelligence, and this association obtains consistently only for Protestants. For all other religions, the values fail to reach statistical significance. Even for Protestants, moreover, the correlations are so low that the hypothesis cannot be said to be confirmed conclusively. In addition, the relationships for the Catholic groups tend to be negative in direction, though mostly not statistically significant. Of course, the measure of fertility-planning success pertains only to the first two pregnancies and it might be argued plausibly that the magnitude of the direct association will increase with the experience of these couples in future years as the control of family size and not only spacing preferences becomes more critical. But this remains to be seen.

These correlations refer to the education of wives and husbands separately, and although the correlation between education of wife

[2] The classification "attended college" ranges from only one year of college through postgraduate education.

[3] This test was developed by Thorndike: see R. L. Thorndike, "Two Screening Tests of Verbal Intelligence," *Journal of Applied Psychology*, 26 (1942), pp. 128–135; and R. L. Thorndike and G. Gallup, "Verbal Intelligence of the American Adult," *Journal of General Psychology*, 30 (1944), pp. 75–85.

TABLE 58

Correlations of Wife's Education, Husband's Education, and Wife's Vocabulary Test Score with Fertility-Planning Success, Number of Children Desired by Wife, and Number of Children Desired by Husband, by Religion and Class

Religion and Class	Fertility-Planning Success			Number of Children Desired by Wife			Number of Children Desired by Husband	
	Wife's Education	Husband's Education	Wife's Vocabulary Test Score	Wife's Education	Husband's Education	Wife's Vocabulary Test Score	Wife's Education	Husband's Education
Protestant total	.14	.15	.19	−.03	.04	−.03	.06	.12
Mixed Catholic total	−.06	−.01	−.07	.10	−.12	−.04	.46	.23
Catholic total	−.11	−.05	.02	.28	.24	.17	.16	.16
Jewish total	.14	.14	.05	.33	.31	.22	.27	.11
All couples	.08	.12	.13	.06	.05	.04	.07	.05

and husband is substantial (.63), there is enough difference to justify analyzing the association between the couple's education and fertility-planning success. The same general pattern of association holds (see Table 59), with a direct relationship appearing for

TABLE 59

Per Cent of Successful Planners, by Education of the Couple and Religion

Education of Couple	All Couples[a]	Religion		
		Protestant	Catholic	Jewish
Both less than four years of high school	49%	47%	59%	[b]
Both attended four years of high school	57	55	56	87
Both attended college	69	74	34	88
Husband more educated than wife	59	62	51	90
Wife more educated than husband	54	58	49	77

[a] Includes the Mixed Catholic group, which is not presented separately because of small frequencies.

[b] Less than 20 couples.

Protestants and an inverse relationship for Catholics. Among Catholics, 59 per cent of couples who did not reach the fourth year of high school report having planned both pregnancies or the last pregnancy while, at the opposite end of the educational scale among Catholic couples who attended college, 34 per cent report this extent of success.

The two categories of couples with educational attainment different for each spouse show little difference in extent of successful fertility planning. The apparent greater success of couples with the husband more educated than the wife in contrast to couples with the wife more educated than her husband is well within the limits of sampling variability.

Do couples who have achieved higher education *want* larger families at this point in the family-building process? Among Protestants virtually no association prevails but among Jews and Catholics there is a definite positive correlation between education of wife and husband with family-size preferences (Table 58). The vocabulary test score achieved by the wife reveals essentially the same pattern of correlations as her education. For the Mixed Catholic group, education is relevant only for the number of children desired by the husband. An examination of the joint educational attainment of both husband and wife adds no further insight beyond the separate correlational analyses.

These sets of relationships pose an interesting question. For both Catholics and Jews, there is a definite positive association between

215

education of the husband and wife and the size of family they wish to have. The interesting point is that education correlates positively with successful fertility planning for the Jewish and Protestant groupings but negatively among Catholics. In other words, better educated Jews want larger families but exercise effective control in planning the spacing of the first two children; the more highly educated Catholics also want larger families but would appear to be taking a path of contraceptive control quite different from that of the Jews. The question thus becomes: why does education exert opposite influence on fertility control in the different religious groupings?

The analysis of the interrelationships among religion, education, and fertility in the Freedman, Whelpton, and Campbell study provides at least partially similar results. In explaining why Protest-ant-Catholic differences in expected fertility widen with rising education, one of the authors writes: "This reflects the fact that among the Catholics, the college educated women expect to have larger families than do the women with only a grade-school educa-tion, while the opposite relationship is found among Protestants."[4] Our data reveal no association at all between education and the number of children desired among Protestants, but there is a direct association between fertility-planning success and education. This may be consistent with the fact that the variable of *expected* fertility used in the study by Freedman, Whelpton, and Campbell can reflect perceptions of future fertility control as well as number of children desired. The author concludes: "Evidently the attitude favoring moderately large families among Catholics is more influential among the better educated than among the less well educated."[5]

Data from the household survey phase of the Indianapolis Study also revealed widening fertility differences between Protestants and Catholics as education increases,[6] although, in this earlier study, an inverse association between education and fertility was observed for couples of both religious categories.

The factor to which we turned for an explanation is church-related education. The hypothesis of a direct relationship between education and fertility-planning success thus becomes refined to mean secular education or exposure to secular values through education. Catholic

[4] Arthur Campbell, "Socio-economic Correlates of Fertility and Fertility Expectations in a Cross-Section of White Married Couples in the United States in 1955," in *Thirty Years of Research in Human Fertility: Retrospect and Prospect*, Milbank Memorial Fund, New York, 1959, p. 110. The data did not permit detailed analyses of the Jewish sample.

[5] *Ibid.*

[6] P. K. Whelpton and Clyde V. Kiser, "Differential Fertility Among 41,498 Native-White Couples in Indianapolis," in Kiser and Whelpton, eds., *Social and Psychological, Factors Affecting Fertility*, 5 Vols., Milbank Memorial Fund, New York, 1946–1958, I, pp. 30–44.

school education is viewed, as noted in the previous chapter, as an experience reinforcing the position of the Catholic church which opposes most techniques of family limitation. If this is the "explanation" of the differences presented above, then we should expect less effective planning among Catholics whose education was in the Catholic schools and colleges. Furthermore, we would expect that as education increases among Catholics who attend church-related schools, fertility planning would decrease on the assumption that additional years of exposure to the teachings of the Catholic church through higher education would tend to make contraception even less available. If this is true, and if there is a direct relationship between education and Catholic school attendance, then the negative relationship between education and fertility planning among Catholics would be explained.[7]

The first of these expectations was confirmed, as described in the previous chapter: Catholics with exclusively church-related education report a lower degree of fertility-planning success than do secularly educated Catholics. The second and third questions have not yet been answered. With respect to the third—the relationship between the number of years of education and the extent of Catholic school training—the answer is also positive. Among Catholic wives, 9 per cent of wives with secular education went to college, compared with 19 per cent of wives some or all of whose education was church-related. The comparable proportions for husbands are 17 and 34 per cent.

The most critical question, however, is whether education and fertility-planning success are related in opposite directions for religiously as opposed to secularly educated Catholics. This hypothesis is tested and confirmed with the appropriate comparisons in Table 60. The relationship is very pronounced. The proportion of successful planners increases with amount of education only for those wives whose education was exclusively secular. Among religiously educated Catholic wives, successful planning declines with increasing education. The comparison is especially striking among the women who went to college: 71 per cent reported as successful planners among the secularly educated contrasted with only 18 per cent in the all-Catholic-schooling category.[8] The comparable proportion for Protestant college women, incidentally, is 70 per cent.

[7] The view that Catholic school education affects fertility should be tempered by the realization that Catholic school graduates undoubtedly come from more religious homes.

[8] Where *both* wife and husband went to college and both had at least some training in the Catholic school system, only 14 per cent of such couples are among the successful planners. The number of Catholic couples with higher but exclusively secular education is too small to permit comparison.

TABLE 60

Fertility-Planning Success of Catholics, by Amount of Education and
Extent of Catholic Schooling

EXTENT OF CATHOLIC SCHOOL EDUCATION	WIVES Per Cent Successful Planners				HUSBANDS Per Cent Successful Planners			
	Less than Four Years High School	High School Graduates	Attended College	All Wives	Less than Four Years High School	High School Graduates	Attended College	All Husbands
None	58%	57%	71%	59%	62%	55%	59%	59%
Some	56	53	33	50	51	56	45	50
All	46	47	18	42	41	42	30	39
Total	55	53	38	52	55	52	55	52

The association among Catholic men is less striking. For each of the three educational levels, the extent of successful fertility planning tends to decrease as extent of Catholic school education increases. However, there is little association at all between educational attainment and fertility planning with extent of Catholic school education held constant. Moreover, the differences among the college group are not as great as noted for wives. Coogan came to the same conclusion from his analysis of Catholic fertility in Florida: "Besides indicating that a Catholic education has a positive bearing on fertility, these data also show that a Catholic education on the part of the wife has more bearing than a Catholic education on the part of the husband."[9] There may be, as has been suggested, real differences in the kind of religious instruction offered in Catholic colleges for women compared to that in all-male or even coeducational Catholic colleges. The implication is that the interpretation of the Church's position on family limitation may be more naive in women's colleges.

Whatever the explanation, the same difference reappears with respect to number of children desired (Table 61). Again the relationships are stronger for women. And again the association is quite sharp. Both amount of education and extent of Catholic schooling correlate positively with number of children desired. As with fertility planning, the association is strongest among wives who attended college, where the correlation with extent of Catholic education and

[9] Thomas Francis Coogan, *Catholic Fertility in Florida. Differential Fertility Among 4,891 Florida Catholic Families*, Catholic University of America Press, Washington, 1946, p. 60.

TABLE 61

Number of Children Desired by Catholics, by Amount of Education and
Extent of Catholic Schooling

EXTENT OF CATHOLIC SCHOOL EDUCATION	WIVES *Mean Number of Children*				HUSBANDS *Mean Number of Children*			
	Less than Four Years High School	High School Graduates	Attended College	All Wives	Less than Four Years High School	High School Graduates	Attended College	All Husbands
None	3.2	3.4	3.4	3.4	3.5	3.4	3.4	3.4
Some	3.5	3.6	4.4	3.7	3.3	3.5	4.3	3.8
All	3.4	4.2	5.1	4.2	3.5	4.0	4.1	3.8
Total	3.4	3.7	4.4	3.7	3.4	3.6	3.9	3.6

family-size preferences reaches .52.[10] The main difference in the two associations, however, is that, unlike fertility planning, there is no evidence of any reversal in family-size preferences among the secularly educated. However, the over-all increase in number of children desired with amount of education is largely a matter of being exposed for a greater length of time to the Catholic school system. The correlation between amount of education and fertility desires is .42 for wives educated entirely in church-related schools, compared to only .08 for wives educated in public schools. The corresponding correlations for husbands are .20 and .01 respectively.[11]

In brief, going to college implies higher fertility for Catholics (women particularly) if the educational experience has religious overtones. College attendance does not apparently affect family-size desires if the education has been exclusively secular. It does increase successful planning, however.[12]

The higher fertility of Catholic college graduates has been noted before in the College Study Report conducted by the Population

[10] These differences in fertility planning and family-size desires are reflected in the length of the most recent birth interval. Among Catholic college women, those with Catholic education took a year less to have the second child, with an interval length averaging just under two years.

[11] The differences between each pair of values is statistically significant.

[12] In his analysis of the fertility of Florida Catholics in earlier decades, Coogan found a widening of fertility differentials between Catholics educated in Catholic as compared to public schools as education increased. Among men for whom sufficient cases at the college level existed to compute rates, he reported only a 1 per cent differential at the grammar school level, 7 per cent at the high school level, and 14 per cent at the college level. At this time, however, an inverse relationship between educational attainment and fertility existed although it was less pronounced for those from Catholic schools than for those from public schools. See Coogan, *Catholic Fertility in Florida*, p. 53.

219

Reference Bureau.[13] In analyses of the fertility patterns of 25 and 10 year college graduates, the report states:

"The reproductive pattern of the Catholic college group is very different from all the others. Though the marriage rate is low, 25-year graduates of Catholic colleges rank second only to the Mormon college graduates in terms of number of children per graduate; they rank highest in number of children per married graduate and per parent. This means that more of the Catholic graduates who marry have at least one child, and more of those with children have more children than do graduates of other colleges.

"Among the 10-year graduates, the men from Catholic colleges have fewer children than those from other colleges, but the women have more than the female graduates of government or Protestant colleges. In terms of children per married graduate or per parent, 10-year graduates of Catholic colleges are exceeded only by 10-year Mormon college graduates.

"The fact that alumni of Catholic colleges rank highest in fertility per married person and per parent in the 25-year group, but well below the Mormon group in the 10-year class, could mean that the fertility of the Catholic group has not been rising as much as that of the Mormon group. It seems more likely, however, that the difference is merely one of age at marriage and age at childbearing. There are indications that Catholics marry somewhat later than Mormons, and continue to have children at older ages. By the time the class of 1946 reaches its 25th anniversary, it is quite probable that in the average number of children per married graduate and per parent, the alumni of Catholic colleges will exceed those of Mormon colleges."[14]

It bears repeating that disentangling the selective effects of who goes to Catholic schools from the effect of the education itself on fertility values has not been accomplished. In view of the importance of the question, however, some effort will be made to collect relevant information on the religiousness of the families of origin in the second interview with these couples. Another intriguing and related question on which data exist but sample size prevents analysis is whether Catholic education in elementary school, high school, or college exerts the greatest influence on subsequent fertility.

[13] "College Study Report—1956," *Population Bulletin*, XII (1956). This report was prepared by the staff of the Population Reference Bureau with P. K. Whelpton and Patience Lauriat.

[14] *Ibid.*, p. 98. As the report indicates, these data treat religion in terms of college administration, not in terms of the graduate. Actually the fertility differences might be even greater than those reported if the comparisons were restricted to graduates of that religion exclusively.

SOCIAL STATUS

Apart from education, the over-all dimension of socio-economic status contains two related but conceptually distinct components—the social and the economic. The educational component, analyzed above, is also involved in this configuration, but it is a temporal antecedent to the couple's current status. The economic component of socio-economic status will be discussed subsequently. At the present, we shall confine our attention to the "social" aspects of socio-economic status.

Several measures have been included in the study designed to tap this variable. Two are fairly conventional: the occupational prestige rating scale developed by North and Hatt[15] and a simple adaptation of Centers'[16] questions on social class self-identification. A third measure was developed specifically for this study which attempts to measure the husband's level of status satisfaction by a series of questions which ask him to evaluate his level of living in terms of how satisfied he would feel if a son of his had the same kind of life.

A fourth variable was designed to measure, in more general terms, the extent to which the wife feels she has achieved her life goals, whatever these may be and however crystallized they might be in the mind of the respondent. Although miscellaneous other factors are involved, the status dimension appears to be the most important element in the responses to items in this scale.

Two additional variables will be included here although they contain elements that do not belong to the status dimension. These are the husband's degree of psychological commitment to work and the wife's level of satisfaction with her husband's job. For the husband, a high level of commitment is defined as an attitude toward work which values this aspect of life as a main source of meaning in his life. For the wife, satisfaction with her husband's job is defined in terms of her perception of the steadiness of his work, hours and working conditions, chance to get ahead, and adequacy of income.

The general hypothesis is that higher social status will associate with a desire for more children and with successful fertility planning. This hypothesis is the same as for the variable of education and for the more narrowly economic dimension of socio-economic status to be presented subsequently. The initial hypothesis for the husband's commitment to work values was that such a commitment would

[15] Cecil C. North and Paul K. Hatt, "Jobs and Occupations: A Popular Evaluation," in Logan Wilson and William L. Kolb, *Sociological Analysis*, Harcourt, Brace, New York, 1949, pp. 464–474.
[16] Richard Centers, *The Psychology of Social Classes*, Princeton University Press, Princeton, 1949.

conflict with familial values and thus tend to be incompatible with additional children. The pretest analysis showed the opposite result, however, indicating a positive correlation between the husband's commitment to work and the number of children he wanted. This unexpected result led to a further hypothesis—that satisfaction with one area of life tends to be associated positively with adjustment in other areas. If this is true, we would expect to find commitment to work values positively correlated with such variables as level of status satisfaction, achievement of life goals, marital adjustment, and the like. The evidence for the existence of such a common factor is, in fact, reasonably clear. Commitment to work values correlates .55 with level of status satisfaction, .34 with extent of wife's satisfaction with her husband's work, .33 and .23 with the husband's and wife's feelings of economic security respectively, and is correlated less strongly but still positively with other "satisfaction" areas.

The relationships of these variables with family-size preferences and fertility-planning success are presented in Tables 62 and 63. None of these variables reveals associations of any magnitude for the total sample. Some relationships exist for the different religious groups, however. Consistent with the positive relation of education to family-size preferences for Jews are the direct associations of occupational prestige, commitment to work values, and status satisfaction. The highest value observed is a correlation of .31 between the prestige rating of the husband's current occupation and the number of children desired by Jewish wives. Among the Catholic sample, these variables also associate positively with the family-size preferences, but although the values are significantly different from zero, the magnitudes are low. The tendency for the measures of the husband's occupational prestige, commitment to work values, and level of status satisfaction to correlate positively with the number of children desired by Jewish wives can be regarded as a result of the communality shared with education. The presumption of a common factor underlying these variables is confirmed by the level of correlations among these variables and with education which range from .40 to .70, averaging .50.

Not a single correlation in Tables 62 and 63 is significantly different from zero within the Mixed Catholic group. The Protestant group, however, reveals a pattern different from that of all three other religious categories. Although no relationships are evident with number of children desired, there is a slight but consistent tendency for these status variables to correlate positively with extent of fertility-planning success. However, the values are low, the six ranging only

222

TABLE 62

Correlations of Husband's Occupational Prestige, Commitment to Work Values, and Level of Status Satisfaction with Number of Children Desired and Fertility-Planning Success

Religion	Occupational Prestige			Commitment to Work Values		Status Satisfaction		
	Number of Children Desired by Wife	Number of Children Desired by Husband	Fertility-Planning Success	Number of Children Desired by Husband	Fertility-Planning Success	Number of Children Desired by Wife	Number of Children Desired by Husband	Fertility-Planning Success
Protestant total	.05	.10	.13	.08	.08	.02	.09	.13
Mixed Catholic total	.04	.19	.07	.01	.09	.03	.08	.03
Catholic total	.13	.07	-.08	.10	-.04	.14	.18	-.06
Jewish total	.31	.19	.07	.19	.07	.22	.15	.10
All couples	.03	.02	.08	.04	.05	.03	.06	.07

223

TABLE 63

Correlations of Wife's Satisfaction with Husband's Work, Achievement of Life Goals, and Social Class Identification with Number of Children Desired by Wife and Fertility-Planning Success

Religion	Satisfaction with Husband's Job		Achievement of Life Goals		Social Class Identification	
	Number of Children Desired	Fertility-Planning Success	Number of Children Desired	Fertility-Planning Success	Number of Children Desired	Fertility-Planning Success
Protestant total	−.01	.10	.01	.14	.12	.14
Mixed Catholic total	.04	.08	−.09	−.16	−.21	.01
Catholic total	.09	.01	.13	.10	.07	−.01
Jewish total	.15	.01	.08	−.06	.05	.08
All couples	.03	.05	.03	.09	.01	.10

from .08 to .14, and only among Protestants does such consistency prevail with this variable.

Thus, the hypothesis initially proffered must be refined: social status does associate positively with number of children desired and with fertility-planning success but only within certain religious categories. The strongest relationships prevail within the Jewish group with number of children desired, an association having a common basis with that observed with education. Among Catholics, only a slight positive relationship of the status variables with family-size preferences exists. No relationships appear among the Mixed Catholic group, and among Protestants a consistent but slight direct association prevails with fertility-planning success only.

This refinement of the hypothesis actually exceeds the limits of the data. In only one of the fourteen tests of the hypothesis in Tables 62 and 63 does the distribution of correlations among the religious groupings justify an assumption of heterogeneity. In strictly rigorous statistical terms, the negligible positive associations for the total sample constitute the firm conclusion. The same generalization applies with both religion and occupational class held constant simultaneously.

ECONOMIC STATUS

The third and final dimension of socio-economic status to be analyzed in reference to fertility is the economic component. The expectation is that couples in better financial circumstances, or those who *feel* economically secure, will desire more children and will have experienced greater success in planning fertility. The first part of this hypothesis appears more plausible when phrased negatively: couples in poorer economic circumstances and who feel economically insecure will prefer to limit the number of children they have. There is no evidence or rationale whatsoever for asserting that every couple has a potential disposition to have a large family contingent only on their ability to afford it. In motivational terms, it makes more sense to conceive of economic conditions as setting limits on fertility which operate only in a very loose sense. Even under the best of financial circumstances, many couples will have small families, and studies of differential fertility have certainly revealed the converse to be true as well.

Since fertility is viewed in this study in a social-psychological frame of reference, the level of income is not a sufficient variable with which to test the hypothesis. Individuals, depending on their reference groups and perceived needs, react differently to the same income. Some couples will feel very secure with an annual income of, say, $6,000, while others will feel very insecure. This phenomenon is obvious and need not be labored. In order to provide a measure of this more subjective individual attitude, indices of "feelings of economic security" were developed for each spouse. Typical questions ranged over topics of: confidence in being able to meet heavy unexpected expenses; possibility of the husband being faced with unemployment; perceptions of the financial future; inclination to worry about bills or debts; and other questions worded in more general terms evaluating the couple's financial situation.

Two internal relationships are of interest: the association between level of income and feelings of economic security and the relationship between the wife's and husband's evaluation.

The correlation of feelings of economic security with the husbands' 1956 yearly earnings[17] are .49 and .36 for wives and husbands respectively. These correlations indicate that a common factor is involved but certainly confirm the fact that income and feelings of economic security are not the same thing. The correlation between the measures of economic security for the wives and for the husbands is .50, which suggests enough disagreement among couples to warrant examination of fertility patterns of types of couples.

Income, but not feelings of economic security, varies significantly with the couple's religion. The median earnings in 1956 for the total sample is $5,600, ranging from a low of $5,300 for Catholics to a high of $6,400 for Jews, differences which for the most part can be explained by the different occupational composition of the religious groups.

The correlations of income and feelings of economic security with

17 Income figures were adjusted to income before taxes.

family-size preferences and fertility-planning success are presented in Table 64 for each religious classification. The association is positive with fertility-planning success, but only for Protestants do the values reach a tangible level, averaging around .20 for the three measures. For the remaining religious categories, the values are indistinguishable from zero. The relationships of these economic variables with the number of children desired reveal only negligible values. Only among Protestant women is there any correlation, but this is low and unexpectedly negative.

In summary, it appears that only the fertility-planning hypothesis is substantiated and this mainly for Protestants. The expected positive association of income and feelings of economic security with number of children desired does not appear, although the observed negative correlations are of questionable stability. Refining the income variable by subtracting fixed housing costs does not produce any difference in the results.

If neither of these variables shows much discriminatory power separately, do they improve when considered jointly and with the couple as the unit? Classifications of feelings of economic security were developed for the couple with each classification further subdivided by the husband's 1956 earnings. For each of these nine classes, the average number of children desired by wife and husband and the proportion of couples who successfully planned either the last or both pregnancies were computed (see Table 65). With respect to number of children desired, there is very little variation at all and what little there is can be attributed mainly to income. Regardless of whether it is the wife's or the husband's family-size desires, the number of children desired decreases slightly with income among all couples except those who feel economically secure, among whom it tends to increase. Couples with the wife feeling insecure and the husband feeling secure are no different in their family-size preferences from couples with the opposite combination. The pattern appears to be for small-family desires to cluster among couples of either high income and low security or low income and high security.[18] This suggests the possibility that a critical intervening variable might be the level of aspiration—that is, the discrepancy between desired and achieved level of living. Such a line of analysis will be pursued further in the next chapter when the variables of mobility and mobility aspirations are discussed.

[18] Some of the frequencies, particularly in the low income-high security classification, are very small. Statistically significant differences exist between the number of children desired by the high security-high income group and the low security-high income category, but not between the low income-high security and low income-low security groups.

TABLE 64

Correlations of Husband's 1956 Earnings and Wife's and Husband's Feelings of Economic Security with Number of Children Desired and Fertility-Planning Success, by Religion

Religion	Husband's 1956 Earnings			Wife's Feeling of Economic Security		Husband's Feeling of Economic Security	
	Number of Children Desired by Wife	Number of Children Desired by Husband	Fertility-Planning Success	Number of Children Desired	Fertility-Planning Success	Number of Children Desired	Fertility-Planning Success
Protestant total	−.15	−.09	.23	−.08	.18	.04	.20
Mixed Catholic total	−.15	.09	.04	−.03	.08	−.08	.12
Catholic total	.03	−.03	.03	.11	−.01	.10	.03
Jewish total	.07	−.03	.06	.07	−.02	.10	.10
All couples	−.10	−.09	.16	.01	.08	.03	.11

TABLE 65

Number of Children Desired and Fertility-Planning Success, by the Couple's Feeling of Economic Security and Husband's 1956 Earnings

Feeling of Economic Security of Couple	Mean Number of Children Desired by Wife 1956 Income				Mean Number of Children Desired by Husband 1956 Income				Per Cent Successful Planners 1956 Income			
	$6,000 and over	$4,000 to 5,999	Under $4,000	Total	$6,000 and over	$4,000 to 5,999	Under $4,000	Total	$6,000 and over	$4,000 to 5,999	Under $4,000	Total
Both feel secure	3.3	3.3	3.1	3.3	3.2	3.3	2.9	3.2	65%	58%	50%	62%
Wife insecure; husband secure	3.0	3.4	3.5	3.3	3.0	3.2	3.4	3.2	76	52	46	56
Husband insecure; wife secure	3.1	3.3	3.4	3.2	3.0	3.2	3.5	3.2	61	51	45	53
Both feel insecure	3.0	3.2	3.4	3.2	2.9	3.1	3.4	3.2	60	59	40	54
Total	3.2	3.3	3.4	3.3	3.1	3.2	3.3	3.2	64	56	43	57

No such pattern exists when variations in fertility-planning success are considered. Although there is a consistent direct relationship with income, even here the differences between the lowest and highest income classes are only around 20 per cent. It is clear, however, that fertility-planning is more sensitive to income than to feelings of security.

CHANCE-TAKING

One hypothesis introduced at the outset is the expectation that income or feelings of economic security is related to casual, irregular contraceptive practice. If this is true, the recent increases in the fertility of the white-collar classes might be thought of more in terms of a relaxation of contraceptive precaution rather than an increase in the number of children actually desired.

To test this hypothesis, information was collected in the interview about the circumstances under which each conception occurred. Those couples reporting unsuccessful planning were divided into two categories: couples who conceived while actually using a method and those who conceived at a time when they "took a chance" and did not use a method. If the hypothesis is correct, one would expect a higher proportion of unplanned pregnancies resulting from chance-taking in the white-collar class.

The results of this analysis, summarized in Table 66, reveal no

TABLE 66

Per Cent of Pregnancies among Accidental and Unplanned
Second Pregnancies, by Occupational Class

| Occupational Class | Per Cent Who Took a Chance | |
	Of Accidental Second Pregnancies[a]	Of Unplanned Second Pregnancies[b]
All Couples:		
White-collar	46%	57%
Blue-collar	58	70
Protestants:		
White-collar	57	62
Blue-collar	67	75
Catholics:		
White-collar	35	56
Blue-collar	47	63

[a] Base includes couples who conceived while actually using a method plus those who had used a method during the interval and conceived while taking a chance.

[b] Base includes not only those using a method and failing and those who had used a method but took a chance and conceived, but also those couples who did not use any method, except those who reported wanting another child as soon as possible and those who gave reasons of religion for nonuse.

such pattern; in fact, the opposite conclusion is more appropriate, although the differences are slight.[19] If the comparison is restricted to those who used contraception during the interval (the second interval), 46 per cent of such couples in the white-collar class conceived their second child while taking a chance, but 58 per cent of such couples in the blue-collar class also conceived under similar circumstances. Even if couples who used no contraception for reasons other than wanting another child as soon as possible or religion are included in the "chance-taking" category, the direction of the relationship remains the same. No exceptions are noted for Protestants or Catholics.

On the possibility that class differences in methods of contraception used might be a factor, the proportion of chance-taking among all accidental second pregnancies was examined separately for each major method. But this refinement does not alter the apparent higher incidence of chance-taking among blue-collar class couples. For white-collar class couples who unsuccessfully used the safe period before the second pregnancy, 36 per cent of the accidental conceptions resulted from taking a chance compared to 46 per cent in the blue-collar class.[20] Comparable proportions of chance-taking among couples who relied on the condom are 64 and 74 per cent, and for diaphragm and jelly, 45 and 68 per cent for white-collar and blue-collar class couples respectively. For the remaining methods, the proportions are about the same.

The reasoning behind the general hypothesis is that chance-taking would increase with feelings of economic security inasmuch as an unplanned pregnancy could more easily be tolerated in such a situation. Or, if a more psychological line of reasoning is preferred, such a conception could be regarded as the unconscious solution to the uncomfortable alternative of having to make a deliberate decision to have another child. Whatever the mechanics of the process at the individual level, the hypothesis calls for a direct relationship between chance-taking and feelings of economic security, a dubious expectation now considering the finding that blue-collar class couples tended to have more pregnancies resulting from chance-taking than did white-collar class couples.

Several types of analyses were undertaken relating feelings of economic security to the circumstance under which conception was

[19] They are significant at the .01 level, however.

[20] Reporting "taking a chance" with the safe period rather than that the method failed presumably means that the couple knew that the time of the month was favorable for conception but ignored this knowledge. Reported failure, on the other hand, probably implies misinformation about the true time of ovulation.

reported to have occurred. The economic security scores of wives and husbands were analyzed both separately and jointly, with income, occupational class, and religion successively controlled. The net result of the whole procedure was a failure to reject the null hypothesis; no association of any type was uncovered.

In conclusion, no credence is lent to the hypothesis that chance-taking is more characteristic of couples with greater feelings of economic security. Moreover, the white-collar classes reveal a higher incidence (among nonplanners) of conceptions occurring while a method was actually being practiced.[21] Of course, as is true of tests of other hypotheses at this juncture of the study, the results of this analysis must be interpreted in the context of only the partially completed fertility picture. Such an association, if it exists at all, may appear at later stages; the hypothesis, therefore, will be retained for further testing in the second phase of the study. All that can be concluded at this stage is that there is no positive evidence at all up to this point.

CREDIT BUYING

Every wife in the sample was asked how often she and her husband used an installment or credit plan in purchasing major items such as cars, furniture, television sets, appliances, refrigerator, and so forth. That this type of activity is, in part, a class phenomenon is evidenced by the fact that over twice as many blue-collar wives report using credit always or usually in their major purchases as do white-collar wives.[22] For each religious category, this class difference prevails; however, there is some religious difference independent of class as well. The main deviation is by the Jews who report comparatively little tendency to buy on credit, an observation consistent with other indications of cautious behavior.

The hypothesis is that couples prone to buy on credit would be ineffective planners of child spacing and family size. The theory is that a lack of self-restraint or self-discipline as manifested in an unwillingness to defer purchases until sufficient money is saved would also be reflected in a failure to realize the possible economic implications of children. Or, to phrase it differently, installment buying is expected to associate with ineffective fertility planning on the assumption that the variance held in common would reflect an

---

[21] The nature and extent of a class bias in reporting the circumstances of conception is unknown.

[22] Again, there may be cultural biases involved in reporting. It is conceivable that persons in the white-collar class may prefer to think of themselves as paying cash for their purchases.

underlying factor of a general lack of caution in many areas of life.

The correlation of credit buying with fertility-planning success is presented in Table 67. The correlation among the total sample is

TABLE 67

Correlations between Regularity of Credit Buying and
Fertility-Planning Success, by Religion

Religion	Fertility-Planning Success
Protestant total	−.07
Mixed Catholic total	.16
Catholic total	−.04
Jewish total	−.26
All couples	−.10

negative as expected, but although statistically significant is negligible in value (−.10). Only among Jews, does the value reach a statistically significant and meaningful level (−.26), but the correlations do not vary significantly either by religion or by religion and class simultaneously considered.

The Relevance of Finances to Fertility

The economic variables examined thus far have revealed extremely little in the way of association with the fertility variables. To assert that economic factors are irrelevant to fertility, even among such a specialized sample, seems like a radical conclusion. It is possible that income ceases to be relevant to fertility either after a certain level of income is reached, or perhaps more significantly during an era of prosperity when family financial futures are viewed optimistically or at least assuredly. Or the answer may be that financial considerations of the kind calculated by many couples are not measured by such variables as income or feelings of economic security.

An attempt was made in the interview to secure a direct indication of the extent to which finances are a relevant consideration in having a child. A question was asked in just these terms: To what extent should couples consider their finances in deciding whether or not to have another child? This direct approach revealed only 9 per cent of all wives replying that financial considerations were not at all relevant, an answer that is most characteristic of the Catholic groups.

The Protestant and Jewish wives reveal the same response distributions (see Table 68). The class difference, which indicates only a slight tendency for finances to be more relevant in the blue-collar class, is less than the Catholic–non-Catholic difference.

TABLE 68

The Relevance of Finances in Decisions to Have Another Child

| Religion and Class | Relevance of Finances | | | | Per Cent Total |
	Very Much	Much	Some	Not at All	
Protestant total	35%	27%	34%	4%	100%
Mixed Catholic total	16	30	41	13	100
Catholic total	20	17	48	15	100
Jewish total	35	27	34	4	100
White-collar total	23	27	41	9	100
Blue-collar total	32	20	39	9	100
All couples	27	24	40	9	100

The relationship of interest is that between the perceived importance of finances in having another child and the number of children desired by the wife (Table 69). The correlation for the total sample is

TABLE 69

Correlations of the Relevance of Finances in Deciding about
Another Child with Number of Children Desired,
by Religion

Religion	Number of Children Desired by Wife
Protestant total	−.27
Mixed Catholic total	−.30
Catholic total	−.40
Jewish total	−.10
All couples	−.37

−.37, reaching its highest value for Catholics (−.40) and the lowest for Jews (−.10). The magnitude of these values (excepting that for the Jewish group) is considerably higher than those observed in similar correlations with income and feelings of economic security.

One obvious difference is that the dependent variable of fertility is contained in the question itself. Another problem is that finances are socially acceptable grounds for rationalizing a family-size orientation that might exist for other reasons.

The correlations for the Catholic groups are in part, but only in small part, a function of religious beliefs. This is indicated by a positive correlation (.19) between the perceived importance of finances and fertility-planning success; a negative correlation with extent of wife's religious education $(-.15)$ and negative correlations averaging about $-.17$ with church attendance and measures of religiousness. The implication of these associations is that Catholics who reply that finances are a relevant consideration in deciding to have another child tend to be Catholics who are less committed to church dogma, but the correlations are far from the magnitude necessary to warrant inferring one variable from the other.

SUMMARY

This chapter has focussed attention on the relationships between three main components of socio-economic status, number of children desired, and fertility-planning success. Most results were presented for each religious grouping separately as well as for the total sample.

In general, the expectation that higher socio-economic status would associate with desires for larger families and with a successful contraceptive record has been only partly borne out and with major exceptions.

With respect to education, only low correlations obtained with fertility-planning success and these were positive in direction only for Protestants and Jews; for Catholics, a negative relationship emerged. For the variable of family-size preferences, positive correlations of greate* magnitude emerged, but only for Catholics and Jews, not Protestants. The negative relationship between education and family-size preferences among Catholics prompted an analysis of church-related education. This analysis proved fruitful and provided the explanation both of the negative relationship with fertility planning and the positive relationship with number of children desired. Catholics with the highest education *and* the most education in religious schools exhibit the least tendency to plan fertility and express desires for an average of more than five children. When these relationships are examined for Catholics whose education was secular, the same types of associations emerge as exist for non-Catholics. This important finding clearly demands a refinement in generalizations about the relation of education to fertility planning.

234

The second general component of socio-economic status, the social dimension, is a cluster of measures of occupational prestige, social-class identification, level of status satisfaction, and a number of related attitudinal measures. The main finding here is a positive association with family-size preferences and successful fertility planning among the Jewish group, a relationship of the same type observed with education. For Catholics, only slight positive relationships appeared and for Protestants little association at all was evident.

The third component of socio-economic status is the economic, including measures of income, feelings of economic security, regularity of credit buying, and the relevance of finances in decisions to have another child. With respect to the first two variables—income and economic security—correlations, quite low in magnitude, exist only for Protestants. As expected, the direction is positive with fertility-planning success, but contrary to the hypothesis, higher income associates with fewer children desired. For the total sample, there is hardly any relationship evident; some suggestion exists that slightly smaller family orientations associate with combinations of high income and low security, and low income on the one hand, and feelings of high security, on the other hand.

The hypothesis that feelings of economic security would produce an atmosphere conducive to contraceptive risk-taking was tested and rejected. At least on the basis of the fertility experience of these couples to date, no such relationship is evident; in fact, there is some indication that couples in the blue-collar occupational class are more prone to chance-taking than those in the white-collar class.

The final two hypotheses examined in this chapter relate to credit buying as a predictor of unsuccessful planning, and the direct perception of the relevance of finances in decisions to have another child with the number of children desired. The regularity of credit buying does correlate negatively with successful fertility planning, but at a tangible level only among Jews. Fairly substantial negative correlations are evident between the perceived relevance of finances in fertility decisions and the number of children desired by the wife for all religious groupings except Jews. For the Catholic groups, these correlations would appear to involve degrees of religiousness; for religious Catholics, there is a slight tendency for financial considerations not to constitute primary legitimate grounds for preventing another pregnancy.

In summary, the analysis thus far suggests that different orders of variables relate to family-size preferences and fertility-planning success for Protestants, Catholics, and Jews. Among Protestants, few relationships have been observed at all. However, the economic component seems to reveal correlations with the fertility variables only for Protestants.

For Catholics, some of the factors affecting fertility appear to be reducible to the degree of adherence to Catholic doctrine. And finally, for Jews the primary associations seem to revolve around education and social status.

Only slight associations between socio-economic status and measures of fertility were reported in the study by Freedman, Whelpton, and Campbell as well. Small and unsystematic economic and occupational differentials were interpreted by the researchers as further evidence of the narrowing of the traditional differentials, a result of the increasing fertility of the higher status groups and the declining fertility among the lower classes. Similar evidence for the narrowing of many of the socio-economic fertility differentials is contained in the recent comprehensive analysis of appropriate census data by Grabill, Kiser, and Whelpton.[23]

Our data would seem to indicate that underlying the contraction of these differentials in actual fertility is an increasing homogeneity of socio-economic differences both in the number of children desired and the effectiveness of fertility planning. This is consistent with the Freedman, Whelpton, and Campbell report, which combines actual with expected fertility.

Although some differences have been ascertained for the different religious groupings, they have been only suggested by the simple analyses thus far conducted. The multivariate analyses in Chapter XIX shed more light on the nature of the underlying factors associated with fertility in the different religious groups. Moreover, the variables discussed in this chapter have not taken into account the effects of *change* in socio-economic status, about which there has been considerable theorizing in connection with fertility. The next chapter will analyze such change in terms of social mobility.

[23] *The Fertility of American Women*, chapters 5, 6, and 7.

Chapter XIV.   Social Mobility

An interest in the dynamic aspects of status follows logically from the analysis of class differences in fertility.[1] The basic theoretical rationale for the inclusion of socio-economic status in the study of fertility is that different occupations, levels of education and of income imply different patterns of values and life interests, which, in turn, possess varying degrees of compatibility with smaller or larger families. However, class level tends to emphasize only the picture at the moment. Many individuals at the same class level have been exposed to a similar environment all their lives, others have been upwardly mobile, and still others downwardly mobile. For some, mobility has been a result of marriage, and for others the product of their own efforts.

It is this dynamic aspect of socio-economic status that has appealed to students of fertility as a possible source of intraclass variations in fertility. The basic hypothesis is simple enough and has been expressed frequently in the literature: the socio-economic and psychological requirements for upward mobility are inconsistent with expenditures of time, energy, and money for children. As a general proposition, this hypothesis appears reasonable enough but numerous qualifications are immediately appropriate. For some persons, the "requirements" may be more exacting than for others. Then there is the question of economic level—the economic costs of another child may not constitute a handicap beyond a certain income level.

Perhaps even more of a complication is the fact that social mobility as measured in objective categories of income or occupational change may not sufficiently reflect level of aspiration.[2] It is probable that decisions about another child or the effectiveness of contraceptive practice are involved with the attitudinal or perceptual aspect of the level of aspiration, an aspect that may be only loosely connected to visible changes in circumstances. Thus, couples who have moved up the scale rapidly may perceive their situation as not requiring so much devotion to the process of moving upward as other couples who may not have moved so rapidly. And, of course, many

[1] Charles F. Westoff, "The Changing Focus of Differential Fertility Research," Milbank Memorial Fund *Quarterly*, xxxi (1953), pp. 24–38. Early theoretical statements were contained in Arsene Dumont, *Dépopulation et Civilization*, Paris, 1890, and his *Natalité et Démocratie*, Paris, 1898. Also see P. A. Sorokin, *Social Mobility*, Harper, New York, 1927.

[2] This proposition has been confirmed in a systematic analysis of the components of social mobility. All in all, nine orthogonal factors of social mobility were determined and described in Charles F. Westoff, Marvin Bressler, and Philip C. Sagi, "The Concept of Social Mobility: An Empirical Inquiry," *American Sociological Review*, Vol. 25, No. 3 (1960), pp. 375–385.

individuals may be extremely ambitious and yet be in a job situation where they have either already reached their ceiling of advancement or in which the rewards are assured over the long-term range. Thus, it seems clear that some measure of mobility aspirations had to be included to tap this more subjective and elusive dimension.

PREVIOUS RESEARCH

Most research in this area has been spotty and frequently reflects utilization of data not collected specifically for the study of social mobility. Nevertheless, the earlier research has indicated some support of the general hypothesis. Bresard and Girard[3] in a study of job changes and intergenerational mobility on a national sample of about 3,000 males in France concluded that "it is in the group of small families that we note the largest proportion of persons who have risen socially."[4]

Berent, in a study of British data,[5] found that when the family size of persons in the same class of origin is considered, those who have moved "up" (intergenerationally) have the smallest families, on the average, and those who have moved "down" have the largest families, with static families having an average size intermediate between the two. On the other hand, when persons of the same present social status are compared, the pattern is reversed. Berent interpreted this difference as "the acquisition of the fertility characteristics of the class into which the sons have moved and the maintenance by them of the family building habits of the class in which they were born."[6] His analysis of intragenerational occupational mobility revealed the expected pattern of upward mobility associated with low fertility.

Goldberg in an analysis of differential fertility of Detroit women having children in the prewar period reports that "mobility has little effect on completed family size. Families having any history of white-collar employment, the stable white, the up and down mobiles, cannot be distinguished from one another . . . Family size consequences of status and social mobility are virtually absent in a two generation urbanite population."[7]

[3] Marcel Bresard, "Mobilité sociale et dimension de la famille," *Population*, No. 3 (1950), pp. 533–566; Alain Girard, "Mobilité sociale et dimension de la famille. Deuxième Partie: Enquête dans les lycées et les facultés," *ibid.*, No. 1 (1951), pp. 103–124.

[4] Bresard, "Mobilité sociale et dimension de la famille," p. 563.

[5] Jerzy Berent, "Fertility and Social Mobility," *Population Studies*, v (1952), pp. 244–260. This study was a report of an inquiry undertaken by the Population Investigation Committee and the Nuffield Research Unit of the London School of Economics into various aspects of the relationship between social stratification and fertility.

[6] *Ibid.*, p. 248.

[7] David Goldberg, "The Fertility of Two-Generation Urbanites," *Population Studies*, xii (1959), pp. 214–222.

Two studies of the relation of occupational mobility to fertility were reported in the Indianapolis Study series. The first report by Kantner and Kiser[8] supported the hypotheses that "families exhibiting intergenerational mobility tend to be smaller than nonmobile couples of comparable status" and that "similar results are found when the analysis is restricted to planned families." The association of mobility with fertility-planning success was less clear but the authors concluded that "the data are not inconsistent with the view that mobility partially overcomes resistances to contraception, giving upwardly mobile couples a position intermediate in fertility planning effectiveness between the levels of effectiveness of origin and destination groups."[9]

The Indianapolis data were also explored to determine the relationship between occupational mobility after marriage and fertility. Riemer and Kiser write:

"The proportions of successful fertility planners and average family sizes by broad categories of occupational mobility after marriage are in general consistent with the notions that upward mobility is at the expense of some deliberate fertility restriction . . . They failed to show, however, that either the total or planned fertility of upwardly mobile couples is as low as that of couples nonmobile at the white-collar level after marriage. . . . It appears that deliberate childlessness, rather than small families accounts for much of the low planned fertility of mobile couples.[10]

The Indianapolis Study was concentrated on variations in fertility among Protestants. A more recent study by Brooks and Henry is focused on the association of occupational mobility with fertility among Catholics. These researchers found a low *positive* relationship between the husband's intragenerational occupational mobility and fertility. The correlation reported, however, was only .05.[11] Their interpretation of the unexpected result of a positive correlation is that it is consistent with the finding of a direct association between socioeconomic status and fertliity. The reasoning, in brief, is that the

[8] John F. Kantner and Clyde V. Kiser, "The Interrelation of Fertility, Fertility Planning, and Intergenerational Social Mobility," in P. K. Whelpton and Clyde V. Kiser, eds., *Social and Psychological Factors Affecting Fertility*, 5 Vols., Milbank Memorial Fund, New York, 1946–1958, IV, pp. 969–1,003.

[9] *Ibid.*, pp. 1,001–1,002.

[10] Ruth Riemer and Clyde V. Kiser, "Economic Tension and Social Mobility in Relation to Fertility Planning and Size of Planned Family," in Whelpton and Kiser, *Social and Psychological Factors Affecting Fertility*, (1954) IV, pp. 1,048–1,049.

[11] Hugh E. Brooks and Franklin J. Henry, "An Empirical Study of the Relationships of Catholic Practice and Occupational Mobility to Fertility," *Milbank Memorial Fund Quarterly*, XXXVI (1958), pp. 222–281.

upwardly mobile will assimilate the fertility values of the status groups toward which they are oriented and, if higher rather than lower fertility is the norm, the mobile couples will conform to this value.[12]

A similar argument is propounded by Boggs following an indication of a slight positive association between husband's level of aspiration and fertility. In his small sample study of a suburban, elite community south of San Francisco, Boggs suggests that "urbanization, prosperity and education may have altered the processes of upward mobility in such a way that children are not now perceived as alternatives to advancement."[13]

From the pretest analysis preceding the present study, the authors come to the following conclusion:

There is a slight but consistent tendency for wives to express desires for larger families if their socio-economic position is favorable, if they feel economically secure, if they do not feel the need to strive to get ahead, and if they feel reasonable confidence about the future and the opportunities they can give their children.[14]

However, a positive correlation of .24 was reported between the husband's intergenerational occupational mobility and the size of family desired by his wife. Similarly, a positive correlation of .26 was cited between income change in the preceding year and number of children desired.[15]

In summary, the results of most of the studies of couples in the early 1940's and preceding decades show the classic inverse relation of fertility to upward mobility. More recent studies suggest a change in this association perhaps not unconnected with the more substantiated reversals of the relationship between fertility and various measures of socio-economic status. But this is by no means clear-cut. What is clear is that the associations are low, that social mobility has been measured in various ways which may not be equivalent, that fertility has also been indexed in different ways, and that religion and socio-economic status may influence the nature and extent of the association.

THE PRESENT ANALYSIS

A number of specific hypotheses have been derived from the basic theme. Instead of presenting each of these at the outset, however, a

[12] *Ibid.*, pp. 267–271.
[13] Stephen T. Boggs, "Family Size and Social Mobility in a California Suburb," *Eugenics Quarterly*, 4 (1957), p. 209.
[14] Frank W. Notestein, *et al.* "Pretest Results of a New Study of Fertility in the United States," *International Statistical Institute Bulletin*, 36 (1958), p. 158.
[15] *Ibid.*, Table 2, p. 159.

series of tests will be made of the general hypothesis that upward mobility is inversely related to desired size of family and directly associated with fertility-planning success. This hypothesis will be examined in the light of a considerable amount of data collected specifically for the purpose.

One general caution must be stated. The selective nature of the sample has had the effect of automatically excluding the extreme low fertility couples (those who are childless or have only one child over a comparable marriage duration) who might most sharply manifest a strong mobility drive. An argument could be developed that an intensely ambitious individual would not marry at all or at least would postpone marriage for a number of years sufficient to depress his potential fertility. This means that the hypothesis is being subjected to a more rigorous test than it might otherwise be—the independent variables are being challenged to discriminate among two-child couples who have had no, one, or two planned pregnancies and who express preferences for two, three, or four or more children. This restriction is acceptable, however, since if the mobility hypothesis is important its demographic implications are most appropriate for the more typical sample represented in this study. The final reservation is implicit throughout the whole analysis of the first interview data: the ultimate test of the hypothesis is future behavior

OCCUPATIONAL MOBILITY

The association of occupational mobility and fertility is analyzed in the context of both changes in occupational class (divided into the white-collar and blue-collar class) and differences in prestige ratings. For the latter analysis, both intra- and intergenerational comparisons are feasible.[16] The extent of change in broad occupational class during the limited period of marriage represented in this sample, however, is very slight. A total of 88 per cent of all husbands were in the same class (either white-collar or blue-collar) at the time of the birth of their second child as they were at marriage.[17] Across generations, however, only two thirds of the husbands were in the same class as either their fathers or fathers-in-law.[18]

The fact that an individual is in a white-collar occupation whose

[16] The small fraction of the sample (about 4 per cent) whose fathers were in farm occupations are eliminated from this analysis and treated separately in the chapter on residence.

[17] Of the remaining 12 per cent, two thirds had changed from a blue-collar to a white-collar occupation and the other one third from the white-collar to blue-collar class.

[18] In both cases, 22 per cent of all sons are in white-collar occupations while fathers or fathers-in-law were classified in a blue-collar occupation. The remaining 13 per cent were cases of downward mobility.

father was in the blue-collar class does not necessarily imply upward mobility, even ignoring income and other nonoccupational dimensions. One has to consider the changes in occupational structure over time throughout the country, since it may be easier in 1950 to be in a white-collar occupation than it was twenty years before. On examination, however, the differences in the proportions of males in the economically active civilian population who are in white-collar occupations in 1950 compared with 1930 is not so great as expected: 30.5 per cent and 25.2 per cent respectively.[19] The difference is even less if the comparison is restricted to males in nonfarm occupations: 35.8 and 33.5 per cent in white-collar occupations in the more recent and earlier period respectively.[20] These small differences, therefore, do not warrant any great concern about adjustments for secular trends. A more refined analysis, of course, would have to take into account the upgrading of skills within these two groupings.

If the general mobility hypothesis is correct, evidence should be discernible in this crude analysis. Thus, in the fourfold tables formed by the white-collar–blue-collar dichotomy across generations, we should expect the lowest fertility among the couples who have moved "up," with the stable groups evidencing indications of higher fertility. These statistics are presented in Table 70 for each religion.

The fertility differences by intergenerational mobility types are extremely small and mostly insignificant statistically. For Protestants, no systematic pattern appears at all. Among Catholics, lower fertility indications seem to characterize individuals currently in the blue-collar occupational class, regardless of class of origin. The higher fertility orientations are found in the white-collar class, mostly among couples whose parental class of origin is also white-collar.

The Jewish group contains only two categories sufficiently large for analysis: wives and husbands in the white-collar class whose parents were in the same class (comprising 59 and 61 per cent of the Jewish totals respectively) and the upwardly mobile group (23 and 22 per cent of Jewish wives and husbands). Among Jews also the fertility differences between the two classes are small but, with the exception of fertility-planning status, do go in the hypothesized direction.

Thus, this limited analysis indicates that upward mobility is associated with lower fertility only among Jews and not very strongly at all. In fact, even in this group, the successful fertility planners are not the upwardly mobile. Among Protestants, the four types might

19 Bureau of the Census, Working Paper, No. 5, *Occupational Trends in the United States 1900 to 1950*, U.S. Department of Commerce, 1958, Table 2.
20 *Ibid.* Calculated from Table 1.

TABLE 70A

Fertility Indicators by Current Occupational Class of Husband, Classified by the
Longest Occupational Class of His Father

Longest Occupational Class of Husband's Father	Husband's Current Occupational Class					
	Protestants		Catholics and Mixed Catholics		Jews	
	MEAN NUMBER OF CHILDREN DESIRED BY HUSBAND					
	White-Collar	Blue-Collar	White-Collar	Blue-Collar	White-Collar	Blue-Collar
White-collar	2.9	2.7	3.8	3.6	2.9	*
Blue-collar	3.0	2.8	3.6	3.5	2.7	*
	PER CENT OF SUCCESSFUL PLANNERS					
	White-Collar	Blue-Collar	White-Collar	Blue-Collar	White-Collar	Blue-Collar
White-collar	71%	53%	51%	62%	91%	*
Blue-collar	61	56	48	49	81	*
	MEAN NUMBER OF MONTHS FROM MARRIAGE TO SECOND BIRTH					
	White-Collar	Blue-Collar	White-Collar	Blue-Collar	White-Collar	Blue-Collar
White-collar	63	59	52	56	68	*
Blue-collar	63	60	58	58	75	*

TABLE 70B

Fertility Indicators by Current Occupational Class of Husband, Classified by the
Longest Occupational Class of His Wife's Father

Longest Occupational Class of Wife's Father	Husband's Current Occupational Class					
	Protestants		Catholics and Mixed Catholics		Jews	
	MEAN NUMBER OF CHILDREN DESIRED BY WIFE					
	White-Collar	Blue-Collar	White-Collar	Blue-Collar	White-Collar	Blue-Collar
White-collar	3.1	3.0	4.0	3.5	2.9	*
Blue-collar	3.1	2.9	3.8	3.4	2.7	*
	PER CENT OF SUCCESSFUL PLANNERS					
	White-Collar	Blue-Collar	White-Collar	Blue-Collar	White-Collar	Blue-Collar
White-collar	66%	66%	48%	58%	87%	*
Blue-collar	66	53	49	53	86	*
	MEAN NUMBER OF MONTHS FROM MARRIAGE TO SECOND BIRTH					
	White-Collar	Blue-Collar	White-Collar	Blue-Collar	White-Collar	Blue-Collar
White-Collar	59	56	51	60	66	*
Blue-collar	67	59	54	57	81	*

NOTE: Asterisk indicates less than 20 cases.

just as well be random samples of the Protestant population as far as fertility is concerned.

Among Catholics the fact of present class is more important than origin, although a white-collar origin apparently raises the fertility orientations of persons currently in the white-collar class.

Each occupation was also coded on the North–Hatt prestige-rating scale, with the differences in scale values representing a crude index of occupational mobility both across generations and within the husband's job history since marriage.

The association of occupational mobility (as measured in prestige terms) with fertility can be summarized conveniently without the aid of a table: for each religious grouping as well as for the total sample, the correlations of all types of mobility comparisons with the number of children desired by the wife or the husband and with fertility-planning success are statistically indistinguishable from zero. Although different combinations of these measures might provide some association with fertility, the initial correlation analyses are so uniformly low that further analysis appears unwarranted. Such a conclusion seems further justified when we consider the crudity of the measurement of prestige. More important for the validity of the general hypothesis is the possibility that changes in occupational prestige may not sufficiently reflect those aspects of change critical to fertility, such as changes in income.

CHANGES IN INCOME

The average income earned by the husband in his first year of marriage was $4,100; by the time his wife was interviewed after the birth of their second child some five years later on the average, his income had increased to $5,600. Not everyone shared equally in this increase, however. Nearly 25 per cent of the wives reported their husband's earnings in the first year of their marriage to be the same as his current income; however, only 5 per cent indicated a decrease in their husband's earnings. Catholic couples experienced the smallest rise in income, an average of $1,200, while Jewish couples had the greatest increase, averaging $2,100. This discrepancy can be partly accounted for by differences in marriage duration, with the Jewish couples having been married an average of fifteen months longer than Catholic couples.

The same generalizations apply when total family income, rather than only husbands' earnings, is considered, except that the modal experience is one of "no change" since the first year of marriage. This difference arises primarily because the wife's contribution to the family income in the first year of marriage when she was working tends to be balanced by the increase in her husband's earnings over the years. Because of this complication, analysis of income change and fertility will be confined to the husband's earnings.[21]

The relationship between income change and number of children desired is negative, though low in magnitude (see Table 71); the

TABLE 71

Correlations of the Change in Husband's Earnings since the First Year of Marriage with the Number of Children Desired by Wife and Husband, Fertility-Planning Success, and Number of Months from Marriage to Second Child

Religion	Number of Children Desired by Wife	Number of Children Desired by Husband	Fertility-Planning Success	Number of Months from Marriage to Second Birth
Protestant total	−.14	−.13	.18	.45
Mixed Catholic total	−.24	−.20	.13	.36
Catholic total	−.14	−.12	.04	.31
Jewish total	−.03	.03	.16	.30
All couples	−.17	−.14	.15	.39

greater the increase in the husband's earnings since the first year of marriage, the fewer children desired. The hypothesized relationship also obtains with extent of fertility-planning success, more success being associated with upward mobility. These relationships are the same for both the white and blue-collar occupational classes and for the religious groupings (although among Jews the relationship with family-size preferences, and among Catholics the association with fertility-planning success, disappeared).

There is a methodological problem implicit in the design of the study of interpreting the meaning of associations between the fertility variables and independent variables such as income change which are tied to the event of the second birth. For example, it is plausible to expect a positive association between income change and the length of birth intervals on the assumption that persons oriented toward financial success will be more likely to defer pregnancies. The correlation for the total sample (Table 71) is .39. Because of the study design, however, the interval between marriage and the second birth

---

[21] The conclusions are identical regardless of which measure of income is used. In order to eliminate the dramatic increases in husband's earnings that would result from an initial level of no income because he was a student during his first year of marriage, the question was phrased in terms of his earnings during the first year he was working regularly.

constitutes duration of marriage. In other words, all couples were interviewed during the first half of 1957, some six months after the birth of their second child which occurred in September 1956. Thus, the only variable is their date of marriage or how long it took these couples to have two children. The interpretive problem stems from the fact that there is a common denominator of *time* in marriage duration and opportunity for increases in income. The income data collected are limited to current income and income during the first year of marriage, and the longer the gap in time separating these two periods (up to a certain point at least), the more likely it is that the change will be greater.

There is no complete solution to this problem, a problem affecting several other independent variables as well. One refinement that does eliminate part of the time dimension is to limit the comparison to the intended intervals[22] of couples who planned both pregnancies, as inferred from the length of time contraception was used before deliberate interruption in order to conceive. The multiple correlation of income change with the intended length of first and second birth intervals is .36. Again, the interpretation is clouded by the under-lying time factor but the over-all conclusion would seem warranted that couples who have experienced increases in income during this early part of their marriage tend to practice contraception more effectively, have their first two children over a longer period of time, and want smaller families.

Several additional analyses were conducted with this variable of income change. One technique which standardizes the time dimension, although it introduces other difficulties, is to calculate the average annual increase in income and correlate it with the interval between marriage and the second conception. This correlation proved negligible. This procedure of course makes the completely unrealistic assumption that income change is distributed evenly over the total marriage period, whereas a few series of increases or changes perhaps accompanying a job change is the more probable expectation.

In any event, the study simply does not contain data detailed enough to connect income change to the months preceding conceptions. This was not an oversight but a realization of the unreliability of income data recalled over time in such detail. A question was asked whether the husband's income for 1956 was different from that of the previous year. Only qualitative answers were sought and the distribution revealed nearly 70 per cent reporting that their income had increased. This is not at all an improbable estimate (about

[22] See Chapter VII for description.

20 per cent reported their income the same as the preceding year and 10 per cent indicated a decline) considering the ages of the husbands and the buoyant state of the national economy in 1956. The distribution is, however, too extreme and the categories too crude to permit analysis of the influence of this factor on the conception of the second pregnancy.

Another consideration provided the basis for one final type of analysis of the relationship between income change and fertility behavior. It could be argued plausibly that relative change in income has more critical psychological implications than absolute change. Thus, an income increase from $2,000 to $4,000 might be more significant than a similar absolute change at the $6,000 level. The correlation of per cent change in income with the number of children desired and fertility-planning success is in the expected direction but the magnitudes are low: —.16 and —.13 with the number of children desired by wives and husbands respectively, and .10 with fertility-planning success. Again, however, the time dimension creates the same problem. Standardizing the per cent change in income by dividing through by marriage duration results in a series of negligible correlations with the fertility variables.

The over-all conclusion to be drawn from these analyses is not one that can be stated confidently because of the complexities in testing the hypothesis which are created by the sample design. In all probability, upward mobility is *weakly* associated with an orientation toward smaller families, longer spacing intervals between births, and successful fertility planning. The second interview with these couples will provide an opportunity to conduct a more refined analysis of the relationship between income change since the second birth and subsequent fertility.

The Perception of the Effect of Children on Mobility

The preceding analysis reveals little indication of any strong association between occupational or financial mobility with fertility. The analysis now turns to the potential effects on fertility of the attitudinal components of mobility. There have been a number of different approaches developed to measure various aspects of what might be termed an "upward mobility orientation" or level of aspiration—that is, to measure the importance attached to mobility values, drive to get ahead, need achievement, aspirations for sending children to college, and the like.

The first question to be answered is whether mothers in their own minds perceive any connection between having children and getting ahead in life. This is obviously not a conclusive test of the behavioral hypothesis—individuals whose behavior is consistent with some theoretical expectation are not necessarily aware of the motivating factors—but it would certainly strengthen interpretation. To obtain some impression of this, the following question was asked of each mother: In what ways, if any, would having another child in the next couple of years affect your chances to get ahead? Judging from the responses, the meaning imputed to "getting ahead" was primarily financial. The modal response to the question was negative—an answer simply of "not at all" or "none"; over 60 per cent of the total sample gave this answer. Although there were no specific expectations about the distribution of responses to this question, the fact that such a high proportion replied negatively is surprising. Among these 60 per cent, there are even a small number who felt that having another child would have a positive effect on their chances to get ahead. Such replies usually carried moral overtones about how it would make the husband work harder, give him a sense of responsibility, bring blessings, and have similar advantages.

At the opposite end of the scale, only a little over 2 per cent felt that having another child would hurt their chances very much. Responses were uniformly cast in the context of financial concerns: "I feel we would never get ahead because we would have to move and our finances just could not take it," or a realization that another child would further delay the mother's ability to work were typical responses.

The remaining responses tended to isolate some single, major unfavorable effect such as having to defer purchasing a home or automobile, or something in this general category. A few women also mentioned their health.

The income level of the respondent is relevant to her responses to this question. Women with low income or who feel insecure economically tended to reply that another child would have an unfavorable effect, although the correlations are not so high as to preclude the operation of other factors.[23]

As expected, the perception of another child as a mobility impediment is associated with a desire for fewer children. The correlations, homogeneous throughout the religion and class categories, are −.20 with wives' family-size desires and −.15 for husbands. Part of this reaction—viewing children as inimical to material progress—may result from a failure to have planned the first two pregnancies successfully. This possibility is supported by its correlation with fertility-

[23] The multiple correlation of the extent to which a child is perceived to affect chances to get ahead with husband's earnings and the wife's feeling of economic security is .33.

planning success, which although low (−.11) is unexpectedly negative.

These results cannot, of course, be relied upon as a test of the mobility hypothesis since the question asked contains the variable of fertility within itself. The analyses which follow can be viewed as more independent tests.

Perception of Opportunities

In an open-class system, opportunities for success are differentially distributed, democratic ideologies notwithstanding. The aspirations of the average American couple are mainly dependent upon the husband's work and their perceptions of the opportunities it affords. Needless to say, jobs vary tremendously in their potential for individual advancement, ranging from those in which the ceiling is reached at a comparatively young age to those in which the proverbial sky is the limit. From the point of view of the wife, her husband's rate of mobility will affect many of the basic facts of her existence—the type of home and neighborhood in which she can expect to live, the clothes she will be wearing, the family automobile, their children's education and a host of other considerations—in short, her level of consumption and style of life. Although the prestige value of her husband's occupational status is doubtless a significant factor in many subtle ways, it is the expected changes in income which can be translated more clearly into the elements deemed relevant to fertility.

We are thus concerned, in this section, with analyzing the implications for fertility of the wife's perception of her husband's opportunities for advancement in his work. Two relevant questions were asked in the interview with appropriate multiple-choice categories: (1) What do you think your husband's chances are for getting ahead in his present line of work? (2) How much is your husband finding it possible to improve his chances for getting ahead? Most women seem to have fairly definite ideas on the subject as evidenced by the few "don't know" responses received. The answers to the first question were distributed as follows: 33 per cent replied "very good," 38 per cent "good," 20 per cent only "fair," and 9 per cent replied "not so good." The second question was answered similarly: 31 per cent replying "very much," 35 per cent "much," 27 per cent "little" and 7 per cent replying "not at all." As expected, the correlation between the two items is high (.75) and justifies combining them in an index labeled "perception of opportunities." The hypothesis with respect to fertility is that wives who perceive their

249

husband's job future with optimism will be less likely to wish to restrict family size. The correlations of the index with the number of children desired by the wife are consistent with this hypothesis, but the values are quite low (see Table 72). Despite the fact that white-collar wives perceive significantly greater opportunities for their

TABLE 72

Correlations between the Wife's Perception of Her Husband's Mobility Opportunities and the Number of Children She Desires

Religion	Number of Children Desired by Wife
Protestant total	.14
Mixed Catholic total	.01
Catholic total	.17
Jewish total	.10
All couples	.09

husbands, on the average, than do blue-collar wives, the correlations are homogeneous throughout the class-religion divisions of the sample.

DRIVE TO GET AHEAD

Changes in income and perceptions of opportunities are not sufficient to describe the entire mobility process. In addition to these components, there is the importance attached to the perceived rewards of success and the level of drive to get ahead. As already noted, the hypothesis that fertility is negatively associated with level of aspiration or ambition has been present in the literature for some time. One of the major orientations of the current study has been to test the validity of this hypothesis. Obviously, this test will be inconclusive as far as actual future fertility is concerned—a shortcoming that will be remedied at least partly by the data collected in the second interview—but the present analysis is appropriate to the question of whether both past contraceptive practice and the total number of children desired are associated with mobility aspirations.

The measurement of mobility aspirations is still at a primitive stage in social research. There are a number of obvious complications in measuring this variable that make it difficult to devise a set of questions that will be equally meaningful to individuals at all socio-economic levels. Another problem is the question of whether to emphasize the economic or the more broadly social aspects of these aspirations. And still another complexity arises with respect to the content of aspirations for women as opposed to men.

Experiments were made in the pretests of this study to develop a satisfactory measure. The net result was to rely on a series of questions (essentially similar for wives and husbands) the format for which had been used in recent studies of mobility aspirations.[24] Although the final product is somewhat different from the previously used versions as a result of the pretests and subsequent modifications of items, the approach is basically the same. The respondent is presented with the question of the value or importance of getting ahead in life (work is emphasized for husbands) as well as with a list of thirteen other values and she is asked whether she would be willing to sacrifice each value in order to get ahead. The list of items ranges over such values as having to leave friends, having to become more active in community organizations not of her own choice, having to keep quiet about religious views, having her husband in a job with opportunity but not security, having her husband spend more time at work, and having to send her children to another school not quite as good. A direct question was also asked whether she would be willing to postpone having another child in order to get ahead.

A similar index was devised for the husbands who completed mail questionnaires in addition to an eight item index on the "importance of getting ahead," but the analytical results are so similar to those revealed by the "drive to get ahead" index that the former will be omitted in the presentation.

The logic of the question structure underlying these indices of "drive to get ahead" is that respondents who feel that these other considerations would be more important than "getting ahead" are revealing lower levels of aspiration than those who would disregard or sacrifice the other values. Of course, there is considerable variation in the extent to which persons are willing to sacrifice these other values, ranging, for example, from 86 per cent of the wives who would be willing to leave friends to 27 per cent who would be willing to keep quiet about their religious views in order to get ahead. Husbands, similarly, are most willing to leave friends (76 per cent), least willing to keep quiet about their religious views (25 per cent). There are only very few wives or husbands who endorse all items positively (5 per

[24] Leonard Reissman, "Level of Aspiration and Social Class," *American Sociological Review*, 18 (1953), pp. 233–242, Russell R. Dynes, Alfred C. Clarke, and Simon Dinitz, "Level of Occupational Aspiration: Some Aspects of Family Experience as a Variable," *ibid.*, 21 (1956), pp. 212–215; Boggs, "Family Size and Social Mobility in a California Suburb." See extensive citations in Westoff, Bressler, and Sagi, "The Concept of Social Mobility."

cent of wives and 2 per cent of husbands) or who would be unwilling to sacrifice any of these values in order to get ahead (2 and 5 per cent respectively). On the average, wives endorse 4.4 items and husbands 3.5 of the total of eight items. There is a slight class difference, with persons in the white-collar class tending to be more inclined to sacrifice other values in order to get ahead. Comparisons by religion indicate lower aspiration scores for Catholics than for Protestants or Jews, a result partially of the differential endorsement of the question on keeping quiet about religious views.

The hypotheses to be tested are that individuals who have a high drive to get ahead will want smaller families and will exhibit more successful levels of fertility control than couples whose aspirations are presumably lower. The correlations, for wives and husbands separately,[25] are presented in Table 73. The correlations with family-

TABLE 73

Correlations of "Drive to Get Ahead" with Number of Children Desired and Fertility-Planning Success

Religion	Number of Children Desired		Fertility-Planning Success	
	Wife	Husband	Wife	Husband
Protestant total	.01	.03	.00	−.12
Mixed Catholic total	−.15	−.18	−.22	−.15
Catholic total	−.06	−.11	−.01	−.11
Jewish total	−.17	−.02	−.12	−.11
All couples	−.10	−.13	−.01	−.08

size desires are in the hypothesized direction but are low in magnitude; in fact, the values for Protestants are zero, although the variability of the correlations throughout the four religious groupings is small enough to have occurred by chance. Nor does holding class constant affect the pattern of homogeneity. An even lower set of values is evidenced with fertility-planning success, but these are unexpectedly negative in sign. Thus, what little association does exist (and for predictive purposes there is none) indicates that poor rather than successful control of fertility associates with a drive to get ahead. This same pattern of association prevailed in the pretest analysis and the explanation advanced then still seems relevant. What type of person is likely to report willingness to sacrifice important social,

[25] A separate analysis of joint classifications for the couple revealed no additional information.

familial, and ideological values in order to get ahead? Is it the individual who is actually moving upward? That the correlations with actual change in income are zero both for wives and husbands makes this explanation unlikely. A rather extensive analysis was undertaken to determine the correlates of these measures of mobility aspiration and very little was found. The only reasonably consistent pattern that emerges may be interpreted as a deprivation response—individuals who feel they are not doing as well as they should or as they would like, tend to report more willingness to sacrifice other values in order to get ahead. It may be that lack of success in planning the spacing of births contributes to this sense of deprivation or that there is an underlying common factor of ineffectiveness. Of course, only those individuals who wanted no children or only one child in order to facilitate mobility but who failed to achieve such fertility control would be eligible for inclusion in the sample; those who succeeded would not.

Income Change and Drive to Get Ahead

There is little evidence from these data that past changes in income are related to mobility aspirations. This may be due to the crudity of measurement, particularly considering the fact that the former is measured over the entire duration of marriage and the latter represents an attitudinal disposition measured at the time of the interview. Regardless of the explanation, it is of interest to raise the question whether different patterns of family-size preferences and fertility control characterize different combinations of changes in income and levels of aspiration. The theoretical expectation is that couples whose record of income change indicates upward mobility and whose drive to get ahead is also high will desire fewer children and will have exhibited more success in fertility control. In order to minimize the temporal biases involved in marriage duration, income change is expressed in terms of the average annual change. On the assumption that relative increases in income would provide a more psychologically meaningful classification, the per cent change in income was computed. Thus, the classification becomes the rather abstract statistic of "mean annual per cent change in income," which is then cross-classified with the indices of "drive to get ahead" dichotomized at the median into high and low scores. The average number of children desired and the proportions of successful planners are shown in Table 74 for each of the resultant categories. As expected, although the pattern is clearer for wives than for husbands, individuals desiring the smallest families tend to be those whose income has

TABLE 74

Number of Children Desired and Proportion of Successful Fertility Planners,
by Change in Income and Drive to Get Ahead

MEAN ANNUAL PER CENT CHANGE IN HUSBAND'S INCOME (mid-point of interval)	MEAN NUMBER CHILDREN DESIRED				PER CENT SUCCESSFUL PLANNERS			
	Drive to Get Ahead				Drive to Get Ahead			
	Low	High	Low	High	Low	High	Low	High
	(wives)		(husbands)		(wives)		(husbands)	
Down 7.5	3.3	3.5	3.3	3.0	68%	57%	75%	57%
No change	3.6	3.5	3.5	3.3	51	52	49	49
Up 5.0	3.3	3.1	3.2	3.0	60	63	67	59
Up 25.0	3.3	3.1	3.2	3.0	61	61	56	66

gone up and who report a drive to get ahead.[26] The expected concentration of successful planners in this group is not revealed however. The main systematic difference is the apparent tendency for couples whose income has not changed to exhibit the lowest proportions of successful fertility planning.

ASPIRATIONS TO SEND CHILDREN TO COLLEGE

The components of mobility aspirations thus far described relate primarily to the respondent's future, with no clear picture of the comparative weight of egoistic or familistic orientations. Many persons conceive of social mobility in terms of the future status of their children and perceive their own role to be that of maximizing opportunities for their children. Such an attitude may or may not derive from a frustration of the parents' ambitions or that feeling of deprivation which is expressed in the familiar phrase "giving my kids the breaks I never had as a kid." Whatever the background of the attitude, the avenue of mobility for the child is perceived clearly to be education. A college education is rapidly becoming a *sine qua non* of entry into managerial, professional, and technical jobs. Thus, the parents' ambitions for their children will tend to take the form of concern that their children be able to take advantage of higher education—a concern which may conflict with having additional children.

A fairly common response encountered in the pretest to the question of why no more children were desired for women who wanted to stop at two was that they felt they could not adequately meet the

[26] For both wives and husbands, the average number of children desired among those whose income has risen and who have a "high" drive to get ahead is significantly (below the .01 level) lower than the average family-size preferences of the remaining groups considered collectively.

costs of raising more than two children. More often than not, this type of reply revealed a concern for the costs of sending children to college, a subject about which there has been much recent publicity. Undoubtedly, many women are using this socially acceptable consideration as a rationalization for not wanting more children for quite different reasons. But at this stage in their family-building process, the question has apparently dawned on many parents in more than a simply abstract way. In light of the proportion of mothers who report already having taken steps to finance their children's college education, a surprisingly high proportion regard the problem with considerable realism. On the other hand, many more mothers expect or hope to send their children to college than will probably ever have to face the actual prospect. Less than 6 per cent of the total sample do not expect to send their children to college! Only one half of one per cent reply that they have not thought about it yet. A total of 57 per cent gave an unqualified "yes" to the question: "Do you *expect* to send your children to college?" Other mothers gave such answers as "depends on the children" (15.5 per cent) or "hope to" or "like to" (12 per cent). The remaining 9 per cent consisted of those who expected to send their son but not their daughter or who qualified their answers in terms of financial considerations.

Obviously there is a good deal of wishful thinking involved, but the answers to the question: "How do you expect this college education to be paid for?" indicated a level of rationality wholly unanticipated. Nearly a quarter of the 1,087 mothers who indicated an expectation or hope of sending their children to college reported that they had already taken specific steps to provide the necessary finances. These provisions were of two main types—educational annuities or some form of insurance provision earmarked specifically for education and miscellaneous types of investment programs. The magnitude of this is impressive,[27] considering that the average age of the oldest child at the time was about three years, implying some fifteen years before the first child would be eligible.

An additional 13 per cent reported that specific steps for financing this education were planned but not yet taken, but the modal response category (44 per cent) represents the mother who reported that financial provisions already exist but without an explicit indication of educational purposes. These are the couples who feel that their savings, income, or insurance is or will be sufficient to bear the costs, an assumption which is undoubtedly unrealistic for many. The remaining 20 per cent are those who have not done anything

[27] Although it is tempting to credit these people with a great deal of foresight, some of the "credit" undoubtedly belongs to the successful insurance salesman.

about it at all—those who have vague plans or hopes, who expect windfalls, or who simply have not thought about it at all.

It would appear that much of this whole attitude toward a college education for children is somewhat exaggerated. In the hope of discerning the intensity of the mother's ambitions for her children, the mothers were further asked whether they would send a daughter or a son of theirs to college even if it meant serious financial hardship. As expected, the education of the male child is considered more important: 72 per cent replied that they would send a son but only 41 per cent[28] would send a daughter to college under such circumstances. Only two mothers in the entire sample replied that they would send a daughter but not a son.[29]

The responses to these questions were assembled in a scale which reflects the strength of the mother's aspiration for her children's education. As expected, considering previous religious and class differences, the highest levels of aspiration are found for Jewish mothers and the white-collar classes. Women with higher aspirations for their children also tend to be women who are well-educated, whose husbands are in the more prestigeful occupations and who themselves are well-educated, wives who perceive good opportunities for their husbands, and women who come from smaller families.[30]

The hypothesis, as suggested earlier, is that mothers who reveal high levels of aspiration for their children's education will view additional children as incompatible with this goal and will thus desire fewer children. The correlations presented in Table 75 indicate no such simple relationship. For the total sample, there is no

TABLE 75

Correlations between Aspiration to Send Children to College
and Number of Children Desired

Religion	Correlation with Number of Children Desired by Wife
Protestant total	.02
Mixed Catholic total	−.05
Catholic total	.12
Jewish total	−.20
All couples	.02

[28] Percentages based on 1,087 couples eliminating those who did not expect to send either child.

[29] Husbands replied to these questions in the same way in the pretest. One of these two mothers had two girls but the other's first born was a son. She felt that the boy could finance his own education if necessary.

[30] These correlations average around .30 in the total sample.

relationship at all. A zero value obtains for both Protestants and Mixed Catholics, while for Catholics there is a positive correlation. Only for Jews does the expected negative association appear. These correlation values differ significantly (at the .05 level) by religion.

Why should Catholic mothers who have the greatest ambitions to send their children to college want to have more children than Catholic women who entertain lower aspirations for their children? The clue to the difference in the association among Catholics and Jews is the positive relationship, for both religious groups, between level of the mother's own educational attainment and level of her aspirations for her children's education. In the previous chapter, the analysis of education revealed sharp differences in the fertility behavior and attitudes of Catholics whose education was secular compared to those whose years of education were spent in religious schools. It was observed that having gone to Catholic schools was associated with greater educational attainment—proportionately twice as many Catholics went to college whose education was either partly or exclusively under religious auspices than Catholics whose training was entirely secular.

The hypothesis that emerges from these patterns of association is that the source of the positive relationship among Catholics between aspirations to send children to college and number of children desired is the religiously educated segment of the Catholic sample. We know that religious education and higher education are positively correlated. We also know that aspirations to send children to college and the mother's own education are positively correlated. We now hypothesize that fertility desires among Catholic mothers whose education was partly or entirely religious will correlate positively with aspirations for their children's education, but that either a negative correlation or no correlation will exist among Catholic women whose education was nonsectarian. If this is correct, we shall have located the source but still not the explanation of the positive correlation for Catholics. The first half of Table 76 confirms this hypothesis. Among Catholics with Catholic school education, the average number of children desired increases with increasing aspirations for children's education, but among secularly educated Catholics, no systematic pattern is visible.[31] Thus, the source of the direct correlation for Catholics between aspiration level and family-size desires can be

---

[31] The difference in the distributions of number of children desired for religiously educated Catholics by aspiration level is statistically significant at the .02 level. No significant difference ($p = .95$) exists among Catholics with secular education.

The categories "some" and "all" Catholic school education were consolidated for convenience; the same patterns prevail for the two groups considered separately.

TABLE 76

Number of Children Desired and Per Cent of Mothers Who Went to College, by Level of Aspiration for Children's Education and Extent of Catholic School Education
(Catholic Women Only)

Level[a] of Aspiration to Send Children to College	Extent of Catholic School Education			
	None	Some or All	None	Some or All
	(Mean number of children desired)		(Per cent who went to college)	
Low	3.2	3.6	2%	6%
Medium	3.5	3.9	11	21
High	3.4	4.2	8	27
Total	3.4	3.9	8	19

[a] The classifications are defined as follows:

Low aspiration includes those who unqualifiedly do not expect to send their children to college, who wouldn't send a child of either sex if it meant serious financial hardship, or who wouldn't send a daughter but might send a son under such circumstances.

Medium level of aspiration includes mothers who expect to send their children to college but might or might not send them if it would mean serious financial hardship, or would send a son but would definitely or probably not send a daughter.

High aspiration includes all mothers who would send both a son and a daughter to college regardless of financial hardship.

attributed to the attitudes of Catholic women who were educated in Catholic schools.[32] Those Catholic women who were educated exclusively in secular schools exhibit the same absence of association as was observed for Protestant women.

Two questions remain to be answered: (1) why do Catholic school educated women who want their children to go to college desire more children than Catholic mothers, also educated within the Catholic system, who have lower aspirations for their children, and (2) why, in contrast, should Jewish women view higher education for their children as incompatible with larger families while for Protestant women and Catholic women who had a secular education apparently such a logical connection does not exist at all? Some direct evidence can be adduced to answer the first question at least. The hypothesis is that extent of the mother's own education will vary directly among women educated in Catholic schools with her aspirations for her children's education, but will not vary systematically among secularly educated Catholic women. In other words, the reason that religiously educated Catholics who have high levels of aspiration want more children than those with lower aspiration levels is that

[32] The correlation for this group is .17, but for women educated outside of the system the correlation drops to .04.

these tend to be the women who themselves had more college education. This hypothesis was tested and confirmed (second half of Table 76).

The situation with respect to these internal differences among Catholics and the other two religious groups, more speculatively, seems to be as follows. The extent of educational attainment by the mother is directly associated with her aspirations for her children's education regardless of religion. But among Catholics, women with higher education tend to have been educated partly or wholly within the Catholic educational system. Thus, among religiously educated Catholics of higher education, there is the combination of higher aspirations for children's education and desires for larger families. One is inclined to speculate that for well-educated Catholics who practice their faith conscientiously, two parallel systems of thought operate in this matter: on the one hand, these women see the social and economic advantages of higher education and want the same advantages for their children; on the other hand, their religion discourages the effective prevention of large families. These women tend to be somewhat better off financially than those with lower education, which may contribute to preventing the logical conflict from coming more sharply into focus, but the more probable explanation is that both educational and religious values are held in somewhat logic-tight compartments. One wishes for both, which is perhaps a form of wishful thinking, but the direct conflict may not become apparent until it is too late to matter. At any rate, at this point in their family history, the limitation of family growth is not perceived as a legitimate means of financing the education of children.

For Jewish women, on the other hand, the inconsistency of the two goals is obviously perceived. This is consistent with the whole general picture of Jewish behavior that has emerged from the analyses throughout this study, a picture which combines a cultural emphasis on education and the rational connection of means and ends. For Jews, education for centuries has been associated with prestige—a condition partly resulting from the intellectual content of Judaism and from the perception of education as a means of escaping some of the social disabilities of minority-group status.

The lack of any association between aspirations to send children to college and number of children desired for Protestants, Catholics not educated in church-related schools, and women in the Mixed Catholic marriages does not readily permit interpretive speculation. This situation, particularly with respect to the Protestant group, has emerged repeatedly in many of these analyses. An association will occur both for Catholics and Jews, perhaps in opposite directions but nevertheless a correlation, while for Protestants more frequently zero correlations seem to prevail. Some speculations about this are included in the Chapter XIX summarizing multivariate analyses.

SUMMARY AND INTERPRETATION

This chapter has been concerned primarily with testing the general hypothesis that upward social mobility is inversely associated with fertility. The test has taken many different forms, with mobility being measured by actual changes in occupational status both within and across generations, changes in income since marriage, perceptions of opportunity, and levels of aspiration both by parents for themselves and for their children.

As a general statement, we cannot conclude that the hypothesis has been consistently supported. The magnitudes of the association can hardly be considered convincing let alone impressive. Also, there are many exceptions in particular tests and in different subsamples. For example, fertility seems largely insensitive to changes in occupation. With the exception of income change, the hypothesis is most consistently and strongly supported for the Jewish group.

On the whole, the statistical results of the analyses of social mobility and fertility are approximately the same magnitude as the interrelationships between the socio-economic status variables and fertility discussed in the preceding chapter. In brief, they are consistent with expectation but hardly impressive. And many of the results are involved with religious preference. It is interesting to reflect that religion in this study, as in many of the analyses in the study by Freedman, Whelpton, and Campbell, exerts a degree of influence very similar to that contributed by socio-economic status in the earlier Indianapolis investigation.

Our review of previous research findings in this area indicated the suggestion of a change in the direction of the association between social mobility and fertility over time. This change is presumed to be connected with the transition from an inverse to a direct association between socio-economic *status* and fertility. The hypothesis assumes that fertility is a value emulated by the upwardly mobile much in the same way as consumer behavior in general.[33] All pictures of life in upper middle class suburbia today emphasize the family, not the individual or other age-sex groups, as the basic social unit. In brief,

[33] Charles F. Westoff, "Some Aspects of Decision Making in the Family Growth Process," in Nelson Foote, ed., *Household Decision Making:* Volume Four, *Consumer Behavior*, New York University Press, New York, 1960.

the family has become fashionable. If this publicly advertised image does in fact mirror contemporary social reality, it may very well constitute one of the main reasons for a lack of a negative association between upward mobility and family size.

It seems desirable, in conclusion, to reiterate the fact that the social mobility hypothesis has been tested only within the limits of the sample studied. It is reasonable to speculate that higher, and more consistently negative, associations between mobility and fertility might obtain if the study had included the possible effects on postponement of marriage, childlessness, and limiting fertility to only one child. This consideration, although it does not in the least obviate the importance of the present analysis, is appropriate to other variables in this study as well and, in conjunction with the uncertainties of the future fertility behavior of the sample, should be sufficient to delimit the generality of our findings.

Chapter XV. Residence and Migration

Clyde V. Kiser
Milbank Memorial Fund

The growth of our country has been accompanied by steady increases in the proportion of population living in urban areas. In 1790, at the time of our first census, only about 5 per cent of our population was urban. The proportion was 40 per cent in 1900 and the 50 per cent level was reached about 1918. At present some 68 per cent, or over two-thirds, of our people live in urban areas.

Furthermore, there is no longer a sharp contrast between urban and rural communities. For a long time the slow means of transportation, symbolized by the horse and buggy, perpetuated sharp lines of demarcation between urban and rural areas. Much of this has been changed by the coming of the automobile, the surfacing of roads, the consolidation of rural schools, and the installation of radios, television, and telephones in rural areas. Thus, many rural residents drive to the city to work and "exurbanites" have their homes in the suburbs and rural areas.

Because of these changes the tripartite division of the population into urban, rural-nonfarm, and rural-farm groups is no longer sufficient, although it is still quite useful. In recognition of the tendency for population to "spill over" the legal boundaries of cities, the concept of "urbanized areas" was introduced in the 1950 Census. These include the central cities of 50,000 and over, together with the contiguous "urban fringes" described in the 1950 definition of urban populations. In recognition of the tendency of much larger areas, including surrounding towns and rural areas, to be more or less economically and socially integrated with the central city, the concept of the metropolitan area or its equivalent has been adopted in many countries. In the United States the term "Standard Metropolitan Area" was introduced in the 1950 Census.[1]

[1] "Except in New England, a standard metropolitan area is a county or group of contiguous counties which contains at least one city of 50,000 inhabitants or more. In addition to the county, or counties, containing such a city, or cities, contiguous counties are included in a standard metropolitan area if according to certain criteria they are essentially metropolitan in character and socially and economically integrated with the central city.

"The criteria of metropolitan character relate primarily to the county as a place of work or as a home for concentrations of nonagricultural workers and their dependents . . .

With respect to population distribution the influence of the metropolitan area in the United States has been both centrifugal and centripetal. The metropolitan area has lured the people from the countryside and small towns. It is now sending many of its inhabitants and newcomers to the suburbs in quest of less crowded living conditions. Thus, whereas there has been an increasing proportion of people living within metropolitan areas, the increase has been especially rapid in the outlying areas. As an example, a recent survey indicated that the twenty-one county tri-state New York region had increased about 14 per cent during 1950–1958. The increase was about 1 per cent for New York City and 25 per cent for the remainder of the area.[2]

The great growth of suburbs probably has been due in part to the coexistence of economic advantages of urban employment and the rural advantages of more spacious living. Probably an important aspect of the "more spacious living" is the real or fancied advantage of single-family dwelling over apartment house life.

The great spurt in the popularity of single-family houses after World War II is attributable to a variety of factors. There was an acute shortage of housing in 1945–1946 when the military services were demobilized. A large percentage of GIs were ready for homes of their own. They were finding brides to the extent that 1946 marked the highest marriage rate on record. Many already had a family with one or two children. All had GI privileges of government-guaranteed, low-interest mortgages, and this facilitated the financing of new homes. Furthermore, despite the standstill in the building of new houses during the war, the techniques for rapid construction of houses on a mass scale had been developed and the opposition of the trade unions to such techniques apparently had been overcome or disregarded. The potentialities of huge developments were increasingly realized. Some decentralization of industry through the establishment of branch plants entailed the mass construction of homes in rural areas. Whatever the reason, there are Cape Cods, colonials, ranch types, and split levels all over the country situated singly and in clusters, in the peripheries of cities and farther out along the highways and back roads, and in spaces that previously were open fields.

This does not mean that apartment houses in central cities are a

"In New England . . . towns and cities were the units used in defining standard metropolitan areas; and . . . a population criterion of 150 persons or more per square mile, or 100 persons or more per square mile where strong integration was evident, has been used."

See U.S. Bureau of the Census, *1950 Census of Population*, Vol. 1, *Number of Inhabitants*, Washington, D.C., Government Printing Office, 1953, p. xxxiii.

[2] *New York Times*, June 15, 1959, p. 29.

drug on the market. On the contrary, they are full and it is still quite a chore to find a "suitable apartment" in most cities. For underneath it all is the great growth of population that this country has experienced since 1940.

In view of the increasing proportion of people living in metropolitan areas and especially in the suburbs of these areas, it is important to secure some better understanding of the reproductive behavior of people living under the widely different conditions existing within metropolitan areas. It is realized that selective as well as determinative factors are involved in the interrelations of fertility and type of residence.[3] Nevertheless, it is important to ascertain the difference between the central cities and outlying areas with respect to fertility and to learn the nature and magnitude of the differentials by type of neighborhood and type of house. Information of this type is not only of interest to the demographer and human ecologist, it is needed for intelligent planning of urban and regional development. Finding that the 1950–1956 increase of population was about 5 per cent for central cities, 17 per cent for the urban fringes, and 56 per cent for remaining portions of metropolitan areas, Woodbury states: "Here is evidence of what many thoughtful observers think is a significant redistribution of population, the early stage of a 'new pattern of settlement' that, if continued, may prove to be a phenomenon comparable in its economic, political, and social consequences to the great urbanization movement of the latter part of the 19th and first part of the 20th centuries."[4] According to Woodbury, this country "lacks a public policy to meet the growing problems of dispersed urban settlement."[5]

In a previous paper the author has provided some background data mainly from census sources regarding the relation of residence and migration to fertility.[6] Those census data have indicated that fertility tends to be inversely related to size of place. Furthermore, within urbanized areas of each size the fertility ratios are consistently and sharply lower for the "central cities" than for the surrounding "urban fringe" areas. Within rural areas of given size or character, the fertility ratios tend to be higher for the "farm" than for the "nonfarm" population.

---

[3] In fact, metropolitan areas rather than cities were chosen as units of study in the present investigation largely because of the assumed tendency for more fertile couples to move into the suburbs.

[4] Coleman Woodbury, "Economic Implications of Urban Growth," *Science*, 129 (1959), p. 1,586.

[5] *Ibid.*, p. 1,585.

[6] Clyde V. Kiser, "Fertility Rates in the United States by Residence and Migration," *Proceedings, International Population Conference*, Vienna, 1959, pp. 273–286.

As for type of house, the Current Population Survey data of April 1946 indicated higher fertility ratios among urban people in single-family houses than in multiple-dwelling units. They indicated higher fertility ratios for urban people in purely residential structures than for those in structures "with business." However, the former type of differential probably accounts for much of the latter type. Among urban white couples living in structures with three or more dwelling units, the fertility ratio was only slightly lower for those in "structures with business" than for those in "structures without business."[7]

With reference to migration, the census data have indicated a strong tendency toward lower fertility ratios among migrants than among nonmigrants.[8] However, they also point up the importance of exceptions and special circumstances. For instance, among white women living in urban areas of the North Central States in 1940, those who were born in the South exhibited higher fertility ratios than did the natives of the North Central States. Southern migrants to the North Central States originate mainly in the states along the Mississippi River and their high fertility appears to be associated with low economic and educational attainment.[9] Thus, the variables of residence and migration sometimes become intertwined insofar as their relation to fertility is concerned. Residence history is in fact also a history of migration.

The data collected in the first phase of the present study offer some further opportunity to examine the relation of residence and migration to certain types of fertility behavior, namely, to relate certain residential and migration characteristics to fertility-planning status with respect to the two existing births, total number of children desired, and intervals between marriage and each birth and between the two births.

The limitations of the "dependent variables" have been described in previous chapters. Briefly stated: (a) the number of children desired may prove to be at variance with the actual future fertility; and (b) the classification of the couples by fertility-planning status necessitated a considerable amount of estimates, assumptions, and arbitrary handling. Also, although the interval data themselves are believed to be quite accurate, certain biases inherent in the study design accompany the cross-classifications of intervals with variables that are functions of time. As will be indicated later, this deficiency

[7] See U.S. Bureau of the Census, *Current Population Reports—Population Characteristics,* Series P-20, No. 18 (June 30, 1948), Table 13.

[8] In the census data, migrants are identified by comparison of place of residence at the time of enumeration with place of birth or place of residence on a given date prior to enumeration.

[9] Kiser, "Fertility Rates in the United States by Residence and Migration," p. 281.

has especial relevance in the data on intervals in relation to number of migrations since marriage.

The chief independent variables on residence include current residence in terms of type of community (central city versus outlying areas),[10] characteristics of street (traffic and residential conditions), and type of house (single-family versus other). The chief independent variables on migration are those concerning number of moves since marriage, whether the moves were within or between cities, and the prospects for being at the present address twelve months hence.

As for limitations of the independent variables, no detailed history of residence since marriage was obtained at the first interview. The respondents were simply asked how long they had lived at the present address, the type of community in which they were reared (large city, small city, town, country), the number of times they had moved since marriage, and whether the moves were within or between cities.

It should also be emphasized that the variable of current residence itself can be studied here only in the context of *large metropolitan areas*. However, within these metropolitan areas, the patterns of residence range from those of the open country to those of the massive apartment houses in cities. In between are the clusters of houses in new "developments," houses along the highways, those in small towns within the shadow of the central city, and the diverse types of houses that have sprung up in the "urban sprawl."

Since religion was found to be an important determinant or correlate of the various measures of fertility, and since it tended to be systematically related to some of the independent variables, most of the analyses have been made separately for at least two religious groups, the Protestants and Catholics. This type of control on religion is especially important with respect to residence because the several religious groups differ markedly with respect to relative proportions living in the central cities and in the suburbs. This means that some of the more detailed analyses are restricted to the Protestants and Catholics because there were not enough Jewish couples to warrant the classifications required.

For these religious groups, some of the tabulations are presented separately for the "white-collar" and "blue-collar" classes. Some are also given separately for couples that planned both children.

---

[10] For present purposes the "central city" for the New York metropolitan area includes the incorporated areas of New York City, Newark, and Jersey City. The "central city" for San Francsico includes that city and Oakland. For the remaining cases the "central city" is coterminous with the legal boundaries of the single cities giving name to the metropolitan areas considered.

RESIDENCE

Central City versus Outlying Areas

As already indicated, the restriction of the study to seven of the largest metropolitan areas results in a considerably higher proportion of Catholic and Jewish couples than would be found in the whole country. Even within the seven metropolitan areas, there are marked differences in residence by religion. Thus, the proportion of all couples in the study who lived in the New York metropolitan area was 17 per cent for the Protestants, 44 per cent for the Catholics, and 66 per cent for the Jews. Likewise, the proportions of couples living in central cities were higher for the Catholics and Jews than for the Protestants. Approximately one third of the Protestants, one half of the Catholics, and three fourths of the Jews lived in central cities as opposed to outlying parts of the metropolitan areas considered.

The suburban selection by religion apparently was much heavier than that by economic status. Within each religious group, the proportion of couples living in the central cities was a little higher for blue-collar workers than for white-collar workers. Furthermore, the median incomes of husbands in 1956 tended to be lower in central cities than in outlying areas for given religion-occupational groups. However, the differences are generally within $600 per year (Table 77).

TABLE 77

Husband's Median Income in 1956 and Distribution of Couples by Religion, Occupational Class, and Type of Residence

Religion of Couple and Occupation of Husband	Total	Number of Couples		Per Cent of Couples		Median Income of Husband in 1956	
		Central Cities	Outlying Areas	Central Cities	Outlying Areas	Central Cities	Outlying Areas
Protestant	473	146	327	31	69	$5,158	$5,578
White-collar	230	67	163	29	71	5,344	5,969
Blue-collar	243	79	164	33	67	5,023	5,222
Catholic	481	249	232	52	48	4,993	5,390
White-collar	200	99	101	50	51	5,232	5,563
Blue-collar	281	150	131	53	47	4,816	5,365
Jewish	125	92	33	74	26	6,385	7,100
White-collar	103	72	31	70	30	6,875	7,300
Blue-collar	22	20	2	91	9	4,900	–
Mixed	86	33	53	38	62	4,950	5,325
White-collar	35	9	26	26	74	–	6,500
Blue-collar	51	24	27	47	53	5,000	4,964
All couples	1,165	520	645	45	55	5,164	5,535
White-collar	568	247	321	43	57	5,538	5,935
Blue-collar	597	273	324	46	54	4,901	5,232

The chief differential between central cities and outlying areas with respect to fertility behavior was that by fertility-planning status (Table 78). The proportions of Protestant couples classified as having

TABLE 78

Fertility Indices by Residence and Religion of the Couple

Residence	All Religions	Protestant	Catholic	Jewish	Mixed Religions
PER CENT OF COUPLES PLANNING BOTH BIRTHS					
Total	41	43	36	67	27
Central Cities	40	36	35	66	18
10,000+	39	44	33	} 70	18
5,000–9,999	55	56	52		} 42
Under 5,000	42	45	34		
MEAN NUMBER OF CHILDREN DESIRED BY WIFE					
Total	3.3	3.0	3.7	2.8	3.3
Central Cities	3.3	3.0	3.7	2.7	3.3
10,000+	3.3	3.0	3.7	3.2	3.4
5,000–9,999	3.2	2.9	3.5	*	3.4
Under 5,000	3.2	3.0	3.7	2.7	3.3
MEDIAN NUMBER OF MONTHS FROM MARRIAGE TO FIRST BIRTH					
Total	17.6	18.2	15.5	28.7	16.7
Central Cities	17.6	17.8	15.3	28.0	15.9
10,000+	16.7	18.8	13.9	28.5	14.0
5,000–9,999	21.3	18.5	22.0	*	25.0
Under 5,000	18.0	18.0	17.2	30.0	15.6
MEDIAN NUMBER OF MONTHS FROM FIRST BIRTH TO SECOND BIRTH					
Total	28.8	28.7	27.1	34.9	27.7
Central Cities	29.9	28.5	28.3	35.3	26.0
10,000+	26.9	28.0	24.8	29.5	23.8
5,000–9,999	29.5	27.3	29.0	–	31.8
Under 5,000	28.2	30.1	23.7	31.0	28.0
MEDIAN NUMBER OF MONTHS FROM MARRIAGE TO SECOND BIRTH					
Total	51.5	52.0	46.3	67.1	51.3
Central Cities	52.6	52.9	46.3	67.3	49.5
10,000+	49.1	50.2	44.4	66.0	52.0
5,000–9,999	55.2	53.0	57.0	*	54.0
Under 5,000	51.0	54.0	45.5	64.0	50.0
NUMBER OF COUPLES					
Total	1,165	473	481	125	86
Central Cities	520	146	249	92	33
10,000+	347	188	120	17	22
5,000–9,999	102	45	42	2	13
Under 5,000	196	94	70	14	18

NOTE: Asterisk indicates fewer than 10 cases.

planned both births ("highly successful planners") were lower in the central cities than in the other areas of the combined metropolitan areas studied.[11]

The proportion of couples planning both births was conspicuously high for both Protestants and Catholics in communities of 5,000–9,999 population, but this may be a chance result of small numbers in such areas. Except for this there was little systematic relation of fertility-planning status to *size of community* within the metropolitan area.

Among the Catholic and Jewish couples in the total sample, the proportions of planners were about the same in outlying areas as in central cities. Within the central cities as a whole, the proportion of couples planning both births was the same (about one third) for Protestants and Catholics. About two thirds of the Jewish couples living in central cities had planned both births (Table 78).

Within the central cities of the New York metropolitan area alone, the proportion of couples having planned both pregnancies was higher among the Catholic than among the Protestant couples. The difference does not stand up as statistically significant because of the small number of Protestant couples in the central cities of this area. However, the New York metropolitan area does appear to differ somewhat from the others with respect to interrelation of religion, residence, and fertility-planning status.

In the combined data for the metropolitan areas except New York, the lower proportion of planners in central cities than in outlying areas held for Catholics as well as Protestants. Within central cities of these areas, the proportion of planners was higher among the Protestants than among the Catholics.

There was not much relation of other aspects of fertility behavior to central city versus other residence. The average number of children desired, the median interval from marriage to each birth, and median interval between births were much the same for residents of central cities as for those of outlying areas. The indices did not differ systematically by size of place within the outlying sections of metropolitan areas. There was not much relation of the fertility indices to type of community in which the wife was reared.

---

[11] Tests of significance by chi-square analysis yielded the following results on the relation of fertility-planning status (couples planning both births versus others) to residence (residence in Central City versus others):

All religions	N	$(P > .05)$
Protestant	S	$(P = .01-.05)$
Catholic	N	
Jewish	N	
Mixed	N	

Some of the above findings are consistent with those of the study by Freedman, Whelpton, and Campbell. Within the metropolitan areas in that study the proportion of "users" of contraception was higher in the suburbs of twelve largest cities than within those cities. This type of differential was much stronger for the Protestants than for the Catholics. Likewise, *within* the twelve largest cities the proportion of users was about the same among Protestant and Catholic wives of comparable age. As stated by the authors, "the proportion of couples who are Users is higher for the Protestant wives of each age who live in the suburbs of the twelve largest cities than for those living elsewhere. However, this consistent pattern of difference in use does not extend to the other aspects of efforts to control conception, such as the time of first use of contraception or fertility-planning status."[12]

The study by Freedman, Whelpton, and Campbell related to white, married women 18–39 years old regardless of number of children. The number of "births by 1955" (when the study was made) tended to be higher in the suburbs than in the central cities for both the twelve largest cities and "other cities of 50,000 or more." The "most likely expected total births" tended to be higher in suburbs than within the legal boundaries of the twelve largest cities. Differentials of both types were stronger for the Protestants than for the Catholics. The authors note, however: "If we exclude the twelve largest cities and compare the women living in other cities of 50,000 or more with the women living in the suburbs of these smaller cities, we find no significant difference in the fertility expectations of the city and suburban groups, either for Protestants or Catholics. Apparently the relative advantages provided for families by suburban living are greater in the larger than in the smaller metropolitan areas."[13]

In general, both the present study and the GAF study point to the need for qualifications regarding the traditional theory of the relation of urbanization to secularized behavior. Perhaps partly because of higher economic status, the Protestant dwellers in suburban areas of large cities may be more secular than those within the central cities insofar as fertility-planning status is concerned. Also, both studies emphasize the fact that by religion the proportion of planned families tends to be highest among the Jewish couples, intermediate among the Protestants, and lowest among the Catholics.

[12] Ronald Freedman, P. K. Whelpton, and Arthur A. Campbell, *Family Planning, Sterility and Population Growth*, McGraw–Hill, New York, 1959, pp. 148–149.
[13] *Ibid.*, p. 312.

Type of Home and Neighborhood

Some of the sharpest relations observed in the present analysis were those between fertility-planning status and characteristics of the home and neighborhood of residence of Protestants in the study (Table 79). In general, the proportion of successful planners was

TABLE 79

Distribution of Protestant and Catholic Couples in all Areas according to Fertility-Planning Status, by Character of Street and House of Residence

Residential Characteristics	Number of Protestant Couples	Per Cent of Protestant Couples Having Planned			Number of Catholic Couples	Per Cent of Catholic Couples Having Planned		
		Both Births	Second Birth (Total)	Neither Birth		Both Births	Second Birth (Total)	Neither Birth
Type of Street								
Residential	411	45%	61%	24%	381	35%	51%	33%
Mixed	60	28	53	30	98	37	55	30
Type of Houses on Street								
Single-Family	352	46	62	22	289	35	52	33
Other	114	31	56	32	190	37	52	32
Traffic								
Local	256	47	63	22	232	35	49	32
Light	129	40	59	24	141	35	52	36
Heavy	84	33	55	36	103	39	55	28
Economic Status of Street								
High and Upper Middle	78	46	67	23	57	42	54	28
Middle	195	43	62	22	171	35	51	30
Lower Middle	149	46	59	26	180	32	48	37
Lower	46	26	48	37	69	43	59	28
Tenure of Home								
Owners	258	50	69	19	219	39	54	29
Others	210	35	50	31	259	33	50	35
Type of House								
Single-Family	334	48	63	22	251	38	53	31
Other	136	29	54	31	230	34	51	33

relatively high for home owners, for occupants of single-family houses, for residents of streets that are predominently residential in character, and for residents of streets that were graded by interviewers as being of high or upper middle economic status. In short, high economic status of the individual families appears to be a common factor in the relationships described above for the Protestants. Some of the relationships were statistically significant at the 1 per cent level.[14] There was no significant relation of the neighborhood and

[14] The chi-squares of the distributions yielded the following results on significance of relation of fertility-planning status to the indicated variables. For these tests two classes by fertility-planning status (planned both births vs. others) and the indicated subdivisions by the other variables were used. The symbols are interpreted as follows: VS (very significant) $P < .01$; S (significant) $P = .01-.05$; N (not significant) $P > .05$.

dwelling variables to fertility-planning status of the Catholic couples.

The relation of fertility-planning status to type of house and neighborhood was much the same among the Jewish as among the Protestant couples. Among the Jewish couples the proportion planning both births was about three fourths for owners and two thirds for others; three fourths for occupants of single-family houses and two thirds for those of other types of houses; three fourths for those living on streets of upper middle class status and one half for those on poor streets. However, because of small numbers of couples in crucial categories, only the last mentioned difference stood up as statistically significant.

Birth Intervals

In view of the more effective use of contraception in the suburbs than in central cities it is perhaps not surprising that among the Protestants the median interval between marriage and first birth was longer for couples living in single-family houses than for the others and longer for couples living on streets that were "mainly residential" than for those on streets of mixed residential-commercial character (Table 80). They were longer on streets in which single-family houses predominated than on streets in which duplex and multiple-dwelling units predominated. Reflecting differences in economic status, the median interval between marriage and first birth was also longer on streets of "light local traffic" than on those of "heavy-through traffic." In general, these same differentials were found among Protestants with respect to interval between first and second births and between marriage and second births. The Catholics exhibited little relationship of birth intervals to type of house or neighborhood.

Couples were also classified by replies of wife to the question as to whether they felt they had enough room for their second child and

	All Religions	Protestant	Catholic	Jewish	Mixed
Type of Street					
Residential vs. Mixed	N	S	N	N	N
Mainly Single-Family Houses vs. Other	N	VS	N	N	N
Traffic					
Local vs. Light vs. Heavy	N	N	N	N	N
Economic Status of Street					
High, Upper Middle vs. Middle vs. Lower Middle vs. Lower	S	N	N	VS	N
Tenure of Home					
Owners vs. Others	VS	VS	N	N	N
Type of House					
Single-Family vs. Other	S	VS	N	N	N

273

TABLE 80

Median Number of Months in Specified Birth Intervals, by Character of Street
and House of Residence, for Protestant Couples

Residential Characteristics of Street and Home	Number of Couples		Marriage to First Birth		First to Second Birth		Marriage to Second Birth	
	All Couples	Couples Planning Both Births	All Couples	Couples Planning Both Births	All Couples	Couples Planning Both Births	All Couples	Couples Planning Both Births
			(months)		(months)		(months)	
Type of Street								
Residential	411	184	19.0	26.7	29.0	32.3	53.6	65.2
Mixed	60	17	15.5	16.2	26.0	31.0	42.8	48.0
Type of Houses on Street								
Single-Family	352	163	20.0	27.2	28.7	32.3	54.4	65.4
Other	114	35	15.5	21.0	28.7	30.6	46.2	56.4
Traffic on Street								
Local	256	121	19.2	27.5	30.6	34.1	54.8	66.8
Light	129	51	18.1	24.5	26.8	29.2	49.7	61.2
Heavy	84	28	16.7	20.0	27.2	29.0	46.2	54.0
Economic Status of Street								
High and Upper Middle	78	36	23.3	32.4	30.5	32.2	60.0	72.0
Middle	195	84	20.7	28.7	31.3	34.0	56.6	68.0
Lower Middle	149	68	16.5	19.5	26.3	29.2	45.9	54.7
Lower	46	12	12.5	18.0	25.0	31.0	37.7	54.0
Tenure of Home								
Owners	258	128	22.7	31.7	31.7	33.3	61.1	70.9
Others	210	73	15.6	17.1	24.6	30.3	42.6	49.4
Type of House								
Single-Family	334	161	20.7	27.7	28.7	32.6	55.0	67.1
Other	136	40	15.1	18.6	28.9	30.7	45.8	51.0
Enough Room for Third Child?								
Yes	212	86	18.4	27.5	29.1	33.0	51.8	66.9
No—But Enough for 2nd	138	66	19.2	23.5	28.6	30.6	53.8	58.4
No—Not Even for 2nd	120	47	16.8	23.3	27.8	32.3	48.0	64.5

whether they would have enough room for a third child. Among both Protestants and Catholics, the average number of children wanted tended to be highest for those stating that they had enough room for a third child. Among Protestants (but not Catholics), the number was lowest for those who said they didn't have enough room for the existing *two* children. The preferred interval from interview to third child was somewhat longer for Protestants and Catholics who reported insufficient room for the existing two children. No consistent relation was found between actual birth intervals and replies to the question regarding sufficiency of room for the second and third children.

As for other fertility indices, we found no striking relation of desired family size to type of neighborhood or home for either the

Protestants or Catholics. Among the Protestants the number of children desired tended to be somewhat higher on streets of lower economic status than on other streets. It tended to be higher for couples in multiple dwelling units than for those in single-family houses. However, the preferred length of the third interval was also somewhat longer among people on streets of the lower-economic status than on the more affluent streets.

Doubtless there are mixed types of influences in the interrelations of birth intervals with type of street and type of house. Ordinarily, there is some selection of couples with children to the neighborhoods believed to be suitable for bringing up a family. On the other hand, residence in desirable neighborhoods and in single-family houses tends to be positively related to economic status.[15] Data restricted to two-child families naturally do not evince the first type of selection. The second type of selection may be present in strong form. There may also be some selection into the better neighborhoods and houses of people who married late or who postponed having their children until they could have the home they wanted.[16] This is indeed strongly

[15] Because of the diverse types of communities and housing outside of central cities within large metropolitan areas, the "single-family house vs. multiple dwelling unit" dichotomy yields a sharper economic differential than does that of "central city vs. outlying areas." Among the Protestants, the proportion of couples classified as white-collar on the basis of the husband's work was 53 per cent for those in single-family houses and 39 per cent for those in other types of houses. Among the Catholics, the respective percentages were 45 and 38. Among all religious groups, the median income of the husband in 1956 was rather strikingly higher for those in single-family houses than for those in other types of houses as indicated below.

	Protestant	Catholic	Jewish
White-collar–Single-Family	$6,222	$5,804	$7,500
White-collar–Other	4,900	5,017	6,286
Blue-collar–Single-Family	5,350	5,300	—
Blue-collar–Other	4,614	4,863	5,000

[16] A side analysis indicated that for both Protestants and Catholics those owning their homes and those living in single-family houses at the time of the 1957 interview were characterized by relatively late age at marriage of wife and husband and by relatively long duration of gainful employment of the wife after marriage. The data are as follows:

TYPE OF HOUSE AND TENURE OF HOME	PROTESTANT			CATHOLIC		
	Median Age at Marriage (Years)		Median Number of Months Wife Worked	Median Age at Marriage (Years)		Median Number of Months Wife Worked
	Wife	Husband		Wife	Husband	
Single-Family House	21.0	23.5	11.6	21.3	24.4	8.6
Others	20.2	22.6	9.9	21.1	23.7	7.7
Home Owners	21.4	23.9	14.6	21.6	24.8	9.6
Others	20.0	22.2	8.1	20.9	23.3	6.7

suggested by the longer birth intervals for home owners than for renters and by the longer intervals for people residing on streets of high rather than low economic status.

MIGRATION

The two chief questions concerning migration that were asked in the study were those concerning number of moves since marriage and type of move (within neighborhood, within city, and between cities). A question was also asked regarding the chance that the family would be in the same house one year later. The coded replies to the latter question were: definitely here, 50–50 chance of moving, definitely move.

Fertility-Planning Status

Among the Protestants, the proportion of couples that planned both births was significantly higher for those that reported no move since marriage than for those reporting one move or more. This held true regardless of whether the migration considered was within the same neighborhood, within the same city, or between cities. Among the Protestants, the proportion planning the second birth (but not necessarily both children) was also higher for the nonmovers than for those that moved but the difference was not statistically significant. There was no instance of significant difference by migration in the proportion of planned births among the Catholic couples (Table 81).

The number of nonmovers among the Jewish group was too small to afford reliable comparison with the movers. However, among the Jewish group, the proportion of couples planning both children was significantly higher for those stating that they would still be in the same house a year hence than for the others.[17]

Birth Intervals

The data yield no systematic relation between birth intervals and number of moves since marriage. In fact, the *similarity* in the median lengths of the intervals by number of migrations is the striking feature. Thus, among the Protestants, the median length of interval between marriage and first birth ranged from about 16 to 23 months (Table 82). Among the Catholics, the range was even narrower: from about 14 to 17. Among Protestant couples of "highly successful" fertility-planning status, the median interval extended

---

[17] The difference between the "definitely here" and "definitely move" groups is significant at the 1 per cent level for "both births." The same is true for the difference between the "definitely move" group and the other two groups combined.

TABLE 81

Fertility-Planning Status of Protestant, Catholic, and Jewish Couples, by Frequency and Type of Migrations since Marriage and by Probability of Living in the Same House Another Year

MIGRATION CHARACTER-ISTICS	PER CENT OF COUPLES PLANNING						NUMBER OF COUPLES		
	Both Births			Second Births					
	Protes-tant	Catho-lic	Jew-ish	Protes-tant	Catho-lic	Jew-ish	Protes-tant	Catho-lic	Jew-ish
Number of Moves									
None	61%	36%	47%	73%	50%	73%	41	107	15
One	42	30	65	54	47	81	84	168	37
Two	43	39	76	57	53	89	87	95	38
Three	42	41	50	60	57	83	85	54	18
Four or More	39	44	88	62	61	100	176	57	17
Average Number of Moves per Year									
None	61	36	47	73	50	73	41	107	15
Moved, but < .33	51	44	75	68	66	88	92	138	52
.33–.49	40	27	67	51	39	85	72	104	27
.50–.99	46	34	68	66	47	88	148	88	25
1.00–4.00	28	36	–	48	50	–	120	44	6
Type of Moves									
None	61	36	47	73	50	73	41	107	15
Within Same Community	40	35	71	57	53	91	63	117	35
Within Same City	35	10	71	52	57	91	60	86	34
Between Cities	42	35	68	61	49	80	300	167	41
Chance of Being Here Next Year									
Definitely Here	44	37	74	66	52	90	223	269	70
50–50 Chance	43	34	68	56	49	77	129	105	31
Definitely Move	41	36	43	57	55	83	113	99	23

from 20 months for couples who moved twice since marriage to 32 for those who had moved four or more times.

There was some tendency among the Protestants for the interval between marriage and first birth to be relatively long at the two extremes of the migration scale—i.e., for those who did not move at all and for those who moved four or more times. As already indicated the nonmovers had a relatively high proportion of highly successful planners. Probably many of them did not move because they had had satisfactory homes and jobs since marriage. As for those moving four times or more, the longer interval may be in part a bias inherent in the nature of the data.

As already indicated, duration of marriage is included as a

TABLE 82

Median Number of Months in Specified Birth Intervals, by Frequency and Type of Migration since Marriage and by Probability of Living in the Same House Another Year, for Protestant Couples

Migration Characteristics	Number of Couples		Marriage to First Birth		First to Second Birth		Marriage to Second Birth	
	All Couples	Couples Planning Both Births	All Couples	Couples Planning Both Births	All Couples	Couples Planning Both Births	All Couples	Couples Planning Both Births
Number of Moves								
None	41	25	23.4	27.8	26.3	30.3	53.0	61.5
One	84	35	16.6	23.4	26.8	31.3	46.4	59.0
Two	87	37	17.8	20.1	25.2	28.0	45.7	48.9
Three	85	36	16.5	21.6	33.1	34.8	55.1	65.1
Four or More	176	69	19.9	32.0	30.8	34.8	60.0	76.2
Average Number of Moves per Year								
None	41	25	23.4	27.8	26.3	30.3	53.0	61.5
Moved, but < .33	92	47	27.3	34.7	38.7	36.1	73.6	78.6
.33–.49	72	29	20.6	27.8	27.6	34.0	62.7	73.5
.50–.99	148	68	18.0	24.9	32.6	32.8	56.0	63.0
1.00–4.00	120	33	14.5	15.7	22.2	26.7	36.0	39.8
Type of Moves								
None	41	25	23.4	27.8	26.3	30.3	53.0	61.5
Within Same Community	63	25	15.8	17.6	28.0	28.0	46.3	50.0
Within Same City	60	21	21.0	33.0	28.6	34.0	60.0	80.4
Between Cities	300	126	17.8	26.2	29.4	33.5	53.3	65.3
Chance of Being Here Next Year								
Definitely Here	223	98	20.8	28.4	30.6	31.6	55.7	63.7
50–50 Chance	129	56	17.2	20.7	27.1	32.2	48.4	64.0
Definitely Move	113	46	16.3	22.0	24.9	32.8	46.5	60.0

dependent variable since it is equivalent to time required for the couple to have two children. However, for reasons already given, selective factors enter into the cross-classification of the present data by migration and duration of marriage. Thus, the longer a couple has been married the longer the opportunity they have had to move several times. This is the same type of bias as that described in other chapters in which duration of wife's employment and amount of change in income are associated with duration of marriage. To some extent, this type of bias affects even the length of the first and second intervals considered separately.

In view of the selections engendered in the classifications by "number of moves since marriage," an experimental reclassification was made according to "average number of moves per year" since marriage. However, this classification was accompanied by an opposite type of bias with respect to duration of marriage. Whereas couples reporting a *large number of moves since marriage* tended to be unduly weighted with long duration of marriage, those with a high frequency of *moves per year* tended to be those with short durations of marriage (Table 82). The percentage of planned families was inversely related to number of migrations per year. The causal nexus may have run as follows: those with maximum number of moves tended to be those married the shortest period—i.e., they experienced the shortest period from marriage to the second birth and hence exhibited relatively low proportions planning both births.

For given numbers of migrations, the interval between marriage and first birth tended to be longer for Protestants than for Catholic couples. Within each religious group, the intervals were relatively long for the couples that planned both births. Within the Protestant but not within the Catholic group, the median intervals tended to be longer for the wives of "white-collar" workers than for wives of "blue-collar" workers.

The median interval from marriage to first birth was about the same for those moving within cities as for those moving between cities. For both Protestants and Catholics, it was a little longer for wives predicting that they rather definitely would not move during the next year than for the remainder.[18] There was less relation of migration to interval between the first and second births than to interval between marriage and first birth.

The data reveal no systematic relation of number or type of moves to number of children desired or to preferred length of the third interval. There was the suggestion of some relation between perceived chances of migration within the forthcoming year to desired fertility. Thus, among the Protestants the average number of children desired was lowest for wives who thought they still would be living in the same house twelve months hence and highest for those who believed that they rather definitely would be living elsewhere. However, the range of variation was small and may well be due to sampling error.[19]

SUMMARY

This present study provides quantitative documentation of certain interrelations between residence and social and economic factors.

[18] A possible selective factor is that the group of people who were not planning to move was weighted by those who had postponed their first birth in order to secure the type of house they wanted.

[19] It is also possible that some selective factor may be involved in that plans to have another child may be associated with plans to move to another house or neighborhood.

Thus, the concentration in New York and also within central cities of the large metropolitan areas is heaviest among Jewish couples and lightest among Protestant couples. Within religious groups, the outlying areas tended to some degree to select couples of relatively high occupational and income status. A much heavier selection of this type is found in comparisons of couples in single-family houses with those in other types of houses.

The study did not yield as many relationships between fertility behavior, residence, and migration as one might have expected from comparable analyses of census data. The chief relation that stood out was the relatively high proportion of successful planners among Protestants living in "desirable" neighborhoods and single-family houses of outlying areas. There was the related tendency for the birth intervals to be relatively long among the same groups. In general, the residential characteristics were more sharply related to the objective indices of past fertility behavior (fertility-planning status and birth intervals) than to the subjective indices of future fertility (desired family size and preferred time of next birth).

As for migration, the proportion of planners was relatively high among the Protestants reporting no move since marriage. The birth intervals tended to be relatively long for wives stating that the couple would still be in the same house twelve months hence. The intervals (especially intervals from marriage to second birth) were also relatively long for couples reporting a large number of migrations (four or more) and relatively short for those reporting a large number of *migrations per year*. These findings point up a bias (inherent in the design of the sample) that accompanies efforts to relate past migration to past intervals. This bias should not be present, in the next phase of the study, in any analysis of migration since the second birth in relation to occurrence and timing of the third birth.

In general, the relationships observed were much weaker for the Catholics than for the Protestants. They appeared to hold for the Jewish couples in so far as the data permitted analysis. Among both the Catholics and the Protestants, the relation of fertility behavior to residence and migration was much the same for white-collar as for blue-collar workers. The relation was much the same for couples planning both births as for all couples.

The sharper relation of socio-economic factors to fertility among Protestants than among Catholics has been found in previous studies. The present data go a step further and indicate that neighborhood and housing conditions are closely related to fertility behavior of the Protestants, but not of the Catholics, in the metropolitan areas studied.

The relation of fertility behavior to residence is a complex one. In the first place, it is selective as well as determinative. In the second place, the selection is varied rather than unilateral. Some selections are channeled by size of family or by prospects for another child, some by economic status and others by other considerations. There is interplay between these factors. A single-family house in the suburbs is good for children, but it is also expensive. Thus, among people of similar family size, the economic selectivity may appear to be paramount; among people of similar economic status the selection with respect to interest in family and children may seem to be dominant.

Finally, it is emphasized that the restriction of the sample to two-child couples probably reduces the variability of the indices of residence and migration as well as the indices of fertility behavior. This may account for some of the failure of the present study to yield sharper relations of the two sets of variables. Possibly more positive results will be secured in the next phase of the study when the occurrence and timing of the third birth will be introduced as dependent variables. On the other hand, it is also possible that the present data may be indicative of a real trend toward uniformity of fertility by residence.

Chapter XVI.   Age and Sex Composition of the Family

This chapter covers several fertility correlates that are familiar to demographers. Demographic studies of fertility repeatedly have shown relationships between age at marriage and completed family size.[1] The evidence is not clear, however, whether this relationship is causal, in the sense that the younger the age at marriage the greater the likelihood of unplanned births, or spurious, in the sense that youthful marriage and a large family are the joint consequence of the parental environment.

Other research demonstrates that fertility and age at marriage between successive generations also are correlated.[2]

Berent,[3] along with Kantner and Potter[4] have more recently investigated family size over successive generations. Berent found a strong relationship, while the latter two found a weak curvilinear association.

Elaborating on their finding of a curvilinear relationship, Kantner and Potter propose three avenues of parental influence. The first has to do with impulse control described as a "complex set of habit patterns resulting from early conditioning that predisposes an individual to immediate action in response to insistent but deferable stimuli." The second has to do with the similarity of knowledge, techniques, and attitudes between generations with regard to fertility planning and birth control that, in turn, affects family size. The third is the social inheritability of a preference for a certain family size.

The explanations offered by Kantner and Potter for their findings are similar to the notion that the correlation between age at marriage and size of family is the joint consequence of the parental environment. A parental environment, by example or attitudes, may encourage early marriage and large families.

Needless to say, neither age at marriage and family size, nor family

[1] D. V. Glass, and E. Grebenik, *The Trend and Pattern of Fertility in Great Britain: A Report on the Family Census of 1946*, H.M.S.O., London, 1954.

[2] K. Pearson and Alice Lee, *On the Inheritance of Fertility in Mankind*. Royal Society of London Philosophical Transactions, Series A, Vol. 192, 1899. See also, E. R. Baber and E. A. Ross, *Changes in the Size of American Families in One Generation*, University of Wisconsin, Madison, 1924.

[3] Jerzy Berent, "The Relationship between Family Sizes of Two Successive Generations," Milbank Memorial Fund *Quarterly*, xxxi (January 1953).

[4] John F. Kantner and Robert G. Potter, Jr., "The Relationship of Family Size in Two Successive Generations," in Kiser and Whelpton, eds., *Social and Psychological Factors Affecting Fertility*, 5 vols., Milbank Memorial Fund, New York (1954) iv, pp. 1069–1086.

size in two successive generations correlate perfectly. Many factors intervene to dilute the correlations. Doubtless, these factors range from the biological (fecundity) to a host of sociological and social psychological variables. The latter two include, among many other possibilities, two variables that will be considered in this chapter—a preference for a particular sex composition and a satisfaction with one's own childhood.

Sex preference has been studied at some length,[5] and it is clear that a number of couples prefer having at least one of each sex rather than, say, all daughters. Also, there is reason to suspect a preference for males. This preference for a male quite plausibly affects the termination of childbearing and, as is argued by Winston,[6] the sex ratio of terminal births. The assumption here is that couples are more likely to terminate childbearing following male rather than female births. To the extent that sex of children is a factor in determining family size and that couples strive for a particular sex or sex combination, it introduces a random element into predictions of family size.

Happiness of childhood has also been included in at least three studies as a correlate of fertility.[7] The reason for its inclusion in this chapter, however, rests on another argument. That is, the parental model, be it a large or small family, is thought to be most emulated if the childhood was happy and, conversely, least emulated if the childhood was unhappy. The expectation is that variation in childhood happiness obscures a strong relationship between the fertility patterns of two successive generations.[8]

It is clear at this point, that each of the variables, age at marriage, sex preference, and size of parental family, is thought to be related to ultimate family size. Less is known, however, about each variable's relationship to desired family size or fertility-planning success, and almost nothing is known about the relationships between these variables and the spacing of first and second births.

[5] For a fairly recent study of fertility and sex composition see: Jeanne E. Clare and Clyde V. Kiser, "Preference for Children of Given Sex in Relation to Fertility," in Kiser and Whelpton, eds., *Social and Psycological Factors Affecting Fertility*, 5 vols., Milbank Memorial Fund, New York (1952) III, pp. 621-673.

[6] Sanford Winston, "Birth Control and Sex Ratio at Birth," *American Journal of Sociology*, XXXVIII (1952), pp. 225–231.

[7] Charles F. Westoff, Philip C. Sagi, and E. Lowell Kelly, "Fertility Through Twenty Years of Marriage: A Study in Predictive Possibilities," *American Sociological Review*, 23 (1958), pp. 449–556. See also, Robert G. Potter, Jr., and John F. Kantner, "The Influence of Siblings and Friends on Fertility," Milbank Memorial Fund *Quarterly*, XXXIII (1955), pp. 246–267; John C. Flanagan, "A Study of Factors Determining Family Size in a Selected Professional Group," *Genetic Psychology Monographs*, 25 (1942), pp. 3–99.

[8] The Indianapolis Study failed to find a direct relationship between fertility and happiness of childhood. See Potter and Kantner, "The Influence of Siblings and Friends on Fertility."

The current study, when completed, will have afforded the opportunity to test whether some of these relationships have persisted despite more and wider knowledge of the means of controlling family size and in spite of what appears to be a growing consensus on family limitation and desired size of family. In addition, the study permits investigations into the lesser known areas, involving relationships among age, sex, birth intervals, and desired size of family.

INFLUENCE OF AGE

Age at Marriage

At least two lines of reasoning lead to the hypothesis relating the wife's age at marriage to the number of children desired by the wife. Firstly, as hypothesized by Baber and Ross, and supported by their limited data, early marriages may indicate dispositions toward large families stemming from parental influences. Secondly, age may be viewed as setting biological limits to childbearing, a fact that a wife may consider in formulating her own family-size preference. It is obvious, however, that the wife's age at marriage is not the only age to be considered. The Baber–Ross hypothesis applies, as well, to the husband's age at marriage. Thus, husband-wife age differences operate to reduce the association between age at marriage and size of desired or ultimate family. Other diluting factors may also readily be listed. Certainly, not all youthful marriages occur as a consequence of a self-induced production quota. Early marriages are also one avenue of escape from an unattractive parental environment.[9] Not all late marriages occur from a lack of interest in marriage and a large family. Doubtless some are determined by lack of opportunity.

Finally, fecundity plays its role in reducing the association between age at marriage and ultimate, if not desired, size of family. In this study, the analogue of low fecundity is the inability to conceive readily. The consequence, extended intervals between births, may lead wives to modify their desired size of family to conform more realistically to their ability to have children.

The extent to which these and other diluting factors actually operate to reduce the association between age at marriage and desired size of family is mainly conjectural. The small negative correlations (Tables 83 and 84) between age at marriage of wife or husband and desired size of family attests to either the importance of the diluting factors or the absence of a strong relationship between age at marriage and desired size of family.

[9] The correlation between childhood happiness and age at marriage, for wives, is .11.

TABLE 83

Correlations between Wife's Age at Marriage and Dependent Variables,
by Religion and Class Categories

Religion and Class	Number of Children Desired by Wife	Number of Children Desired by Husband	Fertility Planning Success	Number of Months from Marriage to First Birth	Number of Months from First Birth to Second Birth	Number of Months from Marriage to Second Birth	Number of Couples
Protestant							
White-collar	−.10	−.10*	.09	.09*	−.11	−.04	196
Blue-collar	−.27	−.20	.14	.30	.07	.22	192
Catholic							
White-collar	−.03	.11	.11	−.04	.15	.08	158
Blue-collar	−.12	−.03	.11	.17	.07	.16	212
Jewish							
White-collar	−.18	−.28	−.08	.01	−.01	−.04	89
Blue-collar	−.22	−.51	.25	.05	.25	.22	21
Protestant	−.17	−.11*	.15	.21	−.01	.11	388
Mixed Catholic	−.19	.11	.06	.17	.05	.15	70
Catholic	−.04	.04	.09	.08	.08	.11	370
Jewish	−.18	−.33	.00	.02	.05	.03	110
White-collar	−.05	.01	.05	.04	−.02	.00	471
Blue-collar	−.13	−.01	.11	.20	.10	.19	467
All couples	−.08	.00	.10	.13	.04	.11	938

NOTE: Asterisk indicates heterogeneities of correlations indicated at 5% level of significance.

Current Age

The hypothesis relating age at marriage to desired size of family implies a relationship between current age (age at birth of second child) and desired size of family. Since a young current age requires either a young age at marriage or a short interval between marriage and the birth of the second child (duration of marriage), it is reasonable to hypothesize that current age is also related to the size of family desired. The possibility that a young current age may be achieved by rapid childbearing provides an additional basis for the hypothesis as well as the further expectation that current age is more closely associated with desired size of family than is age at marriage. Two reasons may be cited for the expected improvement in the correlations. First, the rate of childbearing (duration of marriage) correlates −.36 with desired size of family. Second, those factors that

TABLE 84

Correlations between Husband's Age at Marriage and Dependent Variables,
by Religion and Class Categories

Religion and Class	Number of Children Desired by Wife	Number of Children Desired by Husband	Fertility Planning Success	Number of Months from Marriage to First Birth	Number of Months from First Birth to Second Birth	Number of Months from Marriage to Second Birth	Number of Couples
Protestant							
White-collar	−.03	.00	.00	.12	−.11	−.01	196
Blue-collar	−.10	−.09	.10	.11	.02	.05	192
Catholic							
White-collar	−.10	.02	.15	−.03	.22	.13	158
Blue-collar	−.15	−.06	.07	.16	.09	.15	212
Jewish							
White-collar	−.05	−.27	.11	−.06	.04	−.02	89
Blue-collar	.21	−.04	.11	−.34	.20	−.06	21
Protestant	−.05	−.01	.08	.13	−.05	.04	388
Mixed Catholic	−.04	.13	−.01	.05	−.08	−.01	70
Catholic	−.09	−.01	.10	.06	.13	.13	370
Jewish	.01	−.22	.12	−.13	.08	−.04	110
White-collar	−.03	.00	.05	.04	.00	.02	471
Blue-collar	−.05	.03	.08	.10	.08	.10	467
All couples	−.03	.02	.09	.07	.04	.07	938

dilute the correlation with age at marriage play a weaker role with current age. For example, a couple marrying young to escape the parental environment may or may not have short birth intervals depending on their knowledge of birth control and their fertility intentions.

These latter assertions are certainly consistent with data. Comparisons of correlations (Tables 83 to 86) clearly demonstrate that current age, of husband or of wife, is more closely related to desired family size than is the age at marriage of either spouse.[10] Age at marriage correlates significantly (−.08) with wife's family-size preference and not significantly with husband's fertility desires. On the other hand, current age correlates −.28 and −.19 with the number of children desired by the wife and husband respectively.

[10] Correlations in Tables 89, 92, and 93, with few exceptions, vary nonsignificantly among the religion-class subgroups. For this reason, differences between religions and classes are ignored in this chapter. See Chapter XIX for a multivariate analysis of differences among religious subgroups.

TABLE 85

Correlations between Age of Wife (Current Age) and Dependent Variables,
by Religion and Class Categories

Religion and Class	Number of Children Desired by Wife	Number of Children Desired by Husband	Fertility Planning Success	Number of Months from Marriage to First Birth	Number of Months from First Birth to Second Birth	Number of Months from Marriage to Second Birth	Number of Couples
Protestant							
White-collar	−.27	−.25	.30	.52	.53	.70	196
Blue-collar	−.38	−.29	.31	.53	.54	.72	192
Catholic							
White-collar	−.33	−.15	.25	.37	.63	.67	158
Blue-collar	−.33	−.25	.24	.53	.54	.66	212
Jewish							
White-collar	−.25	−.33	.07	.36	.51	.56	89
Blue-collar	−.43	−.59	.41	.59	.66	.76	21
Protestant	−.31	−.24	.32	.53	.53	.70	388
Mixed Catholic	−.25	−.07	.28	.49	.54	.71	70
Catholic	−.31	−.20	.23	.45	.58	.66	370
Jewish	−.29	−.39	.16	.41	.55	.63	110
White-collar	−.28	−.21	.26	.45	.56	.66	471
Blue-collar	−.31	−.18	.27	.52	.55	.68	467
All couples	−.28	−.19	.27	.48	.56	.68	938

Elimination of the effect of husband-wife age difference results in no appreciable improvement in these correlations. Except for the correlation with first birth interval (Table 87), age difference does not correlate significantly with any of the dependent variables. As a factor that would dilute the correlation between the age variable and desired fertility of either husband or of wife, age difference is of little importance.

For the population examined in this study it appears that neither age at marriage nor husband-wife difference in age has an important association with desired family size or the other dependent variables. Current ages yield the stronger correlations. These latter correlations are partly explained by the observation that marriage duration is included in the measurement of current age of wife and husband.

Number of Siblings

It seems reasonable to regard parental family size as only one index of parental influence supporting, by persuasion or example, particular

TABLE 86

Correlations between Age of Husband (Current Age) and Dependent Variables,
by Religion and Class Categories

Religion and Class	Number of Children Desired by Wife	Number of Children Desired by Husband	Fertility Planning Success	Number of Months from Marriage to First Birth	Number of Months from First Birth to Second Birth	Number of Months from Marriage to Second Birth	Number of Couples
Protestant							
White-collar	−.20	−.21	.20	.51*	.45	.64	196
Blue-collar	−.25	−.22	.27	.49	.51	.68	192
Catholic							
White-collar	−.34	−.19	.28	.35	.59	.63	158
Blue-collar	−.36	−.30	.24	.54	.53	.66	212
Jewish							
White-collar	−.12	−.33	.21	.22	.43	.45	89
Blue-collar	−.17	−.33	.40	.34	.77	.73	21
Protestant	−.20	−.18	.25	.51*	.48	.65	388
Mixed Catholic	−.22	−.08	.28	.49	.54	.73	70
Catholic	−.32	−.24	.25	.44	.58	.65	370
Jewish	−.12	−.33	.26	.24	.51	.51	110
White-collar	−.25	−.23	.25	.43	.49	.61	471
Blue-collar	−.25	−.17	.26	.49	.55	.67	467
All couples	−.24	−.19	.27	.46	.53	.64	938

NOTE: Asterisk indicates heterogeneities of correlations at 5% level of significance.

family size desires or attitudes toward family planning. This notion underlies both the Baber–Ross thesis, which is based on observed correlations, and the Kantner–Potter hypothesis of association between family size in two successive generations.

Obviously, the relationship between parental family size (number of siblings) and desired fertility must be far less than perfect. The married couple is and has been subjected to more than one source of influence bearing on fertility intentions. There are two parental families besides an assortment of friends, relatives, and even neighbors who affect the fertility values of the couple. In addition, doctors, clergy, and counsellors often advise on matters of family size. Moreover, the determinants of family size include method failures and fecundity, and these are factors that make parental family size itself a less than perfect index of parental influence.

Kantner and Potter demonstrate a positive .09 correlation between

TABLE 87

Correlations between Age Difference between Husband and Wife and Dependent Variables, by Religion and Class Categories

Religion and Class	Number of Children Desired by Wife	Number of Children Desired by Husband	Fertility Planning Success	Number of Months from Marriage to First Birth	Number of Months from First Birth to Second Birth	Number of Months from Marriage to Second Birth	Number of Couples
Protestant							
White-collar	.02	.02	−.12	.05*	.00	.03	196
Blue-collar	.16	.08	−.06	−.14	−.06	−.15	192
Catholic							
White-collar	−.12	−.15	.13	−.05	.08	.02	158
Blue-collar	.03	.01	−.04	−.04	−.01	−.02	212
Jewish							
White-collar	.06	−.13	.14	−.10	.06	.03	89
Blue-collar	.50	.47	−.21	−.68	−.02	−.31	21
Protestant	.09	.05	−.09	−.04	−.04	−.06	388
Mixed Catholic	.23	.07	−.10	−.23	−.20	−.25	70
Catholic	−.03	−.05	.03	−.05	.05	.00	370
Jewish	.15	−.02	.08	−.19	.06	−.06	110
White-collar	−.04	−.07	.02	−.01	.01	.01	471
Blue-collar	.12	.06	−.05	−.12	−.03	−.09	467
All couples	.04	−.01	−.01	−.06	.00	−.04	938

NOTE: Asterisk indicates heterogeneities of correlations indicated at 5% level of significance.

size of wife's parental family (number of wife's siblings) and family size before controlling on two sources of variation. When spouses are matched on parental family size and further restricted to effective fertility planners, a .21 correlation results. Here is a clear example of the intervention of other influences and factors to modify the association of family size between successive generations.

In the current study of fertility, desired family size is substituted for completed family size. This substitution of variables presents no logical difficulties and, in fact, there are some theoretical advantages. Desired fertility is not grossly affected by fecundity impairments. Also, the number of planning failures, limited to two births, rarely exceeds the desired size of family. Thus, control on fertility-planning success is, in this case, not as necessary as in the Kantner–Potter analysis. A third advantage is that desire, unlike performance, does not need the cooperation of the spouse.

These considerations suggest that size of parental family is more strongly related to desired fertility than it is to completed family size. However, it should be remembered that the number of children desired, unlike completed family size, probably changes with time.[11] Any prediction about the magnitude of the correlation is hazardous.

The correlations actually observed between number of children desired and size of parental family are .11 and .10 (see Tables 88 and 89) for the husband and wife respectively.[12] Unlike the results

TABLE 88

Correlations between Number of Wife's Siblings and Dependent Variables, by Religion and Class Categories

Religion and Class	Number of Children Desired by Wife	Number of Children Desired by Husband	Fertility Planning Success	Number of Months from Marriage to First Birth	Number of Months from First Birth to Second Birth	Number of Months from Marriage to Second Birth	Number of Couples
Protestant							
White-collar	.18	.02	−.11	−.12	−.06	−.12	196
Blue-collar	.06	−.13	−.10	−.06	.01	−.01	192
Catholic							
White-collar	.04	−.13	−.03	.07	.16	.15	158
Blue-collar	.03	.05	.01	−.11	.01	.04	212
Jewish							
White-collar	−.08	−.04	−.11	.10	−.02	.04	89
Blue-collar	.31	.01	.26	−.14	.18	.05	21
Protestant	.10	−.09	−.13	−.09	−.04	−.07	388
Mixed Catholic	−.14	−.13	.12	−.02	.27	.20	70
Catholic	.00	−.03	.00	−.03	.08	.05	370
Jewish	−.01	−.01	−.02	.04	.11	.09	110
White-collar	.17	.04	−.14	−.07	.02	−.03	471
Blue-collar	.07	.02	−.02	−.11	.04	−.01	467
All couples	.10	.03	−.09	−.09	.03	−.02	938

from the Indianapolis Study data, when spouses are matched on parental family size, the improvement in the magnitude of the correlation is slight and not significant. Curvilinearity is supported by data (see Table 90) only if we disregard the statistical verdict of a

[11] See Chapter XVII for attitudinal factors affecting the number of children desired.
[12] Flanagan, "A Study of Factors Determining Family Size in a Selected Professional Group," p. 26, reports correlations of .33 and .23 with "ideal" size of family.

TABLE 89

Correlations between Number of Husband's Siblings and Dependent Variables,
by Religion and Class Categories

Religion and Class	Number of Children Desired by Wife	Number of Children Desired by Husband	Fertility Planning Success	Number of Months from Marriage to First Birth	Number of Months from First Birth to Second Birth	Number of Months from Marriage to Second Birth	Number of Couples
Protestant							
White-collar	.07	.16*	.14	−.08	.07	−.03	196
Blue-collar	.01	.06	−.09	−.10	.07	.03	192
Catholic							
White-collar	.08	.21	.02	.03	.00	.01	158
Blue-collar	−.05	−.07	.06	.11	.07	.10	212
Jewish							
White-collar	−.13	−.17	−.12	−.01	−.01	−.01	89
Blue-collar	.48	.55	.42	.23	.11	.16	21
Protestant	.03	.08	−.02	−.10	.07	−.02	388
Mixed Catholic	.03	.03	−.12	−.13	.07	−.01	70
Catholic	−.02	.03	.05	.06	.06	.07	370
Jewish	−.03	−.01	.00	.07	.04	.05	110
White-collar	.13	.19	.03	−.03	.01	−.06	471
Blue-collar	.03	.05	−.01	.00	.07	.06	467
All couples	.07	.11	−.04	−.06	.05	−.01	938

NOTE:
Asterisk indicates heterogeneities of correlations indicated at 1% level of significance.

TABLE 90

Number of Children Desired by Wife by Number of Siblings of Wife, Number of Siblings
of Husband, and Number of Siblings of Wife and Husband Jointly

	Siblings								
	0	1	2	3	4	5	6	7	8 or more
	Mean Number of Children Desired by Wives								
Number of wife's siblings	3.2	3.3	3.4	3.5	3.7	4.4	3.8	4.0	3.4
Number of husband's siblings	3.6	3.1	3.5	3.7	3.8	4.1	3.5	3.6	3.3
Husband's siblings approximate wife's siblings	2.9	3.1	3.4	3.6	4.2	3.9	3.7	3.3	3.0[a]

[a] Hypothesis of association supported by analysis of variance test, $\alpha = .05$. The means
suggest nonlinearity, $\eta = .16$.

nonsignificant difference between the correlation coefficient and the correlation ratio. Clearly then, there is a slight tendency to transmit dispositions toward family size from one generation to the next. This tendency, however, is not uniform throughout the sample.

Apparently, happiness of childhood affects the degree to which number of siblings and size of desired family are related.[13] Although the hypothesis that led to the analysis suggesting this generalization was in error, predicting a high positive and not a —.11 correlation among wives with happy childhoods (see Table 91), the data do not dispute the more general assertion of heterogeneity of correlations.

TABLE 91

Correlations between Number of Wife's Siblings and Selected Dependent Variables among Categories of Childhood Happiness

	Happy	Moderately Happy	Unhappy	Total
Number of children desired by wife*	—.11	.14	.05	.10
Fertility-planning success	—.18	—.07	—.06	—.09
Number of months from marriage to first birth	.04	—.10	—.18	—.09
Number of wives	242	672	251	1,165

NOTE: Asterisk indicates correlations among happiness categories are heterogeneous at the 5% level.

The negative correlation must remain an enigma for the moment. The small correlations, .11[14] and —.11 between happiness of childhood and the two variables, number of children desired and number of siblings, offer no clues. Bossard and Boll suggest a "theory of alternating attitudes toward family size" that appears as a promising lead.[15] In essence, they argue, extreme family size is not only not reproduced but there is an overreaction to size.

The present sample may then indicate, if Bossard and Boll are correct, that this overreaction to size is most common among those with recollections of a happy childhood.

In the absence of additional data, further elaboration of this

[13] Responses to two items form the index designed to measure happiness of childhood. The items are: "On the whole, how happy would you say your childhood was?" and "Everything considered, how happy would you say your mother and father's marriage has been?" The alternates are "extremely happy, happier than average, average, and not too happy."

[14] A .07 is reported in Westoff, Sagi, and Kelly, "Fertility Through Twenty Years of Marriage," p. 555.

[15] James H. S. Bossard and Eleanor Stokes Boll, *The Large Family System*, University of Pennsylvania Press, Philadelphia, (1956), pp. 282–284.

thesis does not seem warranted. These data are only sufficient to the task of demonstrating a weak but none the less persistent relationship between desired size of family and number of siblings, a relationship that is positive in sign if no statistical controls are imposed.

Happiness of childhood is only one example of a contingency that modifies the correlation between siblings and desired number of children. There are other similar plausible candidates affecting not only the number of children desired (and thus reducing the effect of parental influence) but the spacing of births as well.

SEX COMPOSITION OF THE FAMILY

Our everyday experiences tell us that prospective parents are concerned about the sex of their as yet unborn children. "I hope it's a boy" or "We want a girl this time" are typical statements indicating sex preferences. The existence of such preferences for individual couples is beyond doubt. How keenly these preferences are held and, more importantly, what effect preferences have on desired family size are two questions having more elusive answers.

Previous statistical studies have indicated a preference for males or a preference for at least one of each sex. In one study, the sex ratios of terminal births were computed for several populations as measures of the effect of an assumed preference for male offspring.[16] The logic of the underlying argument is that success in achieving the desired sex reduces the likelihood of additional children, whereas failure increases the chances of having at least one more child. The implicit assumption is that desired size of family includes a desire for a particular sex composition. Stated differently, couples desiring two children, for example, also desire a son and a daughter. Whether or not fertility will exceed this currently desired size of family is somewhat contingent on the chance phenomenon of sex. If the first two children are, say, daughters, an increase in the number of children desired will follow in the effort to achieve a son.

In another *post factum* study, satisfaction with the sex composition of completed families was used as an index of sex preference.[17] Though both studies were essentially concerned with the same phenomenon—the relationship between family size and sex preference—neither study design was capable of providing conclusive answers. In the former case, bias in the form of underenumeration of female births may have played the telling role, while in the latter case the damaging phenomenon was the extent of rationalization of sex preference to agree with fact.

[16] Winston, "Birth Control and Sex Ratio at Birth."
[17] Clare and Kiser, "Preference for Children of a Given Sex in Relation to Fertility."

Unlike these prior studies, the design of this study will ultimately permit a more direct and therefore more definite investigation of the phenomenon of sex composition and its relationship to fertility—desired and actual. For the present, however, the analysis is limited to the relationship between sex of the first two children and current family-size desires. The next phase will supply the necessary information regarding actual performance.

TABLE 92

Number of Children Desired by Husbands and Wives, by Religion, Class, and Sex of First Two Children

	Mean Number of Children Desired by Wives, by Sex of Children Born				Mean Number of Children Desired by Husbands, by Sex of Children Born			
	MM	MF	FM	FF	MM	MF	FM	FF
White-collar								
Protestant	3.4	2.9	2.6	3.6	3.0	2.8	2.8	3.0
Mixed	3.7	3.7	4.2	3.3	2.8	2.1	3.0	4.1
Catholic	5.0	4.6	4.1	4.9	4.0	3.6	3.4	3.9
Jewish	2.5	2.4	3.1	2.6	2.8	2.8	3.0	2.7
Blue-collar								
Protestant	3.1	2.3	2.5	3.5	2.8	2.6	2.6	3.1
Mixed	4.2	3.6	3.5	3.3	4.1	2.9	3.1	3.5
Catholic	3.8	3.6	3.9	4.7	3.5	3.3	3.6	3.8
Jewish	3.0	2.7	1.8	2.0	3.2	3.0	2.8	2.8
Class totals								
White-collar	3.8	3.5	3.3	3.8	3.3	3.1	3.0	3.4
Blue-collar	3.5	3.0	3.2	4.0	3.2	3.0	3.1	3.4
Religion totals								
Protestant	3.2	2.6	2.6	3.5	2.9	2.7	2.7	3.1
Mixed	4.0	3.6	3.7	3.3	3.5	2.6	3.1	3.8
Catholic	4.3	4.0	4.0	4.8	3.7	3.5	3.5	3.8
Jewish	2.6	2.4	2.9	2.5	2.9	2.8	3.0	2.7
All couples	3.7	3.2	3.2	3.9	3.3	3.0	3.1	3.4

NOTE: M indicates a son; MF, son followed by daughter; FM, daughter followed by son; FF, two daughters; MM, two sons.

Our data (Table 92) provide unequivocal evidence of a relationship between sex of offspring and the number of additional children desired. On the average, couples having children of the same sex desire the most children. The existence of a preference for a sex-balanced family appears well documented. Doubtless, the relationship to actual fertility performance will be different since desired fertility correlates imperfectly with actual fertility.

The Clare-Kiser conclusion seems to imply that sex preference is not an important enough motivating factor to affect the pattern of fertility for more than a few couples. There is evidence to the contrary. Sex of first offspring (see Table 93) affects at least the length of the subsequent birth interval. Birth intervals average three months longer if the first child is a boy. Again, the assumption of a sex preference provides the neatest explanation of this variation in birth intervals[18] and as such implies that sex preference is an important enough motivating factor to affect fertility patterns, including perhaps, family size.

Without further data though, the question of a relationship between sex of offspring and family size remains unresolved. The sex composition of two-child families does affect the number of additional children desired by spouses. Also, birth intervals are affected by the sex of the first child. These are known facts. Implied is a preference for at least one of each sex with a slight favoring of males. Those couples with at least one male desire fewer children than couples with two females.

Summary and Implications

Demographic studies have found that completed family size correlates with age at marriage, size of parental family (number of siblings), and the sex composition of the family. Whether all such correlations are due to rational planning is a question that remains largely unanswered.

The use of number of children desired as a substitute for ultimate family size, early in marriage, is one step toward answering the question just raised. The next step, requiring a longitudinal study design, is the comparison of fertility desires with actual performance. The analysis of data in this chapter is incomplete pending the second step. Nevertheless, even negotiating the first step means a new view that deserves description.

Desired size of family correlates —.08 with wife's age at marriage and —.28 with wife's current age for this sample of two-child couples. The increase from —.08 to —.28 is predictable from the knowledge that wife's current age is the sum of age at marriage and length of birth intervals, both of which correlate with desired size of family. One implication is that for fecund couples the frequently observed correlation between age at marriage and completed family size is hardly one of rational planning and is largely a function of longer exposure to childbearing. Secondly, it implies that for fecund

---

[18] Other explanations are always possible. Compared to a female first child, for example, a male first birth presents greater and more discouraging problems to the neophyte parent. The longer birth interval denotes an understandable hesitancy, on the part of some parents, before chancing another son.

TABLE 93

Mean Number of Months between First Birth and Second Birth, by Sex of First Child, Religion, and Class

	Protestant		Mixed		Catholic		Jewish		Row Averages by Sex	
	Male	Female	Male	Female	Male	Female	Male	Female	Male	Female
White-collar	39.9	32.6	37.9	42.1	31.8	31.7	40.0	37.8	36.8	33.7
Blue-collar	37.1	34.3	36.1	39.3	39.3	35.5	44.2	41.0	38.3	35.5
Column averages by sex	38.4	33.5	36.8	40.4	36.1	33.9	40.7	38.4	37.6	34.6
Within religion differences*	4.9		−3.6		2.2		2.3		3.0	

NOTE: Asterisk indicates that differences between second birth intervals within religions are significant at the 5% level by Fisher's technique of combining probabilities. Difference for the total sample is significant at the 1% level.

couples the spacing of births and not the ultimate size of family is the better index of desired or planned fertility. These implications are consistent with the way in which fertility-planning success correlates with wife's age at marriage (.10), with the current age of the wife (.27), and with desired size of family (−.22). When parity is held constant, the oldest wives not only have the lowest desired size of family and the longest birth intervals, but they are also the most skillful in the planning of births. Age at marriage shows the weaker relationship to fertility-planning success, which again suggests that the former's correlation with completed family size is due to the longer period of exposure to childbearing.

These facts, that age at marriage correlates poorly with desired size of family as well as the ability to control fertility, have further implications. Correlations of family size between successive generations could result from the tendency of an early age at marriage in large parental families.[19] Our data suggest that since the wife's parental family size correlates .10 with her desired size of family, correlations between family size in two successive generations is at least partially one of design.

Two hypotheses are offered as explanations for the weak zero-order associations with desired size of family. First, the desire to replicate the parental model is contingent on the happiness of childhood (as recalled) and, second, desired size of family is not independent of a preference for a particular sex composition.

---

[19] However, data only weakly suggest this explanation. Number of siblings of wife correlates −.03 with wife's age at marriage.

Chapter XVII. Social Relations within the Family

INTRODUCTION

Size of family is in part determined by social relations within the family. Attitudinal and structural variables affect not only the number of children desired but also affect efficacy of fertility planning.

No student of fertility seriously contests this premise. As a consequence, research efforts to establish this near truism empirically have persisted despite negligible results. Most data on the personal orientations of members of a family to each other exhibit only the most tenuous, if any, association with desired or actual size of family or the control of reproduction. Understandably, the paucity of findings has been explained in terms of unsolved problems of measurement or in terms of an unfortunate choice of sample, a sample too homogeneous with respect to attitudinal and structural variables. On the one hand, the nuances of family relationships are but crudely sampled by responses to a few items. On the other hand, white metropolitan families may be homogeneous enough with respect to intrafamilial relations to minimize the explanatory importance of any single attitudinal or structural variable.

While some truths are contained in these speculations, the history of negative or near negative findings suggests still another explanation. Despite efforts to refine specific measures of intrafamilial relations, no improvement in observed correlations is noticeable. The persistently best correlates of fertility are gross social categories. The more unidimensional and pure the measure, the less the way of life is captured. Religion is a better indicator of desired family size than marital adjustment or dominance of wife in running the home. The same once held for an urban-rural residence or ethnic origin. Perhaps the grosser categories yield higher correlations because they summarize many variables. Religion may well include authority patterns, modes of adjustment, the "atmosphere" in the family group, orientation toward children, acceptance of traditional familial roles, and the like.

In fact, a sophisticated theory of the determinants of fertility might lead us to expect only correlations of low magnitude between specific measures of family relations and fertility. Such a theory disposes us to view differential fertility as the consequence of an intricate, complex, and perhaps changing causal network. The effect, for example, of a single aspect of family structure may be suppressed, diffused, or modified by a plethora of uncontrolled contingencies and counter effects. In any event, in this project as in earlier research, the correlations in this area were of low magnitude and tended to reverse in sign, disappear, or be slightly altered with varying conditions or the exercise of even modest controls. Research relating family size to marital adjustment provides one example of weak and varying correlations found between intrafamilial relations and fertility.

Terman reports, "the mean scores (on marital happiness) of childless and nonchildless wives are almost identical."[1] Terman juxtaposes this finding with three prior studies reporting: (a) a positive relationship of family size to marital happiness, (b) no association between family size and marital happiness, and (c) an inverse correlation between marital happiness and family size.[2] Later studies report, "no difference in marital adjustment between couples with no children and those with one child,"[3] and an inverse relationship between number of children and marital adjustment contingent on the attitude of the couple with respect to having children and the success of the couple in controlling fertility.[4]

Another illustration of the same point involves the measure of male dominance. Here two studies report no association.[5] A third, a study of Puerto Rican families, finds weak if not questionable evidence that control of fertility does have some slight association with degree of male dominance.[6] The current study is equally unsuccessful in demonstrating a substantively important connection between dominance of the male and fertility control or desired family size.

Low correlations (whether statistically significant or not) contribute little to an ability to predict or explain fertility. A correlation of .2 accounts for only 4 per cent of the total variance, a small improvement over complete ignorance. Few, if any, unidimensional

---

[1] L. M. Terman, *Psychological Factors in Marital Happiness*, McGraw–Hill, New York, 1938, p. 171.

[2] *Ibid.*, p. 173.

[3] E. W. Burgess and L. S. Cottrell, *Predicting Success or Failure in Marriage*, Prentice-Hall, New York, 1939, p. 259.

[4] See Burgess and Cottrell, *Predicting Success or Failure in Marriage*, p. 260, and Robert Reed, "The Interrelationship of Marital Adjustment, Fertility Control and Size of Family," in Kiser and Whelpton, eds., *Social and Psychological Factors Affecting Fertility*, 5 vols., Milbank Memorial Fund, New York (1950) II, pp. 259–301.

[5] Clyde V. Kiser and P. K. Whelpton, "Summary of Chief Findings and Implications for Further Study," in Kiser and Whelpton, eds., *Social and Psychological Factors Affecting Fertility*, 5 Vols., Milbank Memorial Fund, New York, 1946–1958, v, 1,332–1,333, and P. G. Herbst, "Family Living-Patterns of Interaction," p. 176, in O. A. Oeser and S. B. Hammond, eds., *Social Structure and Personality in a City*, Macmillan, New York, 1957.

[6] Reuben Hill, J. Mayone Stycos and Kurt W. Back, *The Family and Population Control*, University of North Carolina Press, Chapel Hill, 1959, p. 229.

measures of social relationship have approached a correlation of .2 with desired fertility or fertility control. It is misleading to assert, for example, that a male dominant pattern of family decision-making means high fertility when male dominance is also found with low fertility to nearly the same extent.

For predictive purposes, weak relationships can be dismissed, even if "significant" in a statistical sense. There seems little point to an elaborate multivariate treatment to combine variables that explain less than 1 or 2 per cent of the variance of fertility or family-size preference. However, even weak correlations provide clues as to factors affecting fertility.

ADJUSTMENT TO MARRIAGE AND MOTHER ROLE

Ultimate size of family and marital adjustment are undoubtedly associated. Certainly the rejection of null hypotheses of no association between fertility and marital adjustment has been sufficiently frequent to justify this assertion. It is also true that observed associations have all been of small magnitudes. Equally plausible reasons have been given for the expectation of negative or positive correlations. On the one hand, wives who are satisfied with their marriage are more willing to take on the responsibilities and duties that motherhood entails or, on the other hand, children, especially unplanned children, not only create new burdens but upset adult routines, deprive the wife of desired leisure time, and curtail economic and social opportunities.

Somewhat similar reasoning may be applied to the variable of adjustment to mother role. Wives who found it easy to adjust to the role of mother may ultimately have large families. On the other hand, the larger the family, the greater the demands on time and energy and the greater the problem of a satisfactory adjustment.

The substitution of desired family size for ultimate family size among two-child couples merely complicates the problem. The relationship between desires and performance is itself far from perfect and there is reason to suppose that some two-child families have rationalized their family-size desires to equal the present number. If this is true, even associations between family-size desired and the two adjustment variables may be confounded with the efficacy of fertility control.[7]

The observed correlations are hardly consequential. While data

[7] A point suggested by Pratt and Whelpton. See Lois Pratt and P. K. Whelpton, in Kiser and Whelpton, eds., *Social and Psychological Factors Affecting Fertility*, "Interest In and Liking for Children in Relation to Fertility Planning and Size of Planned Family," v, p. 1,212.

TABLE 94

Correlations between Dependent Variables and Personal Orientation Variables

Personal Orientation	Dependent Variables				
	Number of Children Desired by Wife	Number of Months from Marriage to First Birth	Number of Months from First Birth to Second Birth	Number of Months from Marriage to Second Birth	Fertility-Planning Success
Wife's employment duration	−.21	.70	.32	.64	.20
Wife's future work intentions	.04	−.01	.00	.01	.02
Adjustment to mother role	.12	−.07	.06	.00	.07
Age at which children become enjoyable	−.04	.06	.19	.16	.02
Liking for children	.14	−.02	−.08	−.06	.00
Patterns of help available to wife	.00	.01	−.05	−.04	−.03
Wife's marital adjustment	.08	.05	.02	−.05	.09
Dominance in running home	−.02	.02	−.05	−.02	.03
Dominance in social life	−.06	.07	.05	.07	.06
Dominance in nonsocial areas	−.09	.07	.10	.10	.08

(see Tables 94 and 95) are consistent with the notion of positive correlations that vary by planning success categories, the over-all variation of desired family size accounted for by the adjustment measures is less than 2 per cent. What is perhaps equally significant is the fact that the lowest correlations, .04 and .05, occur among couples successfully planning both births. Is marital adjustment to mother role necessarily related to fertility or fertility desires as implied by rationales offered in this and previous researches? There is room for skepticism here, perhaps even room for a completely heretical hypothesis that admittedly cannot be tested by these data. The

TABLE 95

Correlations between Number of Children Desired by Wife and Selected Variables within Fertility-Planning Success Categories

Births Planned Success-fully	Adjust-ment to Marriage	Adjust-ment to Mother-Role	Duration of Employ-ment	Liking for Children	First Birth Interval	Second Birth Interval	Number of Wives
Both births	.04	.05	−.21	.15	−.22	−.25	482
Second only	.13	.23	−.18	.03	−.11	−.23	205
First only	.15	.09	−.22	.36	−.24	−.48	172
Neither birth	.14	.14	−.17	.08	−.09	−.26	306

hypothesis may be a denial of a direct causal link between adjustment to marriage and the number of children desired. Any positive correlation that is observed is due partially to the effect that undesired fertility has upon marital adjustment. To elaborate, where desired fertility is exceeded, adjustment is made more difficult. Since this would be most true for couples initially desiring the fewest children, the consequence is the observed positive correlations. This same reasoning can be used to explain a finding of negative correlation between *completed family size* and either marital adjustment or adjustment to mother role. If family size were largely determined by number of planning failures, the correlation between adjustment and family size would indeed be negative.[8] If planning were completely effective, the association, to be heretical again, would not exist.

Of course this is speculation and it is important, therefore, again to distinguish: what is known—the extremely small positive correlations between the adjustment variables and the fertility variables; and what is conjectural—the possibility of positive, negative, or zero correlations between marital adjustment or adjustment to mother-role and desired or actual fertility. The only support that may be offered for the speculative aspect is that negative, positive, and not even statistically significant correlations have been observed between marital adjustment and actual or desired family size.

ATTITUDES TOWARD CHILDREN AND WORK

Another area that has been examined at some length in the Indianapolis Study is the question of a relationship between fertility and extrafamilial activities, particularly if these involve job or career interests as sources of satisfaction in addition to or in lieu of satisfactions derived from more traditional marital roles.

Implicit in this hypothesis is the assumption that job or career interests are incompatible with or are at least in competition with motherhood as an interest: that the pursuit of one type of interest precludes or places limits on the pursuit of the other type of interest. This assumption appears quite reasonable since for biological reasons alone motherhood usually makes great demands on the time and energy of the wife. In most instances, childbearing removes the

[8] See Robert Reed, "The Interrelationship of Marital Adjustment, Fertility Control and Size of Family," in Kiser and Whelpton, eds., *Social and Psychological Factors Affecting Fertility*, 5 vols., Milbank Memorial Fund, New York (1950) II, pp. 259–301; also Harold T. Christensen and Robert E. Philbrick, "Family Size as a Factor in Marital Adjustment of College Couples," *American Sociological Review*, XVII (1952), pp. 306–312, for similar speculations and supporting data.

mother from the job market for at least a few months or even years. Motherhood also reduces the amount of free time available to the wife, increases her familial responsibilities, and often subjects her to a nearly inflexible routine of child care.

Judging from correlations, however, the number of wives that perceive this logic and plan accordingly appears quite small. Four variables have been selected as bearing on the hypothesis. Two of these, the number of months the wife has worked since marriage and her future work intentions, are intended as indicators of an interest in job or career as an extrafamilial activity. Two other variables are concerned with interests of a familial nature. In particular, these are a generalized liking for children and a liking for babies in preference to older children. The hypothesis takes the form of an expectation that the first two variables are inversely correlated with desired size of family, while the second two variables are directly correlated with desired family size.

The resulting correlations (see Table 94), a −.21 between duration of employment and desired size of family and a .14 between liking for children and desired size of family, encourages the conclusion that the hypothesis was tested and found to be true. Such optimism is, however, premature. The correlations are open to other equally justifiable interpretations. For one, two of the four variables yielded results that did *not* support the hypothesis. Future work intentions and preference for younger children correlated .04 and −.04 respectively with desired family size. Not even the signs of the correlations are as hypothesized.

A second reservation stems from the possibility that duration of employment is really a poor substitute for a an unavailable measure of interest in job or career. All wives do not or need not perceive work as a matter of choice over childbearing. Some may actually work to make fertility economically feasible; others may work to fill available time between marriage and first birth. Then again, even if there is a driving interest in a career, a planning failure would probably terminate employment. Employment duration is more a first interval than a second interval phenomenon, as demonstrated by the correlations which are .70 and .32 respectively, and duration of employment does correlate .20 with fertility planning success.[9]

A third reservation actually follows from the points just made. The number of months *not* spent working also correlates with desired size of family (−.17), which, if duration of employment is considered an

[9] This correlation between fertility-planning status and wife's employment has been isolated before. See Ronald Freedman, P. K. Whelpton, and Arthur Campbell, *Family Planning, Sterility and Population Growth*, McGraw–Hill, New York, 1959, pp, 137–142.

adequate measure of job or career interests, leads to the inference that a lack of career or job interests is also inversely associated with preferred size of family. This antinomy is easily resolved if it is argued that a desire for a small family leads to long birth intervals which in turn permit long duration of employment as well as non-employment between marriage and second birth.

A final reservation perhaps by now superfluous follows from the lack of statistically significant correlation between liking for children and months of employment or future work intentions.

There is neither evidence to support the hypothesis that job or career interests stand opposed to familial interests or, as hypothesized by Pratt and Whelpton, that there exists a direct relationship between extrafamilial participation and interest in and liking for children.[10]

Only the .14 correlation between liking for children and number of children desired offers comfort in the way of evidence for one aspect of the hypothesis. But again this evidence is weak. Apart from the possibility of explaining away the .14 correlation in terms of a sampling quirk or its substantive insignificance, there is reason to question the necessity of such zero-order relationship for wives with two or perhaps more children. If there is a tendency to eventually accept even unplanned children, desired size of family would increase following planning failures. On the other hand, liking for children may remain constant or even decrease as failures in spacing or control of numbers impose greater restrictions and responsiblities.[11] The effect may be to dilute what may otherwise be a stronger relationship, if planning were perfect, between liking for children and desired number of children. In no sense are the correlations in Table 95 offered as a test of this argument. Rather, the .03 and .08 versus the .15 and .36 coefficients are offered as caution signs against assuming too quickly a very simple relationship among liking for children, fertility-planning success, and a desire for children.

A test of this hypothesis obviously involves measurement of change, of desired fertility as well as liking for children and, therefore, must be deferred to the next phase of this study.

[10] Lois Pratt and P. K. Whelpton, "Extra-Familial Participation of Wives in Relation to Interest In and Liking For Children, Fertility Planning, and Actual and Desired Family Size," in Kiser and Whelpton eds., *Social and Psychological Factors Affecting Fertility*, 5 vols., Milbank Memorial Fund, New York (1958), v, pp. 1245–1299.

[11] The hypothesis that liking for children is inversely related to fertility-planning success is no less plausible than the converse hypothesis. See Lois Pratt and P. K. Whelpton, "Interest In and Liking for Children in Relation to Fertilitying Planning and Size of Planned Family," in Kiser and Whelpton, eds., *Social and Psychological Factors Affecting Fertility*, 5 vols., Milbank Memorial Fund, New York (1958), v, pp. 1211–1244. The correlation observed in the present study is zero (Table 94).

PATTERNS OF DOMINANCE AND PATTERNS OF HELP AVAILABLE TO THE WIFE

Family structures vary greatly in their permissiveness and flexibility. Those characterized by egalitarian patterns of husband-wife decision-making obscure the traditional delineations of sex roles within the family. The working mother and the domesticated father are variations of parental roles that are not, at least theoretically, associated with the male dominant family type. The expectation that such crossing of traditional sex roles is to be found among families with egalitarian patterns of husband-wife decision-making is based on the prior assumption that extensive communication between spouses is most likely to be found in the egalitarian household and is a prerequisite if role alternatives are to be successfully explored.

Through this medium of extensive communication, the egalitarian mode of decision-making is presumed to associate with a greater incidence of extrafamilial activities of wives, a greater involvement of husbands in domestic chores, greater success in fertility planning, and lower fertility desires. This latter follows from the assumption that the exploration of other role possibilities implies values competitive with high fertility.

The theme that is developed here is not unrelated to theory that causally relates male-dominant family systems to high fertility.[12] The authority of the male, the low status of the female, the separation of the male from involvement with child-rearing routines, the importance to the male of demonstrating virility in terms of numbers of male offspring as well as the assumed economic value of male children are the elements of the patriarchal system that are thought to be the causal social antecedents of high fertility. The absence of fertility planning and the rigidity of marital roles are also characteristic of such societies.

The egalitarian household, in contrast to the patriarchal household, has as its basis of control a sharing of decision-making between husbands and wives in many important areas of family activities.[13] Authority in the patriarchate is institutionalized and, by definition, is largely vested in the authority of the male. Sociologists contend that modern urban family systems tend toward egalitarianism.[14]

[12] Frank Lorimer, *Culture and Human Fertility*, UNESCO, 1954.

[13] See William G. Mather, "Defining Family Types on the Basis of Control," *The Family*, (March 1935), pp. 9–13, for an early study of some correlates of family decision-making patterns. For more recent study, see Eugene A. Wilkening, "Joint Decision-Making in Farm Families as a Function of Status and Role," *American Sociological Review*, 23 (1958), pp. 187–192.

[14] David Goldberg, "The Fertility of Two-Generation Urbanites," *Population Studies*, XII (1959), p. 221.

Some ramifications of this trend are to be found in the increased employment of women in the work force, the greater use of methods enabling family planning, lower fertility, and the greater involvement of husbands in matters concerned with fertility. Other more speculative hypotheses have even attributed marital instability, delinquency, and "momism" to this denigration of the *male* role.

These generalizations lead to empirical expectations. Presumably, the more egalitarian the household, the fewer the number of children desired by the wife since interests other than fertility may be pursued. Also, the more egalitarian the household, the greater the chance of success in fertility control since there exists both agreement as well as joint responsibility on the desirability and use of control devices.

Three dominance variables were defined and measurements were attempted. These are dominance patterns in running the home, determining the social life, and as a residual category in nonsocial areas. A fourth variable, the extent of help available to the wife was also translated into a measure, on the assumption that this too was related to the pattern of decision-making as well as the willingness or desire to have additional children.

None of these measures correlated with the dependent variables in a manner commensurate with the plausibility of the theory. As may be seen by inspection (Table 94), none of the four variables account for more than 1 per cent of the variation of any dependent variable. Where dominance patterns between husbands and wives approach the egalitarian and wife-dominant pattern, the correlations slightly favor the presence of longer birth intervals, higher fertility-planning success, and a larger number of additional children desired. There are, however, exceptions. Dominance in running the home and the extent of help available to the wife are not significantly related to the dependent variables. Thus, only two of the four variables encourage some generalization of relationship between authority structure and fertility.

These results are no great improvement over those of prior studies. Herbst reports no relationship found between dominance patterns and fertility. The Indianapolis Study proved quite inconclusive. Hill, Stycos, and Back find small and, considering the number of comparisons, nearly random relationships between male dominance and the incidence and efficacy of fertility control.

The success in demonstrating any but trivial relationships between fertility variables and dominance structure within the family has been nil despite variations in the choice of population, the use of different dependent fertility variables, and the care with which dominance patterns are measured.

306

The weight of evidence again favors a review of theory and its implications. What has been said before about the complex etiology of fertility still applies, though as before, the lack of more positive findings may also be attributed to poor measurement. One other tack is also available. Implicit to this and other research is the assumption that the authority structure within the family remains relatively stable and that it affects rather than is affected by fertility.[15] Perhaps the authority structure is subject to change. The birth of a child generally expands the wife's, relative to the husband's, area for decision-making. Also, it may be argued that structure changes with experience and competence. A change in the wife's social, economic, or psychic dependence on the husband, through employment, children, or social activities, essentially increases her own power and ultimately her authority. There is evidence consistent with this notion, though again correlations are weak.

Duration of employment correlates .09 with dominance of wife in nonsocial areas. Also, the younger the wife or the greater the husband-wife age difference, the more dominant the male. And finally, the larger the husband's income, the greater the male dominance. Wolfe reports similar associations.[16] Husband-dominant family types have higher incomes, the wives are younger, and fewer wives have had employment experience.

If, in fact, the structure of authority in the family does change along with change in income, age, work experience, and the like, it is then not too surprising that dominance is not more closely related to the fertility variables.

CONCLUSION

Thus far research has failed to uncover substantively important correlations between fertility variables and specific aspects of the nature and tenor of social relationships within the family. Personal orientations of husbands and wives toward each other, toward marriage, and toward children undoubtedly affect fertility and perhaps even determine fertility to a great degree. Singly, however, the measured variables exhibit only minor associations with fertility. This generalization holds true from study to study, whether the

[15] Exceptions to this generalization number at least two. See Donald M. Wolfe, "Power and Authority in the Family," Chapter 7, pp. 99–117 in Dowrin Cartwright, ed., *Studies in Social Power*, University of Michigan, Ann Arbor, 1959, and David Goldberg, "Some Recent Developments in American Fertility Research," in *Demographic and Economic Change in Developed Countries*, Princeton University Press for National Bureau of Economic Research, Special Conference Series, No. 4, 1960, 137–151.

[16] Wolfe, "Power and Authority in the Family," p. 114.

population is Australian, Puerto Rican, or American urban couples, or whether the population is Protestant, Catholic, or Jewish. (See ancillary Tables 96 to 105.)

Two possible inferences are:

(1) Theory is correct. The causal system of which fertility, desired fertility, and control of fertility are effects is indeed complex or,

(2) To date, little success has been achieved in the construction of valid measures.

The second inference does not exclude the first. The associations that have been isolated to date attest to the complexity involved. The correlates of the fertility variables are many and they are intertwined.

A third inference also follows from the observation that correlations may be altered by controlling variables that describe the past. (Fertility-planning success is one such variable and birth interval length or duration of employment are other likely candidates.) That is, families are always adjusting to new sets of circumstances, circumstances that affect not only future fertility patterns but also affect the relationships between dependent fertility variables and the independent variables. This synthesis of past and present in the process of becoming is best exemplified by the change in the relationship between marital adjustment and desired size of family following a fertility-planning failure.

Implications for future research follow from these inferences. As stated before, multidimensional measures such as religion, urban background, ethnic background, and education, since they summarize patterns of living instead of a single aspect of interaction, promise to be the best single predictors of fertility. The second implication has to do with problems of hypothesis testing. The analysis of data presented in this chapter suggests there is no one single parameter value that describes the association between a specific attitudinal or structural variable and family-size preference. Instead, there is a range of values generated by the intervention of, most often, unknown intrusive factors. A particular value merely reflects the composition of the population and the point at which respondents are in the family-building cycle. The correlations, therefore, are themselves variables and not constants that do or do not differ from zero.

TABLE 96
Correlations between Wife's Marital Adjustment and Dependent Variables within Religion and Class Categories

Religion-Class Category	Number of Children Desired by Wife	Number of Children Desired by Husband	Fertility-Planning Success	Number of Months from Marriage to First Birth	Number of Months from First Birth to Second Birth	Number of Months from Marriage to Second Birth	Number of Couples
Protestant							
White-collar	.18	.20	.11	−.04	−.09	−.07	196
Blue-collar	−.05	−.12	.18	.10	.25	.24	192
Catholic							
White-collar	.14	.16	−.02	.01	−.13	−.10	158
Blue-collar	.06	.05	.13	.11	.08	.10	212
Jewish							
White-collar	.13	−.05	−.09	−.04	−.13	−.09	89
Blue-collar	.21	.00	−.03	−.02	−.32	−.22	21
Protestant	.06	.05	.16	.04	.08	.09	388
Mixed Catholic	.08	−.10	.07	.12	.07	.12	70
Catholic	.10	.10	.07	.07	−.01	.02	370
Jewish	.15	−.04	−.07	−.04	−.17	−.12	110
White-collar	.11	.10	.05	.00	−.10	−.07	471
Blue-collar	.04	.00	.11	.10	.13	.15	467
All couples	.08	.05	.09	.05	.02	.05	938

TABLE 97
Correlations between Adjustment to Mother-Role and Dependent Variables within Religion and Class Categories

Religion-Class Category	Number of Children Desired by Wife	Number of Children Desired by Husband	Fertility-Planning Success	Number of Months from Marriage to First Birth	Number of Months from First Birth to Second Birth	Number of Months from Marriage to Second Birth	Number of Couples
Protestant							
White-collar	.11	.08	.11	−.11	.16	.06	196
Blue-collar	.10	.11	.16	−.02	.03	.02	192
Catholic							
White-collar	.12	.12	−.04	−.09	.07	−.03	158
Blue-collar	.23	.16	.13	−.01	−.02	−.02	212
Jewish							
White-collar	−.08	−.10	.08	−.18	.16	.02	89
Blue-collar	.35	.37	.04	−.35	−.02	−.25	21
Protestant	.10	.10	.13	−.07	.10	.04	388
Mixed Catholic	.01	−.04	−.06	.12	.02	.07	70
Catholic	.18	.14	.06	−.04	.02	−.02	370
Jewish	−.01	−.02	.07	−.21	.12	−.04	110
White-collar	.08	.05	.05	−.11	.12	.01	471
Blue-collar	.16	.13	.10	−.01	.00	.00	467
All couples	.12	.09	.07	−.07	.06	.00	938

TABLE 98

Correlations between Wife's Employment Duration and Dependent Variables within Religion and Class Categories

Religion-Class Category	Number of Children Desired by Wife	Number of Children Desired by Husband	Fertility-Planning Success	Number of Months from Marriage to First Birth	Number of Months from First Birth to Second Birth	Number of Months from Marriage to Second Birth	Number of Couples
Protestant							
White-collar	−.09	−.11	.21	.71	.35	.71	196
Blue-collar	−.27	−.20	.25	.63	.37	.63	192
Catholic							
White-collar	−.28	−.21	−.01	.82	.25	.67	158
Blue-collar	−.20	−.16	.20	.67	.35	.58	212
Jewish							
White-collar	−.04	.02	.34	.73	.08	.47	89
Blue-collar	−.40	−.30	.17	.82	.54	.85	21
Protestant	−.17	−.14	.24	.68	.36	.67	388
Mixed Catholic	−.12	−.07	.08	.54	.27	.53	70
Catholic	−.25	−.19	.12	.73	.32	.62	370
Jewish	−.13	−.05	.27	.75	.21	.58	110
White-collar	−.20	−.17	.17	.75	.27	.65	471
Blue-collar	−.22	−.15	.21	.65	.38	.62	467
All couples	−.21	−.16	.20	.70	.32	.64	938

TABLE 99

Correlations between Wife's Future Work Intentions and Dependent Variables within Religion and Class Categories

Religion-Class Category	Number of Children Desired by Wife	Number of Children Desired by Husband	Fertility-Planning Success	Number of Months from Marriage to First Birth	Number of Months from First Birth to Second Birth	Number of Months from Marriage to Second Birth	Number of Couples
Protestant							
White-collar	−.18	.01	.06	−.01	.04	.04	196
Blue-collar	.12	−.07	−.04	.08	−.04	.04	192
Catholic							
White-collar	.09	.22	.07	−.12	−.01	−.08	158
Blue-collar	.00	.01	.16	.06	.05	.08	212
Jewish							
White-collar	−.03	.04	−.13	−.09	−.07	−.09	89
Blue-collar	.43	.59	−.38	−.45	−.32	−.49	21
Protestant	−.03	−.03	−.01	.03	.00	.04	388
Mixed Catholic	−.01	.07	−.12	.09	.06	.12	70
Catholic	.05	.10	.12	−.02	.02	.01	370
Jewish	.04	.13	−.19	−.15	−.11	−.16	110
White-collar	.01	.13	.00	−.07	.01	−.03	471
Blue-collar	.06	.01	.04	.05	.00	.04	467
All couples	.04	.07	.02	−.01	.00	.01	938

TABLE 100
Correlations between Liking for Children and Dependent Variables within Religion and Class Categories

Religion-Class Category	Number of Children Desired by Wife	Number of Children Desired by Husband	Fertility-Planning Success	Number of Months from Marriage to First Birth	Number of Months from First Birth to Second Birth	Number of Months from Marriage to Second Birth	Number of Couples
Protestant							
White-collar	.15	.00	.00	−.11	−.09	−.12	196
Blue-collar	.09	−.05	−.05	−.01	.04	.05	192
Catholic							
White-collar	.15	.09	−.01	.05	−.15	−.08	158
Blue-collar	.17	−.01	.02	−.01	−.07	−.05	212
Jewish							
White-collar	.10	.17	.01	.05	−.25	−.15	89
Blue-collar	.15	.21	−.05	−.25	−.38	−.40	21
Protestant	.12	−.02	−.02	−.06	−.02	−.04	388
Mixed Catholic	.13	.02	.23	.06	−.05	.00	70
Catholic	.16	.03	.01	.02	−.10	−.06	370
Jewish	.12	.18	.00	−.02	−.28	−.22	110
White-collar	.13	.06	.03	−.03	−.12	−.10	471
Blue-collar	.14	.01	−.02	−.01	.−04	−.03	467
All couples	.14	.03	.00	−.02	−.08	−.06	938

TABLE 101
Correlations between Age at Which Children Are Most Enjoyed and Dependent Variables within Religion and Class Categories

Religion-Class Category	Number of Children Desired by Wife	Number of Children Desired by Husband	Fertility-Planning Success	Number of Months from Marriage to First Birth	Number of Months from First Birth to Second Birth	Number of Months from Marriage to Second Birth	Number of Couples
Protestant							
White-collar	−.07	−.17	.06	.07	.27	.19	196
Blue-collar	−.03	−.03	.07	.16	.17	.21	192
Catholic							
White-collar	−.02	−.08	.09	.08	.08	.13	158
Blue-collar	−.12	−.09	−.05	−.05	.14	.09	212
Jewish							
White-collar	−.01	−.02	−.18	.10	.40	.40	89
Blue-collar	−.14	−.11	.17	.64	.41	.63	21
Protestant	−.05	−.10	.05	.11	.22	.19	388
Mixed Catholic	.12	.07	.01	−.10	.07	.00	70
Catholic	−.08	−.09	.01	.00	.12	.11	370
Jewish	−.05	−.04	−.09	.23	.41	.46	110
White-collar	.00	−.06	.03	.06	.22	.18	471
Blue-collar	−.06	−.04	.01	.07	.16	.15	467
All couples	−.04	−.05	.02	.06	.19	.16	938

TABLE 102
Correlations between Dominance in Running the Home and Dependent Variables within Religion and Class Categories

Religion-Class Category	Number of Children Desired by Wife	Number of Children Desired by Husband	Fertility-Planning Success	Number of Months from Marriage to First Birth	Number of Months from First Birth to Second Birth	Number of Months from Marriage to Second Birth	Number of Couples
Protestant							
White-collar	−.05	−.06	.01	−.01	−.09	−.08	196
Blue-collar	.04	.09	.00	.04	−.09	−.05	192
Catholic							
White-collar	.08	.05	.05	−.04	−.04	−.04	158
Blue-collar	−.09	−.05	.01	−.01	−.05	−.04	212
Jewish							
White-collar	.13	.23	−.03	−.01	−.02	.00	89
Blue-collar	−.40	−.22	−.06	.33	.19	.36	21
Protestant	.00	.02	.01	.02	−.09	−.06	388
Mixed Catholic	.14	.08	.03	.04	.02	.03	70
Catholic	−.01	.00	.03	−.02	−.05	−.04	370
Jewish	.05	.16	−.03	.05	.02	.07	110
White-collar	.00	.00	.04	.02	−.05	−.02	471
Blue-collar	−.05	−.02	.01	.02	−.04	−.03	467
All couples	−.02	−.01	.03	.02	−.05	−.02	938

TABLE 103
Correlations between Dominance in Social Life and Dependent Variables within Religion and Class Categories

Religion-Class Category	Number of Children Desired by Wife	Number of Children Desired by Husband	Fertility-Planning Success	Number of Months from Marriage to First Birth	Number of Months from First Birth to Second Birth	Number of Months from Marriage to Second Birth	Number of Couples
Protestant							
White-collar	−.10	−.02	.10	−.09	.06	−.01	196
Blue-collar	−.05	−.07	.03	.05	.06	.07	192
Catholic							
White-collar	−.09	.01	.00	.10	.05	.09	158
Blue-collar	−.01	−.01	.05	.06	.03	.03	212
Jewish							
White-collar	−.01	−.04	.04	.16	−.03	.08	89
Blue-collar	−.33	−.40	.15	.24	.17	.32	21
Protestant	−.07	−.04	.07	−.01	.06	.03	388
Mixed Catholic	−.02	.22	.05	.26	−.01	.14	70
Catholic	−.05	.00	.03	.08	.04	.06	370
Jewish	−.05	−.09	.06	.17	.00	.11	110
White-collar	−.10	−.01	.07	.06	.04	.07	471
Blue-collar	−.03	−.01	.05	.08	.05	.07	467
All couples	−.06	−.01	.06	.07	.05	.07	938

TABLE 104
Correlations between Dominance in Nonsocial Areas and Dependent Variables within Religion and Class Categories

Religion-Class Category	Number of Children Desired by Wife	Number of Children Desired by Husband	Fertility-Planning Success	Number of Months from Marriage to First Birth	Number of Months from First Birth to Second Birth	Number of Months from Marriage to Second Birth	Number of Couples
Protestant							
White-collar	−.13	.02	.14	.13	.09	.15	196
Blue-collar	−.17	−.11	.17	.13	.16	.18	192
Catholic							
White-collar	−.15	−.13	.09	.01	.03	.02	158
Blue-collar	−.09	.00	.00	.02	.08	.05	212
Jewish							
White-collar	−.19	−.07	.12	.14	.11	.17	89
Blue-collar	.05	−.14	−.10	−.02	.14	.03	21
Protestant	−.15	−.05	.14	.11	.12	.15	388
Mixed Catholic	.12	.04	.00	.08	.10	.12	70
Catholic	−.10	−.05	.04	.01	.06	.03	370
Jewish	−.16	−.07	.06	.11	.12	.15	110
White-collar	−.06	.00	.09	.07	.08	.09	471
Blue-collar	−.12	−.04	.08	.08	.11	.11	467
All couples	−.09	−.02	.08	.07	.10	.10	938

TABLE 105
Correlations between Patterns of Help Available to Wife and Dependent Variables within Religion and Class Categories

Religion-Class Category	Number of Children Desired by Wife	Number of Children Desired by Husband	Fertility-Planning Success	Number of Months from Marriage to First Birth	Number of Months from First Birth to Second Birth	Number of Months from Marriage to Second Birth	Number of Couples
Protestant							
White-collar	−.02	−.15	.02	.01	.15	.09	196
Blue-collar	.01	.04	−.12	.08	−.03	.03	192
Catholic							
White-collar	−.10	−.03	.02	−.09	−.05	−.12	158
Blue-collar	−.01	.04	−.06	−.11	−.14	−.14	212
Jewish							
White-collar	.21	.11	−.04	.28	−.18	.02	89
Blue-collar	−.62	−.42	−.02	.36	.12	.32	21
Protestant	.00	−.05	−.05	.05	.07	.06	388
Mixed Catholic	.20	.15	−.13	−.24	−.34	−.39	70
Catholic	−.04	.02	−.03	−.11	−.11	−.13	370
Jewish	.05	.01	−.04	.30	−.11	.09	110
White-collar	.01	.00	.00	.01	.00	−.02	471
Blue-collar	.00	.03	−.08	.00	−.09	−.06	467
All couples	.00	.01	−.03	.01	−.05	−.04	938

Chapter XVIII. Personality Characteristics

Studies of the relationship between personality characteristics and fertility are still few enough to be quickly summarized. An early study by Flanagan[1] included analyses of the relationships between ideal family size and scores on the Bernreuter Personality Inventory with only slight differences observed. Aside from the pretest analyses preceding the present study, two recent studies have also incorporated some measures of personality characteristics and related them to aspects of fertility. The Indianapolis Study was explicitly directed toward testing several hypotheses in this area. Attention was focused specifically on linking feelings of personal inadequacy, ego-centered interest in children, and fear of pregnancy with effective fertility planning and low planned fertility.

For the most part, little relationship at all was found; occasionally, the evidence contradicted the hypothesized direction of association. For example, the relationship found to exist between feelings of personal inadequacy and fertility planning was opposite from that anticipated: success rather than failure in planning size of family appears in some measure to depend on the presence of the emotionally stable, self-confident, well-satisfied personality.[2] The correlation between feeling of personal adequacy and fertility-planning status was .17 and .20 for wives and husbands respectively. No appreciable association with size of planned family was uncovered. The analysis of "ego-centered interest in children"[3] provided no evidence of any association with the fertility variables. There was some suspicion, however, that measurement was deficient. Fear of pregnancy appeared to be no deterrent to fertility after the birth of the first child.[4]

Another recent treatment of this subject is contained in the analyses of data collected by E. Lowell Kelly in a longitudinal study of marital adjustment covering a period of approximately twenty

[1] John C. Flanagan, "A Study of Factors Determining Family Size in a Selected Professional Group," *Genetic Psychology Monographs*, 25 (1942), pp. 3–99. Flanagan concluded: "In general very little relation was found in this group (Army Air Corps officers and wives) between reported 'ideal family size' and scores on general measures of interests, values, and personality traits." (p. 30).

[2] Charles F. Westoff and Clyde V. Kiser, "The Interrelation of Fertility, Fertility Planning, and Feeling of Personal Inadequacy," in P. K. Whelpton and Clyde V. Kiser, eds., *Social and Psychological Factors Affecting Fertility*, 5 Vols., Milbank Memorial Fund, New York, 1946–1958, III, pp. 741–799.

[3] Marianne De Graff Swain and Clyde V. Kiser, "The Interrelation of Fertility, Fertility Planning, and Ego-Centered Interest in Children," in Whelpton and Kiser, *Social and Psychological Factors Affecting Fertility*, (1954) IV, pp. 801–834.

[4] Nathalie Schacter and Clyde V. Kiser, "Fear of Pregnancy and Childbirth in Relation to Fertility-Planning Status and Fertility," in *ibid.*, IV, pp. 835–884.

years.[5] A large number of personality characteristics from rating scales and conventional inventories, measured after the couples were engaged, were correlated with desired family size (before marriage) and eventual fertility twenty years later.

The personality characteristic most consistently related to both aspects of fertility was "neurotic tendency" as measured in the Bernreuter Personality Inventory. Other scales in this inventory as well as scales from other tests (such as the Bell Adjustment Inventory) seemed to indicate the same basic association: women who showed tendencies toward introversion, submissiveness, inferiority, and poor emotional and social adjustment had fewer children. The correlations of these highly intercorrelated measures with total fertility twenty years later average about .20. The hypothesis is that women who are overly concerned with their own personal problems will lack ego resources sufficient to afford the psychological costs posed by the demands of children for attention and care and, thus, will be likely to have fewer children.

The evidence thus far is inconsistent. The Flanagan study uncovered little evidence of any association between personality characteristics and measures of fertility. If the assumption is made that feelings of personal inadequacy as measured in the Indianapolis Study and the emotional adjustment scales measured in the conventional inventories are basically the same phenomenon (a reasonable assumption considering the items) then there is rather contradictory evidence in connection with fertility. The Indianapolis investigation revealed that the emotionally stable women control the number and spacing of pregnancies more effectively than the women who are less well-adjusted emotionally. However, no relationship of personal adequacy to number of children born was ascertained. On the other hand, evidence from the Kelly data reveals no association of emotional adjustment and fertility-planning success but does indicate negative correlations with fertility itself as well as number of children desired.[6]

In brief, this was the main evidence upon which our study had to build. In view of the objectives of the study, one of which was to explore the motivations underlying family-size preferences and the psychological factors affecting fertility planning, a decision was

[5] See Elliot G. Mishler, Charles F. Westoff, and E. Lowell Kelly, "Some Psychological Correlates of Differential Fertility: A Longitudinal Study," *American Psychologist*, 10 (1955), p. 319 (Abstract); Charles F. Westoff, Philip C. Sagi, and E. Lowell Kelly, "Fertility Through Twenty Years of Marriage: A Study in Predictive Possibilities," *American Sociological Review*, 23 (1958).

[6] This statement is true for both the fertility of the total sample and the fertility of couples who planned all births successfully.

reached to explore the area of personality in comprehensive terms. The selection of particular variables was based on the research summarized above as well as the evidence accumulated in the extensive pretesting program.[7]

THE PERSONALITY VARIABLES

The logic underlying the selection of personality variables is basically the same as that organizing many of the previous hypotheses involving attitudes and values, namely, the perceived compatibility of the demands of children and child-rearing with other requirements, in this case requirements of the personality. A total of eight personality variables was included.

One theme arising out of the previous research discussed above was that unsatisfied dependency needs and immature concern for one's self and one's personal problems would reduce desires for additional children. The variable included to tap this area is termed "generalized manifest anxiety."[8] The manifest anxiety scale has been described as a measure of excitableness, tenseness, and tendency to worry. It is very close in content to other measures of neurotic tendency, emotional instability, and the like.

Nurturance is described by Edwards[9] as: "To help friends when they are in trouble, to assist others less fortunate, to trust others with kindness and sympathy, to forgive others, to be generous with others, to sympathize with others, to sympathize with others who are hurt or sick, to show a great deal of affection toward others, to have others confide in one about personal problems."

A third variable relates to the type of psychological balance existing between impulse and self-control that was deemed relevant to the practice of contraception. Ability to defer the gratification of

[7] Frank W. Notestein, et al., "Pretest Results of a New Study of Fertility in the United States," *International Statistical Association Bulletin*, 36, (1959).

[8] The items comprising these and subsequent indices are listed in Appendix D along with the details of index construction. The Personality Research Inventory developed by David R. Saunders of the Educational Testing Service in Princeton was used in an abbreviated and modified form for all variables except nurturance needs. The complete form consists of 250 items divided into 25 nonoverlapping sets of 10 items, each of which is intended to measure a different personality characteristic. Statistical independence of the 25 traits is the goal of an on-going series of factor analyses of items so that each successive analysis contributes to the relative independence and homogeneity of each scale.

Before this particular test was selected, an extensive pretesting program had been undertaken in an attempt to develop an instrument. The outcome of this venture is described in Elliot G. Mishler, "A Scalogram Analysis of the Sentence Completion Test," *Educational and Psychological Measurement*, 18 (1958), pp. 75–90.

[9] The Edwards Personal Preference Schedule was developed by Allen L. Edwards and is distributed by the Psychological Corporation. An abbreviated form of the original test was used.

impulses was hypothesized to correlate positively with fertility-planning success.

The fourth personality variable has been varyingly labeled self-awareness, introspectiveness, self-acceptance, and self-insight. Persons scoring high on this scale were presumed to be more successful in planning fertility, an expectation confirmed in the pretest.

Individuals vary considerably in their psychological needs for routine and their capacity to accept indefiniteness and uncertainty. Children's behavior is characteristically incompatible with neatness and orderliness and requires considerable flexibility and tolerance. Measures of compulsiveness (meticulousness, rigidity) and tolerance for ambiguity (orderliness, authoritarianism) were included on the assumption that they would correlate with family-size preferences. Compulsiveness was expected to correlate negatively and ambiguity tolerance positively with number of children desired.

Participation in family life is a primary form of group interaction requiring many subtle social skills of interpersonal relations. As in any group endeavor, a premium is placed upon cooperativeness, a response that is learned and incorporated in the personality structure beginning in the early stages of socialization. On the assumption that personal dispositions toward working and solving problems with others, rather than by one's self, would correlate directly both with family-size preferences and efficacy of fertility control, a measure of "cooperativeness" was included.

The final personality characteristic purports to measure the individual's needs to achieve. In modern urban culture, achievement has not yet become synonymous with a large family. Expressed needs for higher achievement were accordingly hypothesized to associate with preferences for smaller families.

TABLE 106

Correlations between Selected Measures of Wife's Personality Characteristics and Number of Children Desired, by Religion

Religious Preference	Manifest Anxiety	Need to Nurture	Compulsiveness	Ambiguity Tolerance	Cooperativeness	Need Achievement
Protestant total	−.05	.02	−.16	.15	.01	−.02
Mixed Catholic total	.05	−.07	−.16	.02	.20	.05
Catholic total	−.13	.12	−.11	.15	.02	.10
Jewish total	−.12	−.15	−.11	.10	−.01	−.04
All Couples	−.07	.06	−.11	.11	.02	.04

RESULTS AND CONCLUSIONS

The correlations between these eight personality characteristics and the appropriate dependent variables were computed for each religious grouping separately. However, statistical tests of homogeneity support only the conclusion that observed intergroup variations in the magnitudes of the correlations could have happened by chance.

Ten hypotheses are tested (in Tables 106 and 107), and in only three instances (anxiety, compulsiveness, and ambiguity tolerance,

TABLE 107

Correlations between Selected Measures of Wife's Personality Characteristics and Fertility-Planning Success, by Religion

Religious Preference	Manifest Anxiety	Defer Impulse Gratification	Self-Awareness	Cooperativeness
Protestant total	−.10	−.01	.06	−.06
Mixed Catholic total	.01	.02	.08	.12
Catholic total	.01	.08	.03	−.04
Jewish total	−.03	.00	.01	−.05
All couples	−.05	.02	.05	−.03

with number of children desired) do the correlations reach statistically significant levels.[10] However, these values at best account for only 1 per cent of the total variance of number of children desired. As a matter of fact, the two personality characteristics that do indicate some association with number of children desired— ambiguity tolerance and compulsiveness—are correlated higher with each other (−.41) than any other paired combination of personality variables. It would be more reasonable to conclude, therefore, that one rather than two underlying factors are involved.[11]

A further analysis investigated the possibility that high impulsiveness would associate with contraceptive chance-taking. No evidence was found in support of this hypothesis.

In short, there is little evidence at this juncture of the study (and little confidence that correlations will improve at later stages) that the

[10] The correlation of −.07 between anxiety and number of children desired is significantly different from zero at the .05 level. The two remaining correlations are significant at the .01 level. That ten and not only three hypotheses were tested affects these probabilities.

[11] The multiple correlation of these two personality characteristics with number of children desired increases only to .13.

area of personality has produced fruitful results. Whether the failure thus far to uncover stable relationships of any predictive value is due more to the unreliability and the primitive level of measurement of personality or to simple invalidity of theory is a critical, though unfortunately moot, question.

Chapter XIX. Summary Multivariate Analysis

The preceding eight chapters have taken the form of testing specific hypotheses about the relationships between single independent variables and indices of fertility. Occasionally, the hypotheses were refined sufficiently to introduce one or two additional variables into the analysis, but the objective in such instances was mainly to eliminate the influence of variables extraneous to the hypothesis. Multivariate analysis, conceived in terms of assessing the impact on fertility of a large number of social-psychological variables considered simultaneously, has been deferred to the end of the report. Having completed the specific hypothesis testing, we have now reached a point appropriate to synthesize the foregoing analyses.

OBJECTIVES

A number of different questions are poseu in this chapter:

1. To what extent can the large number (67) of independent variables be reduced to a lesser number of basic factors?

2. How much of the variation in the dependent variables is held in common with these factors? Is fertility equally "predictable" for the three major religious groups?

3. Is the social-psychological structure underlying fertility the same for each religious group?

4. How much of the variance of the dependent variables is held in common? What is the structure of a factor which maximizes the common variance of the fertility variables? Is it similar for each religious group?

These four questions constitute the basis for the following analyses.[1]

Toward Parsimony of Explanation

A total of 67 variables clearly inhibits easy generalization. Since we are interested primarily in the factors related to our measures of fertility, this number can be reduced according to criteria of redundancy or lack of correlation with any of the three dependent variables (number of children desired, length of birth intervals, and fertility-planning success).

More specifically, the criteria were as follows:

1. Nine of the original variables were eliminated for reasons of

[1] This chapter contains the core of a paper by Charles F. Westoff, "The Social-Psychological Structure of Fertility," *Proceedings, International Population Conference*, Vienna, 1959, pp. 355–366.

redundancy, that is, not enough new information was gained to justify their continued use. An example of this is the husband's income, which corresponds closely to "disposable income," calculated as total family income less regular costs of housing.

2. For similar reasons, the twelve variables for the husband (mainly attitudinal) were also eliminated. This decision was based on a side analysis which revealed that the dependent variables of wife's and husband's fertility desires (measured separately) respond almost identically to the independent variables.[2] This does not include variables such as husband's income, occupational prestige, and the like, which characterize the status of the couple.

3. A total of 46 variables remained to be screened in light of their correlations with the dependent variables. The criterion established is that the variable must correlate with at least one of the three dependent variables in at least one of the three religious subsamples at a level of $\pm.15$ or higher.[3] This figure, although arbitrary, is higher than the minimum value required to justify the assumption of statistical significance at the .01 level. If the correlation reached at least $\pm.15$ in any one of the three religious populations, it was retained for all religions. Thus, the same variables can be compared for all three groups.

Application of this criterion led to the retention of 25 variables,[4] with a twenty-sixth (extent of Catholic school education) included for Catholics only.

The variables retained for multivariate analysis include representatives of the entire range discussed in the last eight chapters. Aside from the fertility measures, the areas of religiousness, social and economic status, mobility, age, siblings, adjustment to marriage and motherhood, personality, and others are represented.

FACTOR ANALYSIS

Although a reduction from 67 to 22 independent variables is substantial, parsimony of explanation calls for still further simplification

[2] The initial correlation matrix provides correlations of wife's and husband's fertility desires with 67 other variables. The correlation of these two series (the correlation of correlations) is .94, varying only slightly for each of the religious subsamples.

[3] The variable, number of wife's siblings, did not reach this level of correlation but was retained because of its predictive value in previous studies, particularly that reported in Charles F. Westoff, Philip C. Sagi, and E. Lowell Kelly, "Fertility Through Twenty Years of Marriage: A Study in Predictive Possibilities," *American Sociological Review*, 23 (1958), pp. 549–556. One or two personality characteristics besides manifest anxiety barely passed the .15 correlation test. In view of the previous evidence on measures of anxiety, enough confidence existed to justify retaining it.

[4] This procedure means that we are capitalizing on chance more in retaining a variable than in eliminating one.

if possible. The technique of factor analysis is ideally suited for such a purpose. Although other techniques of multivariate analysis such as multiple regression techniques are available, factor analysis was selected because it better serves all the objectives described at the outset.

Three factor analyses of the 25 variables for Protestants and Jews, and 26 for Catholics, produced a total of 11 factors for each. Although this represents still further reduction—from 25 to 11 dimensions—[5] our interest lies primarily in isolating the factors relevant for the fertility variables. To accomplish this, simple structure is desirable to facilitate identification of factor content. This approach has the advantage of providing an objectively defined mathematical solution for each factor matrix.[6]

It seems desirable on theoretical grounds to exclude the dependent variables from this solution. The objective of the rotations can then be defined as achieving simple structure among the independent variables[7] and examining the resulting distributions of the loadings of the fertility variables among these factors. These weights are determined by allowing the fertility variables to be distributed proportionately with the independent variables but not to be involved in the simple structure solution itself. The ultimate analytical objective is to compare the factors affecting fertility for each religious grouping. To what extent are the same factors operating? Which factors are unique to each group? These are two of the research questions posed above. The final rotated factor structures appear for Protestants, Catholics, and Jews in Tables 108, 109, and 110 respectively. The 11 factors are identified numerically but there is no meaning to their ordering.

INTERPRETATION OF INITIAL RESULTS

The first results of interest are the communalities (h^2) of the fertility variables for each religious group. The amount of variance accounted for by all 11 factors is consistently lower for Protestants than for either Catholics or Jews for all three fertility variables.

---

[5] Mainly for reasons of convenience, the principal-axes solution for the factor problem was used. According to Thurstone, the principal-axes solution is ideal for the problem of statistical condensation. See L. L. Thurstone, *Multiple Factor Analysis*, University of Chicago Press, Chicago, 1947, pp. 473–510. Also see Sten Henrysson, *Applicability of Factor Analysis in the Behavioral Sciences*, Almqvist and Wiksell, Stockholm, 1957.

[6] The quartimax criterion of simple structure was used. This solution maximizes the fourth moment of the distributions of factor loadings.

[7] Operationally there is no difference between "independent" and "dependent" variables in factor analysis. These terms are used for substantive purposes and consistency with previous analyses.

TABLE 108

Protestants: Rotated Factor Matrix[a]

Variable	1	2	3	4	5	6	7	8	9	10	11	h²
Number of children desired	.17	.11	−.08	.10	.02	.40	−.22	−.04	−.17	−.13	−.41	.48
Number of months from marriage to second birth	−.78	−.15	−.06	.10	−.01	−.10	.25	.09	.12	.24	−.04	.80
Fertility-planning success	−.20	−.01	−.13	.20	.01	−.20	.18	.28	.02	.21	−.08	.30
Husband's annual earnings	−.05	.11	.02	−.01	.01	−.05	.22	.01	.02	.76	−.06	.65
Income change since marriage	−.34	.01	−.03	−.05	.18	.05	.00	−.02	.09	.67	.02	.62
Economic security	.09	.12	−.09	.22	−.28	.03	.18	.01	−.11	.60	.11	.57
Perception of opportunities	.08	.35	−.13	.04	−.18	.21	.02	.08	−.28	.34	.06	.43
Relevance of finances	.05	.01	−.03	−.04	.00	−.02	−.04	.02	−.02	.01	.58	.35
Credit buying	−.08	−.10	.06	−.12	.36	−.06	−.27	.00	−.01	−.15	.00	.27
Aspirations for children's education	−.01	.50	.01	.16	.08	−.06	.08	−.14	.00	.12	.02	.33
Education	.06	.57	−.09	.09	−.06	.11	.43	.15	−.02	.12	.07	.59
Occupational prestige	−.02	.53	−.08	.02	−.21	.01	.32	−.03	−.09	.31	−.13	.56
Wife's employment duration	−.78	−.01	−.05	−.02	−.08	.01	.19	.00	−.01	.11	−.02	.66
Age	−.46	−.09	−.05	.05	.02	−.06	.80	.04	−.08	.18	−.02	.90
Age at marriage	.06	.11	−.03	−.02	−.01	.01	.90	−.03	−.05	.04	.00	.83
Number of siblings	−.03	−.39	.07	.04	.01	−.04	−.19	−.33	−.13	−.20	−.14	.39
Happiness of childhood	.12	.10	−.13	.39	−.05	.03	.13	.15	−.02	.08	.04	.25
Marital adjustment	−.01	.15	−.18	.50	−.07	.01	.04	−.08	−.11	.15	−.05	.36
Adjustment to mother role	.03	−.09	−.06	.42	.15	.06	−.08	.08	−.01	.08	−.02	.24
Manifest anxiety	.00	−.26	.07	−.48	.06	.03	−.05	.04	−.11	.01	.03	.32
Liking for children	.00	.01	−.11	.17	.04	.00	.02	−.11	−.43	−.07	.05	.25
Preference for babies	−.12	−.23	−.01	.19	.06	.06	.00	−.05	.37	.00	.01	.25
Sex identity of children	−.01	.12	−.02	.02	−.02	.59	−.08	.01	.00	.04	−.02	.38
Church attendance	.02	−.02	−.73	.03	−.07	−.02	.05	.05	.05	.05	−.04	.55
Informal religious orientation	−.11	.14	−.69	.08	.07	.04	.12	−.04	−.08	.02	.07	.55

[a] Rotated to simple structure by quartimax criterion, excluding first three variables.

323

TABLE 109

Catholics: Rotated Factor Matrix[a]

Variable	1	2	3	4	5	6	7	8	9	10	11	h^2
Number of children desired	.11	.23	.09	.12	-.14	.03	-.02	.51	-.41	.23	-.22	.64
Number of months from marriage to second birth	-.29	-.46	.11	-.61	.20	-.09	-.02	-.20	.04	-.11	.27	.86
Fertility-planning success	-.04	-.22	.30	-.01	.09	-.14	-.08	-.27	.21	.11	.22	.35
Husband's annual earnings	-.59	-.10	-.01	.14	-.17	.08	-.45	.09	-.03	.02	-.04	.63
Income change since marriage	-.79	-.06	.00	-.09	.02	-.01	.02	-.03	.03	-.02	-.02	.63
Economic security	-.12	.04	.04	-.01	-.09	-.09	-.70	.04	-.10	.03	-.10	.54
Perception of opportunities	-.13	.14	.06	.02	-.22	-.07	-.29	-.09	-.08	.03	-.50	.45
Relevance of finances	.03	.02	.02	-.09	.17	.13	.12	-.60	.16	-.02	-.04	.46
Credit buying	-.20	.25	.04	.02	.24	-.04	.44	-.08	.10	.08	-.14	.40
Aspirations for children's education	-.09	-.04	.01	-.08	-.33	-.15	-.09	.02	-.11	.02	-.12	.18
Education	.00	-.14	.06	.08	-.65	.01	-.12	.20	-.11	-.01	-.11	.54
Occupational prestige	-.23	-.06	-.01	.01	.35	.02	-.21	.08	-.05	-.12	-.31	.34
Wife's employment duration	-.04	-.25	.00	-.72	.03	-.02	.02	-.08	.10	.01	.09	.60
Age	-.10	-.98	.02	-.19	.05	-.02	.01	-.05	.00	-.02	.04	1.02
Age at marriage	.08	-.80	-.06	.18	-.17	.03	-.03	.12	-.04	.03	-.08	.74
Number of siblings	.10	-.11	.02	.05	.56	.05	.12	.18	.07	-.08	-.09	.41
Happiness of childhood	-.02	-.06	.08	-.01	-.28	-.33	.00	.17	-.14	-.11	-.02	.26
Marital adjustment	.06	-.03	.03	-.04	-.03	-.56	-.12	.12	-.06	.07	-.04	.36
Adjustment to mother role	-.02	.14	.33	-.03	.13	-.12	-.06	.08	-.11	.08	-.05	.19
Manifest anxiety	-.10	-.07	-.40	-.01	.16	.06	.14	-.10	.07	.18	.10	.28
Liking for children	.06	.03	-.01	-.05	-.07	-.14	-.03	.04	-.03	.44	-.03	.23
Preference for babies	-.07	.00	-.10	-.04	.13	.03	.04	.10	.14	-.06	.13	.09
Sex identity of children	.02	.07	-.05	.10	.00	.06	-.10	.22	.08	.27	.08	.16
Church attendance	-.02	-.16	.08	.02	-.07	-.06	-.04	.05	-.67	-.05	-.06	.50
Informal religious orientation	-.01	-.13	-.02	.05	-.17	-.15	-.08	.02	-.54	.09	-.01	.38
Catholic school education	.08	.03	-.10	.09	-.04	.11	-.14	.07	-.56	.01	.06	.38

[a] Rotated to simple structure by quartimax criterion, excluding first three variables.

324

TABLE 110

Jews: Rotated Factor Matrix[a]

Variable	1	2	3	4	5	6	7	8	9	10	11	h^2
Number of children desired	-.07	.24	.10	.10	-.43	-.13	-.09	.03	.12	-.48	.10	.55
Number of months from marriage to second birth	-.42	-.30	-.67	.02	.03	-.24	.28	-.05	-.13	.09	-.10	.89
Fertility-planning success	.19	-.05	-.38	.07	-.07	-.30	.31	.02	-.15	-.16	.29	.51
Husband's annual earnings	.10	-.02	-.02	-.22	-.07	.08	9.0	.81	-.05	-.13	-.05	.75
Income change since marriage	-.05	-.04	-.46	-.11	-.04	.12	-.11	.54	-.06	-.03	-.14	.57
Economic security	.00	.19	.03	.21	-.01	.06	.13	.78	.03	-.01	-.03	.71
Perception of opportunities	-.11	.09	.14	.12	.24	-.12	-.08	.58	.07	-.23	.00	.53
Relevance of finances	-.16	.24	.14	-.14	-.02	-.07	.34	-.04	.21	.40	.08	.45
Credit buying	-.08	-.07	-.07	.07	-.03	-.05	-.66	-.28	.01	.20	-.06	.59
Aspirations for children's education	.04	.05	.01	.01	.56	.04	-.01	-.09	.00	-.11	-.02	.34
Education	.07	-.04	.02	-.05	.04	.04	.13	.21	-.07	-.75	.09	.64
Occupational prestige	.01	.06	-.03	-.11	-.02	.00	.04	.23	.24	-.57	-.11	.46
Wife's employment duration	-.10	-.26	-.73	.02	.01	.08	-.02	-.04	.01	-.03	.09	.62
Age	-.16	-.91	-.30	.01	.04	-.09	.07	-.06	-.07	.05	-.03	.97
Age at marriage	.12	-.90	.14	.03	-.05	.11	-.09	-.02	.04	-.07	.06	.88
Number of siblings	-.12	-.25	.01	.55	.01	-.05	-.23	-.12	.05	.19	.12	.51
Happiness of childhood	.16	.18	.40	.05	.04	-.26	.22	.13	.10	-.08	.22	.42
Marital adjustment	.12	.02	.13	.02	-.05	-.30	-.08	.37	.42	.08	.07	.45
Adjustment to mother role	.01	.04	.19	.06	-.05	-.52	-.09	-.15	.00	.19	.04	.38
Manifest anxiety	-.07	-.02	-.16	.09	.07	.16	.16	-.40	-.10	.03	-.24	.33
Liking for children	-.10	.14	.09	-.08	.17	.04	-.15	.04	.28	-.07	.48	.41
Preference for babies	-.70	-.09	-.17	.06	-.02	-.01	.00	.00	-.01	.13	.06	.54
Sex identity of children	.02	.15	.00	.17	-.05	.14	.19	.05	.38	.00	-.07	.27
Church attendance	.17	-.17	.00	-.03	.19	-.03	.07	-.15	.03	.11	.68	.61
Informal religious orientation	.13	.06	-.07	.08	.01	-.03	.12	-.05	-.23	-.28	.56	.50

[a] Rotated to simple structure by quartimax criterion, excluding first three variables.

325

This is an interesting proposition and one that was suspected in the earlier correlations. Why should fertility apparently be more predictable with these variables among Catholics and Jews than among Protestants? One possibility is that the classification "Protestant" no longer signifies homogeneous patterns of behavior to the extent it did historically. This is especially true of this sample which is limited to urban Protestants. From some points of view, it is more revealing to regard Protestants as non-Catholics and non-Jews.

Catholics and Jews, on the other hand, still possess distinctive sub-cultures. Another way of describing the difference is that Catholics and Jews adhere to value systems which are more integrated in the sense of the logical consistency of means and ends. Moreover, the content of these value systems has a relevance for fertility that does not exist for the more heterogeneous Protestant population.

In the case of Catholics, faithful adherence to the norms of Catholicism has direct implications for family size. This may take several forms. Since periodic continence is the technique of child spacing sanctioned by the church, and since this method is less perfected and more difficult to use successfully than other methods, its use results in more pregnancies than occur with other methods. Another connection is implied in observed Catholic preferences for larger families. Although there may be no official church position on the desirability of large families *per se*, the social-psychological supports for such norms are no doubt promoted by misinterpretation at the parish level (i.e., priests may interpret the official position on birth control as implying the virtues of unlimited reproduction). Many Catholics probably have been educated to regard sex as sinful and the rhythm method as not to be used in the spirit of birth control. Just how this set of values is translated into desires for larger families is not altogether clear. It probably involves more than simply rationalization of the probable consequences of an unreliable technique of family limitation. At any rate, the degree of adherence to the norms of the Catholic church, as measured by indices of religiousness, can be expected to furnish an extra predictor of fertility among Catholics that does not exist among non-Catholics.

For Jews, the cultural effects on fertility are more indirect. The Jewish group in the United States, much more than the Catholic minority, is a minority group in the sociological sense of the term. Moreover, Jews have a long history of minority status and its attendant disadvantages, a status that has promoted feelings of both individual as well as group vulnerability. Group solidarity has been one response to the anxieties created by perceptions of a hostile environment. Another response, facilitated by a cultural tradition which esteems intellectual pursuits, is social mobility; the image of the Jew emphasizes middle-class values. Although education is the avenue of social mobility for most persons in American society, among Jews the aspiration is apparently directed more toward professional training. Financial success can be ephemeral; professional skills are more dependable.

In this context, the assumption of family responsibilities can be viewed as an impediment to higher education or as increasing vulnerability. Thus, average age at marriage is oldest for Jews. Once the security of education is achieved, however, inhibitions on fertility can be released. Given the cultural homogeneity of the Jewish group[8] and the emphasis on education, it might be expected that fertility would be more predictable than among Protestants.

NUMBER OF CHILDREN DESIRED

Much of this preceding theorizing is *ex post facto* and suffers all the usual limitations of such theory. In the case of the Jews, the factor analysis clearly points up the importance of education in the fertility pattern (Table 110). Factor 10, for example, which contains most of the variance of education[9] and occupational prestige, also contains the largest single amount of the variance in number of children desired. Another variable loaded significantly with regard to this factor is a perception of finances as relevant in decisions about having children, another component of rational behavior. The factor containing most of the remaining explained variance of family-size preferences (Factor 5) is defined chiefly by aspirations to send children to college. It is interesting to reflect that only among Jews is there evidence in these data of a perceived incompatibility between wanting to send children to college and wanting large families.

The 64 per cent of the variance of family-size preferences of Catholics accounted for by the 11 factors is concentrated mainly in Factors 8 and 9. The former factor is the perception of the relevance of finances in family-size decisions, but this, however, includes only a low loading on education. The latter factor (9) is clearly that of religiousness, containing the common variance of regularity of church attendance, informal religious orientation, and extent of education in the Catholic school system. If this factor were eliminated for Catholics, and if the educational factor were eliminated for Jews, then the total common-factor variance of desired family size explained would be as low or even lower than for Protestants.

[8] The variances of most of the 81 variables are lowest for Jews.
[9] Education of wife correlates .65 with education of husband among Jews.

The variance of family-size preferences for Protestants is also distributed predominantly in two factors (Table 108). As for Catholics, one of these (11) is the factor being measured by the perception of the relevance of finances in fertility decisions. The other factor (6) plays a less important role in determining the variance of family-size desires among Catholics and appears wholly irrelevant among Jews. This factor includes almost all of the common-factor variance of the sex identity of the two children. The variance in common with family-size preference indicates that additional children are desired if the first two children are of the same sex.

FERTILITY-PLANNING SUCCESS

Another generalization emerging from the factor analyses is that fertility-planning success is the least predictable of the three dependent variables. For Protestants and Catholics, the variance controlled is only 30 and 35 per cent; among Jews it reaches slightly over 50 per cent. In addition to revealing the lowest variance control for each religious grouping, the explained variance is distributed over many more factors and hence produces a more complicated structure than either family-size preferences or birth intervals. Consequently, there is a much greater risk that the common factors delineated below may reflect some chance variation.

Even confining our attention to factors in which fertility-planning success contains a loading of at least .20 produces some apparent anomalies as revealed in Factor 6 among Protestants. In this factor, a portion of the variance of fertility-planning success overlaps the much higher correlation between sex identity of the first two children and number of children desired. There is every reason to believe that the sex of the two births is independent of fertility-planning success.[10]

The other factors involved with fertility-planning success for Protestants are: 1, wife's employment duration (essentially a time factor); 4, a factor weakly defined as a family adjustment factor; 7, the factor containing most of the common variance of age and age at marriage; 8, a weakly defined "number of siblings" factor containing that part of the variance of siblings unconnected with the socio-economic status variables; and, 10, what appears to be a social mobility factor.

With Catholics, the picture is slightly less complex. The same two factors (8 and 9) that figure so heavily in the determination of

---

[10] Our attention was directed to this by Frank Lorimer. Unfortunately, the stability of other factors with less obvious problems cannot be ascertained.

family-size preferences are also involved with fertility-planning success. Together they account for one third of the explained variation. The remaining two thirds, however, is distributed among three additional factors: 2, a factor defined mainly by age and age at marriage; 3, a weakly defined factor containing the common variance of low anxiety and successful adjustment to the mother role, and, 11, what may be an occupational achievement factor although its structure is poorly defined.

And, finally, among Jews significant portions of the explained variance of fertility-planning success are distributed among four factors. One factor (3) is defined mainly by the length of time that the wife worked since her marriage, variance held in common with length of birth intervals and income change. Another factor (7) would appear to be a variation on the theme of rationality, reflecting the variance held in common by successful fertility planning, a habit of not making purchases on credit, and the perception of finances as relevant to fertility decisions. A small portion of the variance of long birth intervals also appears in this "cautious planning" factor. The third factor relevant to fertility-planning success among Jews is defined by adjustment to the mother role, Factor 6, a factor not dissimilar to the so-called family-adjustment factor (4) among Protestants. Undoubtedly, there is a selective feature operating in this association. Women who have unplanned pregnancies are not likely to make as easy an adjustment to the demands of motherhood as those who deliberately planned their children. The last factor of relevance to fertility-planning success is religiousness, which among Jews also contains a significant loading on liking for children. The positive association between religiousness and fertility-planning success cannot be explained away by a joint connection with education. One possible explanation, though no direct evidence of this is contained in our data, is that both Judaism and Protestantism stress the social responsibilities of parenthood, one component of which is optimal spacing of births.

Why should the factors affecting fertility-planning success be so diffuse and account for such a comparatively small amount of the total variance? The reasons are not clear, but may include the nature of measurement of the variable, that is, assigning the second pregnancy more weight than the first on the planning success scale. It may, however, be due more to the nature of the variable. Perhaps there is a large random component involved in whether a couple is classified at one or the other end of this scale on the basis of only two experiences. If this speculation is true, one would expect an increase in statistical association with additional experience.

329

BIRTH INTERVALS

The total interval between marriage and birth of the second child reflects the net influence of family-size desires, spacing preferences, fertility-planning success, and ease of conception. Most of the variance of birth intervals is accounted for in the factor matrices: 80 per cent for Protestants, 86 per cent for Catholics, and 89 per cent for Jews. An important reason for the apparent greater success in "predicting" birth intervals than either family-size preferences or fertility-planning success is due to its communality with other variables based on time, such as age, age at marriage, changes in income since marriage, and so forth. The most important single factor for all three populations is one affected precisely by such a problem—the length of time the wife worked since her marriage. Time is the common factor. Among Protestants, three quarters of the explained variance of total interval is located in such a factor (1). Virtually an identical factor is observed for the Jews (3), although smaller portions of the variance of birth intervals are also included in other factors as well (1 and 2). Among Catholics, the factor of wife's employment duration accounts for proportionately less (44 per cent) of the explained variance of birth intervals than it does for non-Catholics. As for Jews, the secondary factor of importance (2) is defined for Catholics by age and age at marriage.

THE FERTILITY FACTORS

The preceding analysis is based on rotations of all 11 orthogonal factors to simple structure excluding the fertility variables. Such a solution is appropriate to the objective of isolating and identifying the underlying structure of the correlates of fertility. Rotation to simple structure facilitates the separation and identification of relatively pure components of the factors and the loadings of the fertility variables in these factors permits assessing their relative weights in the association with fertility.

These rotations resulted in the isolation of only two main factors underlying family-size preferences, but in the case of fertility-planning status much greater structural complexity was evident. There is some overlapping involved, with the same factors in some instances being involved with both fertility variables.

Three further questions are now of interest:

1. To what extent are these fertility variables reflecting a common fertility factor underlying both number of children desired and

fertility-planning success as well as length of birth intervals? This question is of critical importance in assessing the amount of redundancy in statistical associations observed between an independent variable and the different fertility variables. In other words, how "different" are the fertility indices?

2. What would the social-psychological structure underlying such a fertility factor look like?[11] How complex would it be? What weights (factor loadings) would the different independent variables have?

3. How similar is the structure of this factor for each religious group?

Translating these general questions into specific operations involves some compromises. The criterion for rotation is limited to the two variables of number of children desired and fertility-planning success. By eliminating birth intervals from the solution we avoid the complexity of a third dimension, but more importantly we eliminate the substantive problem of the automatic time bias built into the correlations between marriage duration and other variables in the matrix. As the results indicate, however, a substantial portion of the variance of birth intervals is involved in the common fertility factor. This covariance, however, is a genuine component of the fertility factor and not simply an artifact of the study design.[12]

The objective of the analysis is to maximize the loadings of number of children desired and fertility-planning success in a single factor. Since only two variables are involved in this solution, two orthogonal factors were extracted and rotated once, with the first factor representing the common fertility factor in which we are most interested.[13] The results of this rotation are presented in Table 111 for each religious grouping. The communalities (h^2) for the two dependent variables of interest are those derived from Tables 108–110.

[11] It is the answer to this question that necessitates factor analysis. If the first question were the only one, the conventional techniques of partial and multiple correlation would be sufficient.

[12] We wish to avoid capitalizing on the built-in associations between birth intervals and such variables as wife's employment duration, income change, age, and so forth. This does not mean, however, that the variable of time itself is regarded as artificial and hence to be eliminated. The rotations that are presented in this section include that part of the variance of birth intervals which does involve time in a very definite sense.

[13] This was accomplished by the diagonal method of factoring the original correlation matrices, relying on the communalities computed iteratively in the preceding factor analyses. The rotation actually amounts to the same criterion used in the complete centroid method of factoring developed by Thurstone. Although the loadings of fertility-planning success in Table 111 have been reflected in sign (so that a + value indicates high rather than low success), before reflection the absolute sum of the two loadings in the first factor is a maximum (which would be the "general" factor in the centroid method) and their algebraic sum in the second factor is zero.

TABLE 111

Two Factors Including All Common-Factor Variance of Number of Children Desired and Fertility-Planning Success

Variable	Protestants			Catholics			Jews		
	I	II	h²	I	II	h²	I	II	h²
Number of children desired	.60	−.35	.48	.73	−.32	.64	.49	−.56	.55
Fertility-planning success	−.42	−.35	.30	−.50	−.31	.35	−.44	−.56	.51
Number of months from marriage to second birth	−.57	−.21	.37	−.62	−.03	.39	−.55	−.18	.33
Husband's annual earnings	−.36	−.20	.17	.02	−.05	.00	.00	−.12	.01
Income change since marriage	−.32	−.13	.12	−.14	.11	.03	−.20	−.13	.06
Economic security	−.26	−.21	.11	.09	−.13	.02	.09	−.05	.01
Perception of opportunities	.08	−.28	.08	.20	−.05	.04	.10	−.09	.02
Relevance of finances	.22	.42	.22	−.48	.15	.25	−.05	.13	.02
Credit buying	.09	.09	.02	.00	.12	.01	.22	.28	.13
Aspirations for children's education	−.02	−.10	.01	.11	−.12	.03	−.16	.22	.07
Education	−.13	−.22	.07	.30	−.16	.12	.21	−.42	.22
Occupational prestige	−.07	−.27	.08	.17	−.01	.03	.25	−.33	.17
Wife's employment duration	−.40	−.19	.20	−.30	.09	.10	−.43	−.14	.20
Age	−.62	−.17	.41	−.45	−.04	.20	−.48	.10	.24
Age at marriage	−.31	−.04	.10	−.10	−.11	.02	−.19	.16	.06
Number of siblings	.22	.10	.06	.00	−.01	.00	.01	.02	.00
Happiness of childhood	−.05	−.27	.07	.15	−.14	.04	.09	−.17	.04
Marital adjustment	−.11	−.34	.13	.02	−.26	.07	.24	−.07	.06
Adjustment to mother role	−.04	−.35	.12	.09	−.35	.13	−.09	−.06	.01
Manifest anxiety	.05	.22	.05	−.11	.14	.03	−.10	.14	.03
Liking for children	.14	−.11	.03	.12	−.21	.06	.12	−.10	.02
Preference for babies	−.08	−.04	.01	−.07	.08	.01	.05	.12	.02
Sex identity of children	.40	−.18	.19	.12	−.20	.05	.06	.01	.00
Church attendance	−.10	−.32	.11	.31	−.22	.14	−.38	−.11	.16
Informal religious orientation	−.08	−.23	.06	.27	−.07	.08	−.22	−.45	.25
Catholic school education	*	*	*	.37	−.08	.14	*	*	*

NOTE: Asterisk denotes variable not included in the factor analysis.

CONTENT OF THE TWO FERTILITY FACTORS

The loadings of number of children desired and fertility-planning success on the two factors present two patterns of covariation with other variables to be explained. In Factor I, the combination is preference for larger families and a record of less successful planning of the first two births (or vice versa, that is, smaller families desired and a successful fertility-planning record). This first factor accounts for the major portion of the variance of the two fertility variables except among Jews. In the case of Jews, because of an initial *positive* correlation between number of children desired and fertility-planning success, Factor II contains the greater part of the fertility variance (although both factors contain nearly equal amounts).

Focusing our attention first on the content of Factor I, we see a certain pattern of similarity across religions. Preferences for larger families and less successful fertility planning in the past is part of a common factor which includes appreciable loadings for all three groups on: (shorter) birth intervals; (shorter) duration of wife's employment since marriage; and (younger) age. These are the only variables with high loadings appearing in Factor I for each religious grouping. There are, however, significant loadings appearing for only one or two religious groupings. Among Protestants, a "rate of family growth" identification of Factor I is further supported by loadings on income and income change and age at marriage consistent with what might be expected of a family at different stages in its development. In addition, whether or not the first two children are of the same sex is involved in this factor.

For Catholics, the secondary loadings on Factor I tend to cluster about religiousness. There are positive loadings on church attendance, informal religious orientation, and Catholic school education as well as amount of education in general. The extent to which finances are perceived relevant to decisions about additional children is also represented in this factor common to the religiousness and rate of family growth components.

The pattern of secondary loadings on Factor I for Jews is similar to that of Catholics except that higher education is coupled with low rather than high religiousness and the relevance of finances is not involved.

Factor II, combining preferences for smaller families with unsuccessful planning (or vice versa), is the more important factor for Jews in that it contains more of the common-factor variance of the fertility variables than does Factor I. In this factor the educational and occupational prestige variables are more clearly represented.

333

The pattern, although only weakly manifested, reveals low fertility desires coupled with unsuccessful planning in common with lower education, lower occupational prestige, and less religiousness. In reverse, the picture is one of larger family preferences and successful planning combined with higher educational and occupational accomplishment and informal religiousness. (Factor II is, of course, orthogonal to the rate of family development inferred in Factor I.)

Factor II among Catholics and Protestants is not well-defined. Among Catholics, the only loadings worth mentioning seem to suggest a family adjustment factor in which low fertility desires and unsuccessful planning connect with poor adjustment both to the role of mother and marriage.

The difficulty in developing a theory of the structure underlying Factor II among Protestants is that too many variables play a part. In rather loose general terms, the pattern suggests an interrelationship of financial considerations and family adjustment. The common factor has the following characteristics: finances considered relevant to fertility, poor opportunities perceived for the husband in his job, lower income, feelings of economic insecurity, anxiety feelings, lower education and occupational prestige, poor adjustment to motherhood and marriage, unhappy childhood, and, finally, low religiousness. This factor is very weakly defined and there is little justification in speculating further about its meaning.

COMPARISON OF RELIGIOUS GROUPS

The third question posed in this section relates to the similarity of the structures of the fertility factors across religious groups. We have seen that there are some outstanding differences, particularly in that one cluster of variables seems to operate for one group but not another. On the other hand, we have observed striking similarities such as in the case of those variables dominating Factor I.

The similarity of these factors across religious groups can be gauged by correlating the observed values of the factor loadings.[14] Since the same variables were included in each religious group,[15] the correlation can be assessed with the factor loadings serving as paired observations for each variable. Computing three correlations for each

[14] A number of individuals have been concerned with different aspects of the problem of comparing factor structures. See, for example, Ledyard R. Tucker, "A Method for Synthesis of Factor Analysis Studies," *P.R.S. Report No. 984*, Educational Testing Service, March 31, 1951; Raymond B. Cattell, "r_p and Other Coefficients of Pattern Similarity," *Psychometrika*, 14 (1949), pp. 279–298.

[15] The one exception—extent of Catholic school education—is eliminated for these comparisons.

combination of two religious groups permits an assessment of whether the factor structure underlying fertility for Protestants, for example, is more closely similar to that for Catholics or Jews.

The six correlation coefficients (three for each factor) are presented in Table 112. Approximately 50 per cent of the variation in factor

TABLE 112

Correlations between Factor Loadings[a] within Three Religious Groups

Combination	Factor I	Factor II
Protestant and Catholic	.75	.72
Protestant and Jewish	.73	.64
Catholic and Jewish	.70	.48

[a] The number of common variables in the matrix is twenty-five.

loadings is common across religions, which of course means that half of the variability in the patterns is not common. There tends to be greater similarity between Protestants and Catholics and least correspondence between Catholics and Jews in both fertility factors. However, it should be emphasized that no basis exists for evaluating the significance of differences in these values.

SUMMARY AND CONCLUSIONS

This chapter presents a series of multivariate analyses of factors affecting number of children desired, fertility-planning success, and length of interval between marriage and second birth. To summarize these series which are themselves highly condensed summaries would indeed be presumptuous. Only a few of the highlights will be reviewed.

Following the elimination of variables either redundant or un-related to fertility, factor analyses of a large remaining group of variables (25 for Protestants and Jews and 26 for Catholics) were undertaken separately for each sample of couples in order to isolate the underlying factors relevant to the fertility variables and to assess the extent to which the same factors are involved for all three religious categories. The independent variables are mostly of a socio-economic and attitudinal type.

A total of 11 orthogonal factors was found to account for the common variance in each of the three correlation matrices. Each set of factors was rotated to simple structure. The fertility variables were excluded from the mathematical solution, however, and were distributed according to their loadings on the rotated factors.

The fertility variables are least predictable for Protestants from this group of independent variables. For Catholics, the particular factor of religiousness is operative. For Jews, the main factors relate to education and other components of rational behavior. Some sociological speculations for these differences in the predictability of fertility are offered. In general, the factors affecting fertility are only partly the same in the three religious groups.

The structure of factors[16] affecting the number of children desired is comparatively simple, consisting of two factors in each religious category. One of these factors—the perceived relevance of finances in decisions about future fertility—is common to all three religious groups. The variance of interval between marriage and the second birth is also concentrated in a few factors, but interpretation is complicated by the study design which results in a time dimension common to some independent variables as well. The analysis of factors affecting fertility-planning control is the least successful, both in terms of the total variance accounted for as well as the structural complexity of relevant factors. No single factor in fertility-planning success is common to all three groups, although a few seem common to two religious categories.

The summary multivariate analysis was concluded with another set of rotations designed to maximize the loadings of number of children desired and fertility-planning success in a single factor. The structure of this general fertility factor containing high loadings on age, wife's employment duration, and length of birth intervals prompted an identification of a "rate of family growth" dimension. This core is similar for Protestants, Catholics, and Jews, but other variables play a role as well.

[16] The factor structures compared are functions of the initial correlations computed within each of the three religious groupings. If characteristics other than religion had been used to subdivide the sample, the correlations and derived factors might have resulted in different structures. The nature of these differences would depend on the extent to which another control variable would produce heterogeneity of correlations different from religion.

PART IV

RESURVEY

Chapter XX. The Next Phase of the Study

The longitudinal design of this study not only facilitates the determination of the course of fertility but also permits introducing measurements of new variables. This concluding chapter describes the connections between the first and second phases of the study, with particular attention devoted to the implications of the findings described in this report for the content of the second round of interviews.

The second phase of the study concentrates on the correlates of both the occurrence and timing of the third child. The record of fertility planning during the interval[1] provides another observation for the couple's total planning history. The number of children desired or expected at this time will probably more closely approximate ultimate completed fertility and will continue to be of interest as a dependent variable. Furthermore, the fertility experience during the intervening three years provides some basis for estimating the validity of interview data on family-size preferences. And finally, the longitudinal design permits analysis of the impact on fertility and family-size preferences of changes in the couple's circumstances during the intervening years.

Many of the hypotheses formulated in the first phase of the study will be reexamined in the light of the new fertility data. One model of analysis will be to study the extent to which the factors affecting the events and timing of a third pregnancy tend to be unique for that pregnancy or simple extensions of general factors related to preceding stages of the fertility process. In fact, this expectation that correlates would differ with parity was one of the original assumptions underlying the design of this study.

The type of data collected in the second round of interviews was determined both by the basic design of the study and questions stimulated by the analyses of the first interviews reported in the preceding chapters. As suggested above, the primary focus of the second interview is to determine the pregnancy histories during the three and one-half year interval elapsing since the birth of the second child. Data exactly comparable to those for first and second pregnancies have been collected for subsequent pregnancies. The other routine information collected relates to changes in the status of the couple involving dimensions such as income, occupation, employment, and residence. The rest of the interview has been directed

---

[1] The interviewing was scheduled for three years after the first interview (three and one-half years after the birth of the second child) in order to obtain a high proportion who have become pregnant again and to minimize both the average time lag from the event and the number of fourth pregnancies.

toward subjects stimulated by the preceding analyses and the remainder of this chapter will describe these new avenues of interest.

THE FERTILITY VARIABLES

Considerable emphasis was placed on fertility-planning success in the analyses just concluded. In Chapters X through XIX, for example, this variable together with number of children desired and length of birth intervals was included in almost all of the correlational analyses. The measurement of fertility-planning status, however, involves important questions of reliability.[2] As noted in the last chapter, one reason why so little of the variance of fertility-planning status is accounted for by the social-psychological variables in comparison to the other dependent variables is that the respondent's report of the circumstances under which each pregnancy occurred may contain various kinds of error. One partial test of this proposition is possible by repeating a few of the basic questions three years later. This affords some opportunity to test the reliability of an important classification used in other studies as well as this one.

A novel type of information—on knowledge of the ovulatory cycle—was also sought for reasons provoked by this as well as other research. In the present sample, even in the interval between marriage and the first birth, pregnancy delays before first use of contraception are nearly twice as long as those following deliberate interruption of contraception for the express purpose of becoming pregnant. One important reason may be that successful contraceptors tend to know more about the location of the brief fertile period within the menstrual cycle and to be more inclined to use such knowledge to hasten conception. Since we plan to question mothers regarding their knowledge of the fertile period and their use of this knowledge, we will be able to test this hypothesis.

Another reason for interest in this subject is that half of the variation in birth interval is attributable to variation in conception delay. As yet there has been very little investigation of the extent to which these delays are subject to influence by social factors, such as knowledge of the fertile period and deliberate timing of intercourse corresponding to this knowledge.

Beliefs concerning fecundity during the period immediately preceding menopause have also been determined. Whether women

---

[2] The other two primary dependent variables also present problems such as the validity of number of children desired for predicting subsequent fertility performance (which can be partly checked now). Even the measurement of time intervals between births undoubtedly involves some reporting error.

believe this period is especially fertile or sterile may have implications for the practice of contraception by women in their late thirties.

Another addition to the fertility section is an attempt (with only limited confidence in the reliability) to secure some indication of coital frequency. Variations in frequency may be relevant to length of time required to conceive as well as the effectiveness of contraceptive practice.

The final innovation attempts to determine the extent to which sexual behavior is routinized. If it is true that intercourse becomes more regularized the longer the couple has been married, it would be relevant for the prediction of fertility-planning success. The assumption is that routinization reduces chance-taking and the possible consequences of impulsive behavior.

FAMILY COMPOSITION

One approach to the subject of family composition concerns the mother's reactions to the experience of her first two children. One of the rationales for restricting the sample initially to couples with the same number of children is to determine the extent to which family-size plans are affected by the very experience of having children. In a manner of speaking, the hypothesis is that fertility affects fertility. Questions about the mother's perceptions of various problems connected with raising her first two children were included. They cover such topics as health, discipline, sibling relationships, eating and sleeping habits, and other subjects.

Although neither adjustment to the role of mother nor to marriage was highly correlated with the fertility variables measured in the first phase of the study, the two variables have been included again in the second phase. One of the speculations advanced in Chapter XVII, Social Relations within the Family, was that these role adjustments are themselves affected by success in family planning as well as having some bearing on the course of fertility. Measuring the same adjustment variables at two points in time will facilitate disentangling the causal nexus.

One theoretical interest in the study of fertility has focused on communication between husband and wife both in general as well as in the specifics of family planning.[3] The interview schedule designed for the second phase incorporates this focus of interest, but translates it into terms of satisfaction with the way the couple has handled a variety of potential problem areas in their marriage. The underlying

[3] Reuben Hill, J. Mayone Stycos, and Kurt W. Back, *The Family and Population Control,* University of North Carolina Press, Chapel Hill, 1959.

assumption here is that communication *per se* is less relevant than consensus regardless of the extent to which it has been articulated.

The family composition of both the wife and husband has also been explored further by collecting information on their position in the birth and sex order in their parental family. On the assumption that birth order and sex affect opportunities, responsibilities, and affective ties, a number of hypotheses connecting the couple's family positions with present fertility orientations were formulated. Various combinations of position in the sibling and sex order have been hypothesized to associate with attitudes toward ambitions and family responsibilities, reflected both in fertility and age at marriage.

Interest in the activities of the wife has been expanded beyond the record of her work experience to include her participation in organized social activities. The rationale is that extrafamilial activities are associated with effective fertility planning and smaller family preferences.

Visiting is another type of social activity which extends the individual's world, but in contrast to the wife's participation in organized activities is more likely to be familial. The influence of family and kinship ties on fertility is presumably maintained in part by visiting patterns among relatives. The ratio of visiting friends compared to relatives (allowing for migration) gives some indication of reference groups possibly having some bearing on fertility.

Socio-Economic Status

During 1957–1958 the country experienced an economic recession which was felt especially in cities with heavy industry such as Detroit and Pittsburgh. It did not commence, however, until well after our first interviews had been completed (in early 1957). As a result, we fortuitously have something of a "built-in" experiment and with special tabulations will be able to make some analysis of the effects on fertility.[4] In addition to employment and income data, a direct question on how the couple was affected by the recession was included.

Aside from conventional data on income change and occupational mobility, and repeated measures of economic security and perceptions of opportunity, no additions have been made in the socioeconomic domain.

---

[4] At the time of this writing (November 1959) the steel strike poses implications for a second-order economic effect in addition to the recession.

RESIDENCE

Recent research by Goldberg[5] has reemphasized the rural-urban dimension that had given some evidence of being diminished in importance in fertility studies. He has effectively demonstrated that it takes more than one generation of urban living to erase the fertility effects of rural culture. In our first interview we obtained information sufficient only to classify the previous generation.[6] In order to extend the analyses to an earlier generation, we have included appropriate questions in the second interview.

The remaining changes in the measurement of residence have taken the direction of securing more detail on residential history, including the respondents' classification of the urban-suburban-rural character of each place the couple has lived since their marriage.

RELIGIOUS BEHAVIOR

In view of the apparent importance of religion and religiousness for fertility, we have expanded this section of the interview appreciably. First of all, a question on whether the marriage was performed by a minister, priest, rabbi, or other official was included to permit extending our classification of mixed marriages beyond that possible from the data collected originally. In the first phase, a question of whether the marriage was performed by a Catholic priest was asked only if prior questioning had revealed a mixed marriage involving a Catholic. With the new data, it will be possible to classify all marriages by the type of ceremony.

Two other orientations are reflected in the remaining questions in this area. One of the main results of our study thus far has been to uncover a strong relationship among Catholics between extent of education in schools and colleges affiliated with the church and the various measures of fertility. The obvious question left hanging is whether the formal educational system exerts this influence or whether individuals from highly religious home environments are simply selected into the system. In other words, does the formal educational system have an effect on fertility over and above that which would result from parental and home influences? Although this question can be posed clearly, securing the appropriate data is much

[5] David Goldberg, "Another Look at the Indianapolis Fertility Data," Milbank Memorial Fund *Quarterly*, 38 (1960), pp. 23–36; and "Fertility of Two-Generation *Population Studies*, XII (1959), pp. 217–222.

[6] Detroit and Indianapolis residents studied by Goldberg afforded much higher proportions of one-generation urbanites than do the couples in our sample who live in the largest metropolitan areas of the nation.

more difficult and arriving at any conclusive answers in the present study is probably impossible. Nevertheless, some questions have been included that ask the respondent to recall the religiousness of her home life as a child. This will at least facilitate some limited approach to the problem.

The remaining innovation in this section reflects our interest in trying to understand the basis of Catholics' attitudes toward larger families. One hypothesis is that many Catholic women may interpret the position of their church as that of directly favoring fertility and not that of only discouraging the use of family limitation techniques. In the hope of securing some estimate of the extent of such an interpretation as well as perhaps providing a basis for understanding why the more religious Protestants and Jews tend to be successful fertility planners, we have included a question on the wife's interpretation of her religion's position, if any, on the subject of family size.

Whether these innovations will prove fruitful remains to be seen. The second phase of this study provides a testing ground to determine not only the success of such innovations but perhaps more importantly whether many of the relationships described in this volume have been translated into behavior.

344

APPENDICES

Appendix A. Supplement to Chapter IV

Much of the technical detail of Chapter IV has been reserved for summary treatment in this appendix, which is organized into the following divisions:

1. Significance tests
2. Supplementary analyses
   a. douching for cleanliness only
   b. separations
   c. conception waits prior to second and third pregnancies
   d. relative fecundity of couples suspected of premarital conception
3. Classification of noncontraceptor conception waits

SIGNIFICANCE TESTS

When one wishes to test whether two independent samples of conception waits are drawn from the same universe (or from populations with the same distribution), one may use chi-square. An alternative test is the Kolmogorov-Smirnov two-sample test, applicable when both sample sizes are equal or, when sample sizes are unequal, both are 40 or more. This test assumes continuously distributed variables, a fairly realistic assumption for conception waits whose lengths are discontinuous only because of measurement crudities. The Kolmogorov-Smirnov test has two advantages over the chi-square test. First, it is generally regarded as a more powerful goodness-of-fit test than chi-square, though its power tends to decrease as the intervals into which the sample distributions are divided are made broader. Secondly, it is usually easier to compute, since it requires merely constructing a cumulative percentage distribution for each sample (taking care to use the same set of intervals in both samples), observing the maximum difference D between any pair of corresponding percentages, and then determining whether this value of D (multiplied by a coefficient involving the sample sizes) exceeds certain critical values.

However, when analyzing conception waits, one often wants to test a more specific hypothesis, namely, that one sample is drawn from a population representing greater ease of conception than the population from which the other sample is drawn. In statistical parlance, one wishes to test whether the conception waits of one population are stochastically greater than those of the second population. For this purpose L. Goodman has suggested the statistic

$4D^2\, N_1 N_2/(N_1 + N_2)$ where N_1 and N_2 are the two sample sizes and D is the largest difference between cumulative percentages in the predicted direction. This statistic is approximately distributed as chi-square with 2 degrees of freedom. Theoretically, there is no restriction on sample size, but the power of the test weakens as samples become small. Unless sample sizes are very large, the test tends to be conservative. That is, the risk of rejecting the null hypothesis of no differences when the null hypothesis is true is less than calculated, but with a corresponding increase in the opposite risk of not detecting a difference when it actually exists. Hence, in most analyses of this appendix, or Chapter IV, when use of this test does not lead to a rejection of the null hypothesis, it is supplemented with the two-tailed version of the Kolmogorov-Smirnov test, even though the latter is testing a broader hypothesis than ideally desired, and even though the use of two tests means slightly increased chances of a Type I error.

SUPPLEMENTARY ANALYSES

Douching for cleanliness only

Even when used solely for hygienic purposes, douching may exercise a contraceptive effect, and thereby prolong conception waits. If the effect is large, it becomes desirable to exclude those who douche for cleanliness only from analyses of conception waits.

In the present study, only those respondents who report conception delays longer than one year are asked about douching for cleanliness only. Hence the appropriate comparison is between douchers and nondouchers among those reporting conception waits of at least 13 months. If douching used for hygienic purposes prolongs conception waits, then the waits of douchers should be stochastically larger than those of nondouchers, and this fact should emerge, given sufficient sample sizes, even if the two distributions are truncated at 12 months. The comparisons are given in Table A–1, separately for waits before and after first pregnancy, with planned and nonplanned pregnancies distinguished. Two out of three differences are in the predicted direction, though with such small n's statistical significance cannot be expected. When all intervals are combined, douchers and nondouchers average waits of 31 and 27 months respectively after interrupting contraception and 42 and 39 months when not practicing contraception at all. These differences are not great, and this fact, coupled with the small number of identifiable douchers, is regarded as justification for ignoring the distinction in subsequent analyses.

TABLE A–1

Conception Waits for Douchers and Nondouchers in the Absence of Contraception,
by Pregnancy Interval and Circumstance of Pregnancy[a]

Douching Status and Circumstance of Pregnancy	Mean Number of Months from Marriage to First Pregnancy		Mean Number of Months between First and Second Pregnancy and between Second and Third Pregnancy		All Pregnancy Intervals Combined	
	Number	Average Wait	Number	Average Wait	Number	Average Wait (mean number of months)
Contraception interrupted						
Doucher	6	–[b]	12	32.8	18	31.3
Nondoucher	28	24.0	49	28.4	77	26.8
Contraception not used						
Doucher	15	26.1	10	66.3	25	42.2
Nondoucher	71	35.2	90	42.7	161	39.4

[a] Restricted to couples having conception waits of 13 months or longer and reporting no separations.

[b] Average conception wait not computed because of insufficient cases.

Separations

The respondents were asked to report any separations three months or longer and to give the dates when these separations began and ended. Those portions of reported separations not coinciding with pregnancy time or with the one-month allowance for postpartum amenorrhea are coded as separation time (as distinct from contraception or conception wait time). More than 80 first pregnancy intervals contain separation time and approximately 50 of the subsequent pregnancy intervals. Most separations, incidentally, are connected with military service.

A separation may not be total throughout its reported length. An example is the soldier husband who is not seen by his wife when overseas, but is seen occasionally while stationed in the States. Depending whether respondents tend to include or exclude periods of partial separation from their reports of separation, one may expect negative or positive associations between separation time and rates of contraceptive failure or time waited for conception.

Some of the pertinent data are summarized in Table A–2. Wives reporting separations average longer waits for first pregnancy both in the absence of, and after interrupting, contraception. The same is

TABLE A–2

Conception Waits for Separated and Unseparated Couples in the Absence of
Contraception, by Pregnancy Interval and Circumstance of Pregnancy

Separation Status and Circumstance of Pregnancy	Mean Number of Months from Marriage to First Pregnancy[a]		Mean Number of Months between First and Second Pregnancy and between Second and Third Pregnancy	
	Number	Average Wait	Number	Average Wait
Contraception interrupted				
Separation	34	5.97	33	12.94
No separation	316	5.28	618	5.58
Contraception not used				
Separation	41	13.56	9	—[b]
No separation	415	9.37	287	20.4

[a] Excluding cases of suspected premarital conceptions and first pregnancies terminating in miscarriages.
[b] Average conception wait not computed because of so few cases.

true for conception waits following interruption of contraception in subsequent pregnancy intervals. (Insufficient cases precludes a comparison involving noncontraceptors in these later intervals.) None of the three differences is highly significant statistically, although according to the one-tailed Kolmogorov-Smirnov test, one difference associates with a probability between .10 and .20 and another with a probability between .02 and .05. But all three differences are in the same direction. Furthermore, they are consistent with the differences observed in relation to contraceptive failure. In the period before first pregnancy, those separated average 24 failures per 100 years of contraceptive exposure, as compared to 27 failures for those not separated (based on 699 and 6,379 months of exposure). In subsequent pregnancy intervals, those separated average 16 failures per 100 years of exposure, in contrast to 20 failures (based on 917 and 8,206 months of exposure). Accordingly, it seems likely that respondents tend to exclude periods of partial separation from their reported separations, and these periods of partial separation then attenuate the risk of pregnancy during either coded contraception or conception wait time. On this premise, intervals involving separation time are excluded from subsequent analyses.

Conception waits prior to second and third pregnancies

To supplement the analyses of Chapter IV, which treat only conception waits prior to first pregnancy, some results pertaining to conception waits prior to second and third pregnancies are now reviewed.

Table A–3 provides the main comparisons between conception

TABLE A–3

Conception Waits by Pregnancy Interval and Circumstance of Pregnancy[a]

PREGNANCY INTERVAL AND TERMINATION OF PRECEDING PREGNANCY (IF ANY)	CIRCUMSTANCE OF PREGNANCY			
	Contraception Interrupted		Contraception Not Used	
	Number of Wives	Mean Wait (months)	Number of Wives	Mean Wait (months)
First pregnancy interval	340	5.2	458	10.0
Second and third pregnancy intervals	618	5.6	282	20.4
Following miscarriage	60	2.6	28	15.6[b]
Following live birth	558	5.9	254	20.9[c]

[a] All intervals containing separation time are excluded.
[b] One month allowance for postpartum amenorrhea.
[c] Three month allowance for postpartum amenorrhea.

waits before and after first pregnancy. Looking first at the conception delays following interruption of contraception (second column of Table A–3), one observes little contrast between the two periods, the average conception waits being 5.2 months before first pregnancy and 5.6 months after. Nor do the Kolmogorov-Smirnov (one-tailed or two-tailed) or chi-square tests indicate significant differences. Puzzlingly enough, in the later period, conception delays appear shorter when following a miscarriage than when they follow a live birth. Both chi-square and Kolmogorov-Smirnov tests indicate that a difference so extreme has a probability less than .025 under the null hypothesis. No explanation has been found for this unexpected contrast.

As expected, the difference in average conception delay between noncontraceptors and successful contraceptors becomes larger after the first pregnancy, because of the tendency for subfecund couples to feel no need for precautionary measures while nearly all fecund couples do. This difference between reported and inferred conception waits increases from 5.2 versus 10.0 months before first pregnancy, to 5.6 versus 20.4 months after first pregnancy. One also expects the association between nonuse of contraception and subfecundity to be stronger following a live birth than following a miscarriage, because in the latter instance many couples hesitate to resume contraception lest they extend a birth interval already prolonged by

351

pregnancy wastage. Consistent with this expectation, the average conception delay is shorter among noncontraceptors after a miscarriage than after a live birth. The difference, 15.6 months to 20.9, is not statistically significant because only 28 waits follow miscarriage. Unequal periods of temporary sterility may contribute to the difference, though to minimize this factor, 3 months have been allowed for postpartum amenorrhea but only one month for postabortum amenorrhea.

For the sake of completeness, the reported waits of successful contraceptors before second and third pregnancies are tabulated in detail (Table A–4). Waits affected by separation are excluded.

TABLE A–4

Conception Waits prior to Second and Third Pregnancy

Length of Conception Wait (in months)	Percentages		
	Following Birth (n = 558)	Following Miscarriage (n = ⁀0)	Total (n = 618)
1	37.6	56.6	39.5
2	15.4	15.0	15.4
3	11.3	6.7	10.8
4	5.4	8.3	5.7
5 – 6	9.0	3.3	8.4
7 – 9	5.4	5.0	5.3
10 – 12	5.2	1.7	4.9
13 – 24	7.2	3.3	6.8
25 – 48	2.3		2.1
49 – 84	0.9		0.8
85 or more	0.4		0.3
Per cent total	100.1	99.9	100.0
Mean wait	5.9	2.6	5.6

Because of the anomalous contrast between them, waits preceded by miscarriage are distinguished from those preceded by live births.

Relative Fecundity of Couples Suspected of Premarital Conception

Whelpton and Kiser and Tietze have argued—see section on "suggested causes" in Chapter IV—that exclusion of couples suspected of premarital pregnancy gives an upward bias to the first pregnancy waits inferred for noncontraceptors. Critical to their explanation is the assumption that couples suspected of premarital pregnancy are more fecund than others. To test this premise, the conception waits after first pregnancy of couples suspected of premarital conceptions are compared with those of the remainder of the sample. It is, of course, crucial that reported conception waits be compared with reported waits, inferred waits with inferred waits. Doing this, one finds in the present sample that couples suspected of premarital pregnancy average shorter waits after interruption of contraception, 5.2 months as compared to 5.8 (based on N's of 38 and 520) and considerably shorter inferred waits, 11.3 to 25.3 months (based on N's of 24 and 253). According to the Kolmogorov-Smirnov one-tailed test, the probability of differences as large as these under the null hypothesis is between .10 and .20 for the first result, between .01 and .001 for the other. These are low probabilities given so few couples representing premarital conceptions.

CLASSIFICATION OF NONCONTRACEPTOR CONCEPTION WAITS

In Chapter IV, the first conception waits of noncontraceptors are classified into 28-day intervals, namely, . . ., $(-28, -1)$, $(1, 28)$, $(29, 56)$, . . . days, in order to estimate the number of pregnancies occurring during menstrual mid-periods . . ., -2, -1, 1, 2, . . . after marriage. Correctly centered, these intervals have an efficiency which depends on the dispersions of conception waits estimated for couples becoming pregnant during specified menstrual mid-periods. This scatter of estimated conception waits will be estimated in succession for couples conceiving the first menstrual mid-period after marriage, the second, and the jth mid-period after marriage, and finally for couples conceiving the last mid-period before marriage.

In general, the more complete the information collected about such things as length of gestation and time elapsing between marriage and next menstruation, the narrower will be the scatters of conception waits estimated for couples conceiving a particular menstrual mid-period. Only minimal information has been collected from the present noncontraceptors: namely, date of marriage, date first pregnancy terminated, and its outcome. Conception waits are estimated by differencing these two dates (in days) and subtracting 270 or 90 days from this difference, depending whether the first pregnancy ends in live birth or miscarriage. Waits known to be prolonged by separations are excluded.

In the analysis below it is assumed that all marriage and termination-of-pregnancy dates are accurate. Of course, it is realized that some of the dates are inaccurate and some of the errors produced are relatively large. But because there is no way of specifying the distribution of these errors, it is impossible to treat them numerically in the analysis. Accordingly, it seems better to omit consideration of these errors, thereby greatly simplifying notation and discussion, and to treat the results of analysis as giving an upper bound estimate of the efficiency attained by the recommended set of 28-day intervals.

Couples Conceiving the First Menstrual Mid-Period after Marriage

Consider couples conceiving the first menstrual mid-period after marriage with pregnancy leading to a live birth. For a particular couple, let i be the interval between marriage and first birth, this interval being the sum of two components: o, the period between marriage and first ovulation, and p, the pregnancy period lasting from first ovulation until the live birth. The conception wait estimated for the couple is defined by

$$w = i - 270 = o + p - 270.$$

Thus w varies as a function of the variables o and p.

The mean length of p, or $\bar{p}$, is usually put at 270 days.[1] Some idea of the dispersion of p around this mean is gained from a large series of pregnancy lengths collected by Gibson and McKeown.[2] According to these data, which represent 15,861 observations of the period between last menses and a live birth, p has an unimodal, essentially symmetric distribution with a standard deviation in the neighborhood of 15 days. The degree of skewness is small: β_1 is only .84. More than 75 per cent of the cases fall within one S.D. of the mean, which is a larger percentage than would be expected in a normal distribution. But the frequency of extreme deviations from the mean is also greater than would be expected in a normal distribution.

The behavior of o is much harder to specify, depending as it does upon the typical positioning of marriage within the "interovulatory period" between last ovulation before marriage and first ovulation after marriage. In cases where this interovulatory period is 28 days long, o may assume any value from 0 to 28. Now the simplest assumption is that time of marriage is random relative to the interovulatory period, so that the probability of marriage falling in any particular subinterval dx in a 28-day interovulatory span is uniformly $(1/28) \, dx$. This assumption of randomness of marriage date defines a rectangular density with $f(x)dx = (1/28)dx$ for $0 \leq x \leq 28$ and zero otherwise. Using the same assumption of randomness in the more general case of an interovulatory period j days long, we derive, by integration, a value of $j/2$ for $\bar{o}$, the mean of o, and a value of $j^2/12$ for $v(o)$, the

---

[1] See Paul Vincent's recent review of the literature, "Données biométriques sur la conception et la grossesse," *Population*, 11 (1956), pp. 77–81.

[2] Reported and discussed in *ibid.*, p. 81.

variance of o. For reasons discussed a little later, we may assume that interovulatory periods have the same distribution of lengths as do menstrual cycles. Gunn *et al* offer a distribution of menstrual lengths for "healthy" women aged 25–29.[3] Using these as weights for the two series of $\bar{o}$ and $v(o)$ values, one obtains a grand $\bar{o}$ of 14.4 and a grand $v(o)$ of 71.

However, the assumption that marriage dates are distributed randomly relative to the menstrual cycle is not wholly realistic. Undoubtedly, when weddings are being planned a short time in advance, many brides attempt to arrange their marriage dates so that they follow shortly after menstruation rather than immediately before or during menses. The effects of such efforts are to reduce o from 14 and $v(o)$ from 70. When planning is longer range, brides may be more inclined to play it safe by aiming for the middle of the menstrual cycle. To the extent these latter efforts are effective, marriage will shortly precede, coincide with, or shortly follow the middle of the cycle, and so keep o close to 14 days but increasing $v(o)$ above 70. Of course, some of these long-range planners, as they approach marriage and realize they have miscalculated, will change their marriage date to have it come briefly after menses. Quite likely, then, the larger percentage of successful manipulations of the wedding date are of this type which puts the wedding shortly after menstruation. But all these remarks are speculative since no data have been collected concerning either the frequency or the success of efforts to control the marriage date.

With regard to the covariation of p and o, there is little reason to suppose that gestation length and interval between marriage and first ovulation are significantly correlated.

On the basis of all these considerations, and ignoring sampling fluctuations, we estimate the mean of w as

$$\bar{w}=\bar{o}+\bar{p}-270$$
$$=14,$$

where we have substituted $\bar{p}=270$ and $\bar{o}=14$ days. The w-variance is estimated as

$$v(w)=v(o)+v(p)+C(o, p)$$
$$=70+225$$
$$=295,$$

if we ignore the covariance term $C(o, p)$, and substitute $v(o)=70$ and $v(p)=225$.

[3] *Ibid.*, especially p. 76.

However, more important for the purposes of Chapter IV than an estimate of $v(w)$ is an estimate of the percentage of w-values falling within the interval (1, 28) days. Clearly this percentage must be under 75 per cent because only 75 per cent of the p-values are observed in the large sample of Gibson and McKeown to fall within ±14 days of their mean and the dispersion of w-values is necessarily greater than that of the p's. However, $v(p)$ accounts for most of the value of $v(w)$, so that $s(w)$, the standard deviation of w, is not much larger than $s(p)$. Therefore, an assumption that only 50 per cent of w-values fall into (1, 28) appears quite conservative.

Next consider couples conceiving the first mid-period after marriage, but with pregnancy leading to miscarriage. This time w is defined by $o+p'-90$, where p' is the length of pregnancy preceding miscarriage. The behavior of o remains unchanged. The mean of p', or $\bar{p}'$, is not precisely known and may be somewhat under 90 days, introducing a bias, $b=90-\bar{p}'$. Furthermore, according to fragmentary evidence, $v(p')$ is roughly four times as large as $v(p)$.[4] Presumably $C(o, p)$ is negligible. These considerations, with sampling fluctuations again ignored, give

$$\bar{w}=\bar{o}+\bar{p}'-90$$
$$=14+b,$$

where $\bar{o}=14$ and b is an unknown constant not necessarily trivial; and

$$v(w)=v(o)+v(p')+C(o, p)$$
$$=70+4\ (225)$$
$$=970.$$

The relatively large value for $v(w)$ probably means that less than half of these estimated conception waits fall into the interval (1, 28) days.

Couples Conceiving the Second Menstrual Mid-Period after Marriage with Pregnancy Leading to a Live Birth

Here we define i, the interval between marriage and first birth, as $o+m+p-270$, where o and p take the same definitions as before, and m is the interovulatory period between first and second ovulation. In the estimates below, the mean and variance of m, an interovulatory period, are equated with the mean and variance of menstrual cycle length, for which estimates are available. This step seems justified, apart from necessity, because (1) menstrual records kept for one or two years fail to indicate that menstrual lengths are

---

[4] This evidence consists of four distributions published in *Foetal, Infant and Early Childhood Mortality*, United Nations, ST/SOA/Series A/13, New York, I, p. 16.

autocorrelated; and (2) no other mechanism is presently known that would produce a significant correlation between the postovulatory portion of one menstrual cycle and the preovulatory portion of the next.[5]

P. Vincent, using Vollman data, has shown that menstrual cycle length varies with age.[6] Using cycle lengths of women aged 25–29 as a basis of estimation, we obtain a $\bar{m}$ value of 28 days and a $s(m)$ value of 5. Presumably the covariance terms $C(o,m)$ and $C(m,p)$ are negligible. From these considerations we have for the large sample case,

$$\bar{w} = 14 + 28 = 42,$$

$$v(w) = 70 + 225 + 25 = 320.$$

Note that as compared with its value among couples conceiving the first menstrual mid-period after marriage with pregnancy ending in a live birth, $v(w)$ has increased slightly in value from 295 owing to the addition of $v(m)$, with a corresponding slight decrease from 50 per cent in the percentage of estimated conception waits falling into the interval (29, 56) days.

Couples Conceiving the jth Menstrual Mid-Period after Marriage with Pregnancy Leading to a Live Birth

In this more general case, we define i as $o + (m_1 + - - + m_{j-1}) + p$; where o and p are defined as before, and the m_i represent successive interovulatory periods. It seems justifiable to treat the $\bar{m}_i$ as equal to m and the $v(m_i)$ as equal to $v(m)$. There are $(j^2-j)/2$ distinct covariance terms, $C(m_i m_k)$, each appearing twice, and their sum is not negligible because women differ significantly with respect to menstrual cycle length. Thus, we have, as large sample estimates,

$$\bar{w} = 14 + (j-1)\ 28,$$

$$v(w) = v(o) + v(p) + (j-1)v(m) + \Sigma\ \Sigma c(m_i m_k).$$

Clearly as j increases, $v(w)$ increases, meaning that when j is large enough, only a small percentage of estimated conception waits corresponding to jth mid-period pregnancies fall into the interval $(1 + 28(j-1),\ 28j)$ days. However, virtually zero per cent fall into the interval (1, 28) days when $j \geq 4$, and very few when $j = 3$. Hence, the

[5] The first comprehensive review article was L. B. Arey, "The Degree of Normal Menstrual Irregularity," *American Journal of Obstetrics and Gynecology*, 37 (1939), 12–29. See also, D. L. Gunn, P. M. Jenkins, and A. L. Gunn, "Menstrual Periodicity; Statistical Observations on a Large Sample of Normal Cases," *Journal of Obstetrics and Gynecology of the British Empire*, 44 (1937), 839–879.

[6] Vincent, "Données biométriques sur la conception et la grossesse." p. 75.

increase in $v(w)$ with increasing j is not troublesome for purposes of estimating fecundability.

Premarital Conceptions Ending in Live Births

Consider now women conceiving the "last" mid-period before marriage (i.e., in the absence of pregnancy, the next mid-period would have followed marriage). Here estimated conception waits are defined as $i-270=p+o'-270$, where p is the same as before, and $-o'$ represents the period between last ovulation and marriage. Now if the marriage date is viewed as rectangularly distributed over the interovulatory period between last ovulation before marriage and pregnancy-averted first ovulation after marriage, then the behavior of $-o'$ may be equated to that of o. From this it follows, ignoring chance fluctuations, that

$$\bar{w}=\bar{o}'+\bar{p}-270$$
$$=-14 \text{ days, and}$$
$$v(w)=v(o')+v(p)$$
$$=70+225$$
$$=295.$$

Note that the estimated w-variance has the same value as that estimated for couples conceiving the first mid-period after marriage.

Finally, for couples conceiving the jth mid-period before marriage, when $j\geq2$, an obvious extension of the argument above leads to estimates for $\bar{w}$ of $-14-(j-1)28$ days, and for $v(w)$ the same values as estimated for couples conceiving the jth mid-period after marriage.

Appendix B. Supplement to Chapter V

The analyses of Chapter V focused on the contraceptive behavior of the total sample of 1,165 couples, while giving some attention to contrasts among class-religious groups. This appendix is primarily concerned with comparing methods of contraception. The following sequence of topics is considered:

Classifying contraceptive methods
The attraction of multiple methods for accident-prone couples
Reasons for preferring current method
Method loyalty
Method acceptability
Index of fertility-planning success.

A CLASSIFICATION OF METHODS

Sample wives were asked to identify the methods they used before each pregnancy as well as the method or methods they are presently using. Doubtless they did not report all the methods they used. The phrasing of the key question may have encouraged them to overlook any method used only sporadically. Quite likely this incompleteness of reporting varies with pregnancy interval. The earlier the interval, the harder to recall, with the possible exception of the first method used. On the other hand, the many repetitious questions asked about contraception may have led some interviewers and respondents to hurry toward the end of the long section on contraception. If so, the answers about current usage are adversely affected. These speculations are unanswerable. One may only assume incompleteness of reporting, with a likelihood that this incompleteness varies for different pregnancy intervals.

Despite this incompleteness, a few wives mentioned as many as four methods for a single pregnancy interval and indicated how they combined and alternated these methods as well. Separately for each pregnancy interval this information was coded by means of a 10-column code. This code consists of four pairs of columns, identifying a maximum of four methods, plus two additional columns to define how these methods are combined or alternated. Of course, in analysis such a code is unworkable, and it becomes necessary to reduce it to a single-column code with a maximum of ten categories.

About 80 per cent of the time the sample couples report using a single method throughout a pregnancy interval; the remainder of the time they report using multiple methods. Accordingly, six of ten categories are assigned to single methods, namely, safe period, douche, withdrawal, condom, diaphragm and jelly, and "other." The residual "other" category comprises mainly jelly used without the diaphragm and, secondarily, abstinence and suppository.

The remaining four categories constitute use of multiple methods. A distinction is made between "combinations" (two or, rarely, three methods combined and this set of method used throughout a pregnancy interval) and "alternations" (two or more sets of methods used at different times during the pregnancy interval). Since these two types of usage are about equally frequent, it seems appropriate to allocate two categories to each.

With respect to combinations, the safe period united with another method (no method used on "safe days" and the second method on "unsafe days") is defined as a combination and denoted as "combined-safe period." Alternations between combinations involving the safe period are also included in this category, as well as the few combinations of abstinence with another method. This last assignment is made on the premise that respondent and interviewer erred in not reporting these cases as the safe period combined with a second method. Because nearly all other combinations entail adding a douche to a second method, they are pooled and designated "combination-douche."

Alternations are divided into two groups: "alternation-douche," when a douche is alternated with another method (except safe period), and "alternation-other," representing mainly paired alternations of withdrawal, condom, and diaphragm and jelly. Included among the latter are the few cases of "multiple method— no information on groupings." The incidences, by pregnancy interval, of the ten method categories and their subdivisions are given in Table B–1.

THE ATTRACTION OF MULTIPLE METHODS FOR ACCIDENT-PRONE COUPLES

A suspicion arises, and deserves testing, that couples in contraceptive difficulty are prone to use multiple methods.

For instance, the incidence of "alternations" declines with increasing pregnancy order, from 10 per cent of all usage before first pregnancy to 7 per cent for current usage. This decrease fits with the idea that alternating between two or more methods frequently marks a period of experimentation during which the couple appraise various methods, perhaps moving tentatively from one to another. Such periods of experimentation may be peculiarly liable to accidental pregnancy. In other instances, couples may vacillate between

TABLE B–1

Methods of Contraception, by Pregnancy Interval

Method of Contraception	Per Cent of Couples Using Method			
	Before First Pregnancy	Before Second Pregnancy	Before Third Pregnancy	Current Usage
Safe period	14%	19%	19%	19%
Douche	6	5	4	4
Withdrawal	4	5	4	5
Condom	35	29	41	31
Diaphragm and jelly	17	18	15	18
Jelly	4	2	2	2
Other	1	1	1	1
Combined-safe period	4	5	2	7
Alternation between combinations involving safe period	1	2	2	1
Combination-douche	3	3	3	4
Combination-other	0	0	0	1
Alternations-douche	3	3	4	2
Alternations-other	7	6	4	5
Multiple methods—no information on groupings	1	0	1	0
Per cent total	100	98	102	100
Number of couples	607	914	113	983

a method that is disliked but deemed effective and one that is found congenial but ineffective. That the second method is still being used implies that the couple are not yet highly motivated to achieve efficient contraception or else that they find the discipline required by the effective method particularly difficult. According to this line of thought, the couples who alternate methods are a selected group whose failure rate is higher than warranted by the methods they use.

An alternative hypothesis for interpreting alternations is that no such selectivities are involved and that what counts is the methods being alternated and the relative emphasis placed upon them. Thus, for couples alternating between given sets of methods, one anticipates a failure rate somewhere between the rates expected for the most effective and the least effective of the methods involved in the alternation.

An analogous pair of hypotheses may be formulated with respect to combinations. Perhaps it is only the methods involved in the combination that count. That is, for a given combination, the failure rate will be as low, or even lower than, the rate expected for the most effective method included in the combination, since to that most effective method are being added extra precautions. Or alternatively, there are selectivities which insure a failure rate higher than this. For instance, couples taking the most elaborate precautions may tend to be couples who especially fear failure because of past failures.

As a first step toward testing these hypotheses, it is necessary to consider the relative effectiveness of the single methods. Table B–2

TABLE B–2

Effectiveness of Specific Methods of Contraception, by Pregnancy Interval

Method of Contraception	Before First Pregnancy			Before Second and Third Pregnancy		
	Months of Contraceptive Exposure	Failure Rate[a]	Per Cent Successful	Months of Contraceptive Exposure	Failure Rate[a]	Per Cent Successful
Safe period	894	57.7	37%	3,285	33.2	52%
Douche	336	60.7	47	929	33.6	43
Withdrawal	213	22.5	78	1,074	15.6	73
Condom	3,227	17.1	75	6,835	12.3	76
Diaphragm and jelly	1,941	13.6	76	3,738	14.8	73
Other	179	60.3	59	351	41.0	56
Combined-safe period	563	34.1	48	1,221	43.2	32
Combination-douche	346	34.7	47	683	24.6	56
Alternation-douche	245	24.5	64	618	27.2	55
Alternation-other	768	18.8	71	1,161	19.6	67
Total	8,712	25.3	65	19,895	21.1	64

[a] Failures per 100 years of contraceptive exposure.

furnishes failures per 100 years of contraceptive exposure for six single methods, separately for the periods preceding and following first pregnancy. In both intervals safe period, douche, and "other" show failure rates twice as high as withdrawal, condom, and diaphragm and jelly.

Table B–2 also furnishes failure rates for the four categories of multiple methods. These results, studied in comparison with those for the six single methods, suggest that with one exception the failure rates of combinations and alternations vary mainly as a function of the component methods involved.

The category "alternation-other" furnishes the most striking verification of the hypothesis that it is the methods involved, and the relative emphasis placed upon them, which matters and not any selection toward accident-proneness. Since "alternation-other" consists almost wholly of alternating between withdrawal, condom, or diaphragm and jelly, one anticipates failure rates below 20, and these obtain.

More partial verification comes from the category "alternation-douche," representing cases in which the douche-used-alone is alternated with other methods. Approximately 80 per cent of the time the second method is withdrawal, condom, or diaphragm and jelly. Accordingly, if type of method is crucial and if exposure is fairly equally divided between douche and the other method, one expects a failure rate approximately midway between 15 and 60 before first pregnancy, and between 15 and 35 after first pregnancy. The rates observed, 24.5 and 27.2, accord pretty well with expectation, given such small bases of experience (245 and 618 months of contraceptive exposure respectively).

The category "combination-douche" also presents only partial confirmation. This category, which excludes any combinations involving the safe period, consists mainly of douche added to withdrawal, condom, or diaphragm and jelly. Relatively few instances occur of douche added to jelly. Hence, if the particular methods involved are the determining factor and not selection for or against accident-proneness, one would expect failure rates equal or below 20. The rates observed are higher than this, namely 34.7 and 24.6, though lower than those for douche used alone. This result would suggest an exception to the hypothesis except for one consideration: douching may lower the effectiveness of either jelly alone or jelly and diaphragm, and these two methods account for more than 40 per cent of the relevant experience.

The category "combined-safe period" is hardest to theorize about. Using the safe period alone means using no method of contraception during "safe days" and abstinence during "unsafe days." Combining the safe period with another method means using no method of contraception during "safe days" and the second method during "unsafe days." One may argue that safe period alone is more efficient because no method of contraception is more effective than abstinence. But one can also argue the opposite. The couple who use the safe period alone must abstain from sexual relations during the unsafe days and as a result may be more tempted (than the user of safe period in combination) to narrow their definition of unsafe days and to take more chances generally. The net balance of these considerations is entirely conjectural. Thus, there is no clear theoretical basis for calling safe period alone more effective than safe period in combination.

As compared to the failure rates observed for the safe period alone, those observed for the safe period in combination are lower before first pregnancy (34.1 to 57.7) and higher after that event (43.2 to 33.2). Neither of these differences is statistically significant. Nor is the increase in failure rate from 34.1 to 43.2, experienced by safe period combiners before and after first pregnancy, statistically significant.

REASONS FOR PREFERRING CURRENT METHOD

Wives are asked why they prefer the method they are currently using. Their reasons are classified in Table B–3, with percentage

TABLE B–3

Reasons Given by Wives for Preferring the Single Method
They Are Currently Using

Reason for Preferring Current Method	Times Mentioned	Per Cent of Wives
Reliable, safest, most effective	388	49%
My husband prefers it; doesn't interfere with enjoyment of either spouse; most natural	156	20
Church approves it	152	19
Only method I know; never used any other	127	16
My doctor recommended it	127	16
Convenient, no trouble, easy to use; simple	77	10
Not reported	27	3
Clean, not messy	23	3
Physically safe, not harmful to the body	23	3
Other reasons	13	2
Don't know	4	1
Total	1,117	142

distributions given for the 792 couples currently using a single method. The percentages add to more than a hundred because approximately one third of the respondents cite multiple reasons.

Half the wives report reliability as a reason for using their current method. The second most popular theme, cited by 20 per cent of the wives, is "husband prefers it; doesn't interfere with enjoyment of either spouse; most natural." Three less heterogeneous reasons are mentioned by 16 to 20 per cent, namely, "church approves it," "only method I know; never used any other," and "my doctor recommended it." Ten per cent or less allude to such considerations as convenience, cleanliness, or physical safeness.

Certain reasons are more frequently mentioned alone than others.

For instance, church approval is mentioned alone more than 80 per cent of the time, when it is mentioned at all. Reliability is cited as sole reason nearly half the time, but all other reasons are so cited under 40 per cent of the time. These data are contained in Table B–4.

TABLE B–4

Per Cent of Times Particular Reasons Are Reported Alone or
Reported in Combination with Reliability

Reason	Number of Mentions	Per Cent Mentioning It Exclusively	Per Cent Combining It with Reliability
Church approval	152	82%	11%
Reliability	388	45	–
Doctor recommends	127	26	59
Only method known	127	39	51
Husband prefers, etc.	156	38	42
Convenient	77	30	42
Clean	23	30	30
Physically safe	23	23	56
Total	1,073	44	–

Table B–4 also indicates how frequently particular reasons are mentioned in conjunction with reliability. The reason most often paired with reliability is "recommended by my doctor." Presumably a method adopted on medical advice is preferred not just because the doctor recommends it, but because he recommends it as particularly reliable. "The only method we know," is another reason which coincides with reliability more than 50 per cent of the time. Probably confidence in a method lessens incentive to explore alternative techniques. Reliability is somewhat less frequently mentioned in connection with the heterogeneous reason "husband prefers it; doesn't interfere with sexual enjoyment of either spouse; most natural." Reliability least often pairs with "church approval."

Because of infrequent mention, little can be said about convenience, cleanliness, and physical safeness when these reasons are taken separately. Merged into a single category, which might be called "aesthetic considerations," they are cited as sole reason about 30 per cent of the time and are paired with reliability over 40 per cent of the time. These last results imply that aesthetic considerations may sometimes determine choice of method, although probably more often they dictate a preference only when other considerations, such as reliability, fail to establish a definite priority.

REASONS FOR PREFERRING SPECIFIED METHODS

Reasons for preferring seven types of single method are presented in Table B–5. Jelly is treated as a separate category, and this leaves a

TABLE B–5

Reasons for Using Specific Method

Reason for Preference	Per Cent of Wives Currently Using the Method[a]							
	Dia-phragm and jelly	Condom	Jelly	With-drawal	Douche	Safe Period	Other[b]	Total
Reliability	70%[c]	58%	57%	43%	33%	16%	64%	49%
Doctor recommends	54	4	52	–	3	1	21	16
Church approval	–	–	–	11	13	76	29	19
Only method known	12	27	13	13	20	2	7	16
Husband prefers, etc.	23	18	35	36	15	15	–	20
Convenient	11	12	22	11	5	5	–	10
Clean	2	5	–	–	13	–	–	3
Physically safe	3	3	–	4	10	1	7	3
Other	–	7	4	8	8	1	14	6
Number of wives	179	303	23	53	40	180	14	792

[a] Percentages add to more than 100 because of multiple citations.

[b] The breakdown for this residual category is abstinence (8 cases), suppository (4 cases), pessary (1 case) and vasectomy (1 case).

[c] Percentages are italicized when higher than the corresponding per cent in the last column.

residual "other" category comprised mainly of abstinence and secondarily of suppository. Whenever the emphasis upon a reason is disproportionately high, relative to the emphasis displayed by the entire sample, that percentage is *underlined*.

More than half the users of diaphragm and jelly, other, condom, and jelly mention reliability. In contrast, less than half of the users of withdrawal and douche do so and less than one fifth of the safe period users mention reliability.

With regard to reasons other than reliability, these vary according to method. Little can be said about the distinctiveness of reasons given for jelly, other, or douche because of insufficient cases. Diaphragm and jelly users are distinctive for the percentage saying they followed medical advice. Women married to men who use a condom are apt to say it is the only method they know. Wives whose husbands use withdrawal often report that their husbands prefer it. Not un-expectedly, religion is the predominant consideration among safe period users.

Wives currently employing multiple methods are asked why they prefer each method. The reasons reported are about what one would expect from knowledge of the individual methods. This holds for both types of alternation and for combined-safe period. The douche component of combination-douche represents an exception. When using a douche alone or alternately, wives are likely to attribute their use of it to such motives as "only method known," "clean," "safe," "husband prefers it," etc. Only a third mention reliability as a reason, while the proportion saying it was recommended by their doctor is negligible. But more than half the wives combining a douche with another method (other than safe period) do so as an added precaution, and of these, one third say their doctors suggested it.

METHOD LOYALTY

As might be expected, there is a strong tendency to persist with a method once its use is begun. Sixty-seven per cent of the current contraceptors are using the method with which they started. Among couples starting contraception prior to first pregnancy, this proportion is 63 per cent.

Over 70 per cent use the same method in any two successive intervals. It makes little difference whether the successive intervals occur before and after first birth or before and after second birth. This tendency to repeat a method is far stronger than would be expected by chance. If choice of method during successive intervals represented two independent decisions, one would expect repetition of the same method in less than 20 per cent of the cases, a figure far below the 70 per cent actually observed.

There is no tendency to shift away from ineffective methods and toward more effective ones. This has been demonstrated in Table 12, which showed that, among couples practicing contraception two or more intervals, the distributions of methods initially and last used are nearly identical. This means that for each method as many shift away from it as shift to it from other methods. It does not necessarily mean that different methods are alike in the percentage of times they are repeated for two or more consecutive intervals.

Actually different methods of contraception command unequal loyalty. Effective methods tend to be repeated more often than are ineffective ones. For instance, Table B–6 shows that withdrawal, condom, and diaphragm and jelly are more often repeated than douche, jelly alone, alternation-douche. But there are exceptions. Safe period and combined-safe period, though relatively ineffective

TABLE B–6

Per Cent of Times That Specific Method Is Repeated in Two Successive Intervals

Method of Contraception	Before and After First Birth		Before and After Second Birth		Significance of Differences[a]
	Number	Per Cent of Repeats	Number	Per Cent of Repeats	
Safe period	95	78%	172	83%	NS
Douche	37	49	44	55	NS
Withdrawal	24	88	49	69	05
Condom	240	82	272	83	NS
Diaphragm and jelly	110	73	157	78	NS
Other	28	46	29	55	NS
Combined-safe period	32	75	69	70	NS
Combination-douche	23	61	31	68	NS
Alternation-douche	20	60	31	42	NS
Alternation-other	54	52	55	53	NS
Total number using methods	663	–	909	–	–
Total per cent of repeaters	–	72	–	74	NS

[a] Based on the formula $(p_1 - p_2)/\sqrt{pq\,(1/n_1 + 1/n_2)}$, where p_1 is the proportion of repeats before and after first birth; p_2 is the proportion of repeats before and after second birth; $p = (n_1 p_1 + n_2 p_2)/(n_1 + n_2)$; and $q = 1 - p$.

methods, are often repeated. Alternation-other exemplifies an effective method repeated less frequently than average. In general, single methods are more often repeated than combinations, and combinations command more loyalty than alternations.

It seems to matter little whether the two successive intervals precede and follow first birth or precede and follow second birth. In either case the frequencies with which particular methods are repeated are about the same. Significance tests point to only one change of proportion repeating as probably real. This concerns withdrawal, whose proportion of repeaters sinks from 88 to 69 per cent.

An intensive analysis of method shifts has been undertaken in an effort to detect selectivities between method abandoned and method adopted. Such selectivities seemingly exist, although usually the number of cases is insufficient to demonstrate their statistical significance. Moreover, many of them are partly spurious, representing merely a method dropped from a combination or alternation, or else a method added to a single one.

The likelihood of shifting from a method increases when a failure has been experienced with it. However, it does not seem to matter whether the failure occurs as a result of taking a chance or while actually practicing the method. These results are given in Table B–7.

TABLE B–7

Per Cent of Times that Specific Method Is Repeated in the Next Interval, as Related to Experience in the Prior Interval

METHOD OF CONTRACEPTION	PER CENT OF TIMES THAT METHOD IS REPEATED FOLLOWING:					
	Success		Failure while Chance-taking		Failure while Practicing Method	
	Number	Per Cent	Number	Per Cent	Number	Per Cent
Safe period	119	89%	51	67%	72	74%
Combined-safe period	37	76	31	74	26	65
Douche	35	74	20	30	24	29
Condom	348	87	86	71	36	64
Diaphragm and jelly	191	81	39	67	26	50
All methods[a]	932	80	288	63	233	59

[a] Includes withdrawal, other, combination-douche, alternation-douche, and alternation-other, all of which have less than 20 cases in each type of failure.

Several points emerge for specific methods. The distinction between success or failure in the previous interval produces the widest differential in the case of douching and its smallest in the cases of safe-period and combined-safe period, for which rates of repeating remain high regardless of past experience. The distinction between failure while taking a chance and failure while practicing the method assumes its greatest importance for condom and diaphragm and jelly. Results are not given in Table B–7 for five categories of method because of insufficient cases.

ACCEPTABILITY OF CURRENT METHODS

Three pieces of information are available to describe the respondent's attitude toward her present method. First, does the wife mention reliability as a reason for using it? About half the wives do. Second, how does she answer the question: "How confident are you of the reliability of the method you are currently using? Very confident, fairly confident, or not too confident?" Forty-three per cent say "very confident," 42 per cent "fairly confident," and 15 per cent "not too confident." Third, what is her reply to the question: "Do you think you and your husband might change to another method in the future?" Sixty-seven per cent say "no," the remainder answer "yes," "possibly," or "don't know." Marks of an acceptable

369

method are mention of reliability, high confidence, and not expecting to shift from it in the future.

The ten categories of methods vary in their acceptability. Diaphragm and jelly is the most acceptable method, being associated with above median percentages of users who are highly confident, mention reliability, and who do not expect to change in the future. (See Table B–8.) Condom and other (mostly jelly), exhibit two

TABLE B–8

Acceptability and Success Rates of Specific Methods

Method of Contraception	Per Cent Highly Confident	Per Cent Mentioning Reliability	Per Cent Expecting Not to Change	Per Cent Successful[a]
Safe period	29%	16%	82%	48%
Douche	21	33	48	45
Withdrawal	40	46	49	74
Condom	47	62	54	76
Diaphragm and jelly	62	70	91	74
Other	65	66	62	57
Combined-safe period	31	–	63	38
Combination-douche	46	–	64	53
Alternation-douche	41	–	47	58
Alternation-other	31	–	69	69
Total	43	50	67	64

[a] Combines experiences before and after first pregnancy.

percentages above the median. At the other extreme, douche has the lowest acceptability of any method.

Determinants of Acceptability

An important factor in determining the acceptability of a method is past experience with it. In Table B–9, the three measures of acceptability are given for six categories of past experience with current method.

That a tangible association exists between confidence in a method and past experience with it is shown by a .35 coefficient of contingency. When past experience is restricted to success, more than half the wives say "very confident." With failures confined to conditions of taking a chance, the percentage saying very confident remains close to 50 per cent. But it drops to 20 per cent and below when

TABLE B-9

Past Experience with a Method in Relation to Confidence in It, Reasons for
Using It, and Expectation about Abandoning It in the Future

Past Experience with Method	Per Cent Very Confident[a]	Per Cent Mentioning Reliability[b]	Per Cent Expecting Not to Shift[a]
Success only	57%	56%	73%
Success and failure while taking a chance	49	50	73
Success and failure while practicing the method	20	34	72
Failure while taking a chance	47	51	66
Failure while practicing the method	13	29	66
No previous experience	33	50	60
Total	43	51	68

[a] Based on 891 couples currently using single or multiple methods.
[b] Based on 792 couples currently using a single method.

there has been a failure while practicing the method, whether
accompanied by an interval of successful use or not. Thus, a failure
while taking a chance shakes confidence far less than a failure while
practicing the method. When the method is being used for the first
time, the level of reported confidence stands halfway between the
levels reported for the two types of failure.[1]

The association between past experience and mention of reliability as a reason for using the method is much looser, the coefficient of contingency being only .15. The immediate basis for this
low association is the failure of such kinds of past experience as
success, failure while taking a chance, and absence of previous
experience to produce differences. The only distinction that seems
to matter is whether or not there has been a failure while practicing
the method. Given such a failure, only about 30 per cent report
reliability as a reason for using their current method, as compared
with 50 per cent among those not experiencing this type of failure.

It is surprising that reliability is not more consistently mentioned
by wives who are using a method for the first time and especially
those who have experienced only success with it. This result serves
as a reminder that many couples attach importance to other considerations than reliability. However, question order in the schedule may

[1] This association between past experience with, and confidence in, a method is also
shown by the data of Table B-8. For the ten method categories, the rank order correlation
between per cent successful and per cent highly confident is .52. For the six single methods,
the correlation between per cent successful and per cent mentioning reliability is .63.
When failure rates are substituted for per cents successful, these correlations decrease to
.51 and .49.

also be a factor. Preceding the question asking the wife why she prefers her current method is the question asking her about her confidence in it. The wife who answers "very confident" may fear that she is repeating herself if she then answers the next question in terms of reliability and effectiveness. The coefficient of contingency between confidence in method and mention of reliability is .32.

The association between past experience with a method and expecting to change from it is also very weak. The .12 coefficient of contingency involves a chi-square value that might be exceeded by chance nearly 5 per cent of the time. Possibly explaining this near absence of relationship is a selective process whereby those who have failed in the past but then did not shift had special reasons for not doing so and these reasons are still operating in the present. For example, devout Catholics who stay with the safe period method despite failures have religious reasons for saying that they do not expect to change in the future. Then also, a couple may not shift from a method after a failure because they blame themselves and not the method, but for the same reason they have no cause to contemplate a future change. Thus, the low correlation may be partly a function of when the question is asked. Had the wives been asked during pregnancy, a higher per cent of those who had just failed might indicate a resolve to shift methods, which would have generated a higher association between past experience and expectation of a shift.

In addition to past experience with a method, a second important factor determining confidence in a method is the couple's prejudgement of the method's effectiveness on the basis of things heard or read about the method. The fact that methods differ greatly in reputation is demonstrated by Table B–10 which compares levels of confidence among wives employing specified methods for the first time. Despite inexperience with them, wives place considerable confidence in "other" (mostly jelly), diaphragm and jelly, combination-douche, and withdrawal. Somewhat less confidence is placed in condom; less yet is placed in alternation-other. Least confidence is placed in safe period, combined-safe period and douche.

Thus, two determinants may be postulated as controlling confidence in current method of contraception. First is past experience with the method, measured in terms of the six-category classification employed in Table B–9. Second is a residual determinant, the reputation for effectiveness which the method has for the couple apart from their personal experience with it. In any attempt to weigh the relative contributions of the two, the second determinant, being residual, is assigned a weight complementary to that obtained

TABLE B–10

Confidence in Method Which Is Currently Being Used for the First Time

Type of Method[a]	Per Cent Reporting Self as:			Per Cent Total	Number of Wives
	Very Confident	Fairly Confident	Not Too Confident		
Other (mainly jelly)	55%	30%	15%	100%	20
Combination-douche	48	37	15	100	27
Diaphragm and jelly	48	52	0	100	46
Withdrawal	47	53	0	100	15
Condom	32	48	21	100	63
Alternation-other	22	61	17	100	18
Safe period	17	58	25	100	36
Combined-safe period	16	68	16	100	25
Douche	7	53	25	100	15
Total	33	51	16	100	265

[a] Data are not given for alternation-douche because there is only one case.

TABLE B–11

Comparison of Observed Per Cent Highly Confident with Per Cent Expected on the Basis of Past Experience with Method, by Type of Method

METHOD OF CONTRACEPTION	PER CENT HIGHLY CONFIDENT			
	Observed	Expected	Observed Minus Expected	
			Per Cent	Standard Deviations
Safe period	29	40	−11	3.07*
Douche	21	42	−21	2.77*
Withdrawal	40	42	−2	.41
Condom	47	47	–	.10
Diaphragm and jelly	62	46	16	4.30*
"Other"	65	39	26	3.18*
Combined-safe period	31	38	−7	1.22
Combination-douche	46	40	6	.88
Alternation-douche	41	45	−4	.09
Alternation-"other"	31	43	−12	1.71
Total	43	43	–	–

NOTE: Asterisk indicates significant at the .01 level.

for the factor of past experience. For this purpose the Westergaard expected cases procedure is suitable.[2]

Such an analysis, summarized in Table B–11, is aimed at the

[2] S. A. Stouffer and C. Tibbits, "Tests of Significance in Applying Westergaard's Method of Expected Cases to Sociological Data," in A. J. Jaffe, ed., *Handbook of Statistical Methods for Demographers*, U.S. G.P.O., Washington, 1951, pp. 65–70.

question: to what extent do the contrasting levels of confidence expressed towards the ten types of method reflect differences in past experience with them? The first column of figures gives the percentages of users highly confident in each method. The second column gives the percentages expected if the users of each method had the past experience with it that they actually do, but derived the same levels of confidence from each category of past experience as does the entire sample. The third column provides differences: observed percentages less expected percentages. The last column restates these differences in terms of standard deviations. A positive difference means that the users of that method place more trust in it than is average for wives having the same past experience with contraception.

It may be seen that users of diaphragm and jelly and other (mainly jelly) exhibit a greater measure of confidence than would be expected on the basis of their past experience with these two methods. Just the opposite applies to users of safe period and douche. Apparently what they have read or heard about these latter methods have added doubts beyond those accruing from personal experience.

An Index of Fertility-Planning Success

Designing a classification of fertility-planning success has presented special problems in this study. To be useful in the correlational analysis such a classification ideally must rank every couple (the Never Users of contraception as well as the Ever Users) along a single continuum. In the classification developed for this study, planning success is defined to mean delaying a pregnancy as long as desired (of course, slowness to conceive may delay this pregnancy far longer than desired but this aspect is not incorporated). Data are taken from both pregnancy intervals (or all three intervals in cases of a miscarriage). However, behavior since second birth is not represented.

Four levels of planning success are distinguished: highly successful, semi-successful, semi-unsuccessful, and highly unsuccessful. The highly successful have "planned" all pregnancies prior to second birth, while the highly unsuccessful have failed to plan any of these pregnancies. The semi-successful have planned their last pregnancy but failed to plan one earlier pregnancy. Most of the semi-unsuccessful have planned at least one pregnancy but failed to plan their last one; a few have planned their last pregnancy but failed to plan two earlier ones. This classification attaches greater importance to planning successfully the second birth than the first for two reasons. Indirect evidence suggests that many of these couples have felt more strongly about lengthening the interval between their two children than about delaying the first-born's arrival. Also, these couples have usually attempted longer postponements of second pregnancy than first pregnancy. Accordingly, successfully planning the second birth is viewed as a greater contraceptive challenge with more at stake than planning the first birth.

A pregnancy is considered planned under three circumstances: (1) if contraception is stopped in order to conceive; (2) if contraception is not used because of a desire to have the pregnancy as soon as possible; (3) if contraception is not used because of assumed difficulty conceiving. In regard to the last two circumstances, it is reasoned that a woman anxious to have her next pregnancy as soon as possible, or believing herself subfecund, is behaving rationally with reference to her spacing preferences if she does not use contraception. The corresponding circumstances for unplanned pregnancies are: (1) pregnancy occurred while using a method of contraception; (2) pregnancy occurred while taking a chance and omitting contraception; (3) contraception not used for such reasons as religion, ignorance or fear of contraception, aesthetic aversion to contraception, not caring when pregnancy occurred, or not believing that she would become pregnant so soon. With regard to the third circumstance, women who do not use contraception for such reasons as religion or dislike of contraception are, of course, behaving rationally with reference to their larger value systems; but with reference to the single value of child-spacing they are behaving inconsistently; the reasons they give for nonuse are irrelevant to their spacing interests. Indeed, their failure to delay pregnancy is more complete than in the case of those using contraception unsuccessfully. Thus, it is being argued that a large majority wish to delay their pregnancies but that a few are restrained from contraception by values irrelevant to their spacing interests. For instance, the women who plead indifference to spacing are regarded as wanting to delay pregnancy but giving indifference to spacing as a justification for placing other values above spacing values. The only women who are accepted as not wanting to delay a pregnancy are those who explicitly say they did not use contraception because they wanted that pregnancy as soon as possible. Naturally this means that many of the assignments are wholly or partly based on responses given to a "why" question. This is regrettable but seemingly unavoidable.

ASSIGNMENT TO PLANNING CATEGORIES

The 127 Never Users of contraception require special handling. They are asked the reason for their never practicing contraception.

Assignment is made on the basis of answers to this single question. The 15 who give "wanting children as soon as possible" as their *only* reason are classified as highly successful planners. The 18 who cite difficulty conceiving are classified as semi-successful. This constitutes an arbitrary assignment of a heterogeneous group. Some of these couples deserve a rating of highly successful since they did not use contraception before their first pregnancy because they wanted their first child as soon as possible and then discovered their subfecundity. Others did not use contraception before their first pregnancy because of such reasons as religion, ignorance of contraception, and so forth, and therefore merit a rating of semi-successful. Without a question addressed specifically to the first pregnancy interval there is no way of distinguishing the two groups. Hence, it is arbitrary

TABLE B–12

Couples Having Only Two Pregnancies prior to Second Birth:
Assignment to Planning Statuses

Assignment	Behavior before First Pregnancy	Behavior before Second Pregnancy	Frequency
Highly successful	SC	SC	256
	R nonuse	SC	107
	SC	R nonuse	11
	R nonuse	R nonuse	29
			403
Semi-successful	UC	SC	88
	I nonuse	SC	62
	UC	R nonuse	5
	I nonuse	R nonuse	8
			163
Semi-unsuccessful	SC	UC	54
	R nonuse	UC	59
	SC	I nonuse	5
	R nonuse	I nonuse	13
			131
Highly unsuccessful	UC	UC	105
	I nonuse	UC	76
	UC	I nonuse	4
	I nonuse	I nonuse	15
			200

whether they are assigned to the highly successful or the semi-successful rank. The latter has been chosen because of the fewer cases and more intermediate position. Remaining for assignment are the 94 Never Users who give such reasons as religion, indifference about spacing, aversion to contraception, and others. These couples are treated as highly unsuccessful since all their pregnancies are unplanned according to the definitions being followed.

Among the 1,038 Ever Users, 897 had no miscarriage before their second birth and therefore only two pregnancies. The various patterns of planning behavior assigned to each planning group are tabulated in Table B-12, using as notation: SC, successful contraception; UC, unsuccessful contraception; R nonuse, rational nonuse (that is, nonuse because pregnancy wanted as soon as possible or difficulty conceiving); I nonuse, inconsistent nonuse (that is, nonuse for reasons of religion, ignorance of contraception, and so forth).

It may be noted that the highly successful group contains the most cases, followed by the highly unsuccessful, the semi-successful, and the semi-unsuccessful in that order.

Couples having a miscarriage and therefore three pregnancies prior to second birth present a wider variety of types for assignment. Couples planning all three pregnancies are allocated to the highly successful; couples failing to plan all three pregnancies, to the highly unsuccessful. Couples planning their last pregnancy but failing to plan one (but not both) of their previous two pregnancies go into the semi-successful category. Included among the semi-unsuccessful are couples failing to plan their last pregnancy but planning one or both of their earlier pregnancies. Also included in this category are couples who planned their last pregnancy but failed to plan both their previous pregnancies. There are two reasons for assigning this group to the semi-unsuccessful rather than the semi-successful. First, in a fairly clear way these particular couples are less successful than the couples, labeled as semi-successful, who planned their last pregnancy and who failed to plan only one (not both) of their previous pregnancies. On the other hand, it is much less clear that these particular couples are more successful than the couples defined as semi-unsuccessful, who planned both their first two pregnancies though not their last one. Second, the addition of 17 cases to the semi-unsuccessful group is welcome for augmenting the smallest planning group.

The frequencies in the four planning ranks are summarized in Table B-13. The index of fertility-planning success is not used extensively until Chapter XI.

TABLE B–13

Fertility-Planning Status

Fertility-Planning Status	Never Users	Ever Users			Total
		No Miscarriage	Miscarriage First Pregnancy	Miscarriage Second Pregnancy	
Highly successful	15	403	27	37	482
Semi-successful	18	163	5	19	205
Semi-unsuccessful	–	131	16	25	172
Highly unsuccessful	94	200	3	9	306
Total	127	897	51	90	1,165

Appendix C. Index Construction

This appendix contains the items[1] with their distributions and inter-correlations which comprise the summary indices of attitudinal and personality characteristics. As described in Chapter III, Methodology, a decision was reached to rely on simple unweighted summations of items (dichotomized) screened initially through correlational analysis rather than using scalogram analysis. The reasons underlying this decision are detailed in Chapter III and will not be repeated here.

The order of presentation follows that of the appearance of the index in the book. All responses of "don't know" if this response was not an ordered response category or "no response" were assigned randomly in order to score all individuals on a uniform basis. Loadings on the first factor were derived by the Thurstone centroid technique, using the highest correlation coefficient in each column as the estimate of the communality.

In general, purification of an index by item elimination proceeded according to the following criteria:

(a) Items with first factor loadings of less than .5 but greater than .4 are to be considered for exclusion. Such items are retained if the number of items with loadings greater than .5 is three or less.

(b) Items with loadings of .4 or less are to be eliminated from inclusion in the final index.

(c) Items with marginals outside the 10 to 90 range to be eliminated regardless of loadings.

(d) The number of items retained for any index is less than or equal to 8 items. This last criterion is simply a matter of machine and coding convenience.

Most but not all batteries were processed by these criteria.

RELIGIOUSNESS (WIVES)

Aside from reported regularity of church attendance, two other measures of religiousness were developed. The first, labeled "informal religious orientation," combined the responses to two questions posed to the wives ($+$ = high religiousness).

---

[1] The actual interview schedule and supplementary questionnaires are not reproduced because of the amount of repetition of items this would involve. Copies can be secured by request at the Office of Population Research, Princeton University.

Q. 222. Aside from attendance at religious services, how religious-minded would you say you are? Very, more than average, less than average, or not at all?

Very (+)	8.8
More than average	21.7
Average	54.4
Less than average	12.3
Not at all (−)	2.7
Per cent total	99.9
Number	1,165

Q. 228. To what extent is religion included in the home activities of your family? For example, family prayers, reading the Bible or other religious materials, saying grace at meals, and so forth. Would you say a great deal, more than average, a little, or not at all?

A great deal (+)	6.4
More than average	23.2
Average (written in)	2.8
A little	51.7
Not at all (−)	16.0
Per cent total	100.1
Number	1,165

The product-moment correlation between these two items is .52.

A third question was also designed to be included in this index, but the distribution of responses proved too extreme to be useful.

Q. 229. Have you ever gone to see your minister, priest, or rabbi for advice or help on family or personal matters since you've been married?

Yes (+)	9.8
No (−)	90.0
Don't know	0.1
Not reported	0.1
Per cent total	100.0
Number	1,165

The second measure of religiousness is summarized in an index labeled "religiosity." These questions were included in the personality inventory left with the wife at the completion of the interview. A total of 961 women returned usable questionnaires.

Q. 5. Which would you rather teach? Religion *or* English?

Religion (+)	51.7
English (−)	48.0
No response	0.3
	———
Per cent total	100.0

Q. 16. Which is more important to you? Religion *or* Politics?

Religion (+)	93.2
Politics (−)	6.7
No response	0.1
	———
Per cent total	100.0

Q. 27. What would you rather have a son of yours do? Follow a career in the Church *or* follow a career in the Army?

Church (+)	65.1
Army (−)	32.5
No response	2.4
	———
Per cent total	100.0

Q. 38. Would you like to be a missionary?

No (−)	80.6
Yes (+)	18.9
No response	0.4
	———
Per cent total	99.9

Q. 49. Which spouse would you prefer? One who will command admiration *or* one who likes to read religious books?

Admiration (−)	75.2
Religious books (+)	23.3
No response	1.5
	———
Per cent total	100.0

Q. 60. Whom would you rather have been? A famous playwright *or* a great religious leader?

Playwright (−)	57.9
Religious leader (+)	40.2
No response	2.0
	———
Per cent total	100.1

381

Q. 71. Which spouse would you prefer? One who is deeply religious *or* one who is a good provider?

Deeply religious (+)	11.8
Good provider (−)	87.8
No response	0.4
Per cent total	100.0

Q. 81. Would you prefer to read a story with a religious theme *or* a romantic theme?

Religious (+)	25.4
Romantic (−)	73.4
No response	1.2
Per cent total	100.0

TABLE C–1

Correlational Matrix (r_t) and Estimates of First Factor Loadings (k_1)

Question	5	16	27	38	49	60	71	81
5		.54	.40	.33	.45	.57	.52	.42
16	.54		.37	.10	.42	.66	.53	.59
27	.40	.37		.22	.33	.50	.64	.38
38	.33	.10	.22		.29	.48	.50	.34
49	.45	.42	.33	.29		.48	.38	.44
60	.57	.66	.50	.48	.48		.73	.51
71	.52	.53	.64	.50	.38	.73		.58
81	.42	.59	.38	.34	.44	.51	.58	
k_1	.69	.70	.63	.50	.59	.85	.84	.70

Question 16 was eliminated because of an extreme distribution. All other items were retained.

The product-moment correlation between these two measures of religiousness is .45.

Husband's Level of Status Satisfaction (Husband's)

There are four questions measuring the husband's level of status satisfaction, three of which project to his aspirations for his children (+ = high satisfaction). A total of 941 husbands returned questionnaires and form the basis for the statistics below:

Q. 4. I would be satisfied if a son of mine, when he reaches my age, is in the same kind of work that I am now in.

No (−)	56.7
Yes (+)	43.1
No response	0.2
Per cent total	100.0

Q. 14. I would be satisfied if my children receive the same amount of education as I have.

No (−)	65.8
Yes (+)	34.1
No response	0.1
Per cent total	100.0

Q. 15. I am pretty well satisfied with the chances for getting ahead in my present work.

No (−)	34.2
Yes (+)	65.2
No response	0.6
Per cent total	100.0

Q. 19. I would be satisfied if my children, when they reach my age, have the same income and live the same way as I.

No (−)	56.0
Yes (+)	43.8
No response	0.2
Per cent total	100.0

The intercorrelations of these four items and their loadings on the first factor appear in Table C–2.

TABLE C–2

Correlational Matrix (r_t) and Estimates of First Factor Loadings

Questions	4	14	15	19
4		.58	.69	.60
14	.58		.36	.53
15	.69	.36		.48
19	.60	.53	.48	
k_1	.85	.68	.74	.73

All four items were retained for the index.

ACHIEVEMENT OF LIFE GOALS (WIVES)

There are four questions in the interview schedule designed to measure what was previously termed "feelings of personal

383

competence," but which in its revised content is more appropriately described as "level of perceived achievement of life goals" (+ = high achievement). All statistics are based on 1,165 responses.

Q. 127. We all have our own picture of the kind of life we would really like to lead and the things we would really like to do in life. Whatever your picture, how much do you feel that you are reaching it? Would you say very much, much, little, or very little?

Very much (+)	28.9
Much	48.8
Little	17.7
Very little (−)	4.6
Per cent total	100.0

Q. 128. What do you think the chances are of living the kind of life you'd like to have? Do you think they are very good, good, fair, or not too good?

Very good (+)	38.5
Good	43.9
Fair	14.2
Not too good (−)	3.2
Don't know	0.1
Per cent total	99.9

Q. 129. Some people feel they can make pretty definite plans for their lives for the next few years, while others feel they are not in a position to plan ahead. How about you? Do you feel you are able to plan ahead or not?

Yes, able to plan ahead (+)	64.1
Depends, mixed responses	7.7
No, unable to plan ahead (−)	28.2
Per cent total	100.0

Q. 130. Do you feel you now know *and* can look forward to the kind of life you will have ten years from now?

Yes (+)	65.7
Depends; mixed responses	8.8
No (−)	25.4
Don't know	0.1
Per cent total	100.0

TABLE C-3

Correlational Matrix (Product Moment) and Estimates of
First Factor Loadings

Question	127	128	129	130
127		.55	.26	.25
128	.55		.30	.31
129	.26	.30		.47
130	.25	.31	.47	
k_1	.64	.68	.60	.60

All four items were retained for the index.

COMMITMENT TO WORK (HUSBANDS)

There are nine questions in the husband's questionnaire designed to measure the extent of his involvement in work or commitment to work values. All statistics are based on 941 cases (+ = high commitment).

Q. 1. I would much rather relax around the house all day than go to work.

No (+)	88.0
Yes (−)	11.8
No response	0.2
Per cent total	100.0

Q. 6. My work is more satisfying to me than the time I spend around the house.

No (−)	69.4
Yes (+)	30.2
No response	0.4
Per cent total	100.0

Q. 10. If I inherited so much money that I didn't have to work, I would still continue to work at the same thing I am doing now.

No (−)	52.6
Yes (+)	47.2
No response	0.2
Per cent total	100.0

Q. 12. More than almost anything else, it is work that makes life worthwhile.

No (−)	71.2
Yes (+)	27.7
No response	1.1
Per cent total	100.0

Q. 16. Some of my main interests and pleasures in life are connected with my work.

No (−)	42.7
Yes (+)	57.1
No response	0.2
Per cent total	100.0

Q. 18. I have sometimes regretted going into the kind of work I am now in.

No (+)	54.6
Yes (−)	44.8
No response	0.6
Per cent total	100.0

Q. 22. The work I do is one of the most satisfying parts of my life.

No (−)	47.6
Yes (+)	52.0
No response	0.4
Per cent total	100.0

Q. 28. I enjoy my spare-time activities much more than my work.

No (+)	44.3
Yes (−)	54.9
No response	0.8
Per cent total	100.0

Q. 32. To me, my work is just a way of making money.

No (+)	62.1
Yes (−)	37.8
No response	0.1
Per cent total	100.0

TABLE C-4

Correlational Matrix (r_t) and Estimates of First Factor Loadings

Question	1	6	10	12	16	18	22	28	32
1		.34	.51	.40	.36	.26	.43	.58	.53
6	.34		.33	.34	.43	.24	.48	.56	.39
10	.51	.33		.20	.48	.44	.60	.39	.56
12	.40	.34	.20		.29	.07	.23	.22	.08
16	.36	.43	.48	.29		.34	.78	.65	.71
18	.26	.24	.44	.07	.34		.50	.31	.44
22	.43	.48	.60	.23	.78	.50		.64	.75
28	.58	.56	.39	.22	.65	.31	.64		.73
32	.53	.39	.56	.08	.71	.44	.75	.73	
k_1	.66	.61	.68	.37	.79	.51	.86	.79	.81

Question 12 with a factor loading considerably below that of the other items was eliminated and an eight-item index was constructed.

Satisfaction with Husband's Work (Wives)

Five questions were asked to tap the extent of the wife's satisfaction with her husband's job. All statistics are based on 1,165 cases (+ = high satisfaction).

Question	Per Cent Total	Completely satisfied (+)	Very satisfied	Fairly satisfied	Dissatisfied (—)	No response or don't know
145. In general, how well satisfied are you with your husband's present job or work?	100.0	29.0	33.0	31.0	6.5	0.5
146. More wives are more satisfied with some things about their husband's job than they are with others. How satisfied are you, for example, with the steadiness of his work?	100.0	47.4	36.9	10.7	4.7	0.3

387

147. How do you feel
about his hours
and working con-
ditions? 99.9 31.2 27.0 25.1 16.3 0.3
148. How do you feel
about his chances
to get ahead in
his work? 100.0 25.3 34.0 31.2 9.1 0.4
149. And finally, how
satisfied are you
with his income? 100.0 16.3 33.6 40.5 9.2 0.4

TABLE C–5

Correlational Matrix (Product Moment) and Estimate of
First Factor Loadings

Question	145	146	147	148	149
145		.38	.40	.46	.67
146	.38		.23	.31	.26
147	.40	.23		.22	.16
148	.46	.31	.22		.51
149	.67	.26	.16	.51	
k_1	.82	.50	.45	.64	.72

All five items were retained for the index of wife's satisfaction with
husband's work.

FEELINGS OF ECONOMIC SECURITY (WIVES)

Six questions were asked of each wife to measure her feelings of
economic security. All statistics based on 1,165 cases ($+$ = high
security).

Q. 131. All in all, what kind of breaks do you feel you and your
husband are having financially? Very good, good, fair, or
not too good?

Very good ($+$)	21.9
Good	41.1
Fair	26.9
Not too good (or poor) ($-$)	10.1
Per cent total	100.0

Q. 132. Are there times when you feel you have to deny yourself many of the extras you want because of your income?

Yes (—)	62.1
No (+)	37.8
Not reported	0.2

Per cent total	100.1

Q. 133. Suppose you ran into an unexpected heavy expense. Do you feel that your income and savings are enough to handle it?

Yes (+)	50.0
Depends	10.8
No (—)	39.1
Not reported	0.1

Per cent total	100.0

Q. 134. In general, how would you describe your present financial situation? Would you say it is very good, good, fair or not too good?

Very good (+)	8.7
Good	39.7
Fair	39.8
Not too good (—) (or poor)	11.8

Per cent total	100.0

Q. 135. Are you ever faced with the possibility of your husband getting a large cut in income or being out of work for several months?

Yes (—)	18.5
No (+)	81.4
Not reported	0.2

Per cent total	100.1

Q. 136. On the whole, what would you say your financial future looks like? Very good, good, fair or not too good?

Very good (+)	21.2
Good	52.1
Fair	22.8
Not too good (—) (or poor)	3.0
Uncertain, don't know, depends	0.9

Per cent total	100.0

TABLE C–6

Correlational Matrix (r_t) and Estimates of First Factor Loadings

Question	131	132	133	134	135	136
131		.55	.52	.86	.29	.77
132	.55		.54	.58	.18	.49
133	.52	.54		.65	.14	.50
134	.86	.58	.65		.22	.76
135	.29	.18	.14	.22		.46
136	.77	.49	.50	.76	.46	
k_1	.88	.67	.68	.90	.40	.86

Five questions (eliminating question 135 because of its low loading) were retained for the wife's summary index of economic security.

FEELINGS OF ECONOMIC SECURITY (HUSBANDS)

There were seven questions included in the husband's questionnaire to assess the husband's feelings of economic security. All statistics based on 941 cases ($+$ = high security).

Q. 2. I feel that my wife and I have had very good financial breaks since we have been married.

No (−)	36.0
Yes (+)	63.8
No response	0.2
Per cent total	100.0

Q. 5. It is extremely important to me to have a higher income.

No (+)	37.9
Yes (−)	61.8
No response	0.3
Per cent total	100.0

Q. 13. I feel that my present financial situation is very good.

No (−)	61.3
Yes (+)	38.0
No response	0.7
Per cent total	100.0

Q. 20. On the whole, my financial future looks very good.

No (−)	27.2
Yes (+)	72.4
No response	0.4
Per cent total	100.0

390

Q. 24. There are many times when I have to deny myself and my
family things we would like because of our income.

No (+)	29.6
Yes (−)	70.4
No response	—
Per cent total	100.0

Q. 27. I worry sometimes about the possibility of a large cut in
income or being out of work for a while.

No (+)	51.2
Yes (−)	48.6
No response	0.2
Per cent total	100.0

Q. 30. In my present financial situation, I have to worry about
bills or debts.

No (+)	47.6
Yes (−)	52.1
No response	0.3
Per cent total	100.0

TABLE C–7

Correlational Matrix (r_t) and Estimates of First Factor Loadings

Question	2	5	13	20	24	27	30
2		.35	.75	.60	.55	.20	.50
5	.35		.32	.26	.34	.24	.33
13	.75	.32		.77	.56	.23	.56
20	.60	.26	.77		.55	.37	.49
24	.55	.34	.56	.55		.33	.60
27	.20	.24	.23	.37	.33		.31
30	.50	.33	.56	.49	.60	.31	
k_1	.78	.46	.83	.80	.74	.43	.71

Although eliminating questions 5 and 27 with lower loadings
increases the homogeneity of the set slightly, the increase is not
sufficient to counterbalance the advantage of the greater number of
items. A summary index of husband's feelings of economic security
was constructed from all seven items.

DRIVE TO GET AHEAD (WIVES)

Thirteen questions were included in the interview schedule to
measure the wife's drive to get ahead. A response of "Yes" is scored
as indicating high drive. All statistics are based on responses of
1,165 wives.

People feel differently about the importance of getting ahead in life. Some people would give up a lot in order to get ahead, while other people would feel that other things are more important and would not be willing to give them up. Please try to answer each of these questions either Yes or No.

Q. 154. For example, if getting ahead meant that you had to move to a strange part of the country, would you be willing to move?

Yes (+)	79.5
No (—)	20.3
Don't know	0.2
	___
Per cent total	100.0

Q. 155. Would you be willing to entertain people because they were connected with your husband's work, even though you might not like them?

Yes (+)	84.5
No (—)	15.4
Don't know	0.1
	___
Per cent total	100.0

Q. 156. Would you be willing to leave your friends?

Yes (+)	85.7
No (—)	14.2
No response	0.1
	___
Per cent total	100.0

Q. 157. In order to get ahead, would you be willing to become more active in community organizations and clubs not of your own choice?

Yes (+)	49.5
No (—)	50.3
Don't know	0.1
No response	0.1
	___
Per cent total	100.0

Q. 158. Would you be willing to leave your close relatives?

Yes (+)	78.7
No (—)	21.0
Don't know	0.2
No response	0.1
	___
Per cent total	100.0

Q. 159. Would you be willing to postpone having another child?

Yes (+)	67.0
No (−)	32.3
Don't know	0.4
No response	0.3
Per cent total	100.0

Q. 160. Would you be willing to keep quiet about your religious views in order to get ahead?

Yes (+)	27.2
No (−)	72.5
Don't know	0.1
No response	0.2
Per cent total	100.0

Q. 161. Would you be willing to have your husband take a chance on a job that he might be less certain of holding, if it had better opportunities?

Yes (+)	47.2
No (−)	52.1
Don't know	0.5
No response	0.2
Per cent total	100.0

Q. 162. Would you be willing to move to a less pleasant neighborhood temporarily?

Yes (+)	65.1
No (−)	34.9
Per cent total	100.0

Q. 163. Would you be willing to keep quiet about your political views in order to get ahead?

Yes (+)	63.0
No (−)	36.9
No response	0.1
Per cent total	100.0

Q. 164. Would you be willing to live temporarily in less desirable housing?

Yes (+)	63.6
No (−)	36.3
No response	0.1
Per cent total	100.0

Q. 165. If getting ahead meant that you would see less of your
husband because he would spend more time at work, would
you be willing to do this?

Yes (+)	66.9
No (−)	33.0
Don't know	0.1
Per cent total	100.0

Q. 166. And finally, if getting ahead meant you might have to send
your children to another school not quite as good, would
you be willing?

Yes (+)	36.2
No (−)	63.4
Don't know	0.3
No response	0.1
Per cent total	100.0

The item intercorrelations in Table 8 reveal several patterns. In
general, there is a significant level of intercorrelation among all of
the items. However, the fact that the average correlational value is
far from unity and the existence of four clusters of items which
correlate internally at very high levels indicate the presence of more
than one factor.

TABLE C–8

Correlational Matrix (r_t) and Estimates of First Factor Loadings

Question	154	155	156	157	158	159	160	161	162	163	164	165	166
154		.25	.86	.24	.88	.18	.26	.27	.44	.17	.37	.34	.30
155	.25		.41	.70	.31	.28	.28	.23	.33	.36	.24	.35	.29
156	.86	.41		.44	.87	.32	.24	.32	.52	.22	.44	.41	.37
157	.24	.70	.44		.27	.22	.34	.27	.27	.32	.29	.31	.29
158	.88	.31	.87	.27		.22	.21	.31	.43	.20	.41	.26	.41
159	.18	.28	.32	.22	.22		.54	.08	.25	.31	.13	.23	.24
160	.26	.28	.24	.34	.21	.54		.23	.24	.82	.27	.25	.20
161	.27	.23	.32	.27	.31	.08	.23		.34	.20	.38	.19	.20
162	.44	.33	.52	.27	.43	.25	.24	.34		.22	.82	.25	.43
163	.17	.36	.22	.32	.20	.31	.82	.20	.22		.23	.28	.18
164	.37	.24	.44	.29	.41	.13	.27	.38	.82	.23		.24	.48
165	.34	.35	.41	.31	.26	.23	.25	.19	.25	.28	.24		.42
166	.30	.29	.37	.29	.41	.24	.25	.20	.43	.18	.48	.42	
k_1	.69	.60	.80	.59	.72	.45	.61	.43	.68	.55	.65	.50	.55

These clusters are:

Cluster I: Q. 154 (move to strange part of the country); Q. 156 (willing to leave friends); Q. 158 (willing to leave close relatives); average intercorrelations is .87.

Cluster II: Q. 155 (willing to entertain people) and Q. 157 (become more active in organizations); intercorrelate at .70.

Cluster III: Q. 162 (move to less pleasant neighborhood) and Q. 164 (live in less desirable housing); intercorrelate at .82.

Cluster IV: Q. 160 (keep quiet about religious views) and Q. 163 (keep quiet about political views); intercorrelate at .82.

A face examination of the content of each of these clusters lends confidence to the meaning of the high intercorrelations. They are four specific homogeneous subsets of values having empirically defined valences on the general dimension of the "drive to get ahead." The fact that these four clusters incorporate 9 of the 13 items, thus leaving 4 items which do not fall into any clusters, is largely fortuitous. There is no theoretical reason why the remaining 4 items would not have clustered as did the other 9, if the schedule had included additional questions in similar subcontent areas. The chief implication of this imbalance is that any summary score which includes all 13 items weighted equally would disproportionately emphasize the subcontent areas in which more than a single question was asked.

A summary index of eight items (Questions 156, 157, 159–162, 165, and 166) was finally developed after eliminating items involved in redundancies.

Drive to Get Ahead (Husbands)

As in the interview with the wife, the questionnaire for the husband also included thirteen questions. Some are similar or identical in content, others are different. Moreover, the frame of reference set for the husband emphasizes work as well as life in general.

A response of "yes" is scored as a high drive to get ahead. All statistics are based on 941 cases.

Men feel differently about the importance of getting ahead in work and in life generally. Some men would give up a lot in order to get ahead while other men would feel that other things are more important and would not be willing to give them up.

395

Q. 34. For example, if getting ahead meant that you would have to go without any vacation for several years, would you be willing to do this?

No (—)	25.6
Yes (+)	74.2
No response	0.2
Per cent total	100.0

Q. 35. Would you be willing to leave your friends in order to get ahead?

No (—)	23.9
Yes (+)	75.7
No response	0.4
Per cent total	100.0

Q. 36. If getting ahead meant that you would have to live in an undesirable neighborhood temporarily, would you be willing?

No (—)	45.6
Yes (+)	54.1
No response	0.3
Per cent total	100.0

Q. 37. Would you be willing to give up your leisure time in order to get ahead?

No (—)	23.7
Yes (+)	76.1
No response	0.2
Per cent total	100.0

Q. 38. Would you be willing to postpone having another child in order to get ahead?

No (—)	46.4
Yes (+)	53.0
No response	0.6
Per cent total	100.0

Q. 39. To get ahead, would you be willing to move your family to a strange part of the country?

No (—)	26.4
Yes (+)	73.4
No response	0.2
Per cent total	100.0

Q. 40. Would you be willing to do less interesting or less enjoyable work, in order to get ahead?

No (—)	55.2
Yes (+)	44.5
No response	0.3
Per cent total	100.0

Q. 41. If it meant not seeing your wife and children as much as you would like, would you be willing?

No (—)	71.2
Yes (+)	28.5
No response	0.3
Per cent total	100.0

Q. 42. Would you be willing to take some risk to your health in order to get ahead?

No (—)	83.2
Yes (+)	16.2
No response	0.6
Per cent total	100.0

Q. 43. Would you be willing to keep quiet about your political views in order to get ahead?

No (—)	49.1
Yes (+)	50.5
No response	0.6
Per cent total	100.0

Q. 44. Would you be willing to take a chance on a job that you might be less certain of holding, if it had better opportunities?

No (—)	49.7
Yes (+)	49.7
No response	0.6
Per cent total	100.0

Q. 45. If getting ahead meant you might have to send your children to another school not quite as good, would you be willing?

No (—)	73.9
Yes (+)	25.7
No response	0.4
Per cent total	100.0

Q. 46. And finally, if getting ahead meant that you would have to keep quiet about your religious views, would you be willing?

No (—)	74.3
Yes (+)	25.3
No response	0.4
Per cent total	100.0

The intercorrelations among the thirteen items are shown in Table 9. In general, the same results are apparent as were observed in the analysis of the wives' responses. There is a certain advantage to this since it contributes to greater comparability of the two resulting eight-item indices.

TABLE C-9

Correlational Matrix (r_t) and Estimates of First Factor Loadings

Question	34*	35*	36*	37	38*	39	40	41*	42*	43	44	45*	46*
34		.37	.33	.68	.32	.18	.36	.44	.29	.22	.05	.19	.06
35	.37		.47	.31	.43	.70	.35	.42	.19	.29	.21	.49	.37
36	.33	.47		.29	.23	.44	.29	.44	.34	.27	.24	.52	.28
37	.68	.31	.29		.34	.28	.25	.52	.34	.16	−.06	.17	.12
38	.32	.43	.23	.34		.33	.22	.42	.16	.34	.06	.29	.45
39	.18	.70	.44	.28	.33		.28	.51	.29	.28	.31	.43	.25
40	.36	.35	.29	.25	.22	.28		.39	.30	.29	.15	.30	.23
41	.44	.42	.44	.52	.42	.51	.39		.49	.27	.19	.38	.34
42	.29	.19	.34	.34	.16	.29	.30	.49		.32	.33	.34	.31
43	.22	.29	.27	.16	.34	.28	.29	.27	.32		.11	.44	.85
44	.05	.21	.24	−.06	.06	.31	.15	.19	.33	.11		.26	.17
45	.19	.49	.52	.17	.29	.43	.30	.38	.34	.44	.26		.46
46	.06	.37	.28	.12	.45	.25	.23	.34	.31	.85	.17	.46	
k_1	.55	.70	.62	.56	.52	.66	.50	.71	.55	.62	.31	.64	.63

NOTE: Asterisks indicate items retained for index.

The eight (*) items retained for the summary index were selected mainly for the same reasons advanced in the preceding description of the index constructed for the wife's "drive to get ahead." Single items in highly homogeneous clusters were retained with preference given to those revealing highest loadings on the first factor.

IMPORTANCE OF GETTING AHEAD (HUSBANDS)

There were eight questions included in the questionnaire which purport to measure the degree of importance that the husband attaches to getting ahead in life. In the pretest, this variable turned out to be more a measure of felt deprivation—men who had not been successful in their work were more likely to attach greater significance to the importance of "getting ahead" than men whose aspiration-achievement ratio was in closer balance. These questions are not conceived to be independent of "drive to get ahead," but rather represent another approach to the measurement of the same general aspirational dimension.

A plus sign indicates a high level of importance attached to getting ahead. All statistics based on 941 cases.

Q. 3. I feel that the most important thing about work is the chance it offers to get ahead.

No (−)	42.9
Yes (+)	57.0
No response	0.1
Per cent total	100.0

Q. 7. I spend a lot of time thinking about how to improve my chances for getting ahead.

No (−)	28.5
Yes (+)	71.4
No response	0.1
Per cent total	100.0

Q. 9. Getting money and material things out of life is very important to me.

No (−)	46.7
Yes (+)	52.9
No response	0.4
Per cent total	100.0

Q. 17. It is important to me to own material things, such as a home, car, or clothing, which are at least as good as those of my neighbors and friends.

No (−)	52.9
Yes (+)	47.1
No response	—
Per cent total	100.0

Q. 21. I am very anxious to get much further ahead.

No (−)	21.9
Yes (+)	77.9
No response	0.2
Per cent total	100.0

Q. 26. Getting ahead is one of the most important things in life to me.

No (−)	41.9
Yes (+)	57.4
No response	0.7
Per cent total	100.0

Q. 31. It is quite important to me that my children marry persons of at least equal social standing.

No (−)	45.3
Yes (+)	54.4
No response	0.3
Per cent total	100.0

Q. 33. The most important qualities of a real man are determination and ambition.

No (−)	49.1
Yes (+)	50.6
No response	0.3
Per cent total	100.0

The intercorrelations of these eight items and their loadings on the first general factor are presented in Table 10. One question, Q. 31, was eliminated because of its low correlation with the general factor.

TABLE C–10

Correlational Matrix (r_t) and Estimates of First Factor Loadings

Question	3	7	9	17	21	26	31	33
3		.42	.24	.19	.45	.41	.08	.48
7	.42		.32	.11	.70	.55	.02	.27
9	.24	.32		.48	.48	.51	.18	.27
17	.19	.11	.48		.27	.36	.38	.17
21	.45	.70	.48	.27		.75	.15	.39
26	.41	.55	.51	.36	.75		.24	.37
31	.08	.02	.18	.39	.15	.24		.24
33	.48	.27	.22	.17	.39	.37	.24	
k_1	.58	.65	.62	.52	.83	.83	.35	.56

ASPIRATIONS FOR CHILDREN'S COLLEGE EDUCATION (WIVES)

There are four questions in the interview schedule designed to measure the mother's aspirations for her children's higher education.

400

Two of these questions are open-ended and two are multiple choice. All statistics are based on 1,165 cases. A plus sign indicates high aspirations.

Q. 150. Do you *expect* to send your children to college?

Yes (unqualified) (+)	57.0
Depends on children	15.5
Hope to; like to	12.0
Expect or like to send son	3.4
Expect or like to send son, but not daughter	2.0
If can afford; depends on finances	2.2
Depends both on children and finances	1.3
Other responses and other combinations	0.3
Don't know; haven't thought about it	0.5
No; probably not (−)	5.8
Per cent total	100.0

Q. 151. How do you expect this college education to be paid for?

Specific steps already taken or in process (+)	21.6
(Includes investment and educational annuity programs)	
Specific steps planned but not yet taken	11.7
Specific provision in existence but without explicit indication of educational purpose	40.7
(Includes savings, insurance, income, wife working)	
Expected windfalls	10.0
Hopes vague plans	6.3
Don't know, haven't thought about it (−)	3.0
Not reported	0.4
No answer necessary ("No" or "Don't know" to Q. 150)	6.3
Per cent total	100.0

Q. 152. Would you send a *daughter* of yours to college even if it meant serious financial hardship?

Yes (+)	40.9
Depends or don't know	15.1
No (−)	38.1
Not reported	0.2
No answer necessary ("No" to Q. 150)	5.8
Per cent total	100.1

Q. 153. Would you send a *son* of yours to college even if it meant serious financial hardship?

Yes (+)	71.5
Depends or don't know	9.5
No (−)	13.0
Not reported	0.3
No answer necessary ("No" to Q. 150)	5.8
	———
Per cent total	100.1

The four items revealed low but positive intercorrelations (see Table 11). In the correlation analysis, Q. 150 was ordered by the first two response categories and all remaining responses; Q. 151 permitted five categories (grouping below but including "Hopes, vague plans") and Questions 152 and 153 permitted three categories.

TABLE C–11

Correlational Matrix (Product Moment)

Question	150	151	152	153
150		.30	.24	.26
151	.30		.16	.26
152	.24	.16		.54
153	.26	.26	.54	

The cross-tabulation of Questions 152 and 153 reveal an almost perfect scale relationship: only two mothers said "Yes" to the question about sending a daughter to college under serious financial hardship (Q. 152) and "No" to the following question about a son. The following scale classifications were finally developed:

Score	Category	Numerical Distribution
1	Do not expect to send children to college	67
	If it meant serious financial hardship:	
2	wouldn't send either son or daughter	148
3	not send daughter; depends or don't know for son	43
4	depends or don't know for both	74
5	not send daughter; send son	253
6	depends or don't know for daughter; send son	106
7	would send both	474
		———
		1,165

Marital Adjustment (Wives)

There are five questions in the schedule designed to measure marital adjustment. Question 122 is open-ended; the rest are multiple choice. All statistics are based on 1,165 cases. A plus sign indicates good adjustment.

Q. 121. How often do you and your husband have different opinions about the best way to raise or handle the children?

Often (−)	4.6
Sometimes	16.7
Once in a while	43.9
Hardly ever (never) (+)	34.8
Per cent total	100.0

Q. 122. When you get upset about having to take care of the house and the children, is your husband as sympathetic as you would like him to be?

Unqualified Yes (+)	55.5
Qualified Yes; most of the time; ordinarily; guess so; think so	7.5
Neutral: sometimes he is; sometimes he isn't; depends on his mood; not always	1.6
Qualified No; usually no; no, but sometimes he is	3.7
Unqualified No (−)	31.8
Other	
Don't know; can't say; "I don't get upset"	
Not reported	
Per cent total	100.1

Q. 123. In general, compared to most couples you know, how well do you and your husband get along with each other?

Much better (+)	31.9
Somewhat better	27.5
About the same	39.2
Not as well as most (−)	1.4
Per cent total	100.0

Q. 124. Have you ever wished you were not married?

Fairly often (−)	1.6
Occasionally	13.4
Once or twice	27.6
Never (+)	57.3
Per cent total	99.9

Q. 125. Everything considered, how happy has your marriage been?

Extremely happy (+)	36.3
Happier than average	37.0
Average	25.4
Not too happy (−)	1.3
	———
Per cent total	100.0

TABLE C–12

Correlational Matrix (r_t) and Estimates of First Factor Loadings

Question	121	122	123	124	125
121		.08	.19	.18	.24
122	.08		.28	.33	.31
123	.19	.28		.27	.55
124	.18	.33	.27		.51
125	.24	.31	.55	.51	
k_1	.33	.47	.65	.63	.76

Items 123, 124, and 125 were retained for the index. Items 121, 122 were eliminated by reason of their low loadings.

LIKING FOR CHILDREN (WIVES)

There are six items in the schedule designed to measure liking for children. All items have four response categories and except for one item, Question 113, the contents of the items are ordered from negative to positive. All statistics based on 1,165 cases.

Question	Per Cent Total	Less than Most (1)	About the same as Most (2)	Some-what more than Most (3)	Much More than Most (4)
109. Compared to other things you like to do that are not mainly connected with children, how much do you like to read or talk to children?	99.9	9.5	55.3	26.8	8.3

110. Again, compared to other things you like to do, how much do you like looking at pictures of children in ads, store windows, or magazines? 99.9 15.9 46.1 27.3 10.6

111. And, how much do you like showing children new places to go and new things to do? 100.0 3.1 30.8 39.6 26.5

112. How much do you like seeing movies or plays about children, or reading stories about them? 100.0 12.9 47.0 28.1 12.0

113. Compared to other chores, like housekeeping work and things like that, how much do you mind straightening up after children? 100.0 26.8 61.3 8.7 3.2

114. All in all, in comparison to your other interests, how interested are you in spending time with children? 100.0 3.7 32.4 38.9 25.0

TABLE C–13

Correlational Matrix (r_t) and Estimates of First Factor Loadings

Question	109	110	111	112	113	114
109		.38	.46	.32	−.03	.61
110	.38		.49	.48	.04	.35
111	.46	.49		.48	.01	.44
112	.32	.48	.48		.11	.38
113	−.03	.04	.01	.11		−.02
114	.61	.35	.44	.38	−.02	
k_1	.69	.65	.69	.66	.06	.69

Question 113 obviously does not belong to the group and was eliminated from the index.

DOMINANCE PATTERNS (WIVES)

There are six trichotomous items included in the interview schedule designed to measure the dominance pattern between husband and wife in selected areas of decision making. All statistics based on 1,165 cases.

Question	Per Cent Total	I Have Most Say	Both 50/50	Husband Has Most Say	No Response Don't Know
115. In some families the father makes the main decisions about the children, in others he leaves it all to the mother. When it's about the children, who has the most say in your family, you or your husband?	100.0	44.2	49.2	6.6	–
116. Which of you has the most say about other things not mainly connected with the children?	100.0	13.1	59.8	27.1	–
117. Who has the most say about which friends you see most often?	100.1	19.0	68.7	12.3	0.1
118. .... and the most say about what you do together for recreation?	100.0	13.3	73.4	13.1	0.2
119. Which of you has the most say about how to spend the family income?	100.0	25.3	53.0	21.7	–
120. And finally, who has the most say about running the house?	100.0	77.0	19.9	3.1	–

Inspection of the cross-tabulations indicated non-isotropic contingency tables. Evidence of non-isotropy limits measurement to some type of nominal scale. Three such scales were developed, each representing a particular area of husband-wife decision making. These are described in Table C–14.

TABLE C–14

Scale Classifications

SCALE SCORE	CATEGORY	NUMERICAL DISTRIBUTION		
		Home Questions 115, 120	*Social Life* Questions 117, 118	*Nonsocial Areas* Questions 116, 119
1	Husband dominant in both responses	10	65	146
2	Each dominates one	69	46	55
3	Husband dominates and 50/50	24	118	223
4	50/50 on both	151	687	445
5	Wife dominates and 50/50	481	185	199
6	Wife dominant in both responses	430	84	97
	Total	1,165	1,165	1,165

PATTERNS OF HELP AVAILABLE TO WIFE (WIVES)

Four items were included in the interview schedule to assess the degree of help with the children and the house which is perceived by the wife to be available to her. A plus sign indicates perception of adequate help. All statistics are based on 1,165 cases.

Question	Per Cent Total	Almost Any Time (+)	Usually	Only some of the Time	Hardly Ever (−)
101. How often can you count on someone to take care of the children?	100.0	47.9	17.4	20.0	14.7
102. How often can you count on your husband to take care of the children?	100.0	49.4	18.2	17.7	14.7

Question	Per Cent Total	Very Often	Often	Some- times	Hardly Ever
103. How often can you count on someone other than your husband to help you around the house?	100.1	15.8	16.7	26.1	41.5

Question	Per Cent Total	Com- pletely Satis- fied	Very satis- fied	Some- what Satis- fied	Dissatis- fied
104. On the whole, do you feel satisfied with the amount of freedom you have away from the children?	100.0	25.1	29.6	35.9	9.4

TABLE C–15

Correlational Matrix (r_t) and Estimates of First Factor Loadings

Question	101	102	103	104
101		.20	.37	.43
102	.20		.05	.31
103	.37	.05		.47
104	.43	.31	.47	
k_1	.62	.38	.59	.73

Question 102 was eliminated and the remaining three items combined in a summary index.

GENERALIZED MANIFEST ANXIETY (WIVES)

There are nine dichotomous items measuring anxiety. A plus sign indicates high anxiety. All statistics based on 961 cases.

Q. 8. Are your nerves sometimes "on edge" so that particular sounds, such as a screechy hinge, are unbearable and "give you shivers?"

No (−)	38.2
Yes (+)	61.8
	———
Per cent total	100.0

Q. 19. Do you frequently get into a state of tension and turmoil by thinking over the day's happenings?

No (−)	56.3
Yes (+)	43.7
	———
Per cent total	100.0

Q. 30. Do you consider yourself a rather nervous person?

No (−)	50.8
Yes (+)	49.2
	———
Per cent total	100.0

Q. 41. Do you tend to get over-excited and easily "rattled" in exciting situations?

No (−)	49.6
Yes (+)	50.4
Per cent total	100.0

Q. 52. Do you worry, tremble, and perspire when you have some difficult task ahead?

No (−)	58.5
Yes (+)	41.5
Per cent total	100.0

Q. 63. Do you sometimes awaken in the night and, through worrying, have difficulty in going to sleep again?

No (−)	57.8
Yes (+)	42.2
Per cent total	100.0

Q. 74. Are you inclined to worry, without any reason for doing so?

No (−)	56.1
Yes (+)	43.9
Per cent total	100.0

Q. 82. Do you often have fits of "jitters" with trembling or sweating for no good reason?

No (−)	88.8
Yes (+)	11.2
Per cent total	100.0

Q. 89. Do certain small things get on your nerves even though you know they're not important?

No (−)	24.3
Yes (+)	75.7
Per cent total	100.0

TABLE C–16

Correlational Matrix (r_t) and Estimates of First Factor Loadings

Question	8	19	30	41	52	63	74	82	89
8		.46	.44	.24	.44	.36	.35	.62	.39
19	.46		.48	.40	.57	.44	.53	.63	.55
30	.44	.48		.52	.50	.42	.59	.69	.56
41	.24	.40	.52		.43	.29	.47	.55	.42
52	.44	.57	.50	.43		.51	.55	.73	.49
63	.36	.44	.42	.29	.51		.47	.65	.36
74	.35	.53	.59	.47	.55	.47		.70	.63
82	.62	.63	.69	.55	.73	.65	.70		.77
89	.39	.55	.56	.42	.49	.36	.63	.77	
k_1	.60	.72	.75	.59	.76	.64	.76	.94	.76

All items appear worthy of inclusion in an index measuring manifest anxiety. Item 82 was eliminated in keeping with the eight item restriction and the criterion of extreme marginals.

AMBIGUITY TOLERANCE (WIVES)

Eight items were included in the wife's questionnaire to measure her tolerance for ambiguity. A plus sign indicates high tolerance. All statistics are based on 961 cases.

Q. 11. Do you find it nearly impossible to get along with someone who is always changing his mind?

No (+)	54.1
Yes (−)	45.6
No response	0.3
Per cent total	100.0

Q. 22. Would our thinking be a lot better off if we would just forget about words like "probably," "approximately," and "perhaps"?

No (+)	58.1
Yes (−)	41.0
No response	0.9
Per cent total	100.0

Q. 33. Do people who seem unsure and uncertain about things make you feel uncomfortable?

No (+)	49.8
Yes (−)	49.5
No response	0.6
Per cent total	99.9

Q. 44. Do you like to have a place for everything and everything in its place?

No (+)	11.7
Yes (−)	88.3
Per cent total	100.0

Q. 55. Are you in favor of a very strict enforcement of all laws, no matter what the consequence?

No (+)	59.3
Yes (−)	40.4
No response	0.2
Per cent total	99.9

Q. 66. Do you like to keep regular hours and to run your life according to an established routine?

No (+)	35.6
Yes (−)	64.2
No response	0.2
Per cent total	100.0

Q. 77. Do you usually become upset when your daily routines are disrupted by some unexpected event?

No (+)	57.5
Yes (−)	42.2
No response	0.2
Per cent total	99.9

Q. 85. Do you mind things being uncertain and unpredictable?

No (+)	41.8
Yes (−)	57.6
No response	0.5
Per cent total	99.9

TABLE C–17

Correlational Matrix (r_t) and Estimates of First Factor Loadings

Question	11	22	33	44	55	66	77	85
11		.13	.38	.14	.04	.07	.20	.12
22	.13		.12	.14	.15	.06	.15	.03
33	.38	.12		.16	.03	.13	.22	.12
44	.14	.14	.16		.40	.54	.51	.34
55	.04	.15	.03	.40		.09	.08	.02
66	.07	.06	.13	.54	.09		.33	.28
77	.20	.15	.22	.51	.08	.33		.32
85	.12	.03	.12	.34	.02	.28	.32	
k_1	.39	.25	.41	.74	.32	.55	.62	.42

The items retained for the index are Questions 44, 66, 77, and 85.

IMPULSE GRATIFICATION (WIVES)

Ten items were originally included. A plus sign indicates high impulse gratification. All statistics are based on 961 cases.

Q. 2. In spite of other drawbacks, would you prefer the kind of job that offers change, travel, and variety?

No (—)	50.1
Yes (+)	49.4
No response	0.5
Per cent total	100.0

Q. 13. Which is your motto? To take matters of everyday life with proper seriousness, or to laugh and be merry?

Serious (—)	75.4
Laugh (+)	24.0
No response	0.5
Per cent total	99.9

Q. 24. Do you find that your interests tend to be pretty much the same from day to day and month to month?

No (+)	16.5
Yes (—)	83.2
No response	0.2
Per cent total	99.9

Q. 35. Do you go out of your way to see that you have a good time?

No (—)	72.2
Yes (+)	27.7
No response	0.1
Per cent total	100.0

Q. 46. When you are bored do you like to be quiet for a while?

No (—)	47.6
Yes (+)	52.2
No response	0.2
Per cent total	100.0

Q. 57. Are you always looking for new things to do or see or hear?

No (—)	37.7
Yes (+)	62.3
No response	—
Per cent total	100.0

Q. 68. Do you often act on the spur of the moment without stopping to think?

No (—)	38.7
Yes (+)	60.8
No response	0.5
Per cent total	100.0

Q. 78. Are you one of those who drink or smoke more than they know they should?

No (−)	85.7
Yes (+)	13.8
No response	0.4
Per cent total	99.9

Q. 86. Do you cry rather easily?

No (−)	40.6
Yes (+)	59.2
No response	0.2
Per cent total	100.0

Q. 90. Is it important to you that your life be full of change and variety?

No (−)	67.9
Yes (+)	31.5
No response	0.5
Per cent total	99.9

TABLE C–18

Correlational Matrix (r_t) and Estimates of First Factor Loadings

Question	2	13	24	35	46	57	68	78	86	90
2		.10	.08	.17	.07	.27	.14	.23	.10	.41
13	.10		.14	.22	.05	.08	.23	.00	.08	.02
24	.08	.14		.00	.02	.24	.17	.14	.11	.30
35	.17	.22	.00		.02	.37	.13	.12	.12	.28
46	.07	.05	.02	.02		−.02	−.02	.16	.01	.10
57	.27	.08	.24	.37	−.02		.18	.03	.19	.55
68	.14	.23	.17	.13	−.02	.18		.06	.25	.17
78	.23	.00	.14	.12	.16	.03	.06		−.06	.21
86	.10	.08	.11	.12	.01	.19	.25	−.06		.11
90	.41	.02	.30	.28	.10	.55	.17	.21	.11	
k_1	.50	.29	.37	.45	.14	.61	.39	.29	.31	.67

The items retained for the index are Questions 2, 35, 57, 68, 90.

NEED ACHIEVEMENT (WIVES)

Eight items were included to measure the wife's need to achieve. A plus sign indicates a high need for achievement. All statistics are based on 961 cases.

Q. 9. Can you always be counted on to try to do your job regardless of how hopeless it may be?

No (−)	14.5
Yes (+)	85.1
No response	0.4
Per cent total	100.0

Q. 20. Which do you do? Just what comes along as most of the crowd does *or* set yourself a goal of attainment that is quite hard?

Crowd (−)	61.8
Hard (+)	37.8
No response	0.4
Per cent total	100.0

Q. 31. How do failures usually affect you? Discourage you from going on in that line of work *or* spur you to new efforts?

Discourage (−)	37.0
Spur (+)	62.0
No response	0.9
Per cent total	99.9

Q. 42. Do you usually like work that requires accuracy in fine detail?

No (−)	46.9
Yes (+)	53.0
No response	0.1
Per cent total	100.0

Q. 53. Are you a person who generally "sticks to it" when faced by unpleasant obstacles?

No (−)	15.3
Yes (+)	84.1
No response	0.6
Per cent total	100.0

Q. 64. What kinds of goals do you usually set for yourself? Low enough so that you can reach them without too much effort *or* too high for you to reach without a lot of effort?

Low (−)	55.4
Too high (+)	43.2
No response	0.4
Per cent total	100.0

Q. 75. Do you avoid work requiring patience and carefulness?

No (+)	83.9
Yes (−)	15.9
No response	0.2
Per cent total	100.0

Q. 83. Is it important to you to make good use of every minute of your time?

No (−)	57.3
Yes (+)	42.4
No response	0.3
Per cent total	100.0

TABLE C-19

Correlational Matrix (r_t) and Estimates of First Factor Loadings

Question	9	20	31	42	53	64	75	83
9		.31	.31	.19	.51	.17	.34	.33
20	.31		.27	.27	.44	.52	.15	.30
31	.31	.27		.23	.50	.21	.44	.07
42	.19	.27	.23		.24	.25	.58	.24
53	.51	.44	.50	.24		.30	.41	.23
64	.17	.52	.21	.25	.30		.21	.20
75	.34	.15	.44	.58	.41	.21		.04
83	.33	.30	.07	.24	.23	.20	.04	
k_1	.59	.61	.56	.57	.69	.52	.61	.38

The items retained for the index are Questions 9, 20, 31, 42, 53, 64, and 75.

NURTURANCE NEEDS (WIVES)

Eight items were included to measure nurturance needs. A plus sign indicates high needs. All statistics are based on 961 cases.

Q. 10. I like to do small favors for my friends *or* I like to make a plan before starting in to do something difficult.

Do favors (+)	70.7
Plan (−)	28.0
No response	1.4
Per cent total	100.1

Q. 21. I like to treat other people with kindness and sympathy *or* I like to travel and see the country.

Kindness (+)	72.1
Travel (−)	27.0
No response	0.9
	────
Per cent total	100.0

Q. 32. I like to help other people who are less fortunate than I am *or* I like to finish any job or task that I begin.

Help people (+)	47.2
Finish job (−)	51.5
No response	1.2
	────
Per cent total	99.9

Q. 43. I like to help my friends when they are in trouble *or* I like to do my very best in whatever I undertake.

Help friends (+)	58.7
Do best (−)	39.9
No response	1.5
	────
Per cent total	100.1

Q. 54. I like to show a great deal of affection toward my friends *or* I like to say things that are regarded as witty and clever by other people.

Show affection (+)	68.5
Be witty (−)	30.1
No response	1.5
	────
Per cent total	100.1

Q. 65. Are you more likely to blame people for their misfortunes than sympathize with them?

No (+)	81.0
Yes (−)	18.8
No response	0.2
	────
Per cent total	100.0

Q. 76. Do you often go out of your way to comfort people who are unhappy?

No (−)	30.3
Yes (+)	69.4
No response	0.3
	────
Per cent total	100.0

Q. 84. Do you feel that it is important for people to marry only for love?

No (−)	39.1
Yes (+)	60.1
No response	0.7
Per cent total	99.9

TABLE C–20

Correlational Matrix (r_t) and Estimates of First Factor Loadings

Question	10	21	32	43	54	65	76	84
10		.19	.40	.28	.17	.18	.31	.04
21	.19		.22	.16	.24	.33	.25	.02
32	.40	.22		.46	.12	.25	.24	.06
43	.28	.16	.46		.12	.31	.19	.01
54	.17	.24	.12	.12		.23	.32	.11
65	.18	.33	.25	.31	.23		.30	.13
76	.31	.25	.24	.19	.32	.30		.22
84	.04	.02	.06	.01	.11	.13	.22	
k_1	.52	.45	.58	.52	.43	.54	.56	.21

Question 84 was the only item rejected for inclusion in this index.

WORK ALONE PREFERENCE (WIVES)

Seven items were included to measure the wife's preference for doing things by herself as opposed to with other people. A plus sign indicates a preference for working alone. All statistics are based on 961 cases.

Q. 7. Do you like working alone?

No (−)	47.7
Yes (+)	51.7
No response	0.6
Per cent total	100.0

Q. 18. How can you usually solve a problem better? By studying it alone *or* by discussing it with others?

Studying (+)	25.6
Discussing (−)	74.3
No response	0.1
Per cent total	100.0

Q. 29. If you have to learn about something, how would you rather do it? By group discussion *or* by reading a book on the subject in your own time?

Discussion (−)	53.4
Reading (+)	45.9
No response	0.7
Per cent total	100.0

Q. 40. Does it help you to discuss a problem with others before coming to a decision?

No (+)	12.7
Yes (−)	87.0
No response	0.3
Per cent total	100.0

Q. 51. When you must make a number of decisions in a short time, how would you rather make them? Alone *or* with the help of others?

Alone (+)	50.7
Help of others (−)	49.3
Per cent total	100.0

Q. 62. Do you like to do your planning alone, without suggestions from or discussions with other people?

No (−)	68.6
Yes (+)	31.2
No response	0.2
Per cent total	100.0

Q. 73. Do you enjoy working by yourself more than cooperating with others?

No (−)	68.6
Yes (+)	30.6
No response	0.7
Per cent total	100.0

TABLE C–21

Correlational Matrix (r_t) and Estimates of First Factor Loadings

Question	7	18	29	40	51	62	73
7		.25	.22	.22	.16	.24	.62
18	.25		.40	.80	.49	.61	.29
29	.22	.40		.56	.28	.33	.33
40	.22	.80	.56		.66	.62	.18
51	.16	.49	.28	.66		.56	.05
62	.24	.61	.33	.62	.56		.34
73	.62	.29	.33	.18	.05	.34	
k_1	.51	.80	.54	.82	.63	.73	.53

All items were retained for the Index.

SELF-AWARENESS (WIVES)

Ten items were included to measure self-awareness. A plus sign indicates high self-awareness. All statistics are based on 961 cases.

Q. 4. When you make a slip-of-the-tongue do you always notice it yourself?

No (−)	30.2
Yes (+)	69.7
No response	0.1
Per cent total	100.0

Q. 15. When you do something do you always know just why you have done it?

No (−)	65.5
Yes (+)	34.6
Per cent total	100.1

Q. 26. Do you sometimes think you would be happier if you were an animal?

No (+)	95.4
Yes (−)	4.2
No response	0.4
Per cent total	100.0

Q. 37. Are you always aware of what you are doing?

No (−)	40.6
Yes (+)	59.4
Per cent total	100.0

Q. 48. Do you sometimes have thoughts or do things that really surprise you?

No (+)	28.9
Yes (−)	70.9
No response	0.2
Per cent total	100.0

Q. 59. Are you often troubled by guilt or remorse over somewhat unimportant matters?

No (+)	53.0
Yes (−)	46.4
No response	0.6
Per cent total	100.0

Q. 70. Do you find it interesting to think about the reasons why you do certain things?

No (−)	22.2
Yes (+)	77.2
No response	0.6
	———
Per cent total	100.0

Q. 80. Do you think if you really tried that you could deceive a lie detector machine?

No (−)	94.0
Yes (+)	5.6
No response	0.4
	———
Per cent total	100.0

Q. 88. Does it take you a long time to get over being upset after something has gone wrong?

No (+)	66.5
Yes (−)	33.5
	———
Per cent total	100.0

Q. 91. Do you feel that you understand yourself better than most people understand themselves?

No (−)	56.0
Yes (+)	43.5
No response	0.5
	———
Per cent total	100.0

TABLE C–22

Correlational Matrix (r_t) and Estimates of First Factor Loadings

Question	4	15	26	37	48	59	70	80	88	90
4		.30	.17	.22	.12	.02	−.18	−.02	.02	.07
15	.30		.18	.60	.42	.21	.06	.08	−.02	.29
26	.17	.18		.23	.49	.38	.04	.04	.24	−.02
37	.22	.60	.23		.43	.28	.07	.27	.23	.22
48	.12	.42	.49	.43		.26	.27	−.06	.25	.01
59	.02	.21	.38	.28	.26		.04	−.04	.42	.09
70	−.18	.06	.04	.07	.27	.04		−.00	.02	−.10
80	−.02	.08	.04	.27	−.06	−.04	−.00		−.19	.37
88	.02	−.02	.24	.23	.25	.42	.02	−.19		.04
90	.07	.29	−.02	.22	.01	.09	−.10	.37	.04	
k_1	.24	.64	.53	.74	.63	.49	.12	.19	.34	.32

Items retained for the summary index were Questions 15, 26, 37, 48, and 59. The marginal distribution for Question 26 is very extreme, but it was retained, nevertheless, in view of the number of items eliminated.

Compulsiveness (Wives)

Seven items were initially included to measure compulsiveness. A plus sign indicates high compulsiveness. All statistics are based on 961 cases.

Q. 6. Do you sometimes go out of your way to save a few cents, even when the cost of going out of your way is more than what you save?

No (−)	68.2
Yes (+)	31.8
	———
Per cent total	100.0

Q. 17. Do you eat with whatever silverware is provided you in a restaurant, even though it may look like it is not clean?

No (+)	79.6
Yes (−)	20.3
No response	0.1
	———
Per cent total	100.0

Q. 28. Do you always make sure of your facts before making judgments about people?

No (+)	51.3
Yes (−)	48.4
No response	0.3
	———
Per cent total	100.0

Q. 39. Does it annoy you to see a picture hanging crooked in someone else's house?

No (−)	43.2
Yes (+)	56.7
No response	0.1
	———
Per cent total	100.0

Q. 50. Does everything you do have to have a purpose?

No (−)	69.7
Yes (+)	29.9
No response	0.4
	———
Per cent total	100.0

Q. 61. Do you believe that a woman whose children are messy or dirty has failed in her duties as a mother?

No (—)	54.0
Yes (+)	45.7
No response	0.3
Per cent total	100.0

Q. 72. Is it important to you for your home to be clean and straightened up at all times?

No (—)	25.2
Yes (+)	74.7
No response	0.1
Per cent total	100.0

TABLE C–23

Correlational Matrix (r_t) and Estimates of First Factor Loadings

Question	6	17	28	39	50	61	72
6		.01	.27	.10	−.09	−.04	−.01
17	.01		−.12	.12	.09	.10	.05
28	.27	−.12		.07	−.19	.05	−.17
39	.10	.12	.07		.16	.16	.30
50	−.09	.09	−.19	.16		.19	.27
61	−.04	.10	.05	.16	.19		.43
72	−.01	.05	−.17	.30	.27	.43	
k_1	.10	.21		.48	.38	.54	.63

Question 28 was eliminated prior to factoring on the basis of the negative correlations. The final index is composed of Questions 39, 50, 61, and 72. Question 50 was retained despite the low loading in preference to the alternative of a three-item index.

Appendix D. Significance Levels of Correlation Coefficients

TABLE D-1

Coefficients of Correlation Required to Reject the Hypothesis $\rho = 0$ at 5 and 1 Per Cent Levels of Significance

| | Magnitudes of r's by Levels of Significance[a] | | Degrees of Freedom |
	5%	1%	
Total sample	.06	.08	936
Protestant	.10	.13	386
Mixed Catholic	.24	.31	68
Catholic	.10	.13	366
Jewish	.19	.24	108
White-collar total	.09	.12	469
Blue-collar total	.09	.12	465
White-collar			
Protestant	.14	.18	194
Mixed Catholic	.37	.48	26
Catholic	.15	.20	156
Jewish	.21	.27	87
Blue-collar			
Protestant	.14	.18	190
Mixed Catholic	.30	.39	40
Catholic	.13	.18	210
Jewish	.43	.55	19

[a] Calculated by the formula:

$$t = \frac{r \sqrt{N-2}}{\sqrt{1-r^2}}$$

Appendix E. Related Publications

The following is a complete list of articles and papers relating to the plans for the study, preliminary substantive reports, and analyses of other subjects based on study data.

Clyde V. Kiser, "Exploration of Possibilities for New Studies of Factors Affecting Size of Family," The Milbank Memorial Fund *Quarterly*, xxxi, (1953), pp. 436–480.

Charles F. Westoff, Elliot G. Mishler, Robert G. Potter, Jr., and Clyde V. Kiser, "A New Study of American Fertility: Social and Psychological Factors," *Eugenics Quarterly*, 2 (1955), pp. 229–233.

Clyde V. Kiser, "General Objectives and Broad Areas of Interest in a Proposed New Study in Fertility," *Current Research in Human Fertility*, Milbank Memorial Fund, New York, 1955, pp. 115–120.

Elliot G. Mishler, and Charles F. Westoff, "A Proposal for Research on Social Psychological Factors Affecting Fertility: Concepts and Hypotheses," *ibid.*, pp. 121–150.

Philip M. Hauser, "Some Observations on Method and Study Design," *ibid.*, pp. 151–162.

Clyde V. Kiser, Elliot G. Mishler, Charles F. Westoff, and Robert G. Potter, Jr., "Development of Plans for a Social Psychological Study of the Future Fertility of Two-Child Families," *Population Studies*, 10 (1956), pp. 43–52.

Elliot G. Mishler, "A Scalogram Analysis of the Sentence Completion Test," *Educational and Psychological Measurement*, 18 (1958), pp. 75–90.

Robert G. Potter, Jr., "An Analysis of Birth-Spacing Preferences," paper presented at the 1958 Meetings of the Population Association of America, abstracted in *Population Index*, 24 (1958), p. 213.

Frank W. Notestein, Elliot G. Mishler, Robert G. Potter, Jr., and Charles F. Westoff, "Pretest Results of a New Study of Fertility in the United States," *International Statistical Institute Bulletin*, 36, (1959), pp. 154–164.

Robert G. Potter, Jr., "Contraceptive Practice and Birth Intervals Among Two-Child White Couples in Metropolitan America," *Thirty Years of Research in Human Fertility: Retrospect and Prospect*, Proceedings of a Round Table at the 1958 Annual Conference, Milbank Memorial Fund, New York, pp. 74–92.

Philip C. Sagi, "A Component Analysis of Birth Intervals Among Two-Child White Couples in Metropolitan America," *ibid.*, pp. 135–148.

Charles F. Westoff, "Religion and Fertility in Metropolitan America," *ibid.*, pp. 117–134.

Philip C. Sagi, "Interim Report on the Study of Future Fertility of Two-Child Families in Metropolitan America," presented at the annual meetings of the American Statistical Association in Chicago, December 1958. Published in the 1958 *Proceedings* of the Social Statistics Section, 1959.

Charles F. Westoff, "The Social-Psychological Structure of Fertility" presented at the 1959 meeting in Vienna of the International Union for the Scientific Study of Population and published in the *Proceedings*.

Clyde V. Kiser, "Fertility Rates by Residence and Migration," *ibid.*

Charles F. Westoff, Marvin Bressler, and Philip C. Sagi, "The Concept of Social Mobility: An Empirical Inquiry," *American Sociological Review*, 25 (1960), pp. 375–385.

R. G. Potter, Jr., "Length of the Observation Period as a Factor Affecting the Gontraceptive Failure Rate," The Milbank Memorial Fund *Quarterly*, April, 1960, Vol. xxxviii, pp. 140–152.

R. G. Potter. Jr., "Some Gomments on the Evidence Pertaining to Family Limitation in the United States," *Population Studies*, Vol. xiv, No. 1, July (1960).

Robert G. Potter, Jr., "Some Relationships between Short Range and Long Range Risks of Unwanted Pregnancy," The Millbank Memorial Fund *Quarterly*, July 1960, Vol. xxxviii, No. 3 pp. 255–263.

Charles F. Westoff, "The 'Family Growth in Metropolitan America' Study: A Progress Report," presented at the Conference on Family Planning jointly sponsored by The Milbank Memorial Fund and The Population Council, October, 1960, To be published in the Proceedings of the Conference.

Robert G. Potter, Jr., and Philip C. Sagi, "Some Procedure for Estimating the Sampling Fluctuations of a Contraceptive Failure Rate," *ibid.*

Author Index

Anastasi, A., 166
Antonovsky, A., 179
Arey, L. B., 357

Baber, E. R., 282, 284, 288
Back, K. W., 137–140, 175, 299, 306, 341
Bartlett, M. K., 48
Beebe, G. W., 44, 52–54, 57–58, 61
Bell Adjustment Inventory, 315
Bender, S., 52–53
Bendix, R., 189
Bensman, J., 170–172
Berent, J., 238, 282
Bernreuter Personality Inventory, 314–315
Boggs, S. T., 240, 251
Boll, E. S., 292
Bossard, H. S., 292
Bresard, M., 238
Bressler, M., 237, 251
Brooks, H, E., 196, 204, 239
Broom, L., 8
Browne, H. J., 202
Burgess, E. W., 299
Buxton, C. L., 48

Calderone, M. S., 70
Campbell, A. A., 59, 216, 271, 303.
  See Freedman, Whelpton and Campbell
  in subject index
Cattell, R. B., 334
Centers, R., 221
Christensen, H. T., 302
Clare, J. E., 283, 293, 294
Clark, K. E., 35
Clarke, A. C., 251
Collett, M. E., 48
Coogan, T. F., 196, 199, 218, 219
Cottrell, L. S., 8, 299
Crown, S., 35

Davidson, M., 196
Davis, K., 8
Diddle, A. W., 52–53
Dinitz, S., 251
Dumont, A., 237
Dynes, R. R., 251

Eastman, N. J., 46
Edwards, A., 30, 316
Engle, E. T., 48
Eysenck, H. J., 35

Fiske, V. M., 48
Flanagan, J. C., 283, 290, 314–315
Foote, N., 260
Freedman, R., 59, 145, 179, 271, 303.
  See Freedman, Whelpton and Campbell
  in subject index

Gage, N. L., 35
Gallup, G., 213
Gini, C., 47
Girard, A., 238
Glass, D. V., 44, 125, 282
Gold, R. Z., 48, 53
Goldberg, D., 145, 179, 238, 305, 307, 343
Goodman, L., 34, 347
Grabill, W. H., 212, 236
Grebenik, E., 44, 125, 282
Gunn, A. L., 357
Gunn, D. L., 357
Guttmacher, A. F., 48, 52–53, 150
Guttman, L., 35

Hankins, H., 48
Hatt, P. K., 221, 244
Henry, F. J., 196, 204, 239
Henry, L., 47, 62
Henrysson, S., 322
Herbst, P. G., 137, 138, 139, 299, 306
Herrera, L. F., 76, 80, 88, 101
Hertig, A. T., 45, 46
Hill, R., 137–140, 175, 299, 306, 341

Indianapolis Study, 282, 283, 290, 293,
  299, 300, 302, 304, 306. See Freedman,
  Whelpton, and Campbell in subject
  index

Jack, R. W., 52–53
Jenkins, P. M., 357

Kantner, J. F., 239, 282, 283, 288, 289
Kelly, E. L., 13, 144–147, 283, 292,
  314–315, 321

Subject Index

abortions, *see* pregnancy wastage

accidental pregnancies, *see* effectiveness of contraception

adjustment to marriage, 300; birth intervals and, 301, 309; conceptual organization, 165; fertility planning and, 301, 309; hypotheses, 174; measurement of, 403–04; multivariate analyses, 322ff.; number of children desired and, 301, 309; second survey, 341

adjustment to mother role, 300; birth intervals and, 301, 309; conceptual organization, 165; fertility planning and, 301, 309; hypotheses, 174; multivariate analyses, 322ff.; number of children desired and, 301, 309; second survey, 341

age, current age, 287–88; birth intervals and, 287–88; conceptual organization, 165; fertility planning and, 287–88; multivariate analyses, 322ff.; number of children desired and, 287–88, 295

age at marriage, 282, 284–86; birth intervals and, 285–86; conceptual organization, 165; family size and, 284; fecundity and, 284; fertility planning and, 285–86; multivariate analyses, 322ff.; number of children desired and, 284–86, 295; residence type, 275; siblings and, 297; successive generations, 282

age differences, husband-wife, 289; birth intervals and, 289; fertility planning and, 289; number of children desired and, 289

ambiguity tolerance, compulsiveness and, 318; conceptual organization, 176; hypotheses, 317; measurement of, 410–11; number of children desired and, 317–18

anxiety, generalized manifest, conceptual organization, 176; fertility planning and, 318; hypotheses, 316; measurement of, 408–10; multivariate analyses, 322ff.; number of children desired and, 317–18

aspirations, *see* mobility aspirations, education

babies, preference for and age at which babies become enjoyable, 302–04; birth intervals and, 301, 311; conceptual organization, 165; fertility planning and, 301, 311; hypotheses, 302–04; multivariate analyses, 322ff.; number of children desired and, 301, 311

birth, delay, involuntary, 130; voluntary, 103–11; intervals between, *see* birth intervals; postponement, 43

birth control, *see* contraception

birth intervals, adjustment to marriage and, 301, 309; adjustment to mother role and, 301, 309; age at which children become enjoyable and, 301, 311; birth spacing preferences and, 103, 115, 154–55; Catholic education and, 199–02; conceptual organization, 165; as dependent variables, 107–09, 154; dominance and, 301, 312–13; employment duration and, 301, 310; employment type and, 189–91; future work intentions and, 301, 310; help available to wife and, 301, 313; income change and, 244–47; as independent variables, 111–12, 155; "intended" and "residual" components, 103–05, 174, relation of two components, 105–06, 109–11; liking for children and, 301, 311; marriage duration and, 113; migration and, 278; multivariate analyses, 322ff., 330; by neighborhood and religion, 273–75; number of children desired and, 141; occupational mobility and, 242–44; by religion, 183; by religion and class, 188–89; religiousness and, 197–98; by residence and religion, 269; sex composition and, 293, 299; siblings and, 290–91. *See also* preferred birth intervals

birth rate, 5

Catholics, *see* religion, education

church attendance, of Catholics by nationality background, 204–06; conceptual organization, 164; fertility planning and, 197; multivariate analyses, 322ff.; number of children desired